FileMaker® Pro 6 Developer's Guide to XML/XSL

Beverly Voth

Wordware Publishing, Inc.

Library of Congress Cataloging-in-Publication Data

Voth, Beverly.
FileMaker Pro 6 developer's guide to XML/XSL / Beverly Voth.
p. cm.
ISBN 1-55622-043-X (paperback)
1. FileMaker pro. 2. Database management. 3. XML (Document markup language)
4. XSL (Document markup language). I. Title.
QA76.9.D3V685 2003
005.75'65--dc21 2003002416
CIP

2320 Los Rios Boulevard
Plano, Texas 75074

Printed in the United States of America

ISBN 1-55622-043-X

10 9 8 7 6 5 4 3 2 1
0303

All inquiries for volume purchases of this book should be addressed to Wordware Publishing, Inc., at the above address. Telephone inquiries may be made by calling:

(972) 423-0090

Contents

Acknowledgments

First, I must thank Rich Coulombre for recommending that I write this book. Yes, I thank him even though he knows the time and effort needed for such an undertaking! Mostly, I thank Rich for reminding me to put everything in perspective, as life seems to happen while you're writing a book.

The Friday night FileMaker chat group chimed in with so much support to get me going and to keep me going. Among them I found my first technical editor, Chad Gard. Our initial focus was XML in web publishing and Chad's help was invaluable! When XML became another format for import and export in FileMaker Pro, my current technical editor, Doug Rowe, another chat buddy, took on the challenge. Both of these wonderful people are great at taking the "technical" and making it "human." They are busy being great FileMaker Pro developers and you'll find examples from both of them on the companion web sites. Another great FileMaker Pro developer, Jon Rosen, has been helpful in my quest for a publisher.

I could not have written this book without some terrific people at FileMaker, Inc. I have been working with web publishing and databases for a very long time. When FileMaker, Inc. moved in the same direction, I was extremely delighted. They also saw the oncoming freight train, XML, and integrated that technology in many ways. Now you have the chance to understand why we all think this is exciting.

Kevin Mallon has been my main contact and extremely helpful by getting information for me on the products. I think he's more than a public relations person at FileMaker, Inc. I think he's a "believer"!

Jimmy Jones, Dave McKee, Marcel De Maria, and Dave Dumas are among my heros at FileMaker, Inc. They give freely to the FileMaker community, through the mail lists, and support the developers' quest for the ultimate database.

Rick Kalman, technical liaison at FileMaker, Inc., is an "XML devotee," too. Rick and Jay Welshofer have been instrumental in pushing the rest of us into preparing for the journey. You'll find them on the XML-talk list at http://www.filemaker.com/xml/xml_talk.html, and in some of the XSLT examples, http://www.filemaker.com/xml/xslt_library.html.

Wordware Publishing has been so wonderful at taking a chance on me. I could not have finished without Jim Hill, Wes Beckwith, Beth

Kohler, and Paula Price! I just knew that this book would fit in with their other FileMaker Pro titles.

The most understanding bunch of people, my coworkers, family, and friends, have supported me in more ways than one! The Moondudes Extraordinaire, Fred Smith and Herman Adams, let me work on this project when my talents were needed elsewhere at Moonbow Software. But I hear the pride in their voices when they tell clients that "we are writing a book!" It's definitely "we," because I couldn't have done it without their support.

My parents, Duane and Lynne Rabbitt, and sister, Kathy Branch, always knew I could do something like this! They wouldn't let me give up when I had the rest of my life to contend with. My fiance, Jesse Lockard, and his parents, TJ and Carole, also supported me, even though I should have been spending time getting a new life!

Finally, I thank you for taking the time to read *FileMaker Pro 6 Developer's Guide to XML/XSL*. That tells me that you are as interested as I am about XML and how we can achieve something wonderful with it and FileMaker Pro.

Introduction

XML (Extensible Markup Language) is a standardized way of formatting text to facilitate data exchange for machines and humans. Documents are composed of tags, or markup, surrounding the data content. The markup can describe the content or be a generic text or binary data holder:

```
<descriptor>data content</descriptor>
<COL><DATA>field content</DATA></COL>
```

That is all you really need to know about XML and FileMaker Pro 6, unless, of course, you also need some hints as to what to do with that knowledge! This book will help you understand what XML is and how to create XML documents with Filemaker Pro 6 export and web publishing. You will learn how FileMaker Pro XML can be transformed with Extensible Stylesheet Language (XSL) into text, Hypertext Markup Language (HTML), or other XML formats. Other XML formats can be transformed for importing data into FileMaker Pro 6 databases, so you will appreciate why XML is useful to you as a means of data exchanges.

The Design of This Book

Throughout the book, you will find examples of XML and XSL and corresponding FileMaker Pro 6 scripts and functions, if relevant.

Chapter 1 contains a brief history of XML, including samples of markup formatting and how SGML (Standard Generalized Markup Language), HTML, and XML are related. You will learn about the advantages of XML with some examples and definitions of XML terms. Character encoding, Unicode, and how it is used in XML and FileMaker Pro 6 is presented here. XPath, the process for determining the location of data within a XML documents, is also introduced.

Chapter 2 is about exporting and importing XML with FileMaker Pro 6. The first examples of the XML grammars, FMPXMLRESULT and FMPDSORESULT, are discussed here. You will learn how to create manual, calculated, and scripted exports of XML documents. How FileMaker Pro produces related fields, repeating fields, and other field formats in XML exports, imports, and web publishing is discussed. An introduction to XSL is also presented here, along with calculated and scripted imports of XML data into FileMaker Pro 6.

Chapter 3 teaches you about the Document Type Definition (DTD) and how it relates to XML. Many XML formats use a DTD to describe how the document should be formatted. Understanding DTDs is most useful if you are importing and exporting data between FileMaker Pro 6 and other systems. An exercise for creating Document Type Definitions uses FileMaker Pro 6 layout theme files and is included in this chapter.

Chapter 4 explores the DTD further by drilling down into the FileMaker Pro 6 grammars for XML import, export, and web publishing. The FMPXMLLAYOUT grammar is introduced along with more details about the FMPXMLRESULT and the FMPDSORESULT grammars. The Database Design Report found in FileMaker Developer 6 has its own grammar and the discussion of how XML and XSL is used for the report may help you understand these two technologies.

Chapter 5 explains how FileMaker Pro web publishes XML. You will be given suggestions and hints for designing your databases for optimum web publishing. How to make a Hypertext Transfer Protocol (HTTP) request to FileMaker Pro 6 is discussed. You will learn about the use of scripts with web-published databases. Some security hints and tips to add to recommendations by FileMaker, Inc., can be found in this chapter.

Chapter 6 discusses Hypertext Markup Language (HTML) and XHTML. This format for web pages or text pages displayed by browsers is a common method of displaying text, images, and hyperlinks to other documents. XML can be transformed into HTML, thus, detailed information about the HTML elements is presented here. To make HTML documents compliant with XML, XHTML recommendations are also considered. Form requests can be made to web-published FileMaker Pro 6 databases, so the similarities with hyperlink requests can be found in this chapter. The difference for using HTML on smaller browsers, such as mobile telephones, is discussed in this chapter.

Chapters 7 and 8 define the terms for stylesheet transformation of XML with XSL. XPath is explored further here for use with XSL. How browsers handle XSL and how FileMaker Pro uses XSL are also discussed here.

To Be or Not

No attempt is made to assist you in creating databases with FileMaker Pro, but your thoughts will be guided toward designing databases for optimal data exchange with XML. All efforts will be made to explain these design considerations and to help you use XML within your current files. There are excellent resources for working with FileMaker Pro that are beyond the scope of this book. The FileMaker, Inc. web site has example files, a special XML section at http://www.filemaker.com/xml/ and a list of books.

All XML and XSL definitions are taken from the standards and recommendations presented by the World Wide Web Consortium (W3C), http://www.w3.org/. Rather than repeating these documents, you will find simplified examples intended to help you understand how you can use the standards with a minimum of effort. Consult those abstracts and specifications on the W3C web site for the latest changes.

Chapter 1

The Basics of XML

This chapter is intended for the FileMaker Pro database designer. You will be presented with examples of markup languages and a brief history of XML. You will begin to understand why XML can be important to you and how XML documents are structured. You will learn about some of the other standards based on XML for document presentation. If examples of similar usage in FileMaker Pro are helpful, you will find them here next to the XML examples.

1.1 A Brief History of XML

Extensible Markup Language (XML) is based upon SGML (Standard Generalized Markup Language). The simplest explanation of SGML is that it is a method of writing documents with special formatting instructions, or markup, included. A publishing editor makes notations in the margin of a document to alert an author of changes needed to a document. The notations are markup of the document and, indeed, this is where the term "markup" originated. Markup allows the SGML or XML document to be distributed electronically while preserving the format or style of the text. An SGML document contains the content and the markup. The emphasis is placed on the formatting rather than the content, otherwise you would simply have an ordinary document.

SGML can be used to facilitate the publishing of documents as electronic or printed copy. Some programs that read the markup may also translate the styles, for example, to Braille readers and printers. The same document might be viewed on a smaller screen such as those on personal digital assistants (PDAs) or pagers and cellular telephones. The markup can mean something completely different based upon the final destination of the document and the translation to another format. Using stylesheets or transformation methods, a single document with content and markup can be changed upon output.

1.11 Markup Simplified

To help you understand markup, four examples are given in this section. They are based on the same results but have very different means of getting there. The first example illustrates that "there may be more than you see" on a monitor or printed page. The second example uses Rich Text Format (RTF) to show a way to embed formatting in a document for transportability. The third example shows the PostScript file (commands) to produce the desired results consistently on a laser printer. The fourth example uses the nested tag style found in SGML, HTML, and XML documents. You will begin to see how this final markup method can provide the formatting that you don't see, the transportability and the consistency of methods two and three, along with additional information about the document and document contents.

Example 1: Text Containing Bold Formatting

This has **bold words** in a sentence.

Using a word processor or electronic text editor, you may simply click on the word or phrase and apply the text style with special keystrokes (such as Control+B or Command+B) or choose Bold from a menu. On the word processor or computer screen, you can easily read the text, but you do not see the machine description, or code, describing how this text is to be displayed. You may not care how or why that happens, but the computer needs the instructions to comply with your wishes for a format change.

If you save the document and display or print it later, you want the computer to reproduce the document exactly as you designed it. Your computer knows what the stored code (or character markup) means for that text. A problem may arise if you place that code on another operating system or have a different word processor. There may be a different interpretation of the code that produces undesired results. This markup is consistent only if all other variables are equal. The next example uses a text encoding method to change the machine or application code into something more standard and portable.

Example 2: Revealing the Markup in Some Text Editors

```
{\rtf
{This has }{\b bold words}{ in a sentence.
\par }}
```

The above sentence shows Rich Text Format (RTF) markup interspersed and surrounding the words of a document. The characters "{", "}", and "\" all mean something in this document but have nothing to do with the content. Rich Text Format markup is used by many word processors to change the visual format of the displayed text. As each new style is encountered, the formatting changes without changing the content of the document. A document becomes easily transportable to other word processors by using Rich Text Format. Each application that knows how to interpret Rich Text Format can show the intent of the author. This book was composed on a word processor, saved as RTF, and electronically submitted to the publisher. Regardless of the application, electronic device, or operating system used to create the document, the styling is preserved.

Rich Text Format markup adds no other information about the text. We may not know who wrote the sentence or when it was written. This information can be included as part of the content of the document but may be difficult to extract easily. We may have no control over the formatting or be allowed to change it for use with other devices. Using a translation application, we can convert it to the next example, the commands our printer understands.

Example 3: PostScript Printer Commands for the Document

```
%!PS-Adobe-3.0
%%Title: ()
%%Creator: ()
%%CreationDate: (10:29 AM Saturday, May 26, 2001)
%%For: ()
%%Pages: 1
%%DocumentFonts: Times-Roman Times-Bold
%%DocumentData: Clean7Bit
%%PageOrder: Ascend
%%Orientation: Portrait
  // more code here has been snipped for brevity //
%%EndPageSetup
gS 0 0 2300 3033 rC
250 216 :M
```

```
f57 sf
(This has )S
431 216 :M
f84 sf
.032 .003(bold words)J
669 216 :M
f57 sf
( in a sentence.)S
endp
showpage
%%PageTrailer
%%Trailer
end
%%EOF
```

The third example, above, is the same text used in the previous two examples and printed to a file as a PostScript document. It uses a different markup even though it is the same text and same document. PostScript is a language, developed by Adobe in 1985, that describes the document for printers, imagesetters, and screen displays. These files can also be converted to Adobe Portable Document Format (.pdf). The markup retains the document or image style so that it can be printed exactly the same way every time. It is a language that is specific to these PostScript devices. An application can translate this document to make it portable, too.

Example 4: Rules-based Nested Structure Used for Document Markup

```
<? Command: use stylesheet1 for external rules ?>
<document author="Beverly" creationDate="06 AUG 2001">
     <paragraph importance="highest">
          <sentence>This has <b>bold words</b> in a sentence.</sentence>
     </paragraph>
     <paragraph importance="optional">
          <sentence>The styling may be lost.</sentence>
     </paragraph>
</document>
```

Unlike the Rich Text Format, nested markup may also contain a description of the text contents. The markup is often called a tag and may define various rules for the document. Sometimes the rules are internal such as "<b>" and "</b>" or external such as a stylesheet (set of rules) to apply to the whole document or portions of a document.

There can be rules for characters, words, sentences, paragraphs, and the entire document. Characters inherit the rules of the word they are in. Words inherit the rules of the sentence, and sentences inherit the rules of the paragraph. The rules may not be just the formatting or style of the text but may also allow for flexibility in display.

```
<sentence color="blue">Some markup allows for a
<text color="red">change</text> in the document.</sentence>
```

Some formatting rules may also be different and change the inherited rules. All of the characters and words in the sentence above have a rule telling them to be blue. The text color can change to red without changing the sentence's blue color. In this nested markup, only the inner tags make the rule change.

Whether you use Rich Text Format or the nested structure found in SGML, HTML, and XML, changing the content of the words and phrases in the document does not change the style, the format, or the rules. Documents created with markup can be consistent. As the content changes, the style, formatting, and rules remain the same. The portability of documents containing markup to various applications and systems makes them very attractive. Standards have been recommended to ensure that every document that uses these standards will maintain portability.

1.12 The Standard in SGML

Charles Goldfarb, Ed Mosher, and Ray Lorie created General Markup Language (GML) in 1969. These authors wanted to adapt documents to make them readable by various applications and operating systems. They also saw the need to make the markup standard to industries with diverse requirements. Two or more companies could agree on the markup used in order to facilitate the exchange of information. Different standards could be designed for each industry yet could have elements common to them all.

Another requirement for GML was to have rules for documents. To maintain an industry standard, rules could be created to define a document. One rule could define the type of content allowed within the document. Another rule could define the structure of the document. You might say these rules could be the map of the document. If you had the map, you could go to any place on the map. Using this kind of markup, you could locate and extract portions of the document more easily.

GML evolved and was renamed Standard Generalized Markup Language. In 1986 the International Organization for Standardization (ISO) designated SGML as standard ISO-8879. SGML is now used worldwide for the exchange of information.

1.13 SGML Used as Basis for HTML and XML

When the World Wide Web was developed in 1989, Tim Berners-Lee used SGML as a basis for Hypertext Markup Language (HTML). HTML is a document standard for the Internet. Although the set of rules for HTML is limited, HTML still fulfills many of the SGML goals. The HTML markup includes text formatting for the display of content to web browsers and hyperlinks to connect separate documents. An example of this markup for web browsers is shown in Listing 1.1. HTML is application independent, and documents using HTML can be viewed with various operating systems.

Listing 1.1 Example of Hypertext Markup Language

```
<HMTL>
      <HEAD>
            <TITLE>My Document in HTML</TITLE>
      </HEAD>
      <BODY>
            <H1>This Is The Top Level Heading</H1>
            Here is content<BR>
            followed by another line.
            <HR>
            I can include images <IMG SRC="mygraphic.gif"> in a line
            of text!<BR>
            Good-bye for now.<BR>
            <A HREF="anotherPage.html">Go to another page with this
            link.</A>
      </BODY>
</HTML>
```

Unlike SGML, HTML was not originally designed to be open to the creation of new markup. However, custom HTML markup was designed for separate applications, and documents lost some of their ability to be easily portable to other applications and systems. One application had defined a rule one way, and another had defined it differently or could not understand all the rules. Hypertext Markup Language became nonstandard.

1.14 HTML Can Become XHTML

XHTML is a standard for revising HTML to make Hypertext Markup Language documents more compatible with XML. You will learn more about HTML and XHTML in Chapter 6, "Using HTML and XHTML to Format Web Pages." You can also read more about XHTML for the World Wide Web Consortium at the Hypertext Markup Language home page, http://www.w3.org/Markup/. The example of XHTML in Listing 1.2, below, is very similar to Listing 1.1. XHTML is HTML with minor revisions to some of the tags.

Listing 1.2 Example of XHTML

```
<html>
      <head>
            <title>My Document in XHTML</title>
      </head>
      <body>
            <h1>This Is The Top Level Heading</h1>
            Here is content<br />
            followed by another line.
            <hr />
            I can include images <img src="mygraphic.gif" /> in a
            line of text!<br />
            Good-bye for now.
            <a href="anotherPage.html">Links to another page are the
            same in XHTML</a>
      </body>
</html>
```

1.15 XML as a Standard

The World Wide Web Consortium (W3C) set up a task force for recommending a language more useful to electronic transmission and display of documents. They wanted this language to be based on SGML but not as complex. They wanted the language to be more flexible than HTML but maintain standards. The first version of the Extensible Markup Language (XML) specification was presented in 1997 as the "Document Object Model (DOM) Activity Statement," http://www.w3.org/DOM/Activity.

You may see many similarities between HTML and XML. A Hypertext Markup Language document contains a nested structure. With minor adjustments, an HTML document could be an XHTML document and usable as an XML document. However, HTML is used more for display and formatting of the data, while Extensible Markup Language generally separates the data descriptions from the text styles. XML allows the data to be transformed more easily for display on different devices.

1.2 XML Advantages

This section expands upon the goals for XML data exchange and how they can help you as a FileMaker Pro developer. The recommendations for the design of the Extensible Markup Language show some of the advantages this format offers. These XML design goals can be found in the document "Extensible Markup Language (XML) 1.0 (Second Edition), W3C Recommendation 6 October 2000," http://www.w3.org/TR/REC-xml.

- XML shall be straightforwardly usable over the Internet.
- XML shall support a variety of applications.
- XML shall be compatible with SGML.
- It shall be easy to write programs that process XML documents.
- The number of optional features in XML is to be kept to the absolute minimum, ideally zero.
- XML documents should be human-legible and reasonably clear.
- The XML design should be prepared quickly.
- The design of XML shall be formal and concise.
- XML documents shall be easy to create.
- Terseness in XML markup is of minimal importance.

1.21 Why XML Data Exchange is Extensible

Common formats currently exist for exchanging data among applications and systems. Text formats may use fixed-length fields or a delimiter such as a comma, tab, or other character between data types. These formats are wonderfully compact, but they were designed for the days when storage was at more of a premium. These formats rarely offer the description of the type of data. Unless a map is included with the data, you will likely have difficulty extracting specific data. For example, one piece of data as a series of numbers could be an identification key, a telephone number, an account number, or several concurrent number data types. These older formats are often limited in what information can be exchanged.

Text Formats in FileMaker Pro

FileMaker Pro can import and export comma-separated values (.csv), tab-delimited text (.tab or .txt), and other formats. If the first row (or record) of the data contains the field names and the data is comma-separated, the format is of merge (.mer) type. ODBC, JDBC, Web Publishing, and XML use the field names for data exchange. You may think of XML publishing in FileMaker Pro as extending the data exchange already available! You can read "About file formats" in FileMaker Pro Help for more information on the formats available for import and export.

With FileMaker Pro 6, data can be exported as XML in one of two formats. The FMPXMLRESULT grammar uses a metadata format to describe the field names. This is somewhat similar to the merge format, which includes the field or column names as the first record. The actual data is placed in repeating row elements with a column element for each field in the export. The other grammar for FileMaker Pro 6 export, FMPDSORESULT, has less information about the fields but uses the field names as the element names. You can read more about these two grammars in Chapters 2 and 4.

Text Formats in XML

XML documents include the description along with the data. Remember that XML is a markup language for creating markup, so you can create whatever descriptions you want. The goal is to create markup that is "sensible" as well as extensible. The document becomes more human readable by including the description. The document also becomes more machine extractable when the description of the content is included. With XML, the map is included with the document.

A typical XML document may have hundreds of markup tags yet can be quickly searched for a particular one. Imagine looking in a document for a customer whose first name is John. A text editor or word processor can perform a fast search, but how would you know that you have found the correct piece of information? Look at the example in Listing 1.3 for the markup for people, then find all the people who are customers. Finally, search for a customer with the first name of John. You have just narrowed down your search in a hierarchical manner.

Listing 1.3 people.xml

```
<people>
	<vendor>
		<firstname>John</firstname>
```

```
        <company>Paper Cutters</company>
    </vendor>
    <customer>
        <firstname>Jane</firstname>
        <lastname>Doe</lastname>
    </customer>
    <customer>
        <firstname>John</firstname>
        <lastname>Doe</lastname>
    </customer>
</people>
```

The example in Listing 1.3 shows you another advantage of XML: You can extract only the data you need and ignore extraneous data. If all you want is the customer data, the <customer>...</customer> elements are used in a search. Another need may be for vendor information and only those elements are used in the search results. This enables many people who need different information to use the same XML document.

Extensible also means "flexible" when using XML. An XML document may provide alternate versions of text. Listing 1.4, greeting.xml, contains explicit text in a variety of languages (xml:lang). Providing alternate content in the same document can make a document flexible for multiple uses. XML is an international standard and provides for the use of non-English text in the documents.

Listing 1.4 greeting.xml

```
<greetings>
        <!-- English -->
    <greeting xml:lang="en">Hello World!</greeting>
        <!-- French -->
    <greeting xml:lang="fr">Bonjour Monde!</greeting>
        <!-- Spanish -->
    <greeting xml:lang="es">Buenos dias, Mundo!</greeting>
        <!-- German -->
    <greeting xml:lang="de">Guten tag, die Welt!</greeting>
</greetings>
```

XML is also flexible in the way document contents can be transformed for multiple uses. Regardless of platform or application (personal computer, portable digital assistant, or Braille printers and readers, for example), the document can be processed for the proper device. Each application can read the same document and interpret the markup differently. Some of these devices and applications can also write XML. This flexibility opens up much greater communication among many applications and devices. The exchange of information is the key!

1.22 Saving Information for the Future

One of the greatest advantages of documents formatted with XML is that these documents will be accessible long after the devices or methods used to create them are gone. Historical creation and storage of data often relies upon proprietary applications and systems to write and read the documents. The meaning of a document may be lost if that system becomes unavailable. Because XML documents can provide descriptions along with the data, these documents will be easier to interpret later.

The XML standards also provide a partial description of how computer applications should process the XML. This process is called parsing. Some processing is done on a server, and some processing is done within an application on a client machine. Adhering to these standards ensures that in the future documents will be just as useful as they are now.

1.3 XML Document Examples and Terms

XML documents are composed of entities. These entities are storage units for pieces of the document structure. Each entity has a name and can be referenced by its name. The document entities can be parsed or unparsed. Parsed entities are all of the character content of the document and the markup tags. Parsed entities are also called replacement text and are processed like mail merge documents in a word processor. Unparsed entities are all of the non-content and may be text other than XML, graphics, and sound, according to the World Wide Web Consortium, http://www.w3.org/TR/REC-xml#sec-physical-struct. This section discusses XML document terms and gives you examples of these terms.

Note: You will see references to DTDs, Document Type Definitions, throughout this chapter. FileMaker Pro has provided these for you for use with XML publishing on the web or for imports and exports with XML. FileMaker Pro DTDs will be discussed in Chapters 2 and 4. If you wish to write your own Document Type Definitions, see Chapter 3.

1.31 Well-formed and Valid XML Documents

To meet the goals of the XML standard, all documents should be well formed. This means:

1. The document contains at least one entity.
2. The document begins with a root or document element, which is the starting point for XML processors.
3. XML processors build a tree-like nested structure from the text of the well-formed document.
4. All parsed entities are also well formed.
5. All markup is composed of start tags, end tags, or empty tags that are properly nested.

The nested markup in many of the listings in this book is indented for reader convenience, but this is not a requirement for a well-formed XML document. In some cases the tab and return characters are considered viable to the XML document, and extraneous indentation can invalidate the document. Study the needs for your data exchange and don't introduce extra data.

The well-formed XML document has one or more elements: root element, parent elements, and child elements. The XML document in Listing 1.5 starts and ends with a root element, but the name of the element can be anything. All the elements are properly formatted with a start and end tag or empty tag. The child elements are nested within the parent elements, and all elements are within the root element.

Listing 1.5 Properly nested markup tags in a document

```
<root>
    <parent>
        <child>
            <grandchild />
        </child>
    </parent>
</root>
```

The same document could be compacted with no white space and still follow the rules for well-formedness:

```
<root><parent><child><grandchild /></child></parent></root>
```

Conforming XML parsers and processors should verify that a document is well formed. If not, they stop processing and produce a report as soon as any errors are encountered. Improper nesting of elements causes a typical error.

XML parsers can be validating or nonvalidating. A valid XML document has an associated Document Type Definition (DTD), but not all XML documents require a DTD. An XML formatted document can be well formed and not valid. However, a valid XML document must be well formed.

A Document Type Definition is a list of the "fields" that are allowable in a particular XML document type. However, in XML they are not called fields but entities. The DTD contains the entities with element names, attributes of those elements, and the rules governing the entities and the document. For data exchange in a business-to-business situation, the DTD can be the map of the entities of a document. Creating well-formed and valid documents increases the accuracy of the data in those documents. Creating well-formed and valid XML documents also helps standardize the data to assist the exchange of information. There are many DTDs, schemas, XML grammars, and other XML standards such as MathML (Mathematical Markup Language), SMIL (Synchronized Multimedia Integration Language), and XBRL (Extensible Business Reporting Language).

1.32 Data Validation in FileMaker Pro

You have a similar way to assist with data integrity (validity) in FileMaker Pro. When you create a FileMaker Pro database file, you add fields in the Define Fields dialog. You define a field by naming the field and setting it to one of these data types: text, number, date, time, container, calculation, summary, or global. To further define the field, you can specify options to automatically enter specific data, to validate the data entered, and to store the field's index or recalculation as needed. Figure 1.1 shows the Define Fields options dialog for setting validation in FileMaker Pro. The following exercise restricts a number field to only allow number values.

Exercise 1.1 Validate Field Data Entry

1. Open the Define Fields dialog by choosing **File**, **Define Fields...** or using the keyboard shortcut **Command+Shift+D** on Macintosh, or **Control+Shift+D** on Windows.
2. Type **Age** in the Field Name box and select the **Number** radio button. Click the **Create** button to define the field. Now click the **Options...** button and select the **Validation** tab.

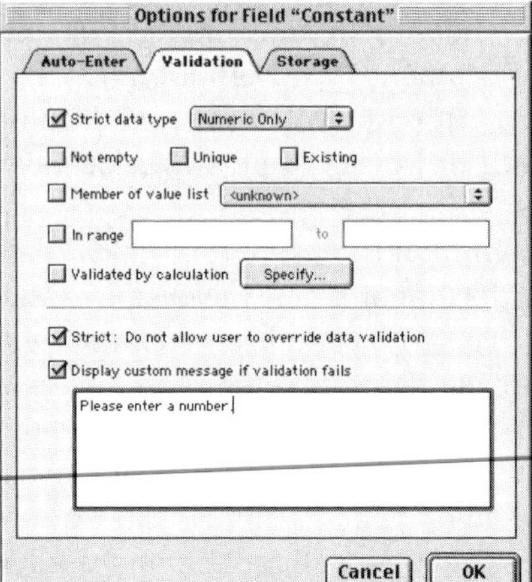

Figure 1.1: FileMaker Pro Define Fields Options dialog

3. Check **Strict data type** and select **Numeric Only** from the pop-up. Close the Options dialog box by selecting **OK** or pressing **Enter** on your keyboard, and close the Define Fields dialog by selecting the **Done** button.
4. Enter Layout mode by choosing **View**, **Layout Mode** or using the keyboard shortcut **Control+L** on Windows or **Command+L** on Macintosh.
5. Place the new field on the layout if it is not already there by choosing the menu item **Insert**, **Field**.
6. Choose **View**, **Browse Mode** or use the shortcut **Control+B** on Windows or **Command+B** on Macintosh.
7. Enter the Age field by pressing the **Tab** key or by clicking into the field. Enter any number and tab out of the field or click anywhere else on the layout. You should not get a warning message.
8. Create a new record by choosing **Records**, **New Record** or the shortcut **Command+N** on Macintosh or **Control+N** on Windows.
9. Enter **abc** into the Age field. After you leave the field, you will be presented with the warning: "This field is defined to contain numeric values only. Allow this non-numeric value?" and the buttons: "Revert field," "No," and "Yes." This dialog will allow you to override the warning if you select Yes. This override feature can be valuable at times but not if you want to have a valid number field.

10. Open the Define Fields dialog again and select the **Age** field. Click on the **Options** button and change the validation to provide a custom warning message. Check **Strict: Do not allow user to override data validation** and **Display custom message if validation fails**, then type **Please enter a number** in the field.
11. When you enter **abc** in the Age field, you get your custom message and the validation cannot be overridden. Figure 1.2 shows this custom message.

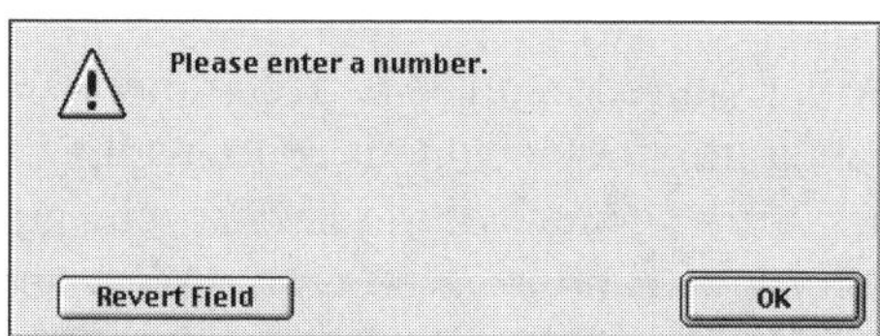

Figure 1.2: FileMaker Pro invalid entry alert dialog

Using a DTD to validate an XML document or setting the validation on fields for FileMaker Pro data entry provides for reliability of the information exchanged. Your XML documents should be well formed and valid. You will see in Chapter 2 how FileMaker Pro exports your data in a well-formed and valid XML document. Examples of the terms in DTDs will be discussed in Chapter 3, "Document Type Definitions (DTDs)." Document Type Definitions for the three XML document types published by FileMaker Pro will be discussed in Chapter 4, "FileMaker Pro XML Schema or Grammar Formats (DTDs)."

1.33 XML Document Structure

An application that opens or reads files needs to know the type of document to process. Few applications are capable of processing all file types. Often the file type is determined by the file extension (.txt, .sit, .exe, .csv, .jpeg, .FP5, or .html) or the Creator Code and File Type on the Macintosh operating system. Sometimes the file type will also be embedded in the document itself. For example, you will find "%PDF" at the beginning of a Portable Document Format file created by Adobe Acrobat or "GIF89a" at the beginning of a Graphics Interchange Format (.gif) file.

Well-formed XML documents begin with a prolog. This opening statement tells the XML parser the type of file it will be processing. The XML document prolog contains an optional XML declaration, one or more miscellaneous entities (comments and processing instructions), and optional Document Type Declarations. An HTML document, for example, can be a well-formed XML document with minor corrections to the standard HTML markup. The well-formed HTML document includes the XML declaration in the prolog. You can read more about the other optional elements of the prolog in section 2.8 of the XML specification, "Prolog and Document Type Declaration," http://www.w3.org/TR/REC-xml#sec-prolog-dtd. Examples of XML declarations are listed below.

```
<?xml version="1.0" encoding="encoding type" standalone="yes" ?>
<?xml version='1.0'?>
<?xml version="1.0" encoding="ISO 8859-1" ?>
```

The version attribute is required in all XML declarations. When you include the version attribute, the document contains the information used should there be future versions of the XML specifications. The current version number is 1.0 and is based on the W3C Recommendation as of October 6, 2000, http://www.w3.org/TR/REC-xml.

The encoding attribute, optional in the XML declaration statement, specifies the character sets used to compose the document. This encoding attribute uses Unicode Transformation Formats (UTF-8) as the default. The 256 letters, digits, and other characters we commonly use for transmitting text are called ASCII (American Standard Code for Information Interchange) characters and are a subset of UTF-8. ASCII may also be called ISO 8859-1 or Latin-1, although only the first 128 characters of all these formats may be the same depending upon platform and font faces.

XML processors must be able to read both UTF-8 and UTF-16 encoding. UTF-16 allows for more characters, such as would be used to compose ideographical alphabets. Graphical alphabets could be symbols, icons, or Asian characters. You may specify other UTF or encoding types. See "Unicode vs. ASCII" in section 1.42 of this chapter, for further explanation and examples of encoding types. Three common encoding types are listed below.

```
encoding="UTF-8"
encoding="UTF-16"
encoding="ISO-8859-1"
```

FileMaker Pro and UTF-8

According to the *FileMaker Pro Developer's Guide*, p. 7-8, "About UTF-8 encoded data": All XML data generated by the Web Companion is encoded in UTF-8 (Unicode Transformation 8 Bit) format... UTF-8 encoded data is compressed almost in half (lower ASCII characters are compressed from 2 bytes to 1 byte), which helps data download faster.

Note: Because your XML data is UTF-8 encoded, some upper ASCII characters will be represented by two or three characters in the text editor—they will appear as single characters only in the XML parser or browser. An example of this type of encoding is shown in Listing 2.4.

The new XML parser in FileMaker Pro 6 uses a larger set of encodings. The FileMaker Pro Help topic "Importing XML data" states: "FileMaker uses the Xerces-C++ XML parser which supports ASCII, UTF-8, UTF-16 (Big/Small Endian), UCS4 (Big/Small Endian), EBCDIC code pages IBM037 and IBM1140 encodings, ISO-8859-1 ("Latin1"), and Windows-1252." You can find additional information FileMaker Pro supports for encodings by typing "UTF" in FileMaker Pro Help under the Find tab.

Standalone Documents

Standalone is also optional in the XML declaration statement. If standalone="yes," there are no external markup declarations associated with this document. The XML processor needs to know whether to process or skip these. If standalone="no," then you will need to specify the location of the external declarations. A document can have both embedded markup declarations and external markup declarations. Documents that might have external calls could contain references to stylesheets or graphics and sounds. The following prolog tells the processors to look for external definitions and where to find them.

```
<?xml version="1.0" standalone="no"?>
<!ENTITY % image1 SYSTEM "http://www.mydomain.com/images/image1.gif">
%image1;
```

1.34 Document Type Declarations (DOCTYPE)

You may have seen Document Type Declarations in web pages. The Document Type Declaration (DOCTYPE) should be one of the first statements in an HTML document, because it is part of the prolog of the document. The DOCTYPE tells more about the document and where the definition for this type of format can be found. A common declaration for an HTML 4.0 document follows.

```
<!DOCTYPE HTML PUBLIC "-//W3C//DTD HTML 4.0 Transitional//EN"
  "http://www.w3.org/TR/1998/REC-html40-19980424/loose.dtd">
```

They may sound similar, but Document Type Declaration (DOCTYPE) should not be confused with Document Type Definition (DTD).

However, the declaration (DOCTYPE) can point to the location of any definition (DTD) to which a particular document should conform.

Tip: While using an HTML editor, you may have the option or preference to check the syntax of your document as you edit. You can specify how strict (precise) the document should be if you insert the DOCTYPE statement first. When you check the document, the editor should warn you if you have not followed the rules according to the specified DOCTYPE. Good HTML editors will tell you what the error is and where it is located in your document.

Let's analyze the parts of the DOCTYPE declaration. Only the topElement is required. Each of the other parts may be optional but occur in the declaration as follows:

```
<!DOCTYPE topElement availability "registration//organization//type label
    definition//language" "URL">
```

topElement is the root element (first significant markup) found in the document; "HTML" is the default for web pages. Remember that the DOCTYPE is part of the prolog and is placed above the root element in the document. Valid documents must have this element match the root element.

availability is a "PUBLIC" or a "SYSTEM" resource. Documents used internally or references to documents related to this one would have "SYSTEM" availability.

registration is "ISO" (an approved ISO standard), "+" (registered but not approved by the ISO), or "–" (not registered by the ISO). The International Organization for Standardization might not register XML or HTML DOCTYPEs.

organization is a unique label of the owner ID or entity that created the DTD. Common organizations are "IETF" (Internet Engineering Task Force) and "W3C" (World Wide Web Consortium).

type is the type of object being referenced. "DTD" is the default.

label is a unique description for the text being referenced. "HTML 4.0," for example, refers to the version of these recommendations.

definition is the type of document. "Frameset," "Strict," or "Transitional" are common definitions for HTML documents. Strict documents have more limited markup but can be used across a broader set of devices.

language is the two-character code of the language used to create the document. "EN" is English and "ES" is Spanish. The ISO 639 standard is used for this code, which are the same codes used for the "xml:lang" attribute. Here, language is used for the entire document, although specific elements in the document can still be redefined by using "xml:lang."

URL (Uniform Resource Locator) is the location of the DTD.

You can name your own document type. This is the only required element of the DOCTYPE statement. You should remember this naming suggestion: Stick with alphanumeric characters and the underscore character and you cannot go wrong! Also avoid any combination of the letters "X" or "x," "M" or "m," and "L" or "l," in that order, when naming your document type, as these are reserved.

DOCTYPES can contain internal Document Type Definitions (DTDs) or external DTDs. Internal DTDs stay with the document and can only be used with that document. You are making the definition of the document in itself. External DTDs can be used for multiple documents and are referenced by the PUBLIC location, or if used internally, by the SYSTEM location as relative path to the document. Listing 1.6 shows some examples of XML documents with external DTD references. Compare them to the code below, which is complete with internal DTD:

```
<?xml version="1.0" standalone="yes" ?>
<!DOCTYPE myDoc [<!ELEMENT myDoc (#PCDATA)>]>
<mydoc>Here's the text!</mydoc>
```

Listing 1.6 XML documents with external DTD references

```
Example 1:
<?xml version="1.0" standalone="no" ?>
     <!DOCTYPE myDoc SYSTEM "myDoc.dtd">
<myDoc>
     <head>This is the first element of my document</head>
     <main>
          <para>Now I can add content.</para>
          <para>Each line is another child of the main element</para>
     </main>
</mydoc>

Example 2:
<?xml version="1.0" standalone="no" ?>
<!DOCTYPE html PUBLIC "-//W3C//DTD XHTML 1.0 Strict//EN"
     "http://www.w3.org/TR/2000/REC-xhtml1-20000126/DTD/
       xhtml1-strict.dtd">
```

```
<html xmlns="http://www.w3.org/1999/xhtml" xml:lang="en" lang="en">
    <head>
        <meta http-equiv="content-type" content="text/html;
          charset=utf-8" />
        <title>New Document</title>
    </head>
    <body>
        <div>
            Because this is strict XHTML, every tag needs
              &quot;closure&quot;<br />
            Including the break just inserted before this line
              and the meta tag in the head.
        </div>
        <div>
            Also note the way the quote mark is encoded around
              the word closure.<br />
            You will see this later as a predefined entity in
              Element Content.
        </div>
    </body>
</html>
```

1.35 Processing Instructions

You can include processing instructions in your document prolog. Processing instructions begin with "<?" and end with "?>." Although the XML declaration in the prolog has similar markup, it is not used as a processing instruction. You may find processing instructions used to reference an XSL (XML Stylesheet Language) document. Use processing instructions rather than comments if you wish the XML processor to see them.

```
<? target ?>
```

The target is the name of the application to receive the instruction. Because the end of this special markup is "?>," do not use these characters in your target declaration. The code below shows examples of the processing instructions that FileMaker Pro produces if you use a stylesheet. In section 5.2, "XML Request Commands for Web Companion," you will see the request for stylesheets.

```
<? xml-stylesheet href="headlines.css" type="text/css" ?>
<? xml-stylesheet href="headlines.xsl" type="text/xsl" ?>
```

1.36 Comments

When you create documents, you may wish to add comments near any statements that need further clarification. Comments should not contain any important part of the document as any processing may ignore them. However, some processors may use comments or they may be helpful to humans reading the document. Comments may be anywhere in the document; they are not only for inclusion in the prolog of the document.

Comments are placed outside any other markup. Comments are simply created using "<!--" at the start of the comment and "-->" at the end. These characters are reserved, so they should not be used anywhere else in a document. Additional "--" or "-" should not be used within any comment. Any white space is ignored, so you may have spaces and returns in a comment. Example comments can be found in Listing 1.7.

Listing 1.7 Example comments

```
<!-- THIS IS A COMMENT -->
<!-- THIS IS ALSO
A COMPLETE COMMENT
ALTHOUGH IT SPANS MULTIPLE LINES -->
<!-- While it is permissible to begin and end the comment next to the -->
<!-- markup, it may be easier to read if you include some white space -->
<!-- as well. This is an ILLEGAL comment. Note the additional dash at -->
<-- the end: --->
```

Using Comments to Test HTML Documents

Comments can be very useful when checking HTML and CDML documents for accuracy in the markup, including FileMaker Pro replacement tags, such as "[FMP-Field: myField]". This can be a valuable tool when troubleshooting or debugging a problematic document. You may place comment tags around a large portion of the document so a browser will not process this part of the document. If the result is as you desired, move the comments around a smaller portion and check again. Errors in HTML and CDML markup can be found easily this way.

Be careful when commenting out table elements. If you place the comment tags around complete tables or rows, you will not receive browser errors. If you need to be more precise, add the comment around the contents of a particular table cell but not the tags themselves. Listings 1.8 and 1.9 show the proper placement of comments inside of HTML table code.

Listing 1.8 Comments around table cell

```
<table>
    <tr>
        <td>content here</td>
    </tr>
    <tr>
        <td><!-- a new row --><td>
    </tr>
</table>
```

Listing 1.9 Comment around table row

```
<table>
    <tr>
        <td>content here</td>
    </tr>
    <!-- <tr>
        <td><!-- a new row --><td>
    </tr> -->
</table>
```

Comments for Future Reference

Comments may also be valuable if more than one person is helping create a document. Notes to others can be provided in the comments. Additional examples of comments are shown in Listing 1.10.

Listing 1.10 Single-line or multiple-line comments

```
<!-- === NEW RECORD BEGINS HERE === -->
<!-- *** do not revise this section -->
<!-- *** -->
... your static document text here ...
<!-- *** -->
<!-- *** end "do not revise" -->
... free to edit text here ...
<!-- === NEW RECORD ENDS HERE === -->
<!-- ******************************
    * make comment highly visible *
    ****************************** -->
<!-- created by me on 09 MAR 1999 -->
<!-- revised by you on 21 MAR 2000 -->
```

1.37 Elements and Attributes

Each XML document has one or more elements. These elements are the entities where the content is declared. The construction of the element is simply the type of element as the name of the tag. Elements have a start and end tag. The tag name is the same for the start tag with "/" added to the end tag:

```
<elementName>content</elementName>
```

An empty element contains no content but may have attributes:

```
<elementName />
<elementName></elementName>
<elementName attrName="attrValue"/>
<elementName attrName="attrValue" attr2="too!" />
```

The question arises whether to place a space before the "/>" in the standalone empty element. Should you use "<emptyElement/>," "<emptyElement />," or simply make all elements paired ("<empty></empty>")? Section 3.1, "Start-Tags, End-Tags, and Empty-Element Tags," of the XML specification http://www.w3.org/TR/REC-xml, states that the empty element tag is composed of "<" followed by the name of the element, zero or more occurrences of spaces and attribute name/value pairs, ending with an optional space and "/>". For human readability, the space before the final characters in the empty element may be preferable. Another suggestion is made by the XHTML 1.0 recommendation: section C.2, "Empty Elements," http://www.w3.org/TR/xhtml1/, to always include the space for compatibility with browsers and other applications that may read or write HTML and XHTML.

Tag Names

Tag names may contain one or more of the following (in any combination): letter, number, period (.), dash (-), underscore (_), and colon (:). These tag names should begin with a letter, underscore, or colon. You should avoid the use of these reserved words (in any combination of upper- and lowercase): "XML" or "xml". Section 2.3, "Common Syntactic Constructs," of the XML specification http://www.w3.org/TR/REC-xml#sec-common-syn, gives some ideas of how names are to be constructed for elements and attributes in an XML document. The World Wide Web Consortium suggestions allow for more than alphanumeric characters and the underscore in element and attribute names. However, you may have discovered that different systems use the period, dash, and colon to signify something special on each system. To maintain the portability of your documents, you should carefully consider the names you choose. For example, you may use lowerUppercase notation for element and attribute names, such as <myElement myPositive="yes" myNegative="no" />.

Attributes

Attributes are found in the start tag or empty tag for elements and are composed of name and value pairs. Attributes are used to refine the definition of the element. You do not want to name your attributes the same within a single element, but the same attribute name may be used for different elements. Generally, one piece of information is included in each attribute, although an element may have one or more attributes.

Attributes should always be quoted in element start tags and in empty elements. Attributes can use double or single quotes, but the quotes surrounding any single element must match (for example, <element myAttribute="bad quotes' /> is incorrect). Try to avoid "smart quotes" (also called curly quotes), as they may be interpreted incorrectly in documents that need to be read by different applications and systems. Listing 1.11 shows proper element attributes.

Listing 1.11 Examples of elements with attributes

```
<elementName attributeName="attributeValue" />
<child firstborn="yes" />
<child firstborn='yes' />
<child firstborn="yes">
     <firstName>Dawn</firstName>
</child>
<pen color="#EEEEEE" pattern="1" size="2" />
<fill color="#FF00FF" pattern="" />
```

1.38 Element Content

The content of most elements is your information. The content is the text or character data that you want to pass along from one application or system to another. Any text that is not considered markup is character data. You could think of this character data as the leaves on a tree. In the family tree metaphor, any branch can have multiple branches. Therefore, elements can also contain other elements. When an element contains character data and other elements, that element has mixed content. Listing 1.12 mixes content with other elements inside the root element element1.

Elements used for XML export or XML web publishing in FileMaker Pro do not contain mixed content. You may encounter XML documents using this format for the elements and need to understand the structure if you are importing XML into FileMaker Pro.

Listing 1.12 Example of mixed content

```
<element1>
      <element2>Some text here</element2>
      Some content to element1
      <emptyElement3/>
      <emptyElement4></emptyElement4>
</element1>
```

Character data can be composed of any letters, numbers, or symbols. The XML processors need to know if you are using characters as markup or as a part of your text content. The comparison symbols greater than (>) and less than (<) might be interpreted incorrectly if used in a computation statement. You might also be writing an XML document about markup that contains text that you do not want to be processed as markup. There is unique markup used to tell the processor to not parse the literal contents. You can see this unique markup in Listing 1.13. The only special character sequence is the "]]>" pattern, so you must not use this pattern anywhere in your content. You may, however, use the "<![CDATA[" beginning pattern within the content. The XML processors are looking for the end of the character data ("]]>") after encountering the beginning pattern.

Listing 1.13 Markup for raw or unparsed data

```
<![CDATA[your data goes here]]>
<![CDATA[This text contains less than and greater than in a calculation,
  so must be treated in a special way. Is 1 > 2 (one greater than two)?
  No, 1 < 2 (one is less than two).]]>
<![CDATA[In your HTML document if you want to hide data in an input form,
  use this: <input type="hidden" name="myField" value="">.]]>
<![CDATA[
      The text can be many lines & contain
      values that might otherwise be converted.
      ]]>
<![CDATA[An example of an XML prolog statement is: <?xml version="1.0"
  encoding="encoding type" standalone="yes" ?>.]]>
```

Another way to include data that might otherwise get translated is to use predefined entities. The characters are encoded so that they will be passed through the XML parser but can be converted by the displaying application. The encoding uses the reserved character "&" (ampersand) followed by the entity name and ";" (semicolon). These entities are found in Table 1.1 and are used in the examples in Listing 1.14.

Table 1.1 Some predefined entities

Character	Entity	Name
&	&	ampersand
<	<	less than
>	>	greater than
'	'	apostrophe or single quote
"	"	double quote

Listing 1.14 Character data using predefined entities

```
<element1>This has a greater than symbol in the function:
  if(a &gt; b).</element1>
<company>Brown &amp; Jones Excavating</company>
<title>&quot;Gone With the Wind&quot;</title>
```

1.39 The Element Tree Completed

Putting all of the element information together, you can build a well-formed XML document. You can have empty elements or elements containing data and other elements. You can have comments to further describe your tree, but they are not crucial to the structure of the tree. The image of the tree (Figure 1.3) follows the rules for the XML document in Listing 1.15.

Figure 1.3

Listing 1.15 The complete tree

```
<?xml version="1.0" standalone="yes" ?>
<!DOCTYPE tree [
<!ELEMENT tree (BRANCH)>
<!ELEMENT BRANCH (branchlet, twig)>
<!ELEMENT branchlet (#PCDATA)>
<!ELEMENT twig (#PCDATA)>
]>
<tree>
     <!-- the root or trunk of the tree has some main branches -->
     <BRANCH>
          <!-- a BRANCH can have branchlets and twigs -->
          <branchlet>
               <twig>leaves</twig>
                    <!-- empty element (no leaves) -->
               <twig/>
               <twig>leaves</twig>
          </branchlet>
```

```
        <branchlet>
            <twig>leaves</twig>
            <twig>leaves</twig>
        </branchlet>
        <twig>leaves</twig>
    </BRANCH>
    <BRANCH>
        <branchlet>
            <twig>leaves</twig>
        </branchlet>
        <branchlet>
            <twig>leaves</twig>
            <twig>leaves</twig>
        </branchlet>
    </BRANCH>
</tree>
```

1.4 XML Character Conventions

To keep XML documents well formed, you should remember the requirements and recommendations for naming elements, attributes, and documents. While the recommendations are not requirements, you may find later that they facilitate the exchange of data. Here you will learn about white space and end-of-line characters, and how Unicode and ASCII, the standards for character representation, are used in XML documents. More about the name of entities, such as links, can be found in section 1.51, "URI, URL, and URN."

1.41 White Space and End-of-Line Characters

White space is not just the space character between words. White space is a set of invisible characters that perform visual spacing of the words and lines of text. These characters are introduced in Table 1.2. White space is important if you are displaying or printing text. The beginning of this paragraph, for example, would be difficult to read if there were no spaces between the words or if a new line began at the wrong place. Below is an example of improper white space.

```
Whitespaceisnot justthespac
echaracter betweenwords.
```

White space in an XML document is important if the character is retained within your content where you intended, but it is ignored otherwise. White space in an HTML document is compressed down to one character, even in the content. Multiple spaces become one space in HTML but are ignored in the markup in the XML document. Using white space to make a document more human readable is permissible (and advisable) because the XML processor does not attach significance to it. Since white space is ignored in the markup by the XML processors, you will want to avoid using white space in any element or attribute name. You and the XML processors would have difficulty determining the element name in the example below because of the use of improper white space.

```
<!-- incorrect element -->
<an element name attribute="here you go" />
<!-- should be: -->
<anElementName attribute="here you go" />
```

Table 1.2 White space characters

Character	ASCII	Unicode
space	32	#x0020
horizontal tab	9	#x0009
carriage return	13	#x000D
line feed	10	#x000A

The end-of-line character is the special white space that we rarely see as we type a new line or a new paragraph of text. You press the Return or Enter key and magically you can begin typing to the left and one line down in the document. You do not actually see any "character" there, although one or more exists in the electronic document. Your word processor or text editor may have a utility to toggle the display of white space on and off. The paragraph symbol (¶) may be shown at the end of a line or paragraph if the toggle is on.

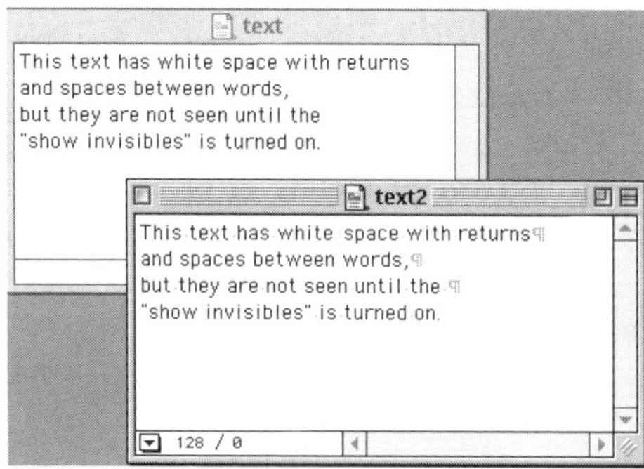

Figure 1.4: Showing invisibles

Where Do We Get These End-of-Line Characters?

If you have ever typed on an old manual (non-electric) typewriter, you probably pulled a lever to return the carriage (the type head) to the left margin and you made the roller feed the paper up one line (or more for multiple spacing). When the process for document composition is automated, printers and teletype machines have to be given precise instructions for everything they do. The two instructions for the location of the print head are carriage return and line feed. The return to the beginning of a line does not necessarily mean that you want the line to feed down at the same time. Separating these two instructions allows for printing text on top of text in the same line and creating unique symbols or simulated graphics from a limited set of characters.

Using the End-of-Line Characters

Electronic typewriters and computers include a Return or Enter key for the end-of-line action. A single keystroke sends a signal to the system processor, which takes the return to the left margin and moves down a line when the text is displayed on a monitor or as a printed document. A new line is created when the instruction for end of line is received. We also may see the text flow to the next line if the screen is a particular width. This is not a new line but is called text wrap and is the continuation of the same line. End-of-line or new line instructions may be called a hard return or end of paragraph. Hard returns occur only where you specifically press the Return or Enter key.

The end-of-line character is different on various systems. On Macintosh, the end-of-line character is the carriage return. The UNIX operating system uses line feed for the end-of-line character. Carriage return and line feed are both utilized on the Windows operating system. The document is stored with these invisible characters wherever there is an end of line. Sometimes they are not interpreted correctly by applications if the document is written on one system and read on another. You may have seen text appear incorrectly or contain a box character to replace the invisible character it cannot interpret.

XML documents can be processed on any operating system. If the document contains carriage returns, line feeds, or any combination of these two characters, an XML processor may convert the end of line to the line feed character (Unicode #x00010) after processing. This keeps the document consistent for further processing.

1.42 Unicode vs. ASCII

There are so many ways to say the same thing and so little time! We have graphical representations for many of our spoken languages. These are our written languages. Machines need a way to transmit a representation of our spoken and written languages. Just like typing white space characters, other characters on a computer keyboard send a signal for each key or combination of keys. This signal is a numerical representation of the key pressed. Most keyboards use the standard ASCII 256-character set, and often a sort will use the ASCII numerical value. Some of the ASCII characters can be found in Listing 1.16. An exercise to create the ASCII character set in HTML is also included in this section.

Listing 1.16 Sample ASCII codes and character representation

```
65   A
66   B
67   C
97   a
98   b
99   c
191  ø
59   ;
49   1
50   2
51   3
184  π
60   <
163  £
```

This representation can be used to translate text from one written language to another representation of the same language. Note these special symbols: the Greek pi (π), Scandinavian o-slash (ø), and British pound symbol (£). However, the American Standard Code for Information Interchange (ASCII) is quite limited for use internationally. ASCII omits a way to represent Japanese, Chinese, symbols, and other highly ideographical languages. ASCII can also be limiting if different applications and systems do not translate the numerical representations identically.

Exercise 1.2 Create Your Own ASCII Table

1. Open FileMaker Pro.
2. Create a database called **ASCII.FP5** and define these four fields:
   - ASCII (number)

- Character (calculated, text result, = "&#" & ASCII & ";")
- HTML (text)
- gCounter (global number)

3. Create the script Create ASCII Table:

```
Set Error Capture [ On ]
Show All Records
Delete All Records [ No dialog ]
# Comment: Set the counter to zero
Set Field [ "gCounter", "0" ]
Loop
  New Record/Request
  Set Field [ "ASCII", "gCounter" ]
  Set Field [ "HTML", "If(ASCII = 0, "<html><head><title>ASCII
    TABLE</title></head>
    <body><table border=0>¶
    <tr><th>ASCII</th>
    <th>Character</th></tr>¶", "") &
    "<tr><td>" &ASCII & "</td><td>" & Character & "</td></tr>¶" &
  If(ASCII = 255, "</table></body></html>", "")" ]
  Set Field [ "gCounter", "gCounter + 1" ]
  Exit Loop If [ "gCounter = 256" ]
End Loop
Export Records [ Filename: "ASCII.html"; Export Order: HTML  (Text) ]
 [ Restore export order, No dialog ]
```

After you perform the script and export this table, you can open the document in a text editor to see the results. You can also open the document in your browser to see the characters created. You may get different results from the same document if you change the font type or size in your browser preferences. Viewing the same document on different systems may also produce different results as the character mapping may be different.

A standard (ISO/IEC 10646) has been devised for representing characters used for electronic transmission. Information about the International Organization for Standardization can be found at http://www.iso.ch/iso/en/ISOOnline.frontpage. This representation of characters is called Unicode. If you tested the above exercise, you may have seen how the same character may not be precisely rendered the same by changing your browser default font. The Unicode standard was created to avoid these problems. Unicode attempts to include characters such as those used for scientific symbols and non-English text characters, thus making it a UNIversal CODE set. Only the first 128 characters are the same in Unicode and the ASCII table.

1.43 Names Using Alphanumeric Characters

The use of white space can cause problems when naming your XML elements. Other characters not in the ASCII and Unicode tables might also be a problem for all systems to process. Even within those first 128 characters, you will have control characters that may not be visible. If you follow the recommendation of only using alphanumeric characters for naming entities, you will be assured of compatibility with most systems and applications. The common letters and numbers have ASCII and Unicode equivalents. These ranges can be found in Table 1.3.

Table 1.3 Alphanumeric, ASCII, and Unicode equivalents

Characters	ASCII	UTC Unicode
0-9	48-57	#x0030-#X0039
A-Z	65-90	#x0041-#x005A
a-z	97-122	#x0061-#x007A

FileMaker Pro Help makes recommendations for naming fields. Figure 1.5 is a screen shot of this information. The same recommendations might apply to all object names, such as file names, value list names, relationship names, layout names, and script names. Your preference may work well for single databases or complete sets of databases, but for XML or any web publishing, you may need to reconsider current choices.

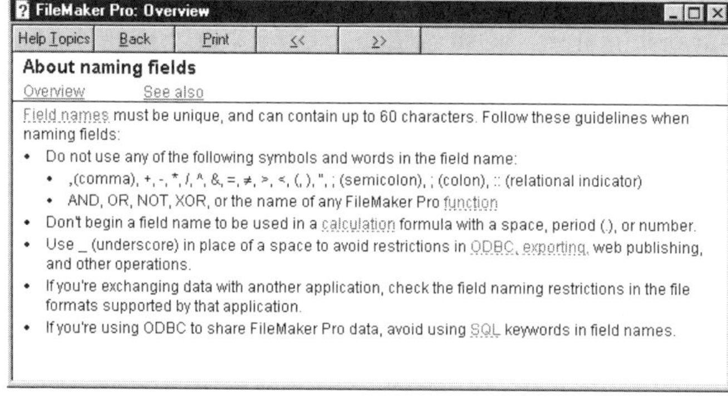

Figure 1.5: Naming fields in FileMaker Pro

1.5 Beyond Basic XML—Other Standards

So far we have studied well-formed and valid documents containing data and other elements. XML is a language that allows other standards to be built upon it. Included in the list of additions to the XML family is XSL (XML Stylesheet Language). You will read more about XSL and how it can be used to transform XML data into neatly formatted output in Chapter 7.

The World Wide Web Consortium has also recommended additional standards for interconnecting documents and addressing precise locations within XML documents. Among these other XML standards are XPointer and XPath, which extend XML. This section gives an overview of each of these and the URI (Uniform Resource Identifier) standard for identifying and locating resources used by XML documents. These recommendations have been grouped together here, as they often work together. However, they can also work independently.

Keep in mind that this section is a very basic overview to help you understand these additions to XML, parsing of XML with FileMaker Pro, and how these standards work with XML and FileMaker Pro. Remember, too, that the specifications and recommendations may change, although it is unlikely that these changes will affect the current technology. The changes may enhance the current specifications just as XPath and XPointer have added to the functionality of XML. You may consult the World Wide Web Consortium for the latest information, http://www.w3.org/.

1.51 URI, URL, and URN (The Uniform Resource Standards)

Uniform Resource Identifiers (URIs) encompass all references to web files: text, images, mailboxes, and other resources. URIs include URLs (Uniform Resource Locators): ftp, gopher, http, mailto, file, news, https, and telnet, common protocols for accessing information on the Internet. Some examples of these are found in Listing 1.18. Remember that the World Wide Web is only a part of the Internet. URIs may be used in XPaths and XPointers if they refer to an address on the Internet.

Another URI type is the URN (Uniform Resource Name). The URN has globally persistent significance; only the name of the resource need be known, not the location of it as in the URL. The Uniform

Resource Name can be associated with Uniform Resource Characteristics (URC), which allows descriptive information to be associated with a URN. A URN can also have a URL. A more complete URL is found in Listing 1.17.

Listing 1.17 URL with more information

```
<link href="http:anyserver/documents/myPaper.txt">
      <author>Me!</author>
      <date>03 JAN 1999</date>
      <revised>05 FEB 1999</revised>
      <title>My Important Paper</title>
</link>
```

Uniform Resource Identifiers can be absolute or relative. Relative paths assume the current document location, and every link from there builds upon the path. A document can have a BASE path specified at the beginning of the document.

Warning: While the password may be included in a URI, it is not advisable, as it may be a security risk. The URI format is:

```
protocol user : password @ host : port / path document ? query # fragment
```

Listing 1.18 Example URIs

```
http://www.mydomain.com/mypage.html
ftp://username:password@server.domin.org/
file:///myDesktop/Documents/fmpxmllayout_dtd.txt
urn:here://iris
mailto:me@mydomain.com?subject=Inquiry%20About%20Your%20Site
ftp://anonymous@server.domain.net:591/index/images/downloads/
telnet://myServer.edu/
http://myDomain.com/fmpro?-db=myDatabase&-lay=web&-format=-fmp_xml&-findall
news:comp.databases.filemaker
https://secureServer.net/thisLink.html#sectionThree
```

The Request For Comment (RFC) document number 2396 was written to specify the standards for Uniform Resource Identifiers. This document, "Uniform Resource Identifiers (URI): Generic Syntax," can be found at http://www.ietf.org/rfc/rfc2396.txt. Notable are the standards for naming these URIs. You should read this list of standards for naming.

Suggestions for naming URIs include using the alphanumeric characters: a-z, A-Z, and 0-9. Any character not within these ranges can be escaped or translated to an octet sequence consisting of "%" and the hexadecimal representation of the character. This means that the space character is often encoded as “%20” in a URL so that it may pass safely as a valid URI. There are other characters used to format a URL that are reserved to specify the format of the URL. These are: “;”, “/”, “:”, “#”, “%”, “@”, “&”, “=”, “+”, “$”, and “,”. There are also unreserved characters that may be used for specific purposes: “-”, “_”, “.”, “!”, “~”, “'”, “(”, and “)”. Characters listed as unwise to use include: “{”, “}”, “|”, “\”, “^”, “[”, “]”, and “`”. If you stick with the alphanumeric characters for your own naming standards, you are less likely to disrupt any usage for the URI itself.

Mailto Is a Special URL

Another document, “RFC 2368, The mailto URL scheme,” http://www.ietf.org/rfc/rfc2368.txt, gives us more specifics for the mailto protocol. This particular URI is often used to send email and can easily be created from calculations in a FileMaker Pro field. The most basic form of this URI is mailto:yourEmail@yourDomain.com. It simply provides the protocol (mailto) and the Internet address. To send the same message to multiple people, you may list them all after the protocol as comma-separated values. An example mailto format is shown here:

```
mailto:joe@hisDomain.com,betty@herDomain.net?body=This%20is%20a%20short%
  20message.
```

The body of the message can be included in a mailto URI, but since the URI cannot contain spaces (or other reserved characters), these are converted. The body attribute was never intended to include a very large message. Some email cannot be sent without a subject, so that also can be included in the URI. The subject must also be converted or encoded. The space character is %20. Additional attributes are separated with the “&”, so if your subject or message body contain this character, change it to “&”. The “from” is implied by the email application sending the message. The mailto protocol is often used on web pages as a hyperlink. You can use double or single quotes for the link, but do not include these within the URI.

Mailto as a link:

```
<a href="mailto:Joe_Brown@eddress.org?subject=Call%20Me!&body=I&apos;
  ll%20be%20at%20home%20today%20&amp;%20tomorrow." >call me</a>
```

The link, as it appears in an email client:

```
to: Joe_Brown&eddress.org
from: me@myDomain.com
subject: Call Me!
I'll be at home today & tomorrow.
```

You can create this link by calculation and use the OpenURL script step in FileMaker Pro to "send" the message. It actually opens your email client if one is mapped as the default and pastes these fields into the proper location of the new email. In the process of pasting into the proper locations, any encoding is converted back. In reality, your email client may be retaining these for sending and receiving, but you do not see them. The message must still be sent by you; it may only be placed in your "outbox" by FileMaker Pro. Using the Web Companion external function Web-ToHTTP is a convenient way to convert errant characters that might need it.

The calculation:

```
SendMessage = "mailto:" & ToField &
"?" & External("Web-ToHTTP", subjectField) &
"&" & External("Web-ToHTTP", bodyField)
```

The script step:

```
OpenURL [ no dialog, SendMessage ]
```

FileMaker Pro Help will help you use the OpenURL script step correctly for each platform. If you use OpenURL to send email, it will use whatever your default email client is in the URL.DLL for Windows. On a Macintosh, the Internet Config settings will determine which email client will send the message. On Macintosh OS X, the Send Mail script step with mail.app is not supported in the first release of FileMaker Pro for OS X. Also, remember that some browsers do not process the mailto protocol properly. Several FileMaker Pro plug-ins may be used in conjunction with web-published databases for sending and receiving email.

1.52 XPath

XML Path Language (XPath), http://www.w3.org/TR/xpath, is a language for addressing parts of an XML document and is used by XPointer and XSLT (Extensible Stylesheet Language Transformations). XPath expressions often occur in attributes of elements of XML documents. XPath uses the tree-like structure of an XML document and acts upon the branches or nodes. The nodes are not merely the elements of the document, but also include the comments, processing instructions, attribute nodes, and text nodes. The human family tree has aunts, uncles, cousins, grandparents, sisters, brothers, parents, sons, and daughters. XPath uses similar designators for the branches of the XML tree. All of the branches of the tree (axes) are related to each other.

We'll look again at the people.xml example, shown in Listing 1.19, to understand the XPath language.

Listing 1.19 people.xml

```
<people>
    <vendor>
        <firstname>John</firstname>
        <company>Paper Cutters</company>
    </vendor>
    <customer>
        <firstname>Jane</firstname>
        <lastname>Doe</lastname>
    </customer>
    <customer>
        <firstname>John</firstname>
        <lastname>Doe</lastname>
    </customer>
</people>
```

The child:: is a direct node from any location or the successor of a particular location source. The child node is also the default and can often be omitted from an XPath.

```
<anyNode>
    <child>
    </child>
</anyNode>
```

In the people.xml example, the children of people are vendor and customer. There are multiple customer children. There could also be multiple vendor children. The element firstname occurs as a child of vendor or customer; however, company is only a child of vendor. Because the child is the default node in the path, you can specify firstname with the XPath format as full or shortcut:

```
people/vendor/firstname
root::people/child::vendor/child::firstname
root::people/child::customer/child::firstname
people/customer/firstname
```

The descendant:: is a sub-part of a node and can be children, grandchildren, or other offspring. The descendants of people are vendor, firstname, company, customer, and lastname. An example is shown here:

```
<anyNode>
    <descendant1>
        <descendant3></descendant3>
    </descendant1>
```

```
    <descendant2 />
</anyNode>
```

The ancestor:: is the super-part of a node, so that the ancestor contains the node. If we use firstname from our example, it has the ancestor's vendor, customer, and people. Not all firstname elements have a vendor or customer ancestor.

```
<ancestor>
    <anyNode></anyNode>
</ancestor>
```

The attribute:: node is relative to the referenced node and can be selected with the name of the attribute.

```
<node attribute="attrName" />
```

The namespace:: node contains the namespace. More about the namespace will be discussed in Chapter 7 with XSL.

The self:: node is the reference node and another way to specify where you already are, but it may be used in conjunction with ancestor or descendant (ancestor-or-self:: and descendant-or-self::).

XPath expressions (statements) have one or more location steps separated by a slash ("/"). The location steps have one of the above axis items, a node test, and an optional predicate. The node test is used to determine the principal node type. Node types are root, element, text, attribute, namespace, processing instruction, and comment. For the attribute axis, the principal node type is attribute, and for the namespace axis, the principal node type is namespace. For all others, the element is the principal node type. The predicate will filter a node-set with respect to the axis to produce a new node-set. This is the real power of XPath using the syntax shortcuts, functions, and string-values as the predicate to select fragments of an XML document.

Table 1.4 XPath shortcuts

*	Selects all matches. This is similar to the notation in UNIX for all, or the wildcard for zero or more characters in FileMaker Pro's find symbols. Searching people.xml for people/vendor/* selects the elements firstname and company. If you searched for */*/firstname, you would select every firstname element with two ancestors. In our example, this would select all matches for firstname. Should this element be the same path from the root, you could easily extract all firstnames in this document.
/	As the first character in an XPath statement, selects the root or parent of the document. A quick way to navigate back to the root is to use the "/" shortcut. Navigating the XML document starts at this root point. If you happen to end up at vendor/company, for example, and wish to navigate to customer/lastname, you can quickly get back to the root of the document with /customer/lastname because customer is a child of the root element.

//	Selects all elements that match the criteria within and including the current node. This is equivalent to the descendant-or-self::node(). Using our people.xml example again, we can quickly select *all* firstname elements with //firstname. Regardless of the descendant level for this element, it is selected.
@	Specifies an attribute and is equivalent to attribute::. The example <element attribute="attrName" /> can be written as element/attribute::attrName or element[@attrName].
.	Selects the context node and is equivalent to self::node(). As you address a particular location, it is convenient to include where you are rather than needing to use the full name of the element. For example, if you were at the element customer and wished to get the children of this element, you would use ./firstname and ./lastname. Since the child:: axis can be implied, "./firstname" is the same as "firstname."
..	Selects the parent of the context node and is equivalent to parent::node(). This is similar to UNIX URI paths used to go up a directory, such as <img src="../images/mypic.gif">. If you are in the /customer/firstname element and want to return to vendor/firstname, you can go back up a level with ../firstname.
[]	Gives the position of the child in a family. child[1] is the first child. These square brackets are also used when a test of the value of the element is needed: parent[child="test"]. We have two children of people called customer. We can navigate to the second occurrence of this child with /customer[2].

XPath String-Values

Each of the nodes has a value returned by the xsl:value-of function. This is the key to getting the content of your XML document. This section explains each node's string value.

The root() node string-value is the concatenation of the string-values of all text node descendants of the root node. If you want the text of the entire document, this will give it to you. Take note that white space will be ignored and you will lose the meaning of the individual elements. One possible benefit of using this value is to search an entire document for a particular value. In our people.xml example, the root is the outermost element, <people>...</people>. The value of the root() is all the text (contents) of all the elements in the document.

The element() node string-value is the concatenation of the string-values of all text node descendants of the element node. The element can have text and other elements, so all text of a particular element is returned here. The value of vendor is John Paper Cutters. The value of customer[1] is Jane Doe.

The attribute() node string-value is the value of the attribute of the parent element. However, the attribute is not a child of the element. If you had an element, <customer preferred="yes">... </customer>, the attribute preferred has the value "yes."

The namespace() node is like the attribute node, as an element can have a namespace. The string-value of the namespace node is the URI or other link specified in the namespace. Namespaces will be discussed more fully in Chapter 7.

The processing instruction() node has the local name of the processing instruction's target. The string-value of the processing instruction node is the part of the processing instruction following the target. A common processing instruction is for an XSL stylesheet. The value of <?xml-stylesheet href="headlines.xsl" type="text/xsl" ?> is the target, headlines.xsl.

The comment() node string-value is the content of the comment not including the surrounding markup (<!-- and -->). The comment <!-- here is a comment --> has a string-value of "here is a comment."

The text() node contains the character data in the element that is the string-value of the text node. The value of /vendor/firstname/text() is the same as the value of /vendor/firstname or John.

XPath Functions

There are additional functions as a part of the XPath language. These can extract more precisely the particular text you need. FileMaker Pro has similar text functions such as Left(text, number) or MiddleWords(text, start, number). These additional XPath functions are not discussed here. The standards are changing, and these new functions may not be fully supported by all XML processors at this time. Your particular choice of XML parser may allow you to use the full set of functions. See Chapter 6 for some of these XPath functions.

XPointer Related to XPath

XML Pointer Language (XPointer) is another method of extracting the content of an XML document. Some applications use XPointer or a combination of XPointer and XPath to parse the XML data tree. The notation is different from XPath and uses the locators root(), child(), descendant(), and id().

root() is similar to XPath "/" or the entire document. The paths to the elements are based off the root() with a "." dot notation. For example, root().child().child() would be similar to "/parent/child."

id() is similar to root() but is a specific element's ID attribute. Because the ID of an element is unique for each element in an XML document, it does matter what path the element is on. The XPointer request for "ID(890)" will jump right to that element and return the element and any of its descendants. Listing 1.20 is a small XML document used to explain the XML Pointer Language.

Listing 1.20 Example for XPointer references

```
<elements>
     <element ID="23469">xyz</element>
     <element ID="123" />
     <element ID="890">
          <element ID="57">1245</element>
     </element>
</elements>
```

The child() node has some parameters that will narrow down which child. The first parameter is a number or "all." The number is the number of the child in the document. "root().child(1).child(3)" is the same as calling "ID(890)" because the third child of the first element of the entire document has the ID attribute of 890. The parameter of "all" will return all elements in a path. "root().child(1).child(all)" returns all elements except the first element.

```
child(# or all, NodeName, AttributeName="")
```

The descendant() node is similar to the child() node, except it can be anywhere as a reference to any element's descendants.

You can read more about XPointer at http://www.w3.org/TR/xptr. This book does not use this language in any of the examples.

1.6 Reading More about XML

If you wish to get the most recent information about XML, you may want to visit the World Wide Web Consortium (W3C) at http://www.w3.org/. Most of the documents use a format called Extended Backus-Naur Form (EBNF) notation. You may have used a similar notation if you ever performed grep (from UNIX command global/regular expression/print) or regular expression searches.

Conclusion

You have been presented with some basic XML history, document structure, and suggestions for valid and well-formed XML. This chapter made no attempt to be comprehensive, and you have been provided references for further study. However, these basics are sufficient to help you with the XML usage in FileMaker Pro.

XML import and export with FileMaker Pro 6 is discussed in Chapter 2, and exporting and importing XML with XSL stylesheets is discussed in Chapter 8. You can read more about DTDs and FileMaker Pro XML schemas in Chapters 3 and 4. If you have successfully set up Web Companion for Instant or Custom Web Publishing with FileMaker Pro, you may wish to skip to section 5.2, "XML Request Commands for Web Companion." If you want to understand Web Companion a bit more and learn how to set it up for XML publishing, see section 5.1, "Setting Up Web Companion for XML Requests." You may also find "Security with Web Companion" in Chapter 5 helpful.

Chapter 2

XML Import and Export with FileMaker Pro 6

In FileMaker Pro 6, you can export and import using the new application programming interface (API) called, appropriately, "XML." This plug-in is located in the System folder on the Windows operating system and the FileMaker Extensions folder on the Macintosh operating system. Unlike other plug-ins, the XML plug-in does not need to be enabled, as it is always available. The XML plug-in uses the Xerces XML parser and the Xalan processor to import and export XML. You can read more about the parser and processor at http://www.apache.org or through your favorite Internet search engine.

An XML export or import is very similar to other text export or import options in FileMaker Pro. You don't need to know how to web publish to export and import XML data with FileMaker Pro 6. There is a slightly different dialog for specifying the XML format for export and for specifying the use of an optional stylesheet. The following examples show you how the XML exports and imports differ from other text exports and imports in FileMaker Pro 6.

2.1 XML Export

This section will present the FileMaker Pro 6 Export options for XML. The first example uses the FMPDSORESULT grammar. The second example uses the FMPXMLRESULT grammar. FileMaker Pro 6 uses two different grammars for XML Export, and these will be discussed later in this chapter and in Chapter 4, "FileMaker Pro XML Schema or Grammar Formats (DTDs)." Special field export considerations will also be discussed in this section.

2.11 Setting Up XML Export

To set up a manual export with XML, choose File, Export Records. Navigate to a directory and name a file to export. Add the appropriate extension, such as ".xml" for a simple export. You may be using another extension, ".txt" or ".htm" for example, if you transform the exported data by choosing a stylesheet. Select XML for the Type and click the Save button. So far this XML export has been similar to other exports such as tab-separated text or comma-separated text. The XML export is just another type of text export. Figure 2.1 shows where this type of export differs from the other types of exports.

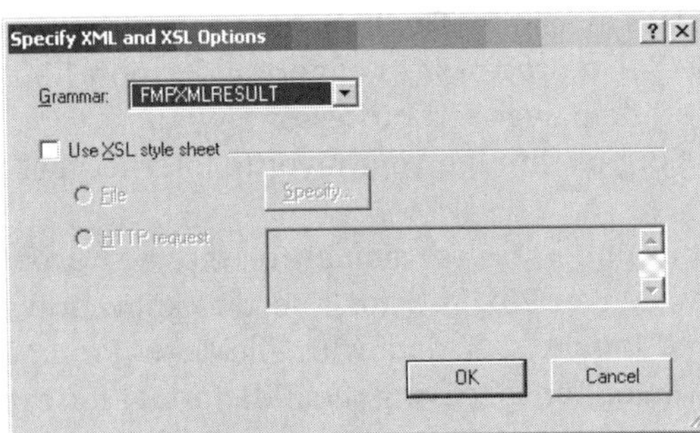

Figure 2.1: Specify XML export options

Choose the FMPDSORESULT grammar, but do not select the Use XSL stylesheet check box. XSL stylesheets will be discussed in Chapter 7, with instructions for exporting and selecting the stylesheet option. After you choose the FMPDSORESULT grammar, click the OK button and you will be presented with the next dialog, shown in Figure 2.2. Again, you are given a dialog for XML export.

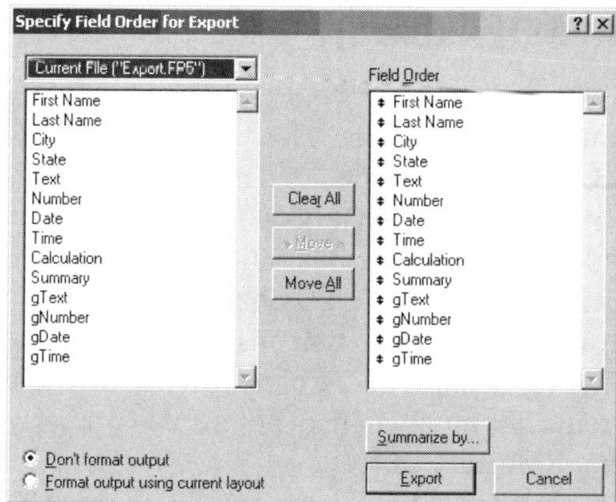

Figure 2.2: Select fields to export

In the Specify Field Order for Export dialog, you have several options. Click a field and the Move button to select a field for export. You may, optionally, double-click a field on the left to move it to the right Field Order box. You may rearrange or clear fields in the Field Order list. The number of records depends upon the found set prior to export, and the record order for export depends on any sort performed prior to export.

Another option is chosen by selecting a relationship on the left to export any related fields. Related fields and the other two options, formatting output or summarizing output, will be discussed later in this chapter. To see an example of a simple export, only select fields in the Current File.

Click the Export button and a text file is created with the name you specified. You may view your XML file with any text editor. To see the tree-like structure of your data, some HTML editors will reformat the text with indentations. The Microsoft Internet Explorer browser also has a default stylesheet that will reformat the XML with indentations. While it's convenient to see this structure as a "pretty-print," the XML parsers do not need to have the text reformatted.

Warning: Do not reformat your XML exported text, as HTML editors may insert unwanted white space (spaces, tabs, and returns). This reformatted text with extra characters may not be what you want for your XML output. Some of the examples in this book have extra tabs and returns to make the code easier to read.

2.12 FMPDSORESULT Export

The FMPDSORESULT grammar creates elements with the name of each field as the name of each element. This format more closely resembles other XML schema or grammars that you may have seen. If a field name has a space, the FMPDSORESULT export will convert each space to an underscore character (_). XML element names should not have any spaces. The FileMaker Pro 6 Help topic "XML FMPDSORESULT Grammar" also recommends that you do not name your fields with a leading number. The export will be correct, but element names beginning with numbers may not display properly in a browser or with other XML parsers.

Each record in the found set will be exported with the ROW element. Two attributes for the ROW element are RECORDID and MODID. FileMaker Pro automatically creates a record ID value each time a record is created, duplicated, or imported. The record ID is unique for each record in a single database. The value is not sequential and should not be used as a key match field in relationships, but it may be used to find a unique record. You can see the value of the RECORDID in your database by creating a calculation field = Status(CurrentRecordID). The MODID is the same as the FileMaker Pro function Status(CurrentRecordModificationCount) and is incremented each time a record is changed and committed. You can read more about Status(CurrentRecordID) and Status(CurrentRecordModificationCount) in FileMaker Pro Help.

The FMPDSORESULT grammar also creates some elements to describe the data being exported. ERRORCODE is a special element showing an error, if any. If the found set of records is empty, the menu item Export Records is grayed out and you cannot export an empty set of records. You should not get any error with FileMaker Pro 6 XML export. If you do get an error, you can find a list of the error codes in the Help topic "Status(CurrentError) Function." More information about error codes can also be found in Chapter 5, section 5.5, "Error Codes for XML."

The DATABASE element shows the name of the file that created the export. The LAYOUT element is empty if you don't click the Format output using current layout option in the Specify Field Order for Export dialog. An example FMPDSORESULT export is shown in Listing 2.1. Notice the field names as elements and the underscore for spaces in the field names.

Listing 2.1 Simple XML export with FMPDSORESULT

```
<?xml version="1.0" encoding="UTF-8" ?>
<FMPDSORESULT xmlns="http://www.filemaker.com/fmpdsoresult">
    <ERRORCODE>0</ERRORCODE>
    <DATABASE>Export.FP5</DATABASE>
    <LAYOUT></LAYOUT>
    <ROW MODID="0" RECORDID="1">
        <First_Name>Beverly</First_Name>
        <Last_Name>Voth</Last_Name>
        <City>London</City>
        <State>KY</State>
    </ROW>
</FMPDSORESULT>
```

The order of the fields exported is not of importance when using XML unless you need to import the fields in the same order. You will see later that the XML structure is very flexible, as only the required data can be extracted when needed. Using a stylesheet to display the XML as a presentation document, the fields First_Name and Last_Name can be placed in the resulting display as Last_Name, comma, space, and First_Name. If you did not sort prior to export, the stylesheet can loop through the XML elements and extract the data in a sorted fashion.

The next export, with FMPXMLRESULT, is different from the FMPDSORESULT in structure. The found set and sort order can be used prior to any export. Stylesheets can be used to transform FMPDSORESULT and FMPXMLRESULT. Read more about stylesheets in Chapter 7.

2.13 FMPXMLRESULT Export

The FMPXMLRESULT is more similar to a spreadsheet with rows and columns. The field names are enclosed inside the NAME attribute of each FIELD element. Spaces in field names are less important with this grammar because the names are enclosed in double quotes. Each FIELD element is in the METADATA element. The list of field names at the beginning of XML documents is similar to the first row of a spreadsheet with the column names. The content of each field is inside a COL and DATA element. Listing 2.2 shows a simple export with FMPXMLRESULT. The PRODUCT and DATABASE elements may have different attribute values in your export. Compare this export with the export in Listing 2.1.

Listing 2.2 Simple XML export with FMPXMLRESULT

```
<?xml version="1.0" encoding="UTF-8" ?>
<FMPXMLRESULT xmlns="http://www.filemaker.com/fmpxmlresult">
    <ERRORCODE>0</ERRORCODE>
    <PRODUCT BUILD="08/09/2002" NAME="FileMaker Pro" VERSION="6.0v3" />
    <DATABASE DATEFORMAT="M/d/yyyy" LAYOUT="" NAME="Export.FP5"
      RECORDS="1" TIMEFORMAT="h:mm:ss a" />
    <METADATA>
        <FIELD EMPTYOK="YES" MAXREPEAT="1" NAME="First Name"
          TYPE="TEXT" />
        <FIELD EMPTYOK="YES" MAXREPEAT="1" NAME="Last Name"
          TYPE="TEXT" />
        <FIELD EMPTYOK="YES" MAXREPEAT="1" NAME="City" TYPE="TEXT" />
        <FIELD EMPTYOK="YES" MAXREPEAT="1" NAME="State" TYPE="TEXT" />
    </METADATA>
    <RESULTSET FOUND="1">
        <ROW MODID="0" RECORDID="1">
            <COL>
                <DATA>Beverly</DATA>
            </COL>
            <COL>
                <DATA>Voth</DATA>
            </COL>
            <COL>
                <DATA>London</DATA>
            </COL>
            <COL>
                <DATA>KY</DATA>
            </COL>
        </ROW>
    </RESULTSET>
</FMPXMLRESULT>
```

There are some elements included with the FMPXMLRESULT export that are not a part of the FMPDSORESULT export. The name of the database is the value of the attribute NAME in the DATABASE element. Additional attributes are found for the DATABASE element. The DATEFORMAT and TIMEFORMAT attributes specify how these types of fields are formatted. The date and time export may depend upon your computer's date and time control panel settings at the time the database was created or cloned. More information about date and time exports is discussed in section 2.2, "Special Export Considerations." The DATABASE element also shows the number of records in the database in the RECORDS attribute. This RECORDS value is the same as the FileMaker Pro function Status(CurrentRecordCount). The name of the layout is in the LAYOUT attribute but is empty when using XML export if you didn't choose the Format output using current layout option in the Specify Field Order for Export dialog.

The XML document created with FMPXMLRESULT can be transformed with stylesheets or other XML parsers. The COL and DATA elements are not the names of the fields, so you must understand the order of the fields in the export. The METADATA and FIELD elements are in the same order as the COL and DATA elements, so you can use these as a map of the XML data.

2.14 FMPDSORESULT vs. FMPXMLRESULT

Which grammar is the best for you to use for XML export? It may depend upon what you need to do with the exported data. The field names become the element names with FMPDSORESULT, but the FMPXMLRESULT may be more flexible without the names of the fields. Both grammars may be used for export and transformed with XSL stylesheets. Both formats can be parsed with FileMaker Pro calculations. The FMPDSORESULT will show you the field names and help you understand XML formats. Make a test export of a limited number of records and fields to help you decide whether to use FMPXMLRESULT or FMPDSORESULT.

The size of the text file exported may also determine which grammar to use. Because FMPDSORESULT uses the field names, the size of the export can grow if the field names are lengthy. FMPXMLRESULT uses "<COL><DATA></DATA></COL>" for each field, so if your field names are seven characters or less, the FMPDSORESULT may produce a smaller file size. Table 2.1 illustrates this comparison. Two fields and the same set of 100 records are used for all the exports. Export one uses the field name _col_data, and export two uses the field name serialNumber. You can see how the size of the file with FMPDSORESULT can quickly increase if you use longer field names. More fields and more records of data will increase the file size using the FMPDSORESULT.

Table 2.1 Export file size comparisons

Field Name	FMPXMLRESULT	FMPDSORESULT
_col_data	6833 characters	6494 characters
serialNumber	6836 characters	7094 characters

A final argument for using FMPXMLRESULT or FMPDSORESULT may depend upon whether you will be importing this data back into a FileMaker Pro 6 database. FMPXMLRESULT is the only grammar used for XML import. If you have data exported with FMPDSORESULT, you can transform it into FMPXMLRESULT to import. The XSL stylesheet option is used to transform the elements. An example of this type of stylesheet is found in Chapter 8, section 8.2, "Transform FMPDSO-RESULT into FMPXMLRESULT."

2.2 Special Export Considerations

This section will discuss the XML export of special field types such as number, date, time, global, summary, and container fields. XML export of fields with layout formatting is also discussed along with related fields, repeating fields, font styles, value lists, and other special considerations, including the field names.

2.21 Character Encoding

The XML element content (or value of the element) is the FileMaker Pro field content. Text is returned between the element tags and may be encoded as UTF-8. Special characters in the field names or content may be displayed strangely if you view the XML in a text editor. The characters may be encoded to represent two characters. One example of this encoding is for the o-slash character. As text, it is often displayed as "ø." The double-byte o-slash, or ASCII 191, may be displayed in the web browser source or a text editor as two characters, "√" and "π." The character will display correctly as "ø" in the browser window.

Exercise 2.1 Export Double-byte Characters

Use the database in Chapter 1, ASCII.FP5. Export and create the text file ascii.html and view the file in a browser. Copy all of the result and paste into any text editor. Save the file as ascii.txt. Alternately, you can save the resulting web page as plain text. The copied or saved HTML table should have converted the space between the two columns to the tab character and placed a carriage return at the end of each table row. This text format (tab-separated text) can be used to import or create a FileMaker Pro database. Create a new database with the ascii.txt file. Export with FMPXMLRESULT or FMPDSORESULT the two fields in the new database. View the exported XML in a text editor to see the double-byte representation for these characters.

Listing 2.3 shows a small portion of the ascii.xml created. The ASCII characters 195 through 200 show the double-byte export. The next listing, 2.4, shows the correct rendering of this character in the browser.

Listing 2.3 Sample double-byte XML export characters

```
<ROW MODID="1" RECORDID="37449"><COL><DATA>195</DATA></COL><COL>
  <DATA>√É</DATA></COL></ROW><ROW MODID="1"
RECORDID="37450"><COL><DATA>196</DATA></COL><COL><DATA>√Ñ</DATA></COL>
  </ROW><ROW MODID="1"
RECORDID="37451"><COL><DATA>197</DATA></COL><COL><DATA>√Ö</DATA></COL>
  </ROW><ROW MODID="1"
RECORDID="37452"><COL><DATA>198</DATA></COL><COL><DATA>√Ü</DATA></COL>
  </ROW><ROW MODID="1"
RECORDID="37453"><COL><DATA>199</DATA></COL><COL><DATA>√á</DATA></COL>
  </ROW><ROW MODID="1"
RECORDID="37454"><COL><DATA>200</DATA></COL><COL><DATA>√à</DATA></COL>
  </ROW>
```

Listing 2.4 ASCII characters 195 through 200

```
195  Ã
196  Ä
197  Å
198  Æ
199  Ç
200  È
```

Test your field names and contents with a small set of found records. Perform the exports using FMPXMLRESULT and FMPDSORESULT. Look at the XML documents in a web browser or text editor. Microsoft Internet Explorer has a built-in stylesheet to render the XML with indents. The browser window will display your field names and contents correctly, even if you use any of the double-byte characters. If you view the source of the XML document in the browser, you will see the two characters representing the double-byte characters.

There are some other characters that will get encoded upon export as XML. Because XML uses some of these characters for tags, they are encoded within the field contents. Table 2.2 shows these characters and how they are encoded. Other characters may be converted in other exports, such as returns and tabs within fields. The return-in-field character gets converted to a vertical tab with other text exports from FileMaker Pro. When you use XML export, these white space characters in a field are not converted but may be invisible until viewed in a text editor. You can read more about white space and encoding in Chapter 1, section 1.41, "White Space and End-of-Line Characters." These encoded characters are also the predefined entities seen in Table 1.1.

Table 2.2 Encoded ASCII Characters

ASCII	Character	Encoding
34	"	"
38	&	&
39	'	'
60	<	<
62	>	>

You should be aware of character conversion and encoding when you export XML, import XML, or use XML for web publishing with FileMaker Pro. Most parsers and processors will correctly handle the conversion for you. But you may need to check for the occurrence of any of these special characters in your XML documents.

2.22 XML from FileMaker Pro Related Fields

This section discusses related fields and how FileMaker Pro 6 displays these fields in both of the XML grammars. In the exercise below, you will create two databases, set up the relationship between them, and export the data. The FMPDSORESULT and FMPXMLRESULT exports produce different results when using related fields. Test both of these grammars to see which one is better for your needs.

Exercise 2.2 Create Related Data XML Results

You do not need to have any related fields displayed on a layout to export these kinds of fields, but you must have valid relationships. Any parent record without related child records will return empty elements. If you use a calculated relationship and temporarily disable the relationship on any given record, there will be only one set of empty related data exported for that record. Whether you use FMPXML-RESULT or FMPDSORESULT grammar for XML export, the contents of each valid related field is returned in DATA elements.

The number of DATA elements returned per field per record depends upon the number of valid related records. For example, if you have a parent with three related fields and record one has two valid related records, those three fields will have two DATA elements each. If the next parent record has five valid related records, the export will create five DATA elements for each related field in the export. A small example for FMPXMLRESULT is shown in Listing 2.5.

If the parent record has no related child records, only one set of empty elements is returned. The FMPXMLRESULT returns "<COL><DATA></DATA></COL>" for every empty related field. This empty element allows the XML export to hold a place for a related field, even if empty, so that the same number of columns is exported. The FMPDSORESULT returns just the related field name as empty elements with no DATA elements. A small example of an XML export with FMPDSORESULT is shown in Listing 2.6.

Listing 2.5 FMPXMLRESULT export of related fields

```
<!-- not a complete export -->
<METADATA>
      <FIELD EMPTYOK="YES" MAXREPEAT="1" NAME="relationshipName::
        fieldOne" TYPE="Text" />
      <FIELD EMPTYOK="YES" MAXREPEAT="1" NAME="relationshipName::
        fieldTwo" TYPE="Text" />
      <FIELD EMPTYOK="YES" MAXREPEAT="1" NAME="relationshipName::
        fieldThree" TYPE="Text" />
</METADATA>
<RESULTSET FOUND="2">
      <ROW MODID="0" RECORDID="1">
            <COL>
                  <DATA>A</DATA>
                  <DATA>B</DATA>
                  <DATA>C</DATA>
            </COL>
            <COL>
                  <DATA>5</DATA>
                  <DATA>6</DATA>
                  <DATA>7</DATA>
            </COL>
            <COL>
                  <DATA>a</DATA>
                  <DATA></DATA>
                  <DATA></DATA>
            </COL>
      </ROW>
      <ROW MODID="0" RECORDID="2">
            <COL>
                  <DATA></DATA>
            </COL>
```

```
            <COL>
                  <DATA></DATA>
            </COL>
            <COL>
                  <DATA></DATA>
            </COL>
      </ROW>
</RESULTSET>
```

The number of rows in a portal on any layout is not a consideration for an export of related fields. For example, if you have a portal displaying five rows and have twelve related records, those other rows may be available on the layout if you have provided a scroll bar for the portal. However, all twelve related records would be exported.

Listing 2.6 FMPDSORESULT export of related fields

```
<!-- not a complete export -->
      <ROW MODID="0" RECORDID="1">
            <relationship.One>
                  <DATA>A</DATA>
                  <DATA>B</DATA>
                  <DATA>C</DATA>
            </relationship.One>
            <relationship.Two>
                  <DATA>5</DATA>
                  <DATA>6</DATA>
                  <DATA>7</DATA>
            </relationship.Two>
            <relationship.Three>
                  <DATA>a</DATA>
                  <DATA></DATA>
                  <DATA></DATA>
            </relationship.Three>
      </ROW>
      <ROW MODID="0" RECORDID="2">
            <relationship.One></relationship.One>
            <relationship.Two></relationship.Two>
            <relationship.Three></relationship.Three>
      </ROW>
```

Exercise 2.3 Create Related XML Exports

This exercise will show you how related field data is displayed in the XML produced by FileMaker Pro 6.

1. Create a main database, **COMPANY.FP5**, with these fields: Co_ID (number, auto-enter serial, primary key field) and CompanyName (text).

2. Create a related database, **EMPLOYEES.FP5**, with these fields: Em_ID (number, auto-enter serial, primary key field), Co_ID (number, secondary key field), Department (text), and EmployeeName (text).
3. Create a relationship called **CoID** in COMPANY.FP5 to EMPLOYEES.FP5, matching the fields "Co_ID." Allow creation of related records in this relationship.
4. Create a Layout named **web** and place the related fields on this layout along with the two fields in this database. (Remember that a portal is not needed for web publishing or XML export of related fields.) For data entry convenience, show the portal with four or five rows on this layout or on another layout.
5. Create a new record in COMPANY.FP5 and add related data through the portal. Leave some of the related fields blank.

```
RECORD 1: Co_ID=1, CompanyName=Herbson's Pices
```

Co_ID	Em_ID	Dept	Name
1	5	Seasons	Rosemary Thyme
1	6	Pickles	Elvis Parsley
1	7	Chutney	

6. Perform the XML Export with FileMaker Pro 6. The results are shown in Listing 2.7. Choose **File**, **Export Records**. Name the new file **companyExport.xml** and choose the Type of **XML**. Click the **Save** button. In the Specify XML and XSL Options dialog (Figure 2.1), select the Grammar **FMPXMLRESULT**. Ignore the Use XSL stylesheet check box for now and click the **OK** button. In the Specify Field Order for Export dialog, select these fields: **Co_ID** and **CompanyName** from the current file (Company.FP5). Choose the **CoID** relationship and select the fields: **CoID::Em_ID**, **CoID::Department**, and **CoID::EmployeeName**. Click the **Export** button and save the file.

Listing 2.7 FMPXMLRESULT export in FileMaker Pro 6

```
<?xml version="1.0" encoding="UTF-8" ?>
<FMPXMLRESULT xmlns="http://www.filemaker.com/fmpxmlresult">
      <ERRORCODE>0</ERRORCODE>
      <PRODUCT BUILD="08/09/2002" NAME="FileMaker Pro" VERSION="6.0v3" />
      <DATABASE DATEFORMAT="M/d/yyyy" LAYOUT="" NAME="COMPANY.FP5"
        RECORDS="1" TIMEFORMAT="h:mm:ss a" />
```

```
    <METADATA>
        <FIELD EMPTYOK="YES" MAXREPEAT="1" NAME="Co_ID"
          TYPE="NUMBER" />
        <FIELD EMPTYOK="YES" MAXREPEAT="1" NAME="CompanyName"
          TYPE="TEXT" />
        <FIELD EMPTYOK="YES" MAXREPEAT="1" NAME="CoID::Em_ID"
          TYPE="NUMBER" />
        <FIELD EMPTYOK="YES" MAXREPEAT="1" NAME="CoID::
          Department" TYPE="TEXT" />
        <FIELD EMPTYOK="YES" MAXREPEAT="1" NAME="CoID::
          EmployeeName" TYPE="TEXT" />
    </METADATA>
    <RESULTSET FOUND="1">
        <ROW MODID="2" RECORDID="1">
            <COL>
                <DATA>1</DATA>
            </COL>
            <COL>
                <DATA>Herbson&apos;s Pices</DATA>
            </COL>
            <COL>
                <DATA>5</DATA>
                <DATA>6</DATA>
                <DATA>7</DATA>
            </COL>
            <COL>
                <DATA>Seasons</DATA>
                <DATA>Pickles</DATA>
                <DATA>Chutney</DATA>
            </COL>
            <COL>
                <DATA>Rosmary Thyme</DATA>
                <DATA>Elvis Parsley</DATA>
                <DATA></DATA>
            </COL>
        </ROW>
    </RESULTSET>
</FMPXMLRESULT>
```

This export is similar to the MERGE format export. The field names are returned as <FIELD> elements within the <METADATA> element. Any field names with spaces are contained in quotes with the FMPXMLRESULT. The related fields are shown with the name of the relationship, a double colon (::), and the name of the field. Finally, encoding has been performed on the data. The apostrophe in the DATA element in the first ROW and second COL has been encoded as "'".

7. Perform the same export, but this time choose **FMPDSORESULT** and see how the related fields are exported. Listing 2.8 shows that the field names become the element names. Related field names are converted to the name of the relationship, a single period (.), and the name of the related field. As with unrelated fields, any spaces in the relationship name or the field are converted to the underscore character (_).

Listing 2.8 FMPDSORESULT export in FileMaker Pro 6

```
<<?xml version="1.0" encoding="UTF-8" ?>
<?xml version="1.0" encoding="UTF-8" ?>
<FMPDSORESULT xmlns="http://www.filemaker.com/fmpdsoresult">
     <ERRORCODE>0</ERRORCODE>
     <DATABASE>COMPANY.FP5</DATABASE>
     <LAYOUT></LAYOUT>
     <ROW MODID="2" RECORDID="1">
          <Co_ID>1</Co_ID>
          <CompanyName>Herbson&apos;s Pices</CompanyName>
          <CoID.Em_ID>
               <DATA>5</DATA>
               <DATA>6</DATA>
               <DATA>7</DATA>
          </CoID.Em_ID>
          <CoID.Department>
               <DATA>Seasons</DATA>
               <DATA>Pickles</DATA>
               <DATA>Chutney</DATA>
          </CoID.Department>
          <CoID.EmployeeName>
               <DATA>Rosmary Thyme</DATA>
               <DATA>Elvis Parsley</DATA>
               <DATA></DATA>
          </CoID.EmployeeName>
     </ROW>
</FMPDSORESULT>
```

2.23 Repeating Field Data

Defining the number of repetitions in the Field Definition dialog creates repeating fields. Click the Options button and choose the Storage tab in the dialog. Check the Repeating field with a maximum of __ repetitions option. Enter the number of repetitions and click OK to close the Options dialog. Repeating fields are displayed on a layout by placing the field on the layout, and selecting Format, Field Format. Enter the number of repetitions in the Show __ of field's ## defined repetitions option. You may show 1 to the number of defined repetitions for the field. You can select the orientation of Vertical or Horizontal for each repeating field display on the layout.

Tab-Separated Export of Repeating Fields

When you select a repeating field for export and use the tab-separated text type, the ASCII character 29 (HEX 0x1D) is placed between the repetitions. The number of repetitions exported is based upon the last repetition, not the number of repeats displayed on the layout. For example, if you define a field with ten repetitions and enter something into the sixth repetition, six items will be exported with the ASCII 29 between the items. An empty repetition will have the ASCII character 29 and no other characters, but only if one of the repetitions following it has data.

It's important to understand how FileMaker Pro handles repeating fields for export when the type is tab-separated text. FileMaker Pro uses the character between the repeats if you need to import fields with repetitions. It is also important to remember that other applications may not handle this special character if you use the exported data anywhere else. We'll now see how the export with XML is different from a tab-separated text export but similar to related fields.

Exercise 2.4 XML Export of Repeating Fields

1. Define a text field named **Repeat** in the Company database used in the previous exercises.
2. Click on the **Options** button, select the **Storage** tab, and enter the number of Repetitions as **10** in the Options dialog.
3. Place the field on your layout and set the field format to display five of the field's ten repetitions. Place the field on another layout and display all ten of the field's repetitions.
4. Enter data into the repeating field as shown in the table below:

Repetition	Data
1	One
2	Two
3	
4	Four
5	
6	Six

5. Go back to the main layout with only five repetitions displayed. You cannot see the final data entered on the other layout.
6. Export as XML using the FMPXMLRESULT. Add the **Repeat** field to the list of fields to export. To easily see the repeating field in XML, remove the related fields at this time. Listing 2.9 shows the result with the fields Co_ID, CompanyName, Repeat, and Constant.

Listing 2.9 FMPXMLRESULT export of a repeating field

```
<?xml version="1.0" encoding="UTF-8" ?>
<FMPXMLRESULT xmlns="http://www.filemaker.com/fmpxmlresult">
    <ERRORCODE>0</ERRORCODE>
    <PRODUCT BUILD="08/09/2002" NAME="FileMaker Pro" VERSION="6.0v3" />
    <DATABASE DATEFORMAT="M/d/yyyy" LAYOUT="" NAME="COMPANY.FP5"
      RECORDS="1" TIMEFORMAT="h:mm:ss a" />
    <METADATA>
        <FIELD EMPTYOK="YES" MAXREPEAT="1" NAME="Co_ID"
          TYPE="NUMBER" />
        <FIELD EMPTYOK="YES" MAXREPEAT="1" NAME="CompanyName"
          TYPE="TEXT" />
        <FIELD EMPTYOK="YES" MAXREPEAT="10" NAME="Repeat"
          TYPE="TEXT" />
        <FIELD EMPTYOK="YES" MAXREPEAT="1" NAME="Constant"
          TYPE="NUMBER" />
    </METADATA>
    <RESULTSET FOUND="1">
        <ROW MODID="3" RECORDID="1">
        <COL>
            <DATA>1</DATA>
        </COL>
        <COL>
            <DATA>Herbson&apos;s Pices</DATA>
        </COL>
        <COL>
            <DATA>One</DATA>
            <DATA>Two</DATA>
            <DATA></DATA>
            <DATA>Four</DATA>
            <DATA></DATA>
            <DATA>Six</DATA>
            <DATA></DATA>
            <DATA></DATA>
            <DATA></DATA>
            <DATA></DATA>
        </COL>
```

```
            <COL>
                  <DATA>1</DATA>
            </COL>
            </ROW>
      </RESULTSET>
</FMPXMLRESULT>
```

The most noticeable difference when exporting a repeating field with XML is the MAXREPEAT attribute for that FIELD element. We defined the field to have ten repetitions and placed five of them on the layout. The XML export uses the defined maximum as the value for MAXREPEAT for that repeating field. The next difference from the tab-separated text export is how the XML export shows all of the repetitions, even if they are empty or not displayed on the layout. There are ten DATA elements created with the field repetition contents and the ASCII character 29 is not used. The FMPDSORESULT grammar also uses all ten of the repetitions for the XML export, as seen in the next listing.

Listing 2.10 FMPDSORESULT export of a repeating field

```
<?xml version="1.0" encoding="UTF-8" ?>
<FMPDSORESULT xmlns="http://www.filemaker.com/fmpdsoresult">
<ERRORCODE>0</ERRORCODE>
<DATABASE>COMPANY.FP5</DATABASE>
<LAYOUT></LAYOUT>
<ROW MODID="3" RECORDID="1">
      <Co_ID>1</Co_ID>
      <CompanyName>Herbson&apos;s Pices</CompanyName>
      <Repeat>
            <DATA>One</DATA>
            <DATA>Two</DATA>
            <DATA></DATA>
            <DATA>Four</DATA>
            <DATA></DATA>
            <DATA>Six</DATA>
            <DATA></DATA>
            <DATA></DATA>
            <DATA></DATA>
            <DATA></DATA>
      </Repeat>
      <Constant>1</Constant>
</ROW>
</FMPDSORESULT>
```

Repeating fields use the same format as related fields when you export as XML in FileMaker Pro 6. The DATA element contains the values for related and repeating fields. All of the defined repetitions are exported, but only the number of related records are used in the XML cxport. What about related repeating fields if they both use the DATA element? Create a repeating field in the Employee database used in the above examples. Set the number of repetitions to 2 or 3 and enter data in some of the repetitions. Now try to use the repeating field in your XML export. You will get this message: "This export type does not support related repeating field. Only the first item from each repeating field will be exported."

2.24 Number, Date, and Time Field Formats

Fields can be formatted on a layout to constrain the actual data entered. Among these fields are the number, date, and time types. Enter Layout mode and click once on a number field. You can choose Format, Number from the menus or right-click your mouse to display the dialog box shown in Figure 2.3. Control+click on the number field will also produce the contextual menu for that object (the number field). Numbers can be formatted as Boolean, and text up to seven characters can be displayed for non-zero and zero values. Numbers can also be formatted as decimal with options for currency notation. Other options are shown in the dialog and can be found in the Help topic "Specifying formats for fields containing numbers."

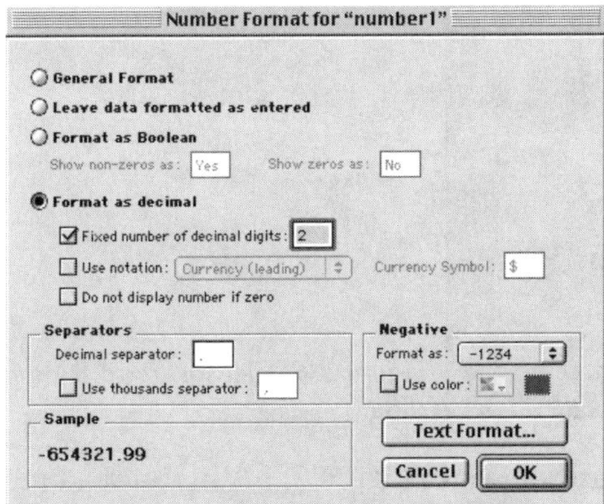

Figure 2.3: FileMaker Pro Number Format dialog

Numbers in fields are only displayed on a layout with these formats. The values of the numbers in the field do not change. XML results will return this value, not the formatted displayed value. You must specify the Format output using current layout option in the Specify Field Order for Export dialog when you export XML if you want to retain any of the layout formatting for numbers.

Another option for exporting a number as you want it is to create a calculation of type text. For example, the number 12.5 may be formatted as $12.50 on your layout. The calculated field (text type result) "dollars" might be defined as:

```
"$" & Int(number) & Case(Int(number) <> number, "." & Left(Middle(number,
  Position(number, ".", 1, 1) + 1, Length(number) - Position(number, ".",
  1, 1)) & "00", 2), ".00")
```

Note: The above calculation does not round a number as it might be formatted on the layout. For example, 1.657 might be formatted as $1.66 if two decimal places are specified. The calculation may be revised to account for this possibility.

The format of dates on a layout is controlled just like the format of numbers. The Date Format dialog is shown in Figure 2.4, and you can read more about the date formats in the FileMaker Pro Help topic "Specifying formats for date fields." Your operating system formats for dates will also have an influence on the display and entry of these dates. If you change the date and time format on your operating system, FMP will respond. The results are still as entered.

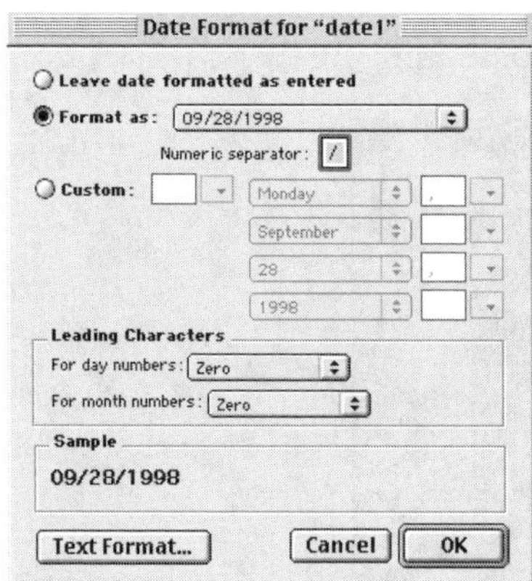

Figure 2.4: FileMaker Pro Date Format dialog

Time format options are shown in Figure 2.5. You can read more about these in the Help topic, "Specifying formats for time fields." The time format is also a function of your operating system. You can reformat a time field by selecting the field in Layout mode. Choose Format, Number, and make your selections, or use the contextual menu for the field to open the format dialog. You can have different formats for the same field on different layouts.

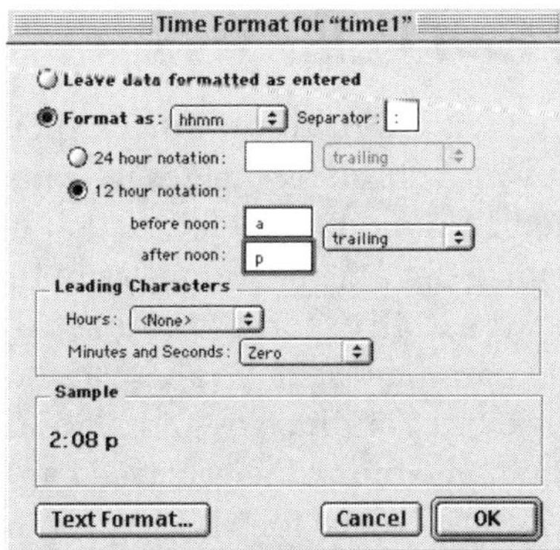

Figure 2.5: FileMaker Pro Time Format dialog

All of these formatting options for numbers, dates, and times will be exported differently if you export as XML and choose the layout format option. You may also export calculation fields or post-process numbers, dates, or time with a formatting command. XSL has functions to change the display of numbers. Other applications may have options for reformatting number, date, or time data.

2.25 Formatted Text and XML Export

Text within FileMaker Pro fields may be formatted with font type, font size, font color, and several different combinations of styles. Among the styles, you can specify a field to have, for example, Plain, Bold, or Italic, or Bold and Italic styles. This formatting can be set when you select a field in Layout mode and select Format, Text from the menu or Text Format using the contextual menu. Additionally, formats for the contents of a text field or individual words or phrases can be applied by using the Format menu, contextual menu, or Text Formatting toolbar. The text format of a field in Layout mode is the default style for that field. A field may have layout text formatting and different manual text formatting.

Text formatting data will not be retained upon export from FileMaker Pro. The data in each field is converted to plain text, except for the special characters noted at the beginning of this chapter. The XML export does not use the layout text formatting or any manual text formatting, even if you select the Format output using current layout option in the Specify Field Order for Export dialog.

2.26 Container Fields and Value Lists

Container fields are not exported with XML or any other export format. You may read more about web publishing images in container fields in the "Request for Image in a Container Field" section in Chapter 5. If you store a path to an image in a field, you may use that path or image name as a reference in the XML export to retrieve the image for later presentation. An image path may be any valid URI.

The ExportFM plug-in can extract your images and place them in a directory on your computer. The name of the image saved can be a field in the database and used as a reference for XML export. Information about ExportFM can be found at http://www.nmci.com/. Other plug-ins may also assist you in saving your images if they are already stored in a database file. See the FileMaker Inc. web site for a list of current plug-ins, http://www.filemaker.com/plugins/index.html/.

Fields may be formatted on a layout using value list options of Pop-up list, Pop-up menu, Check boxes, or Radio buttons. The format for these fields does not change the value of the field contents when XML export is used. Just the value of the field contents is returned with XML. You can read about value lists and XML web publishing in Chapter 5.

The values of a value list used on a layout may be obtained by using the design functions. The function ValueListNames (Status (CurrentFileName)) will return the names of all the value lists in the current database. You can get the values by using the design function ValueListItems (databaseName, valueListName). If you create calculations or script a Set Field[] calculation for any of the values, a field can contain the value list items. The items in the field will be return-delimited upon export as XML.

2.27 Global Fields, Calculated Fields, and Summary Fields

Any one record does not own global fields, so if you select a global field for export as XML, it will be used in every ROW (record). The size of your XML document can increase greatly when you export global fields with data. If you need to use a constant value in your presentation, consider setting these one time in a stylesheet. You will learn more about XSL variables, XSL parameters, and XML entities in Chapter 7.

Calculated fields in FileMaker Pro can result in text, number, date, time, or container output. Except for calculated fields of container type, all calculated fields would be exported as plain text.

Summary fields may also be exported as XML. See the FileMaker Pro Help topic "Exporting data from FileMaker Pro" for information about using the Summarize by option. If you sort the records by a field, that field may be used in a summary export. Or you may include the summary field with every record. The type of field and whether you presort before export may determine the value of any exported summary field.

2.28 Final Thoughts on XML Export with Filemaker Pro 6

Your XML export may produce unexpected results. Always test small sets of records in your databases for special characters in relationship names, field names, and the field contents. Perform an XML export with each of the two grammars, FMPXMLRESULT and FMPDSO-RESULT, to see if either format is preferable for your particular export. Consider the formatting for numbers, dates, and times if you use these types of fields in your XML export.

Text loses all font formatting, such as bold, when exported or web published as XML. Container fields cannot be exported, but references to the real location of images may be used if a field with this information is exported. Value lists are not used for XML export, but the contents of fields selected by value lists are exported. Only the first related repeating field value is exported. Consider exporting from a related database rather than the parent database if you need to include a related repeating field.

An XML export can faithfully return the characters entered into any field, regardless of layout formatting. Calculated fields and summary fields are exported as plain text. These types of fields might not need to be exported if you are presenting your data with XSLT. Many processors have functions to calculate and summarize for you. XML export of data in fields truly follows the XML design goals in Chapter 1, section 1.2, "XML Advantages."

2.3 Scripted XML Exports

Once you perform a manual export of XML from FileMaker Pro, you can set up a script to perform the export. You must preselect the fields with the manual export, or allow the user to select fields by unchecking the Perform without dialog option for the Export Records script step. Remember that the found set and sort order is used in the XML export. You may include a find and sort in your script or use a manual find and sort with the export script. The scripted export is similar to the manual export.

2.31 Setting Up Scripted XML Exports

Using the Export.FP5 sample file, manually export one record with all the fields. Create a script called ExportPlain. Choose the script step Export Records and check the Restore export order and Perform without dialog options for this script step. Next, click the Specify File button and you will be presented with an Export Records to File dialog to specify the file name and file type and to navigate to the location for saving the file. Call the file ExportPlain.xml and select the XML type. Click Save and you will get the Specify XML and XSL Options dialog as shown in Figure 2.1.

Choose the FMPXMLRESULT grammar and ignore the stylesheet selection for now. When you click the OK button, your export script will be saved with the last manual export field order. The script step will look like this in the Script Definition dialog:

```
Export Records [Restore, No dialog, "ExportPlain.xml", "FMPXMLRESULT"]
```

If you print the script, you may see the fields used in the export, as in Listing 2.11.

Listing 2.11 Printed export XML script

```
ExportPlain
     Export Records [ Filename: "ExportPlain.xml"; Grammar:
"FMPXMLRESULT"; Export Order: First Name (Text), Last Name (Text),
  City (Text), State (Text), Text (Text), Number (Number), Date (Date),
  Time (Time), Calculation (Calculation), Summary (Summary), gText (Text),
  gNumber (Number), gDate (Date), gTime (Time) ]
          [ Restore export order, No dialog ]
```

If you create the script and change the fields to export or forgot the manual export before creating the script, you may save the changes by editing the ExportPlain script and choosing Replace by the Export Order radio button in the dialog. If you have made no manual changes prior to editing the script, you will not get the dialog. If you do not wish to change the Export Order, leave Keep selected and close the dialog by clicking the OK button.

You may choose a stylesheet to be used when you export these records as XML at a later date. You may perform the manual export, create the script, and add or change the stylesheet options. Remember to check Replace to assure that the new stylesheet information is saved with the script. More information about using stylesheets with exports is covered in Chapter 7. There, you will set up a scripted export with an XSL stylesheet.

2.32 Export to RTF with EZxslt

Before we move on to importing XML with FileMaker Pro, you may want to take a look at an application that can help create an XSL stylesheet to transform your XML export into an RTF (Rich Text Format) document. Chaparral Software & Consulting Services Inc., of Calabasas, California, has created EZxslt. This method is similar to creating a mail merge formatted document.

You make a document in Microsoft Word and select locations where you want your data to be inserted. You may use the field names in your database for easier matches when you export the data. Once you highlight the field names, save your document as a template using the RTF option. Open your template with EZxslt and it will create your XSL stylesheet for use with the template you just created. There are two options to create the stylesheet. You may specify the record separator, such as two blank lines (the default), one space, a page break, or no separator. Depending upon your record separator, this method may produce a new page for each record. You may also choose the character encoding of the stylesheet.

The newly created stylesheet will list all of your fields and the export order so that they will match the stylesheet. Create a scripted export and arrange the fields in the correct order. You can then specify the stylesheet to produce your RTF document with all of your data inserted. You can read more about EZxslt at http://www.ezxslt.com.

2.33 Exchange Data between FileMaker Pro and QuickBooks Using XML

You can find detailed information about the FileMaker Pro plug-in FileBooks Link at http://www.filebookslink.com/. A fully functional trial version comes with sample files and documentation. FileBooks Link provides two-way data exchange between FileMaker Pro and QuickBooks and works with FileMaker Pro 4.0 through 6.0 and QuickBooks 2002 to 2003 editions.

QuickBooks is the most popular small business accounting and bookkeeping application. The current version for Windows OS uses qbXML for real-time data exchange. Information about the QuickBooks application can be found on the Intuit web site at http://quickbooks.intuit.com/.

2.4 XML Import

FileMaker Pro can export with both the FMPXMLRESULT and FMPDSORESULT grammars. Only the FMPXMLRESULT grammar may be used for import. If you export from FileMaker Pro with FMPXMLRESULT, you may import the data directly into another FileMaker Pro database. The import steps and dialogs are similar in XML as with the other text imports. For the import setup below, make a sample FMPXMLRESULT export from any of your databases and use the file for import back into the same file.

2.41 Setting Up for XML Import

Choose File, Import Records. The contextual menu will show four options: File, Folder, XML Source, and ODBC Source. If you select File, you may navigate to an XML file and import, but FileMaker Pro will make a "best guess" as to the file type. Even if you have the ".xml" extension on the file name, the file may be imported as tab-separated text. The exported XML file is not delimited for this kind of import. You must still specify the type of file. When you choose XML Source, you will be presented with the Specify XML and XSL Options dialog. Figure 2.6 shows this to be different from the export XML dialog as seen earlier in Figure 2.1.

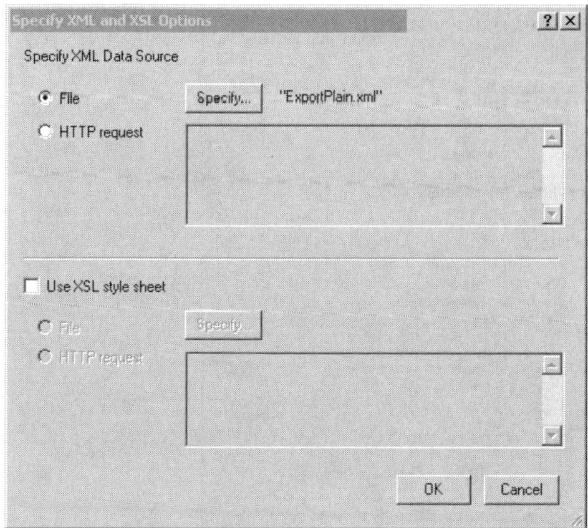

Figure 2.6: Import XML dialog

You may import any XML document found on your local disks or any mounted drives on your network. As long as you can see the file on the network, you may choose it for import. The second option to import XML is to specify an HTTP request. You can select any XML file that is available through the Internet, provided you have permission to get the file. HTTP requests for FileMaker Pro web publishing are discussed in Chapter 5. If you don't know how to make an HTTP request, you may find the information in Chapter 5 useful. Usually, if you have permission to get a file, you will be given the URI to enter into the dialog. For now, ignore the stylesheet selection.

Choose File and you will be given the Open File dialog to navigate to your XML file. After you select the file, click the OK button. Remember that only XML using the FMPXMLRESULT grammar will import correctly into FileMaker Pro. If you have the correct grammar for your XML document, you will be presented with the familiar Import Field Mapping dialog as seen in Figure 2.7.

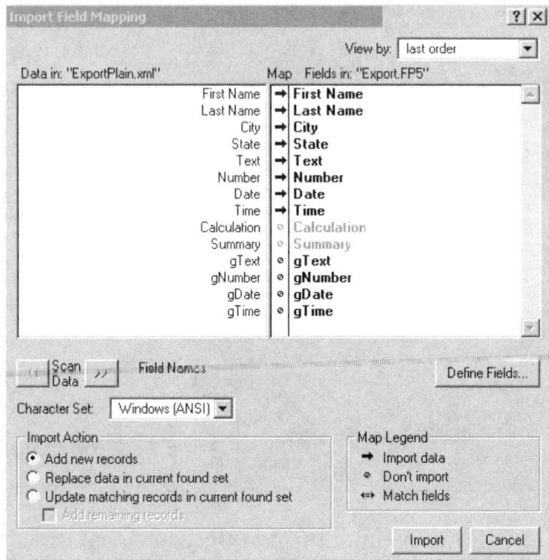

Figure 2.7: Import Field Mapping dialog

You may view the fields by "matching names" or any of the other options. If the XML file has the names of the fields the same as the importing database, the fields will match by name. You may move the fields around and select or deselect the mapping for the fields. As with other FileMaker Pro imports, you may add new records, replace the data in the current found set, or update matching records in the current found set. Click the Import button to bring the data in from the XML document. You can read more about the import options in section 11 of the FileMaker Pro Help topic "Importing data into an existing file." If your field names do not match and you want to import your XML easily, the examples in Exercise 2.5 will show you different ways to do this.

2.42 FMPXMLRESULT Import

The FMPXMLRESULT grammar is the only method of importing XML data into FileMaker Pro. The correct structure of the XML document for importing into FileMaker Pro 6 is necessary. You will get errors when you try to import XML that does not comply with the FMPXML-RESULT grammar. The error dialogs may give you a clue to what is wrong when you import XML. Export a small set of records from any database that you may be using for XML import. Select FMPXML-RESULT and study the structure of the saved XML document. Chapter 4 has more detail about this XML document structure. For many XML documents the structure rules are called Document Type Definitions. Chapter 3 discusses general DTD terms.

Here are a few warnings about importing XML into specific field types in FileMaker Pro: Repeating fields do not import correctly into FileMaker Pro 6 at this time. Only the first repeat will be imported. Related field data should be imported directly into the related child file rather than the parent file. Related fields are not available in the Import Records dialog, so you cannot make any matches for import. Container fields do not import (or export) when using XML. Global fields import once, and calculation or summary fields may be imported into noncalculated fields. Date and time data may import as text and be incorrectly formatted, such as two-digit years instead of four-digit years.

Exercise 2.5 Manual Transformations with FileMaker Pro

The following are XML import examples. The first one will show you how to change the field names for import. The second example uses the same principle and shows you how to create an XSL stylesheet with the changed field names for use with Export or Import. The third example uses a FileMaker Pro database to help you create the stylesheet.

Example 1: Export, Edit the FIELD Elements, and Import

By simply editing the NAME attributes of the FIELD elements, you may be able to import the FMPXMLRESULT format directly into a new database. This test uses the example databases Export.FP5 and Import.FP5. The only difference between the two databases is in some of the field names. Export.FP5 has First Name and Last Name. Import.FP5 has FirstName and LastName. You can make the same test with any of your own files. Make a backup copy of any databases used in this test. Make a second copy of any file, rename it, and edit some of the field names in the Define Fields dialog.

Use the example database Export.FP5 and export the fields First Name, Last Name, City, and State. Export as FMPXMLRESULT and save the export as a script. At this time do not specify an XSL stylesheet. Look at the exported XML file in a text editor if you want to see the result. Do not make any changes to the file and close it.

Now import the XML file into Import.FP5 and use the "matching names" option. The field names FirstName and LastName in the new file do not match, as shown in Figure 2.8. If you have used your own databases, import into your second file with the changed field names. You may find the correct fields and move them to match and then import. This task isn't so difficult with just a few fields but can be complex with many fields! Continue the import or select Cancel.

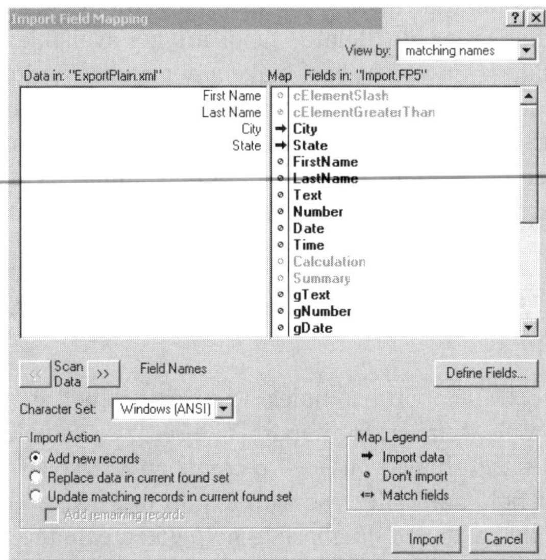

Figure 2.8: Import mismatched fields

Open the XML file again in a text editor. Very carefully find the NAME attributes of the FIELD elements. The NAME="First Name" can be edited to be NAME="FirstName", for example. Change any other field names, whether you use your own databases or the examples, and save the XML document without changing anything else. Try the import again and select matching names. If you get any errors when you import, try the export again and carefully change the field names in the resulting XML document.

Example 2: Transform with a Simple Stylesheet

Changing the field names each time you want to export XML and import into a new database with different names can be time consuming if you need to perform the task multiple times. A simple XSL stylesheet can be created and used with the export or the import. The transformation takes place when you export, and the new XML will import directly. Or you can export to a file and use the XSL stylesheet with the import. As with Example 1, make a manual export and create a script to save the export options, especially the fields order. If you export only a record or two, the XML document should open easily in an XML or text editor.

Create the following XSL document in a text editor and save it as NameChange.xsl.

```
<?xml version="1.0" encoding="UTF-8" ?>
<xsl:stylesheet version="1.0" xmlns:xsl="http://www.w3.org/1999/XSL/
  Transform" xmlns:fmp="http://www.filemaker.com/fmpxmlresult"
  exclude-result-prefixes="fmp">
<xsl:output method="xml" version="1.0" encoding="UTF-8" indent="no" />
<xsl:template match="/">
<!-- REPLACE THIS AREA -->
<xsl:copy-of select="./fmp:FMPXMLRESULT/fmp:RESULTSET" />
</FMPXMLRESULT>
</xsl:template>
</xsl:stylesheet>
```

In the above stylesheet you will need to paste part of your exported XML. Open the XML in a text editor and find the root element "<FMPXMLRESULT>" and the end element "</METADATA>." Copy these two elements and everything in between. Paste into the stylesheet instead of the "<!-- REPLACE THIS AREA -->" line. Change the NAME attribute values for every FIELD element that will be different in your new database. Save the XSL document like the example in Listing 2.12.

Listing 2.12 NameChange.xsl

```
<?xml version="1.0" encoding="UTF-8" ?>
<xsl:stylesheet version="1.0" xmlns:xsl="http://www.w3.org/1999/XSL/
  Transform" xmlns:fmp="http://www.filemaker.com/fmpxmlresult"
  exclude-result-prefixes="fmp">
<xsl:output method="xml" version="1.0" encoding="UTF-8" indent="no" />
<xsl:template match="/">
<FMPXMLRESULT xmlns="http://www.filemaker.com/
  fmpxmlresult"><ERRORCODE>0</ERRORCODE><PRODUCT BUILD="08/09/2002"
  NAME="FileMaker Pro" VERSION="6.0v3"/><DATABASE DATEFORMAT="M/d/yyyy"
  LAYOUT="" NAME="Export.FP5" RECORDS="" TIMEFORMAT="h:mm:ss
  a"/><METADATA><FIELD EMPTYOK="YES" MAXREPEAT="1" NAME="FirstName"
  TYPE="TEXT"/><FIELD EMPTYOK="YES" MAXREPEAT="1" NAME="LastName"
  TYPE="TEXT"/><FIELD EMPTYOK="YES" MAXREPEAT="1" NAME="City"
  TYPE="TEXT"/><FIELD EMPTYOK="YES" MAXREPEAT="1" NAME="State"
  TYPE="TEXT"/></METADATA><xsl:copy-of select="./fmp:FMPXMLRESULT/fmp:
  RESULTSET" /></FMPXMLRESULT>
</xsl:template>
</xsl:stylesheet>
```

Perform the export in the old file again and this time specify the stylesheet in the dialog, as seen in Figure 2.9. You may save the export in a script step and it might be similar to this:

```
ExportTransformedWithXSL
    Export Records [ Filename: "ExportTransformed.xml"; Grammar:
      "FMPXMLRESULT"; XSL (from file): "NameChange.xsl"; Export Order:
       First Name (Text), Last Name (Text), City (Text), State (Text) ]
         [ Restore export order, No dialog ]
```

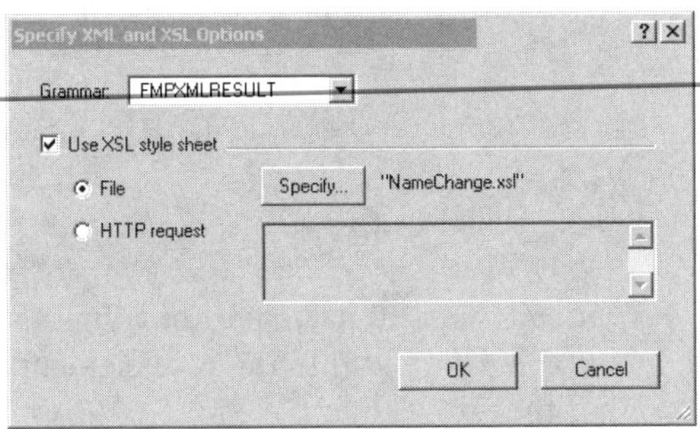

Figure 2.9: Export XML dialog with stylesheet

The exported XML has been changed (transformed) by the XSL stylesheet. If you look at ExportTransformed.xml in a text editor, you may see what appears in Listing 2.13. The field names are correct for matching names in the new file, and the data has been directly copied from the old file.

Listing 2.13 ExportTransformed.xml

```
<?xml version="1.0" encoding="UTF-8"?><FMPXMLRESULT xmlns="http://
  www.filemaker.com/fmpxmlresult"><ERRORCODE>0</ERRORCODE><PRODUCT
  BUILD="08/09/2002" NAME="FileMaker Pro" VERSION="6.0v3"/><DATABASE
  DATEFORMAT="M/d/yyyy" LAYOUT="" NAME="Export.FP5" RECORDS=""
  TIMEFORMAT="h:mm:ss a"/><METADATA><FIELD EMPTYOK="YES" MAXREPEAT="1"
  NAME="FirstName" TYPE="TEXT"/><FIELD EMPTYOK="YES" MAXREPEAT="1"
  NAME="LastName" TYPE="TEXT"/><FIELD EMPTYOK="YES" MAXREPEAT="1"
  NAME="City" TYPE="TEXT"/><FIELD EMPTYOK="YES" MAXREPEAT="1" NAME="State"
  TYPE="TEXT"/></METADATA><RESULTSET FOUND="1"><ROW MODID="50"
  RECORDID="1"><COL><DATA>Beverly</DATA></COL><COL><DATA>Voth</DATA></COL>
  <COL><DATA>London</DATA></COL><COL><DATA>KY</DATA></COL></ROW>
  </RESULTSET></FMPXMLRESULT>
```

Import the new XML file ExportTransformed.xml into the database Import.FP5. Do not specify the stylesheet because the data has already been changed with the export. Select matching names and all of your names should match.

You can also use the stylesheet with an import. First export your records with FMPXMLRESULT, but use the script you created so that the field order is the same as in the XSL above. Do not use the stylesheet for export. Open the Import.FP5 file and select File, Import Records, XML Source. This time select the same stylesheet, NameChange.xsl. The XML parser and the XSLT processor in FileMaker Pro 6 will transform the XML as it is imported.

Example 3: Create a Stylesheet with FileMaker Pro

Doug Rowe, of Robyte Consulting in Jacksonville, Florida, has taken this transformation concept another step. Using the FileMaker Pro Design functions, he reads the field names into a FileMaker Pro file. His demo file will change the names and save the XSL stylesheet using the Troi-File plug-in. You can use the example XSL_Import.fp5 to read in your field names and manually change the names. Remember that the order of the fields in the export from the old database must be the same as the order of the fields in the created XSL.

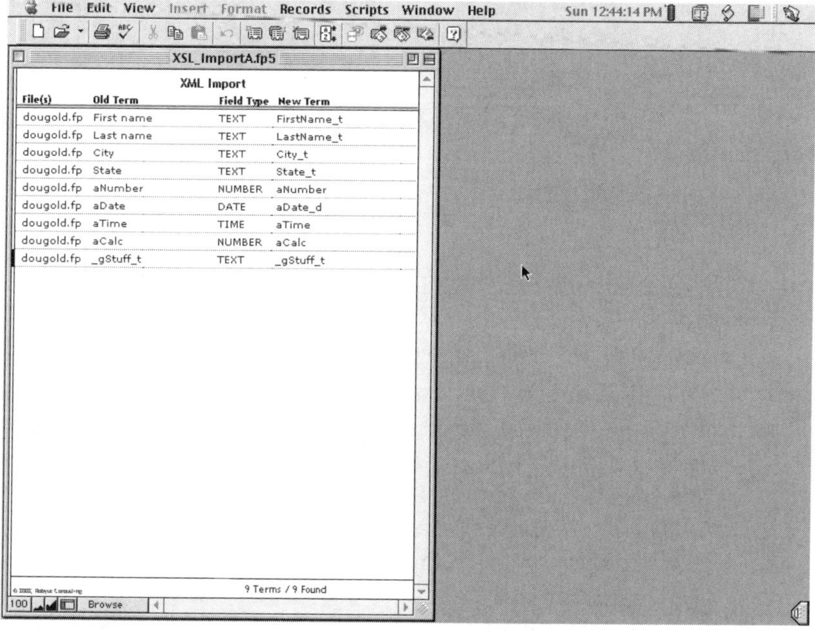

Figure 2.10: XLS_ImportA.fp5

2.43 Scripted XML Import

Just like the XML export, you can script the import of XML data. Take a look at the import dialog in Figure 2.11. Compare this to Figure 2.6. The scripted XML import contains one more option that is not available with the manual XML import. With the scripted import, you can specify a field to contain the path to a file for import or the path for an HTTP request to import.

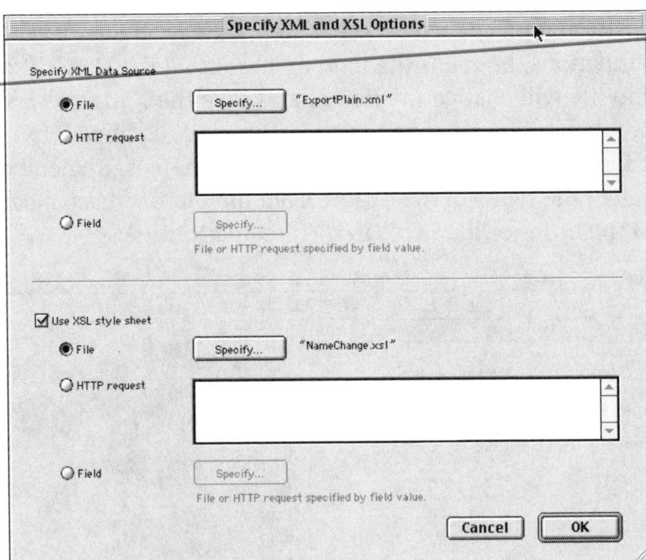

Figure 2.11: Scripted Import XML dialog

If the file or HTTP request returns the FMPXMLRESULT grammar, you can import directly and use the Import Field Mapping dialog, as seen in Figure 2.7. If the file or HTTP request is not the FMPXMLRESULT grammar, you can specify an XSL stylesheet by file, HTTP request, or a field with the file path or HTTP request.

The import script ImportPlain is shown below. The options are shown in the printed script:

```
ImportPlain
    Import Records [ XML (from file): "ExportPlain.xml"; Import
      Order: First Name (Text), Last Name (Text), City (Text), State
      (Text), Text (Text), Number (Number), Date (Date), Time (Time) ]
          [ Restore import order ]
```

2.44 FileMaker Pro XML Import and Other XML Schemas

The structure of your XML documents may not match the FMPXMLRESULT grammar. An example XML document is shown here:

Listing 2.14 Sample XML with multiple levels

```
<?xml version="1.0" encoding="UTF-8" ?>
<customers>
   <customer id="123">
      <name>Joe Brown</name>
      <invoices>
      <invoice id="987">
      <date>11/12/1997</date>
        <total>25.75</total>
        <items>
           <item id="1">
              <qty>3</qty>
              <description>Trucks</description>
              <color>Blue</color>
              <price>5.15</price>
           </item>
           <item id="2">
              <qty>2</qty>
              <description>Trucks</description>
              <color>Red</color>
              <price>5.15</price>
           </item>
        </items>
      </invoice>
      <invoice id="859">
      <date>12/05/1997</date>
        <total>4.00</total>
        <items>
           <item id="3">
              <qty>1</qty>
              <description>Cars</description>
              <color>Blue</color>
              <price>4.00</price>
           </item>
        </items>
      </invoice>
      </invoices>
   </customer>
   <customer id="352">
```

```
    ....
  </customer>
</customers>
```

If you study the example in Listing 2.14, you'll see that the root element is <customers>. If you were to design FileMaker Pro databases for this information, you might create the file ORDERS.FP5. You could design the file to be "flat" and contain the smallest piece of information (the element <item>) to be one record per item. Each record might contain these fields: customerID, customerName, invoiceID, invoiceDate, invoiceTotal, itemID, itemQty, itemDescription, itemColor, and itemPrice. You would need to retrieve the information for customerID and customerName for each invoice and for each item in each invoice. The three items ordered by customer name "Joe Brown" would be the three records in this hypothetical flat file:

123	Joe Brown	987	11/12/1997	25.75	1	3	Trucks	Blue	5.15
123	Joe Brown	987	11/12/1997	25.75	2	2	Trucks	Red	5.15
123	Joe Brown	859	12/05/1997	4.00	3	1	Cars	Blue	4.00

A flat database file such as the example above may be sufficient for a small set of data. But you can see that data is duplicated unnecessarily. The XML document shows the data in the tree structure. Only the necessary information is available. By design, the child elements inherit the parent's information. Even though the document is "flat," it really contains relational data. The next example places the related XML information where needed.

You could create three related files: CUSTOMERS.FP5, INVOICES.FP5, and ITEMS.FP5. The relationship match field customerID would be in all three files. The relationship match field invoiceID would be in the INVOICES and ITEMS files. Table 2.3 shows the databases and the fields in each file:

Table 2.3 Related files from XML

CUSTOMERS	customerID, customerName
INVOICES	customerID, invoiceID, invoiceDate, invoiceTotal
ITEMS	customerID, invoiceID, itemID, itemQty, itemDescription, itemColor, itemPrice

The XSL stylesheets for importing the XML shown in Listing 2.14 into FileMaker Pro 6 will be presented in Chapter 7. For now, these examples illustrate the XML that you may encounter and thoughts on designing the databases for importing XML from other sources. Study the structure of XML documents and find the patterns of data. Some data may be in elements and some data may be in attributes, such as customerID, invoiceID, and itemID. Elements that repeat within an XML document may be good candidates for separate databases and individual records.

2.5 Calculated Export of XML

FileMaker Pro exports with the FMPXMLRESULT and FMPDSORESULT formats. You may need to transform the exported data with a stylesheet for use with other applications. An XSL stylesheet may be used to make the transformation as you export. Stylesheets can be applied to XML after an export as well. To help you understand the logic of XSL, in this section we'll use some common FileMaker Pro functions and script steps to create calculated exports as XML.

Sometimes it may be just as easy to create a quasi-export with FileMaker Pro text functions and scripts. The structure of the XML in Listing 2.14 will be the result for this example of calculated export. The calculated export of HTML in Exercise 1.2 was used to create an ASCII table. The same principles can be used to create calculated XML export. The calculation for the HTML is as follows:

```
Case(ASCII = 0, "<html><head><title>ASCII TABLE</title></head>¶<body>
  <table border=0>¶<tr><th>ASCII</th><th>Character</th></tr>¶", "") &
  "<tr><td>" &ASCII & "</td><td>" & Character & "</td></tr>" &
Case(ASCII = 255, "¶</table></body></html>", "")
```

The above calculation is simple enough. The first Case statement appends "header" information before the first record. The middle part is repeated for every record, and the final Case statement appends "footer" information after the last record. The first and last record use the ASCII numbers 0 and 255 to determine the first and last records.

The FileMaker Pro function Status(CurrentRecordNumber) = 1 can also be used to determine the first record, and Status(CurrentRecordNumber) = Status(CurrentFoundCount) can also be used to determine the last record of a found set. To help us see the required double quotes in the attribute calculation, a global text field named "q" will contain a double quote character. For our example, the element <items> will be the root element (first and last):

```
<!-- first record -->
Case(Status(CurrentRecordNumber) = 1, "<?xml version=" & q & "1.0" & q &
  " encoding=" & q & "UTF-8" & q & " ?><items>", "") &
```

```
<!-- last record -->
& Case(Status(CurrentRecordNumber) = Status(CurrentFoundCount),
  "</items>", "")
```

The database ITEMS.FP5 is used for the following example. The fields in this database are custID, invoiceID, itemID, itemQty, itemDescription, itemColor, and itemPrice. Use a calculation field or a Set Field[] script step in a loop through the item records. Each of the item elements will be calculated, taking the values from the field contents in the database:

```
"<item id=" & q & itemID & q & ">" &
"<qty>" & itemQty & "</qty>" &
"<description>" & itemDescription & "</description>" &
"<color>" & itemColor & "</color>" &
"<price>" & itemPrice & "</price>" &
"</item>"
```

Put the two code snippets above together as shown in Listing 2.15. Export just the calculated field as tab-separated text to get the result.

Listing 2.15 Calculated items XML and result

```
Case(Status(CurrentRecordNumber) = 1, "<?xml version=" & q & "1.0" & q &
  " encoding=" & q & "UTF-8" & q & " ?><items>", "") &
"<item id=" & q & itemID & q & ">" &
"<qty>" & itemQty & "</qty>" &
"<description>" & itemDescription & "</description>" &
"<color>" & itemColor &"</color>" &
"<price>" & itemPrice & "</price>" &
"</item>"
& Case(Status(CurrentRecordNumber) = Status(CurrentFoundCount),
  "</items>", "")
<!-- the result, if the calculated field is exported "calcItems.xml" -->
<?xml version="1.0" encoding="UTF-8" ?><items><item id="3"><qty>1</qty>
  <description>Cars</description><color>Blue</color><price>4</price></item>
<item id="1"><qty>3</qty><description>Trucks</description><color>Blue
  </color><price>5.15</price></item>
<item id="2"><qty>2</qty><description>Trucks</description><color>Red
  </color><price>5.15</price></item></items>
```

The above calculation is only a part of the information needed to complete the XML seen in Listing 2.14. For example, the items are all listed, but there are no elements telling us to which invoice they belong or to which customer. If you use the invoiceID as a match field back to the INVOICES from the ITEMS file, you can use the invoiceID relationship to also use the related fields in your calculation. A custID relationship can also be created back to the CUSTOMERS file to get the information for the calculated export.

Createc global number fields to test the changes in customerID and invoiceID as you loop through the records _customerID and _invoiceID. Sort the records by customerID and invoiceID and create the sort script:

```
Sort CustomerID InvoiceID
    Sort [Restore, No dialog]
```

The following script will loop through the records, create the export field XMLinvoices in each record, and place parent elements around child elements. Export the field as tab-separated text and view the document in the Microsoft Internet Explorer browser.

Listing 2.16 Calculated invoices XML and result

```
Loop Create Export for Invoices and Items
    # "<!-- set up variables -->"
    Set Field [ _invoiceID , "" ]
    # "<!-- sort to get customers and invoices together -->"
    Perform Script [ Sub-scripts, "Sort CustomerID InvoiceID" ]
    # "<!-- begin loop for invoices -->"
    View As [ View as List ]
    Loop
        Perform Script [ Sub-scripts , "Create Export for
          Invoice Items" ]
        If [ Status(CurrentRecordNumber) = 1 ]
            Set Field [ XMLinvoices , "<?xml version=" & q
              & "1.0" & q & " encoding=" & q & "UTF-8" & q
              & " ?><invoices>" ]
        Else
            Set Field [ XMLinvoices , "" ]
        End If
        If [ _invoiceID <> invoiceID ]
            If [ _invoiceID <> "" ]
                Set Field [ XMLinvoices , XMLinvoices &
                  "</items></invoice>" ]
            End If
            Set Field [ _invoiceID , invoiceID ]
            Set Field [ XMLinvoices , XMLinvoices &
              "<invoice id=" & q & invoiceID & q & "><date>"
              & Month(invoiceID INVOICES::invoiceDate) & "/"
              & Day(invoiceID INVOICES::invoiceDate) & "/"
              & Year(invoiceID INVOICES::invoiceDate) &
              "</date><total>" & invoiceID INVOICES::
              invoiceTotal & "</total><items>" & XMLitems ]
        Else
```

```
            Set Field [ XMLinvoices , XMLinvoices & XMLitems ]
        End If
        If [ Status(CurrentRecordNumber) = Status(CurrentFoundCount) ]
            Set Field [ XMLinvoices , XMLinvoices &
              "</items></invoice></invoices>" ]
        End If
        Go to Record/Request/Page [ Next, Exit after last ]
    End Loop
    View As [ View as Form ]
<!-- the result, if the calculated field is exported "calcInvoices.xml" -->
<?xml version="1.0" encoding="UTF-8" ?><invoices><invoice
  id="859"><date>12/5/1997</date><total>4</total><items><item
  id="3"><qty>1</qty><description>Cars</description><color>Blue
  </color><price>4</price></item>
</items></invoice><invoice id="987"><date>11/12/1997</date><total>25.75
  </total><items><item id="1"><qty>3</qty><description>Trucks</description>
  <color>Blue</color><price>5.15</price></item>
<item id="2"><qty>2</qty><description>Trucks</description><color>Red
  </color><price>5.15</price></item></items></invoice></invoices>
```

Challenge: You can revise the calculations and scripts to include the CUSTOMER elements <customers>, <customer id="nn">, and <name>. A single field can contain a maximum of 64,000 characters, so you may need to store each loop step result in a single field in a separate file, one record per step. There are also many fine FileMaker Pro plug-ins that can assist you with calculated XML export. You can find a listing of these at http://www.filemaker.com/.

2.6 Calculated Import of XML

You can create scripts to parse XML to read the data into FileMaker Pro. The process is very similar to the calculated export of XML, only in reverse order. The first priority is getting the text of the XML document into a field. Remembering the field size limit, you may want to read smaller portions of the document with a file plug-in. The second priority is analyzing the structure of the XML document to see where there might be related data. See the example in Listing 2.14 and decide if you will be parsing the entire document into a flat database or into multiple related databases. If the elements in the XML document repeat, they probably should become separate records whether related or not. The next two sections show you some options for parsing (reading) the XML elements and getting the contents of an XML document.

2.61 Troi-Text Plug-in

An easy way to look at the structure of XML documents is to use the Troi-Text plug-in. There are specific external functions that will help you parse the element paths (or nodes) of the XML document. You can read more about the Troi-Text plug-in at http://www.troi.com/. One of the functions of this plug-in, External("TrText-XML"), has two parameters that can be used to get the contents of a node (elements path) and attributes of the element.

```
External("TrText-XML", "-getnode|node|XMLsource")
External("TrText-XML", "-getattributes|node|XMLsource")
```

The XMLsource is the XML document or fragment of an XML document. The plug-in reads the XML source in a field or as a literal or a calculated value. The node can be entered as an XPath expression starting from the root element, such as root/parent/child[3]/child. The expression can be read from a field, or as a literal or calculated value. Each path element is separated by a "/" and multiple occurrences of an element can be extracted by using the XPath predicate "[n]".

```
<!-- XPath Expression for node -->
FMPXMLRESULT/RESULTSET/ROW[3]
```

Using the -getnode parameter for the above node would return the entire set of <COL> and <DATA> elements for the third ROW element. This would be the data for the third record. The attributes returned, using the -getattributes parameter, would be RECORDID="nnn" and MODID="nnn" for the third ROW.

2.62 Calculated Parsing of XML

The elements in an XML document have a pattern of "<" and elementName at the beginning of a node. The end of the node is always "/>" for an empty element and "</", the elementName, and ">" for elements with or without content (data or other elements). We can use these patterns and native FileMaker Pro functions to parse XML documents.

First determine how many occurrences of a starting element are in the document. The function PatternCount(text, string) will return the number of times a string pattern occurs in some text. The string parameter in PatternCount() will be counted regardless of case or where the pattern occurs within a word. Use the XML in Listing 2.14

and search for "customer"; the results of the PatternCount() function are shown here:

PatternCount(XMLdoc, "customer") -> 6
PatternCount(XMLdoc, "CUSTOMER") -> 6
PatternCount(XMLdoc, "customers") -> 2
PatternCount(XMLdoc, "item") -> 10

PatternCount is just looking for a pattern. The element names will appear in the start tag and end tag or empty tag. You must work with a full word and a space, "/", or ">" to count the number of times a starting element occurs in the XML document. Valid starting elements can be <elementName>, <elementName attribute="">, <elementName/>, <elementName attribute=""/>, <elementName />, and <elementName attribute="" />. PatternCount() will still not distinguish between <ELEMENT> and <element>, but for our needs, the calculation is sufficient:

```
elementCount = PatternCount(XMLdoc, "<" & elementName & " ") +
  PatternCount(XMLdoc, "<" & elementName & ">") + PatternCount(XMLdoc,
  "<" & elementname & "/")
```

This would be the same as the XPath expression:

```
count(//elementName)
```

Next determine the starting position of the element. The FileMaker Pro function Position() uses the parameter for the text to search (XMLdoc), the pattern of the search string ("<" & elementName), the character to start the search (1), and the occurrence of the search string from the start (Predicate). Position() also does not give a different result for the case of the search string; for example, Position(text, "string", 1, 1) is the same as Position(text, "STRING", 1, 1). We will be using the starting position regardless of attributes in an element or whether it is empty. Search for the pattern "<" and elementName, based upon the occurrence found in the Predicate number field.

```
elementStart = Position(XMLdoc, "<" & elementName, 1, Predicate)
```

We can revise the above calculation to account for the space (" "), slash ("/"), or greater-than (">") characters that will appear after an element. Calculate each of these possibilities and add them together, as only one will match the element:

```
elementSpace = Position(XMLdoc, "<" & elementName & " ", 1, Predicate)
elementSlash = Position(XMLdoc, "<" & elementName & "/", 1, Predicate)
elementGreaterThan = Position(XMLdoc, "<" & elementName & ">", 1,
  Predicate)
elementStart = elementSpace + elementSlash + elementGreaterThan
```

Determine the ending position of the element and whether it is an empty element or not, based upon the starting position of the element. The Case() function is used to test for an element end tag ("</" & elementName & ">") or the default of the first occurrence of "/>" after the element name (as in an empty element). If the element has an end tag, the end position for the node becomes the start of the end tag plus the length of the end tag. If the element is empty, the end position is after the "/>" for that element.

```
elementEnd = Case(PatternCount(XMLdoc, "</" & elementName & ">"),
Position(XMLdoc, "</" & elementName & ">", 1, Predicate) +
Length("</" & elementName & ">"),
Position(XMLdoc, "/>", cElementStart, 1) + 2)
```

Finally, we use the Middle() function to extract the element. Test first for an empty Predicate field. Verify that the number in the Predicate field is really greater than or equal to the elementCount. If you ask for element[3] and there are only two elements, you will get no results. If both tests fail, the default text result is empty ("").

```
Case(IsEmpty(Predicate), "", elementCount >= Predicate, Middle(XMLdoc,
  ElementStart, ElementEnd - ElementStart),"")
```

The attributes can be extracted with the calculation below. You can further refine and parse the names of the attributes and each of the values. (Hint: The attributes always are spaced and have "=" between the name and value pairs with the values in double or single quotes.)

```
Trim(
Substitute(Substitute(
Middle(cElementNode, Position(cElementNode, "<" & elementName, 1, 1) +
  Length("<" & elementName), Position(cElementNode, ">", 1, 1) -
  Length("<" & elementName)),
"/>", ""), ">", "")
)
```

Using calculated parsing, the XPath expression "//item[2]" would return the attribute (id="2") and the following:

```
<item id="2">
<qty>2</qty>
<description>Trucks</description>
<color>Red</color>
<price>5.15</price>
</item>
```

This section only has a small sampling of the possibilities with parsing in FileMaker Pro. Using plug-ins and/or built-in functions, you can manipulate text formatted as XML. The FileMaker Pro functions are used to transform the XML into other formats. Some of these examples also may help you understand XSL and how it transforms the XML into other text formats. XSL transformation uses the Xerces processor in FileMaker Pro. You can read more about XSL in Chapter 7.

2.7 Debugging XML Export and XML Import

The special considerations presented in section 2.2 of this chapter may provide you with the most help when working with XML. You also can avoid some of the extra work by forcing the user to enter clean data into your databases. For example, numbers that must contain two and only two decimal places will always be correctly formatted if shown with XML exports.

The return in a field will be exported as a return with XML export. If you intend for a field to have one value with no returns, you may use field validations to prevent this. You may also export a calculated field. Depending upon the processor used, you may be able to check for the return character and remove it before presenting the data. In most cases, starting with clean data will ensure proper XML exported results.

2.8 Encrypting Your Data

You can create calculations to scramble your data before sharing with XML web publishing or XML export. You can supply a calculation to unscramble and give the "key" only to select users. Several encryption schemes can be used. One method of encryption is ROT13. This method rotates the characters 13 characters away from the original. While this method can scramble the data, it is a common encryption method and the data can be easily unscrambled by applying the same rotation again. Another way, the Data Encryption Standard (DES), is found on this web site: http://www.itl.nist.gov/fipspubs/fip46-2.htm. A more recent method of encryption is the RC6 standard. You can read more about this cryptography on the RSA Laboratories web site, http://www.rsasecurity.com.

There are two FileMaker Pro plug-ins that can create encrypted (scrambled) data.

The Troi-Coding plug-in performs several kinds of scrambling, including ZLIB compression, ROT13, encryption with DES, and signature generation. Sample scripts using the plug-in are shown in Listing 2.17. Because this text may be transmitted on the Internet, the text can be converted to ASCII characters in the range of 45 to 127 (some special characters, all of the English alphabet, and all of the numbers). Look at your sample file ASCII.FP5 for these characters. These encrypted fields can be served safely on the Internet. If the end user has the correct key, the Troi-Coding plug-in can decrypt them. You can find this plug-in on this web site: http://www.troi.com/.

Listing 2.17 Troi-Coding encryption and decryption

```
Set Field [ result, External("Troi-Compress", myTextField) ]
Set Field [ myTextField, External("Troi-Decompress", result) ]
Set Field [ rotatedField, External("Troi-Rotate13", myTextField) ]
Set Field [ myTextField, External("Troi-Rotate13", rotatedField) ]
Set Field [ secretField, External("Troi-Code", " -encryptDES|" &
  gDecryptionKey & "|" & textField) ]
Set Field [ textField, External("Troi-Code", " -decryptDES|" &
  gDecryptionKey & "|" & secretField) ]
Set Field [ result, External("Troi-TextSignature", myTextField) ]
Set Field [ result, External("Troi-EncodeSafeAscii", myTextField) ]
Set Field [ myTextField, External("Troi-DecodeSafeAscii", result) ]
```

ProtoLight, http://www.geocities.com/SiliconValley/Network/9327/, has the Crypto Toolbox plug-in that performs multiple encryption techniques. First, the text is converted with ROT13. Next, Crypto Toolbox uses the RC4 Compatible or RC6 Compatible schemes. Finally, this plug-in uses a TextToASCII conversion so that the resulting text can be easily sent as email, passed on a web page, or otherwise transported through the Internet. Example script steps are shown below in Listing 2.18. This plug-in also can obtain the VSN (volume serial number) of the C drive on Windows or the MAC (Ethernet) address on Macintosh (will return creation data+time when NIC is missing). Using this information, your access can be keyed to a particular machine.

Listing 2.18 Crypto Toolbox encryption and decryption

```
Set Field [ result, External ("crypt-SetKey", passwordToUse) ]
Set Field [ secretField, External ("crypt-Encrypt_RC4", myTextField) ]
Set Field [ myTextField, External ("crypt-Decrypt_RC4", secretField) ]
Set Field [ secretField, External ("crypt-Encrypt_RC6", myTextField) ]
Set Field [ myTextField, External ("crypt-Decrypt_RC6", secretField) ]
```

When you encrypt your data, it can ensure that only a user with the correct decryption key will be able to retrieve the data. There are field size limits, so this option may not work for all of your database records, but sensitive fields can be encrypted. Remember to remove the original data from any database that is web published if you are relying on field encryption for security.

Where to Go From Here...

The next chapter is about DTD (Document Type Definitions) used by XML to validate documents. The XML used by FileMaker Pro theme files is discussed here. If you want to understand DTDs and how they are used with XML and how to write one, Chapter 3 should be read. Chapter 4, "FileMaker Pro XML Schema or Grammar Formats (DTDs)," expands on the understanding of Document Type Definitions and the grammars used by FileMaker Pro. Chapter 4 also covers the Database Design Reports created with FileMaker Pro Developer.

Chapter 3

Document Type Definitions (DTDs)

This chapter covers the interaction between an XML document and a basic road map for the structure of that XML document. Here you will learn about Document Type Definitions (DTDs) and the rules for creating them. You will be presented with an exercise to create a DTD for the FileMaker Pro theme files, which are used by the New Layout/Report assistant. The exercise is provided to further explain how XML and DTDs work together. Finally, the differences between DTD and schema formats are discussed.

With DTDs, you can define the type of document and define what makes it valid based on the allowable elements and content. Being valid is a good reason to create these definitions, although it is not a requirement for well-formed XML documents. With a Document Type Definition, XML documents are not only valid to the XML processors, but also to an industry that wants to share information and maintain standards for document exchange.

Document Type Definitions can be listed in the XML document or referenced by a link to an external document. Listings 3.1 and 3.2 show examples of the internal and external DTDs. External references can use the same DTD for multiple documents. In this way, a company could keep all documents valid with a single external Document Type Definition. Like the XML it defines, external DTDs can be reused.

Listing 3.1 XML document with an internal DTD

```
<?xml version="1.0" standalone="yes" ?>
<!DOCTYPE myDoc [
<!ELEMENT myDoc (head, main)>
<!ELEMENT head (#PCDATA)>
<!ELEMENT main (para)>
<!ELEMENT para (#PCDATA)>
]>
<myDoc>
	<head>This is the first element of my document</head>
	<main>
		<para>Now I can add content.</para>
		<para>Each line is another child of the main element</para>
	</main>
</myDoc>
```

Listing 3.2 XML document with external DTD

```
"mydoc.xml"
<?xml version="1.0" standalone="no" ?>
<!DOCTYPE myDoc SYSTEM "myDoc.dtd">
<myDoc>
	<head>This is the first element of my document</head>
	<main>
		<para>Now I can add content.</para>
		<para>Each line is another child of the main element</para>
	</main>
</myDoc>
"myDoc.dtd"
<!DOCTYPE myDoc [
<!ELEMENT myDoc (head, main)>
<!ELEMENT head (#PCDATA)>
<!ELEMENT main (para)>
<!ELEMENT para (#PCDATA)>
]>
```

There are variations on the Document Type Definition. The World Wide Web Consortium adopted XML Schema as a recommendation. These are more complete in describing a document. Schemas, or XML Schema Documents (XSD), will be discussed at the end of this chapter. FileMaker Pro uses and produces DTDs, so these are presented here and in Chapter 4. Current DTD specifications are defined in "Extensible Markup Language (XML) 1.0 (Second Edition)," http://www.w3.org/TR/REC-xml.

3.1 Creating a Basic XML Document Containing a DTD

You can create your own Document Type Definitions using the suggestions in this chapter. Begin an XML document with a prolog containing the Document Type Declaration and define at least one element. The first ELEMENT definition matches the document type and is the root element of the XML document. Your definitions may list elements, attributes, entities, and notations. The specific requirements for each of these definitions are listed in your particular document. The name of the XML document does not need to match the root element or DOCTYPE; it is only used in Listing 3.3 for convenience.

Listing 3.3 mydoc.xml

```
<?xml version="1.0" standalone="yes"?>
<!DOCTYPE mydoc [
<!ELEMENT mydoc ANY>
list your definitions here
]>
<mydoc>
</mydoc>
```

3.11 The Relationship between DTD Element Names and FileMaker Pro Field Names

When creating the definitions, you can use the field names in your FileMaker Pro database as the ELEMENT names. Remember the previous cautions about naming elements and attributes with no spaces and using only alphanumeric characters in these names. When FileMaker Pro publishes XML with the FMPDSORESULT, it converts spaces in field names to underscores and may convert other characters. A field named "oSlashø" is acceptable but gets converted with a double-byte character to "oSlash√π." The field name "til~de" or "pipe|name" may stop the XML parser. Also, try to avoid elements or field names that begin with "x," "m," and "l" (upper- or lowercase), because these are reserved and may cause unpredictable results if used at the beginning of element names.

Exercise 3.1 Check Your Field Names

Run tests with one record published to XML to see if there may be a problem with your field names.

Export from your database one record using FMPDSORESULTS. Look at the field names.

Run the same test with FMPXMLRESULTS and notice the difference. The XML processor is less likely to get stuck on the field names "oSlashø," "til~de," or "pipe|name" when using FMPXMLRESULTS. The differences in these two Document Type Definitions will be discussed in Chapter 4.

Another test can be done to verify how a field name may look to the web browser. Create a calculated text field named cFieldsHTTP with the following formula:

```
Substitute(Substitute(External("Web-ToHTTP", FieldNames(Status
  (CurrentFileName), Status(CurrentLayoutName))), "%0" & "d", "¶"), "%0"
  & "a", "")
```

Web Companion must be enabled to use this External function. To see the field names as a list, the end-of-line characters have been converted back to the return-in-field character (¶).

These tests can help tell you if your field names are acceptable or may cause problems as DTD element names. Also, look at the results you get when you display the ASCII characters on the web. Exercises 1.2 and 2.1 can help you see what will happen to your element names with XML Export or XML web publishing in FileMaker Pro.

3.2 Elements in the DTD

The element is the basis for most of the markup in the XML document. In the previous chapter, the exported XML used the field names for the element markup names if you requested FMPDSORESULT. You can use FMPXMLRESULT to produce metadata and generic elements, but it is much easier to see the correlation between the elements as field names and the Document Type Definition if you use FMPDSORESULT in your request.

In Chapter 2 you learned that elements could contain content or other elements or be empty. To define the element, use the keyword <!ELEMENT (case sensitive) followed by the name of the element. If you are using FMPDSORESULT, this is your field name. After the

element name, define the content that this element can contain. End the statement with ">".

```
<!ELEMENT theNameOfTheElement contentSpecification>
```

The above statement in the DTD is not a processing instruction, such as "<? Do this ?>" or other markup. A declaration for a particular element or attribute is made by starting the statement with the exclamation point (!). The end of the statement does not need to become an empty markup. Do not add the slash (/) at the end of the statement.

The content specification for an ELEMENT can be EMPTY, ANY, show the childrenList, or be of mixedType. EMPTY elements can have attributes but have no content. Elements with the content specification ANY can contain any of the other elements listed in the DTD. No element type may be declared more than once in the definition. Element types are shown below:

```
EMPTY Element Definition
<!ELEMENT firstname EMPTY> <!-- definition -->
<firstname /> <!-- as it appears in the XML document -->
ANY Element Definition
<!ELEMENT base ANY> <!-- definition -->
<base>
    <!-- all other elements in this document can be used here -->
</base>
```

Listing 3.4 Element definition with children

```
<!-- definition -->
<!ELEMENT customer (firstname, lastname, shipAddr, shipCity, phone)>
<!ELEMENT firstname (#PCDATA)>
<!ELEMENT lastname (#PCDATA)>
<!ELEMENT shipAddr (#PCDATA)>
<!ELEMENT shipCity (#PCDATA)>
<!ELEMENT phone (#PCDATA)>
<!-- as these appear in the XML document -->
<customer>
    <firstname>Johann</firstname>
    <lastname>Bach</lastname>
    <shipAddr></shipAddr>
    <shipCity>Leipzig</shipCity>
    <phone></phone>
</customer>
```

Mixed elements contain content and children. The definition must use the keyword #PCDATA, followed by the pipe character (|), which means or, and the list of children. PCDATA means parsed character data and can contain any text content or markup. The definition lists #PCDATA in a mixed data element, followed by the pipe character (|) and other children. However, the content data can occur before, after, or between children elements, as shown here:

```
<!ELEMENT customer (#PCDATA | childrenlist)+>
<customer>
      <firstname>Johann</firstname>
      Johann Bach
      <lastname>Bach</lastname>
</customer>
```

To further define the children of an element, shortcuts are used in the Document Type Definition. Multiple children are listed in the order they will appear in the document and are separated by commas. Each child can be required, optional, occur zero or more times, or occur one or more times. The question mark (?) is used at the end of the element name or sequence of names to make them optional. This means they may appear but are not required in the document. If they do appear, they are used only once.

The asterisk (*) is used to specify that an element or sequence of elements appears zero or more times in the document. It is similar to the optional element (?) but may appear multiple times, if at all. To designate an element as required with one or more occurrences allowed, use the plus sign (+) at the end of the element or sequence of elements. This shortcut needs to be included if you have an element with PCDATA and children. You may mix shortcuts along with nested parentheses. We will use people.xml, as shown in Listing 3.5, from Chapter 1 to illustrate mixed elements and shortcuts. Listing 3.6 shows the DTD created for this XML document.

Listing 3.5 people.xml

```
<?xml version="1.0" standalone="no" ?>
<!DOCTYPE people SYSTEM "people.dtd">
<people>
      We can use the people element for mixed content.
      <vendor>
            <firstname>John</firstname>
            <company>Paper Cutters</company>
            <phone>555-7894</phone>
      </vendor>
      <customer>
            <firstname>Jane</firstname>
            <lastname>Doe</lastname>
            <phone location="work">555-1234</phone>
```

```
        <phone location="home">555-1235</phone>
    </customer>
    Wow! I can intermix the PCDATA between elements.
    <customer>
        <firstname>John</firstname>
        <lastname>Doe</lastname>
    </customer>
</people>
```

Listing 3.6 people.dtd

```
<!DOCTYPE people {
<!ELEMENT people (#PCDATA | vendor* | customer*)>
<!-- the root element, people, can contain content and/or zero or more
  occurrences of vendor or customer -->
<!ELEMENT vendor (firstname?, company, phone)>
<!-- firstname is optional for a vendor, but company and phone are
  required one time -->
<!ELEMENT customer (firstname, lastname, phone+)>
<!-- phone can occur multiple times for customer, but once for vendor -->
<!FLEMENT firstname (#PCDATA)>
<!-- this element needs to be defined only once, even though it is a child
  of vendor and customer -->
<!ELEMENT phone (#PCDATA)>
<!-- we should define the attribute list for phone at this point -->
<!ATTLIST phone
location (work | home | pager)?>
<!ELEMENT company (#PCDATA)>
<!ELEMENT lastname (#PCDATA)>
]>
```

3.3 Attributes in the DTD

Attributes are listed after the element they identify in the Document Type Definition. Attribute definitions use the keyword !ATTLIST, followed by the name of the element and the name of the attribute. Attributes can be of string type, tokenized type, or enumerated type. Attributes can also list a default value if there is one. You can include attributes in element start markup or empty element markup. Attributes should contain something unique and be brief, pertaining only to the element it refines.

```
<!ATTLIST theNameOfTheElement theNameOfTheAttribute typeOfAttribute
  defaultIfAny>
```

String type attributes are CDATA (or character data) and only contain content, not markup. Most attributes will probably be string type. String type attributes may not be specific enough, so tokenized or enumerated attribute types can be defined. Tokenized type attributes include an ID for an element. These ID values will be unique for each element in the document, much like the record ID that Filemaker Pro assigns to each record. Enumerated attribute types can list a precise choice of values, as shown in Listing 3.7. If you validate a field in FileMaker Pro to contain only values from a list, it could have an enumerated attribute. Attributes can also have default values, just as FileMaker Pro fields can have auto-enter data.

Default types of attributes can be required and always have a value. This default type of attribute uses the keyword #REQUIRED. If the attribute is optional, use the keyword #IMPLIED as the default value, as seen in Listings 3.8 and 3.9. A default value for an attribute is designated with the keyword #FIXED, and the value should be added automatically by the XML processors. Default values can be listed as a pipe-separated (|) choice list and can include the literal value in quotes. Because these are attribute lists, you can define all the attributes for a single element together, as seen in Listing 3.9.

Listing 3.7 Elements with single attribute and default values

```
<!ELEMENT phone (#PCDATA)>
     <!ATTLIST phone location (work | home | pager | mobile) "work">
<!-- the element "phone" has an attribute of "location" -->
<!-- it is not a required attribute of the element -->
<!-- if it is used, the allowed values and a default are listed -->
<!ELEMENT constant (#PCDATA)>
     <!ATTLIST constant value CDATA #FIXED "1">
<!-- the element "constant" has one attribute, "value" -->
<!-- the fixed content of the attribute is "1" -->
```

Listing 3.8 An element with multiple attributes and separate definitions

```
<!ELEMENT line (#PCDATA)>
     <!ATTLIST line width "1">
     <!ATTLIST line height "1">
     <!ATTLIST line color #IMPLIED>
     <!ATTLIST line fill #IMPLIED>
```

Listing 3.9 An element with multiple attributes and one definition

```
<!ELEMENT line (#PCDATA)>
     <!ATTLIST line
          width "1"
          height "1"
```

```
        color #IMPLIED
        fill #IMPLIED>
```

Listing 3.10 Attribute list for element IDs

```
<!ATTLIST record
     SerialNumber ID #REQUIRED>
<!-- there should be a unique piece of data for each element named
  "record" -->

<!ATTLIST ROW
     RECORDID ID #REQUIRED
     MODID CDATA #REQUIRED>
<!-- this is for results from an -fmp_xml or -dso_xml request -->
<!-- each row (record) is unique in a single database -->
```

The creation of definitions for elements and attributes for a particular XML document is demonstrated in the next section. You can read more about the construction of element definitions in the document "Extensible Markup Language (XML) 1.0 (Second Edition)," http://www.w3.org/TR/2000/REC-xml-20001006#elemdecls. Attribute definitions are in the same document found at http://www.w3.org/TR/2000/REC-xml-20001006#attdecls.

3.4 A DTD for FileMaker Pro Themes

New in FileMaker Pro 5, 5.5, and 6 is an easier way to create layouts for data entry and reports. Choosing a standard style for all the layouts and reports in a set of databases can provide a sense of consistency throughout the set. The New Layout/Report assistant uses the default files included when you install FileMaker Pro. These theme files are XML formatted and may be viewed or changed with a text editor program. You can change the values of the attributes in any theme document and create new themes. Any theme that you create and rename can be added to the Themes folder, and it will appear in the dialog list when you create a new layout. A sample of the New Layout/Report dialog is shown in Figure 3.1.

Be very careful to include the .fth extension to the filename for any themes you create or they may not be available for use by the New Layout/Report assistant in FileMaker Pro.

If you make any errors when you change the text in a theme, the dialog may show unpredictable results even for good theme files.

3.41 Every Layout Must Have at Least One Part

There are utilities available to assist you in creating custom themes. Theme Creator, for one, is available for download at http://www.themecreator.com/. You can import existing themes, edit them, and save them with new names. All the error checking is done for you in creating a well-formed XML theme file. This free FileMaker Pro solution contains over 11,000 colors, including many popular Pantone colors. You can add your own custom colors and create custom color palettes.

Layouts in FileMaker Pro can have default values based on a chosen theme or you can set values for a single object on the layout. Using Command+click in Macintosh or Control+click in Windows on any object on the layout will set the attributes of that type of object as a default. The default theme attributes will be used the next time you create a new object of the same type. FileMaker Pro uses these defaults and the XML theme files to create the layout elements for part background color, field and text colors, borders, and fonts.

Only new layouts can be created with the New Layout/Report assistant. You cannot change an existing layout with any of the default or custom themes. You could also use these XML theme files as stylesheet information if you want to web publish your data.

3.42 Creating a New Layout

Choose View, Layout Mode and then Layouts, New Layout/Report. There are six layout types. Standard form is used for general data entry and reports. Columnar list/report is where summaries are generally located. Table View is a quick listing of columns of fields. Labels can be selected from a list of standard sizes or customized for repeating items on one page. Envelope reports are a standard envelope size for placing the address and return address on an envelope. The last layout type is blank and provides a layout with only a header, body, and footer. You can revise any layout after it is created, including those using themes.

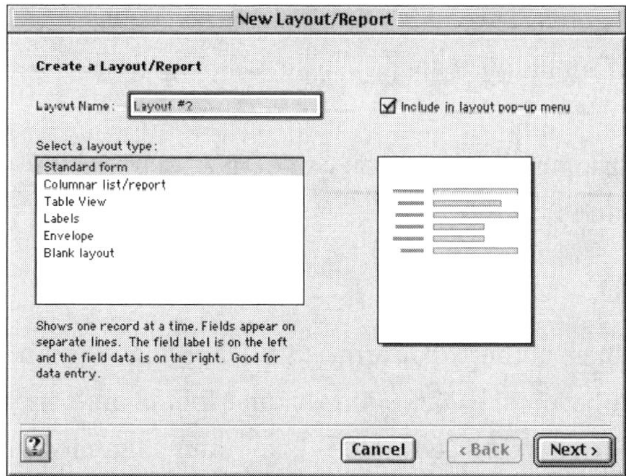

Figure 3.1: Create a New Layout dialog

If you select Standard form layout type and click the Next button, you will be asked to choose the fields you want on your layout. The next dialog will ask you to select a theme. Any valid theme file will appear in this list. Some themes appear to be similar. Lavender is listed as a Lavender Screen theme and a Lavender Print theme. Click on them one at a time and look at them in the preview. You should notice the header, body, and footer colors change. The text styles may also change. These object styles are all stored in the XML document for that theme. Lavender has one theme file, "Lavender.fth," but has two themes, "Lavender Screen" and "Lavender Print."

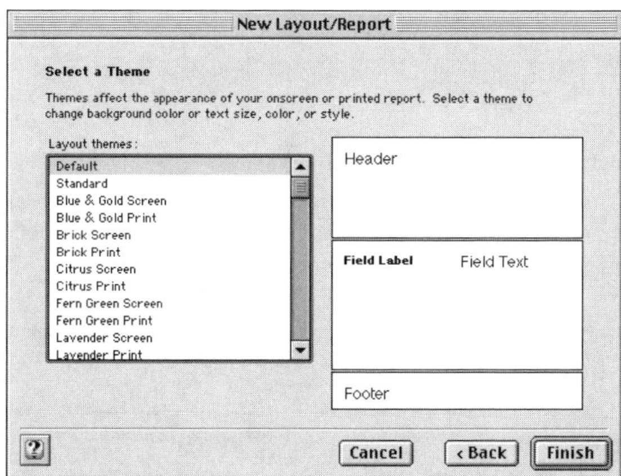

Figure 3.2: Themes from the Themes folder

Theme files contain definitions for these layout objects:

1. Theme name (there can be more than one theme in a theme file)
2. Title Header
3. Header

4. Leading Grand Summary
5. Leading Subsummary parts (you can define up to ten per theme)
6. Body
7. Trailing Subsummary parts (you can define up to ten per theme)
8. Trailing Grand Summary
9. Footer
10. Title Footer
11. Field baselines, borders, background fill, and font characteristics
12. Layout Text borders, background fill, and font characteristics
13. Field Label borders, background fill, and font characteristics

We will use the Lavender theme information to create a Document Type Definition for theme files. Only the New Layout/Report assistant uses these theme files, and they do not need to be validated with a DTD. Exercise 3.2 will help you understand Document Type Definitions. The theme files will be used in Chapter 4 to explain how to parse (read XML) into FileMaker Pro. You can use these theme files as stylesheets for your web published databases, so understanding the structure will be helpful.

Standard themes included with FileMaker Pro 5:

Blue_gold.fth
Brick.fth
Citrus.fth
Fern_green.fth
Lavender.fth
Ocean_blue.fth
Softgray.fth
Teal.fth
Wheat.fth

In addition to the themes listed above, there are new themes included with FileMaker Pro 5.5 and 6:

Aqua.fth
Hc_Black.fth
Hc_pumpkin.fth
Hc_White.fth
Windows_standard.fth

All these theme files may have multiple themes, and each theme will be listed in the New Layout/Report assistant. Any themes you create will also be listed if they are well-formed XML files and conform to the standards for FileMaker Pro theme files.

Create a Document Type Definition (DTD) for Themes

Look at the theme called "Lavendar.fth" located in the Themes folder of the FileMaker Pro folder. Make a copy of this file and open it with a text editor such as Notepad on Windows or SimpleText on Macintosh. You may find the text all running together with no apparent line breaks. You can change the end-of-line character(s) in your text editor to make this more legible. If you change the extension from ".fth," which means FileMaker themes, to ".xml," you can view the file in Microsoft Internet Explorer 5 for Macintosh or Windows. The Internet Explorer browser creates a document tree for displaying the XML. The indented style of the tree will make it easier to see the elements and subelements.

Immediately, you see that the first line declares this document to be a well-formed XML document. <?xml version="1.0" standalone="yes" ?> is the prolog for the theme document. All the elements are paired markup or empty markup with attributes. The theme document contains no content in the elements, only elements, attributes, and comments. The first element (root element) is also the Document Type. We will use a theme file to create a DTD for FileMaker Pro themes. While it is not necessary to have a valid theme document, the following exercise will help you see how DTDs are created.

Exercise 3.2 Create a Document Type Definition for FileMaker Pro Theme Files

1. Create the DTD with the root element as the document type and first element.

```
<!DOCTYPE FMTHEMES [
     <!ELEMENT FMTHEMES ()>
<!-- continue adding elements and attributes -->
]>
```

2. Look at the document and see that the only child element of FMTHEMES is FMTHEME, so we will list this in the definition. The element FMTHEME must occur at least once and can be repeated, so we add the "+" symbol to indicate one or more occurrences.

```
<!DOCTYPE FMTHEMES [
     <!ELEMENT FMTHEMES (FMTHEME)+>
```

```
<!-- continue adding elements and attributes -->
]>
```

3. The first two children elements of FMTHEME are THEMENAME and VERSION. One of each of these elements occurs in the document.

```
<!DOCTYPE FMTHEMES [
      <!ELEMENT FMTHEMES (FMTHEME)+>
      <!ELEMENT FMTHEME (THEMENAME, VERSION)>
<!-- continue adding elements and attributes -->
]>
```

4. As you study the XML tree, you may see other elements that seem to repeat. The children of the layout parts are very much the same. To summarize these, the following example will help us continue to build the DTD. The parts have not been all listed but condensed to "_____PART." The summary below shows the similar elements that are children of each of the parts. The unique child element PARTNUMBER only occurs in the subsummary parts.

```
<FMTHEMES>
      <FMTHEME>
            <THEMENAME VALUE=""  HINT=""/>
            <VERSION VALUE="ver. 1.0" />
            <THEMEDEFAULT VALUE="" />
            <____PART>
                  <PARTNUMBER VALUE="" />
                  <FILL COLOR="" PATTERN="" />
                  <TEXT>
                        <CHARSTYLE FONT="" SIZE="" STYLE="" COLOR="" />
                        <EFFECT VALUE="" />
                        <FILL COLOR="" PATTERN="" />
                        <PEN COLOR="" PATTERN="" SIZE="" />
                  </TEXT>
                  <TEXTLABEL>
                        <CHARSTYLE FONT="" SIZE="" STYLE="" COLOR="" />
                        <EFFECT VALUE="" />
                        <FILL COLOR="" PATTERN="" />
                        <PEN COLOR="" PATTERN="" SIZE="" />
                  </TEXTLABEL>
                  <FIELD>
                        <BASELINE>
                              <PEN COLOR="" PATTERN="" SIZE="" />
                              <ONOFF VALUE="" /> <!-- "ON" or "OFF" -->
                        </BASELINE>
                        <BORDER>
                              <PEN COLOR="" PATTERN="" SIZE="" />
                              <SIDES VALUE="" />
                        </BORDER>
```

```
                        <CHARSTYLE FONT="" SIZE="" STYLE="" COLOR="" />
                        <EFFECT VALUE="" />
                        <FILL COLOR="" PATTERN="" />
                    </FIELD>
                </____PART>
            </FMTHEME>
        </FMTHEMES>
```

5. If you collapse the tree by clicking on the "-" in front of a line in the browser, you will see the other children of FMTHEME. These are all the layout parts used to create a report. There can be multiple leading or trailing subsummary parts. The element PARTNUMBER is used to designate which subsummary is used. The value of this part number is 0-9.

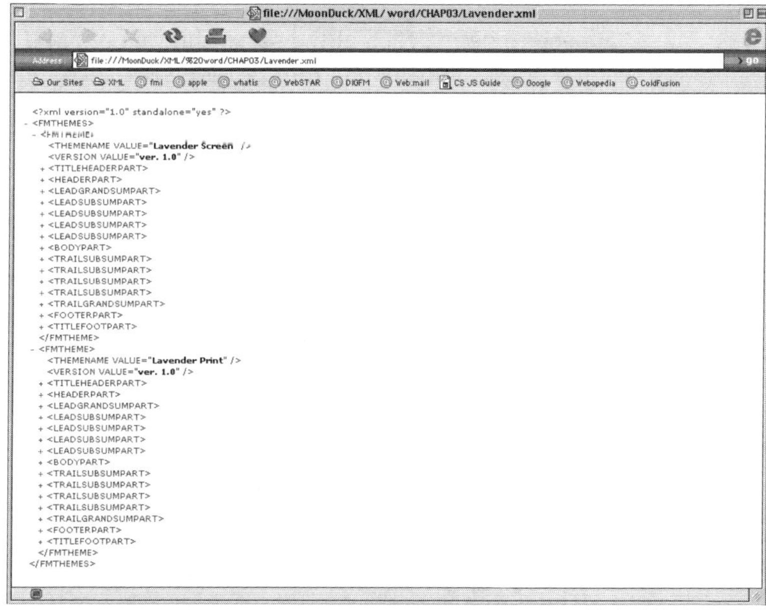

Figure 3.3: Theme file viewed as XML tree

6. We can add the part elements to our definition for the FMTHEME element. These are optional for each theme and there may be multiple subsummaries. We use the "?" around the parts element list and "*" by the subsummary parts. Remember that the layout parts are optional, but there must be at least one part in every layout.

   There is another child element of FMTHEME not shown in the Lavender.fth theme. That element is optional but may be used. The THEMEDEFAULT element supplies any elements that may be missing or invalid in a theme file. When you set the font or the border color of items, for example, in layout mode they become the default for the next object of the same type you add to the layout. These defaults are used if the value of THEMEDEFAULT is "current"; otherwise "standard" is used and takes the values that would be set the first time FileMaker Pro creates a new database.

```
<!DOCTYPE FMTHEMES [
     <!ELEMENT FMTHEMES (FMTHEME)+>
     <!ELEMENT FMTHEME (THEMENAME, VERSION, THEMEDEFAULT,
       (TITLEHEADERPART, HEADERPART, LEADGRANDSUMPART,
       LEADSUBSUMPART*, BODYPART, TRAILSUBSUMPART*,
       TRAILGRANDSUMPART, FOOTERPART, TITLEFOOTPART)?) >
<!-- continue adding elements and attributes -->
]>
```

7. We need to define each of the part's children of FMTHEME. If the element has no further children, it receives the content specification for that element. For all the elements of the document, any element without a start and end element is EMPTY.

   At this time, we can also begin to add the attributes for the first three children. Attributes may be added anywhere in the document, but it is easier to understand if they can be defined just after the elements to which they belong. Note that the !ATTLIST uses the element name as its type, and the next item is the name of the attribute. Any other specifications for the attribute follow the name of that attribute.

```
<!DOCTYPE FMTHEMES [
     <!ELEMENT FMTHEMES (FMTHEME)+>
     <!ELEMENT FMTHEME (THEMENAME, VERSION, THEMEDEFAULT,
       (TITLEHEADERPART, HEADERPART, LEADGRANDSUMPART,
       LEADSUBSUMPART*, BODYPART, TRAILSUBSUMPART*,
       TRAILGRANDSUMPART, FOOTERPART, TITLEFOOTPART)?) >
     <!ELEMENT THEMENAME EMPTY>
          <!ATTLIST THEMENAME
               VALUE CDATA #REQUIRED
               HINT (WIN | MAC)>
     <!ELEMENT VERSION EMPTY>
          <!ATTLIST VERSION
               VALUE CDATA "ver. 1.0">
     <!ELEMENT THEMEDEFAULT EMPTY>
          <!ATTLIST THEMEDEFAULT
          VALUE #IMPLIED (current | standard)>
<!-- continue adding elements and attributes -->
]>
```

THEMENAME is an empty element, as it has no children or content. The attribute VALUE is CDATA (character data) and is required. THEMENAME also has the attribute HINT, which is optional but tells which platform version of FileMaker Pro the theme was created on. The platform listing is valuable if you want to preserve characters that otherwise change, for example, option+o for the character o-slash (ø).

VERSION is also empty and has one attribute. The attribute has the same name as in the THEMENAME element, but we define it to be of VERSION type. VALUE here is CDATA and contains the default string "ver. 1.0". THEMEDEFAULT is empty with the attribute VALUE. Since there are only two choices for this value, we list them with the "|" between them to mean we can use either. "|" is the symbol for "or."

8. Define each of the layout part elements and any optional children of each. The PARTNUMBER element is added to the subsummary parts. Since the parts can contain the same children elements, we group them together and then define the children.

```
<!ELEMENT TITLEHEADERPART (FILL, TEXT, TEXTLABEL, FIELD)?>
<!ELEMENT HEADERPART (FILL, TEXT, TEXTLABEL, FIELD)?>
<!ELEMENT LEADGRANDSUMPART (FILL, TEXT, TEXTLABEL, FIELD)?>
<!ELEMENT LEADSUBSUMPART (FILL, TEXT, TEXTLABEL, FIELD, PARTNUMBER)?>
<!ELEMENT BODYPART (FILL, TEXT, TEXTLABEL, FIELD)?>
<!ELEMENT TRAILSUBSUMPART (FILL, TEXT, TEXTLABEL, FIELD, PARTNUMBER)?>
<!ELEMENT TRAILGRANDSUMPART (FILL, TEXT, TEXTLABEL, FIELD)?>
<!ELEMENT FOOTERPART (FILL, TEXT, TEXTLABEL, FIELD)?>
<!ELEMENT TITLEFOOTPART (FILL, TEXT, TEXTLABEL, FIELD)?>
```

9. Continue to define the detail elements of the layout parts, any of their children, and attributes. FILL is the background color and pattern chosen for a part when it is selected in layout mode. FILL is also used inside the text, field label, and field definitions.

```
<!ELEMENT FILL EMPTY>
      <!ATTLIST FILL
            COLOR CDATA #IMPLIED
            PATTERN CDATA #IMPLIED>
<!-- colors are the HEX values for red, green and blue, #RRGGBB -->
<!-- patterns are: (1-64 | none = 1| solid = 2 | ltgray = 8 |
  gray = 7 | dkgray = 6) -->
<!-- for example: "<FILL COLOR='#FF00FF' PATTERN='SOLID' />" -->
<!ELEMENT PARTNUMBER EMPTY>
      <!ATTLIST PARTNUMBER
            VALUE CDATA #IMPLIED>
```

```
<!-- (this can be a single digit, 0-9) -->
<!-- for example: "<PARTNUMBER VALUE='3' />" -->
```

10. Comments can be added to your DTD for clarity or to further define the attributes. If these values are not explicitly listed with the attribute, any value can be used. For example, instead of CDATA in the VALUE attribute for the element PARTNUMBER, you could be specific. One of these values must be used and "0" is the default, as seen in this example:

```
<!ATTLIST PARTNUMBER
     VALUE (0 | 1 | 2 | 3 | 4 | 5 | 6 | 7 | 8 | 9) "0">
```

11. TEXT is any text on the layout that is not field or field labels. TEXTLABEL is the label created by FileMaker Pro when you place a field on the layout and is the field name. FIELD is the field attributes and has two additional children that TEXT and TEXTLABLE do not have, BASELINE and BORDER.

```
<!ELEMENT TEXT (CHARSTYLE, EFFECT, FILL, PEN)?>
<!ELEMENT TEXTLABEL (CHARSTYLE, EFFECT, FILL, PEN)?>
<!ELEMENT CHARSTYLE EMPTY>
     <!ATTLIST CHARSTYLE
          FONT CDATA #IMPLIED
          SIZE CDATA #IMPLIED
          STYLE CDATA #IMPLIED "plain"
          COLOR CDATA #IMPLIED>
<!-- font name(s) in Title Case and comma separated list -->
<!-- point size for the font -->
<!-- style can be plain or multiples of any of the other options
  (depending on platform 'rules') -->
<!-- plain OR ( bold & italic & (strikeout or strikethru) & (underline
  or wordunderline or dblunderline) & (smallcaps or uppercase or
  lowercase or titlecase or subscript or superscript) & (condense or
  extend)), all optional with "plain" as the default -->
<!-- for example: "<CHARSTYLE FONT='Helvetica, Arial, Sans Serif'
  SIZE='12' STYLE='bold, italic' COLOR='#FF0000' />" -->
<!ELEMENT EFFECT EMPTY>
     <!ATTLIST EFFECT
          VALUE  #IMPLIED (emboss | engrave | dropshadow | none)
            "none">
<!-- since there are only a few values, we list them and include the
  default -->
<!-- for example: "<EFFECT VALUE='EMBOSS' />" -->
<!ELEMENT PEN EMPTY>
     <!ATTLIST PEN
          COLOR CDATA #IMPLIED
          PATTERN CDATA #IMPLIED
          SIZE CDATA #IMPLIED>
```

```
<!-- this is the same attribute name as font, but is the line size
  (0 = none, -1 = hairline, otherwise 1-12) -->
<!-- for example: "<PEN COLOR='#000033' PATTERN='NONE' SIZE='-1'
  />" -->
```

12. FIELD is the final element listed and shows only the two unique children, BASELINE and BORDER, as the other element definitions are already in the document.

```
<!ELEMENT FIELD (CHARSTYLE, EFFECT, FILL, PEN, BASELINE, BORDER)?>
      <!-- the first four elements have been previously defined -->
      <!ELEMENT BASELINE (PEN, ONOFF)?>
            <!-- PEN has been defined as an element -->
            <!ELEMENT ONOFF>
                  <!ATTLIST ONOFF
                        VALUE #IMPLIED (on | off) "off">
                        <!-- by default the baseline is off -->
            <!-- for example: "<BASELINE>
                                <PEN VALUE='2' />
                                <ONOFF VALUE='ON' />
                        </BASELINE>" -->
      <!ELEMENT BORDER (PEN, SIDES)?>
            <!ELEMENT SIDES>
                  <!ATTLIST SIDES
                        VALUE CDATA #IMPLIED>
                  <!-- (sides can be top, bottom, left, right or any
                    combination of these, space separated) -->
            <!-- for example: "<BORDER
                                <PEN VALUE='1' />
                                <SIDES VALUE='TOP LEFT' />
                        </BORDER>" -->
```

The *FileMaker Pro Developer's Guide* says that "on/off" is for field borders on p. 5-8 and for field baselines on p. 5-6. PEN SIZE="0" determines if the border on a field is off. There is no other way to show the field baseline; p. 5-6 is correct.

13. Put this all together as a basic DTD. If you want to be more precise, go back and change those attributes with just CDATA. Note that this DTD only has elements, attribute lists, and comments. There is no parsed character data, so you do not see #PCDATA.

```
<!DOCTYPE FMTHEMES [
      <!ELEMENT FMTHEMES (FMTHEME)+>
      <!ELEMENT FMTHEME (THEMENAME, VERSION, THEMEDEFAULT,
        (TITLEHEADERPART, HEADERPART, LEADGRANDSUMPART,
        LEADSUBSUMPART*, BODYPART, TRAILSUBSUMPART*,
        TRAILGRANDSUMPART, FOOTERPART, TITLEFOOTPART)?) >
      <!ELEMENT THEMENAME EMPTY>
            <!ATTLIST THEMENAME VALUE CDATA #REQUIRED>
```

```
<!ELEMENT VERSION EMPTY>
     <!ATTLIST VERSION
          VALUE CDATA #IMPLIED "ver. 1.0">
<!ELEMENT THEMEDEFAULT EMPTY>
<!ATTLIST THEMEDEFAULT
          VALUE #IMPLIED (current | standard)>
<!ELEMENT TITLEHEADERPART (FILL, TEXT, TEXTLABEL, FIELD)?>
<!ELEMENT HEADERPART (FILL, TEXT, TEXTLABEL, FIELD)?>
<!ELEMENT LEADGRANDSUMPART (FILL, TEXT, TEXTLABEL, FIELD)?>
<!ELEMENT LEADSUBSUMPART (FILL, TEXT, TEXTLABEL, FIELD,
  PARTNUMBER)?>
<!ELEMENT BODYPART (FILL, TEXT, TEXTLABEL, FIELD)?>
<!ELEMENT TRAILSUBSUMPART (FILL, TEXT, TEXTLABEL, FIELD,
  PARTNUMBER)?>
<!ELEMENT TRAILGRANDSUMPART (FILL, TEXT, TEXTLABEL, FIELD)?>
<!ELEMENT FOOTERPART (FILL, TEXT, TEXTLABEL, FIELD)?>
<!ELEMENT TITLEFOOTPART (FILL, TEXT, TEXTLABEL, FIELD)?>
<!ELEMENT FILL EMPTY>
     <!ATTLIST FILL
          COLOR CDATA #IMPLIED
          PATTERN CDATA #IMPLIED>
<!ELEMENT PARTNUMBER EMPTY>
     <!ATTLIST PARTNUMBER
          VALUE CDATA #IMPLIED>
<!ELEMENT TEXT (CHARSTYLE, EFFECT, FILL, PEN)?>
<!ELEMENT TEXTLABEL (CHARSTYLE, EFFECT, FILL, PEN)?>
<!ELEMENT CHARSTYLE EMPTY>
     <!ATTLIST CHARSTYLE
          FONT CDATA #IMPLIED
          SIZE CDATA #IMPLIED
          STYLE CDATA #IMPLIED "plain"
          COLOR CDATA #IMPLIED>
<!ELEMENT EFFECT EMPTY>
     <!ATTLIST EFFECT
          VALUE #IMPLIED (emboss | engrave | dropshadow |
            none) "none">
<!ELEMENT PEN EMPTY>
     <!ATTLIST PEN
          COLOR CDATA #IMPLIED
          PATTERN CDATA #IMPLIED
          SIZE CDATA #IMPLIED>
<!ELEMENT FIELD (CHARSTYLE, EFFECT, FILL, PEN, BASELINE,
  BORDER)?>
<!ELEMENT BASELINE (PEN, ONOFF)?>
     <!ELEMENT ONOFF>
          <!ATTLIST ONOFF
               VALUE #IMPLIED (on | off) "off">
<!ELEMENT BORDER (PEN, SIDES)?>
```

```
                <!ELEMENT SIDES>
                    <!ATTLIST SIDES
                        VALUE CDATA #IMPLIED>
    ]>
```

As an extra challenge, create a Document Type Definition for the FileMaker Pro labels. You will discover that these are also XML files and used by the New Layout/Report assistant. The document LabelsUS.flb is found in the Labels folder of the FileMaker Pro folder. (Your label file may have a different name or you may have more than one file, depending upon installation.)

3.5 Entities in the DTD

An entity, by dictionary definition, is anything that exists. We used the term in Chapter 1 to mean all the parts that make up an XML document. We also used the term to mean predefined entities and showed Table 1.1, with these characters: & (ampersand), < (less than), > (greater than), ' (single quote or apostrophe), and " (double quote). Since the characters themselves are used to form markup or element tags, we need a way to include them in the content of the elements or the information of our document. Another usage for the term entities is to provide a standard set of shortcuts (or replacement text) to common words or phrases.

Table 3.1 Review of the predefined entities

Character	Entity	Name
&	&	ampersand
<	<	less than
>	>	greater than
'	'	apostrophe or single quote
"	"	double quote

The predefined entities are needed to keep us from tripping over our own markup characters, and we do not need to declare them in our DTD. FileMaker Pro will automatically create the predefined entities for us. We could call them shortcuts so we do not have to add a complex set of instructions each time they are used. We can create our own shortcuts or entities by declaring general entities.

```
General Entities
<!ENTITY entityName replacementText>
<!ENTITY mos "My Own String">
```

```
Parameter Entities
<!ENTITY % entityName entityDefinition>
```

3.6 Document Type Definitions (DTDs) vs. Schema/XSD

A schema is a plan, map, diagram, or outline. The Document Type Definition is a schema, because XML processors use it to validate a document. If the document follows the rules or "map" of the DTD, the XML is valid. However, the World Wide Web Consortium recently approved the recommendation for creating and using XML Schema Documents (XSD). These rules are far more complex than for DTDs, but they also provide a broader range of information about the document and the markup, which defines the document contents.

The DTD provides a map to the structure of the XML document, but Document Type Definitions have limited rules to describe the document. Data types cannot be specified, so a number is just another piece of text. The data cannot be tested against validation rules, such as containing only uppercase letters or constraining the length of the data field to two characters. The schema recommendation should provide for greater means of specifying the data. You can learn more about the schema on the World Wide Web Consortium site, http://www.w3.org/XML/Schema.

3.61 DTD for FileMaker Pro Plug-ins

Troi Automatisering, http://www.troi.com/, is a FileMaker Pro plug-in developer. Peter Baanen has designed an XML Software Description based on the XML Schema Document (XSD) in an effort to standardize the submission of plug-in information to the FileMaker, Inc. web site, http://www.filemaker.com/products/search_plugins.html, and to various other web sites. With this plug-in information standard, one XML document could be submitted to each of these web sites, allowing each one to extract the information on new plug-ins. The same XML document could be used to produce an announcement for emailing or printing. The description becomes a template for submitting similar information. The full Troi XML Software Description can be found at http://www.troi.com/info/xsd/, but for an example, some of the document is provided in Listing 3.11. You can see that this type of schema is very similar to the DTD and XSD.

Listing 3.11 Sample definitions for XSD plug-in

```
<!ELEMENT vendor (name,address,city,state,zip,country,phone,fax?,
  email,url?) >
<!ELEMENT name (#PCDATA)>
<!ELEMENT address (#PCDATA)>
...
<!ELEMENT product (name,version,last_release,short_description,
description,price,currency,
info_url?,changes?,
contact name, contact_email,
support_contact_name, support_contact_email,
marketing_contact_name, marketing_contact_email,
engineering_contact_name, engineering_contact_email,
available_for+, fmp_plug_in?) >
```

3.7 More about Document Type Definitions

In the next chapter, each of the three FileMaker Pro DTDs is also called a schema or a grammar. The FMPXMLLAYOUT, FMPXMLRESULT, and FMPDSORESULT definitions are similar but produce very distinct XML documents. Each of them will be further explained so that you may better understand the use of DTDs with XML documents. Chapter 4 contains the schema/grammar information for the Document Design Report, found in FileMaker Pro Developer. The import and export of XML with FileMaker Pro 6 uses two of these grammars, FMPXML-RESULT and FMPDSORESULT, which will also be reviewed in Chapter 4.

Chapter 4

FileMaker Pro XML Schema or Grammar Formats (DTDs)

FileMaker Pro uses three different Document Type Definitions to return the XML results from an HTTP action request. The definitions are called schema, or grammar formats, by FileMaker Pro, and they follow the World Wide Web Consortium recommendation for creating DTDs. The first schema, FMPXMLLAYOUT, defines what layout information will be returned when the -format is -fmp_xml and the action is -view. The other two definitions, FMPXMLRESULT and FMPDSORESULT, are the schemata for field level information to be returned in distinct formats. The DTD or schema that you choose to use in any XML request to FileMaker Pro may depend upon what information you are extracting from the database. We will explore these data formats and the DTD for the Document Design Report XML documents.

The grammar formats for FMPXMLLAYOUT, FMPXMLRESULT, and FMPDSORESULT are normally installed with FileMaker Developer or FileMaker Unlimited as the HTML files fmpxmllayout_dtd.htm, fmpxmlresult_dtd.htm, and fmpdsoresult_dtd.htm, respectively. With FMP 6 the fmpxmlresult_dtd.htm and fmpdsoresult_dtd.htm files are installed with a normal install. You can view these files in a text editor, but they are formatted for viewing in a web browser. This chapter continues to explain the standards for writing DTDs by reviewing the

FileMaker Pro Document Type Definitions. As demonstrated in Chapter 2, FileMaker Pro 6 uses the FMPXMLRESULT grammar for the export and import of XML. The FMPDOSRESULT grammar can be used to export XML from FileMaker Pro 6. The FMPXMLLAYOUT grammar is only available from an HTTP request to Web Companion when web publishing FileMaker Pro. See Chapter 5, "XML and FileMaker Pro Web Publishing," for information about setting up FileMaker Pro for web publishing and about making HTTP requests.

The examples in this chapter use the sample files available in the FileMaker Templates folder. The templates are installed in the FileMaker Pro 6 folder and may be used as the basis for your own FileMaker Pro solutions. They may be used to recreate the code listings found here. The steps necessary to create the results will be presented with the path to the template file.

Note: The Internet Explorer browser will apply a default stylesheet to an XML document. This will make it "pretty-print" with indentations for each level of the XML tree. It also has convenient handles (-/+) to collapse or expand these levels. It is an easy way to see the structure of an XML document. The Netscape browser does not have this default stylesheet for XML, and you may only see the contents of the data without any element tags. Common text editors and word processors may also display the XML document in different ways.

4.1 FMPXMLLAYOUT Schema/Grammar

This simple example of the FMPXMLLAYOUT grammar uses the database Contact Management.fp5, which can be found in the FileMaker Pro 6 Folder, FileMaker Templates. Sections of the grammar are interspersed with the XML results on the following pages to show the kinds of information returned for one layout, "Form - Main Address," in the database. The FMPXMLLAYOUT grammar defines the standard for this kind of document and is available only with FileMaker Pro custom web publishing. You can read more about setting up FileMaker Pro for custom web publishing in Chapter 5. The example HTTP request to the Contact Management.fp5 database in the following example uses -format=-fmp_xml and the -view action. Replace the "localhost" domain with your IP address or server name and port, if necessary:

```
http://localhost/fmpro?-db=Contact%20Management.fp5&-lay=Form%20-
  %20Main%20Address&-format=-fmp_xml&-view
```

The definition for the FMPXMLLAYOUT grammar to create the result begins:

```
<!DOCTYPE FMPXMLLAYOUT [
     <!ELEMENT FMPXMLLAYOUT (ERRORCODE, PRODUCT, LAYOUT, VALUELISTS)>
          <!ATTLIST FMPXMLLAYOUT xmlns CDATA #REQUIRED>
```

The first line declares the document type to be FMPXMLLAYOUT. The next line defines the first or root element to be named FMPXMLLAYOUT. This element has four children: ERRORCODE, PRODUCT, LAYOUT, and VALUELISTS. The FMPXMLLAYOUT element has one required attribute, xmlns, which has a value and is composed of character data (CDATA).

The first two lines in the XML result from the HTTP request to Contact Management.fp5 show the results:

```
<?xml version="1.0" encoding="UTF-8" ?>
<FMPXMLLAYOUT xmlns="http://www.filemaker.com/fmpxmllayout">
```

This well-formed result begins with the XML document prolog. This prolog conforms to the standard by including the version attribute with a value of "1.0". The prolog also specifies the language-encoding attribute, which shows that the document conforms to the UTF-8 character set. The prolog is followed by the opening root element of the document, FMPXMLLAYOUT, with the xmlns (XML Name Space) attribute. The xmlns is not a real link to anywhere but a unique identifier for this type of document. Namespaces are discussed more fully in Chapter 7.

The grammar continues to define the first child element of the root element ERRORCODE. This element is never empty and contains parsed character data:

```
<!ELEMENT ERRORCODE (#PCDATA)>
```

An error code is returned and is 0 (zero) if the request encountered no problems. The error code is the same error code produced by the database if you have a script error. You can find a list of errors in FileMaker Pro Help under the topic “Status(CurrentError).” Specific Web Companion errors are discussed in section 5.5, “Error Codes for XML.”

The XML result shows:

```
    <ERRORCODE>0</ERRORCODE>
```

The second child element of FMPXMLLAYOUT root element is defined in the grammar:

```
<!ELEMENT PRODUCT EMPTY>
     <!ATTLIST PRODUCT
          NAME CDATA #REQUIRED
          VERSION CDATA #REQUIRED
          BUILD CDATA #REQUIRED>
```

This element, PRODUCT, is an empty element but contains the three required attributes describing the application programming interface (API) that created the document. The API, which published this XML from the database, is the Web Companion. The attribute BUILD lists the date of the product, followed by the NAME and VERSION attributes. Depending upon what version of FileMaker Pro you are using to web publish, you may get one of the following results:

```
<product build="8/3/2000" name="FileMaker Pro Web Companion"
  version="5.0v6" />
<PRODUCT BUILD="03/09/2001" NAME="FileMaker Pro Web Companion"
  VERSION="5.5v1" />
<PRODUCT BUILD="5/4/2002" NAME="FileMaker Pro Web Companion"
  VERSION="6.0v1" />
```

4.11 Layout Information

The third child element of FMPXMLLAYOUT is defined with one child element and two attributes:

```
<!ELEMENT LAYOUT (FIELD*)>
     <!ATTLIST LAYOUT
          DATABASE CDATA #REQUIRED
          NAME CDATA #REQUIRED>
```

The next portion of the result from the XML request, as shown in Listing 4.1, shows the LAYOUT element, followed by the required DATABASE attribute with the name of the database as the value of the attribute. The required NAME attribute has the name of the layout as its value. The definition for the LAYOUT element specifies its child element, FIELD, to be a repeated element zero or more times (*). The FIELD elements are listed between the LAYOUT start and end markup. The number of field elements returned depends upon the number of elements on the layout in the HTTP request.

Listing 4.1 Layout and field information results

```
<LAYOUT DATABASE="Contact Management.fp5" NAME="Form - Main Address">
     <FIELD NAME="First Name">
```

```
            <!-- code snippet for brevity, see Listing 4.2 for
              full code -->
      </FIELD>
</LAYOUT>
```

If the LAYOUT element has no fields on it, the LAYOUT element is returned as an empty element. Create a new layout and do not place any fields on it. The following shows the request to the layout “blank” and the XML fragment result:

```
http://localhost/fmpro?-db=Contact%20Management.fp5&-lay=blank&-format=
  -fmp_xml&-view
<LAYOUT DATABASE="Contact Management.fp5" NAME="blank" />
```

Warning: Fields placed on a layout by a copy-drag from a field with a value list will include the previous value list. If the value list is deselected in the new field, the old value list is still returned in the XML result. If you plan to use the FMPXMLLAYOUT information, place a field on a layout by choosing Insert, Field from the menu or by dragging the Field tool from the status area. Then format any fields individually to a specific value list.

4.12 Field Information

Each FIELD element has one required child element and one required attribute, the name of the field:

```
<!ELEMENT FIELD (STYLE)
      <!ATTLIST FIELD
            NAME CDATA #REQUIRED>
```

The STYLE element is an empty element that has two attributes, TYPE and VALUELIST. This element describes how the field is formatted on the layout and if it has an associated value list. The pop-up list value for field "Address Type 1" in Listing 4.2 is "Address Type List". On another layout, "Form - Similars" in the Contact Management.fp5 database, some of the fields are plain “edittext” and others are formatted with a radio button value list “Similarity Criteria.” The definition for the STYLE element is shown here:

```
<!ELEMENT STYLE EMPTY>
      <!ATTLIST STYLE
            TYPE (POPUPLIST | POPUPMENU | CHECKBOX | RADIOBUTTONS |
              SCROLLTEXT | SELECTIONLIST | EDITTEXT) #IMPLIED
            VALUELIST CDATA #IMPLIED>
```

The TYPE attribute can have any of the values listed in the DTD. The "|" (pipe) symbol means any of the values may be used in the attribute list. If a field is formatted as a standard field with "Include vertical scrollbar" checked, the TYPE attribute would have a value of "SCROLLTEXT." Any standard field (including merge fields) will have a TYPE value of "EDITTEXT." The value of the TYPE attribute "SELECTIONLIST" is not currently used. The standard value list formats for fields on a layout are pop-up list, pop-up menu, check boxes, and radio buttons. The fields with a value list will also show the name of the value list in the VALUELIST attribute.

Listing 4.2 Fields formatted on a layout

```
<LAYOUT DATABASE="Contact Management.fp5" NAME="Form - Main Address">
	<FIELD NAME="First Name">
		<STYLE TYPE="EDITTEXT" VALUELIST="" />
	</FIELD>
	<FIELD NAME="Company">
		<STYLE TYPE="EDITTEXT" VALUELIST="" />
	</FIELD>
	<FIELD NAME="Image Data">
		<STYLE TYPE="EDITTEXT" VALUELIST="" />
	</FIELD>
	<FIELD NAME="Title">
		<STYLE TYPE="EDITTEXT" VALUELIST="" />
	</FIELD>
	<FIELD NAME="Phone 1">
		<STYLE TYPE="EDITTEXT" VALUELIST="" />
	</FIELD>
	<FIELD NAME="Phone 2">
		<STYLE TYPE="EDITTEXT" VALUELIST="" />
	</FIELD>
	<FIELD NAME="Email">
		<STYLE TYPE="EDITTEXT" VALUELIST="" />
	</FIELD>
	<FIELD NAME="Notes">
		<STYLE TYPE="SCROLLTEXT" VALUELIST="" />
	</FIELD>
	<FIELD NAME="Similars Tab Label">
		<STYLE TYPE="EDITTEXT" VALUELIST="" />
	</FIELD>
	<FIELD NAME="Street 1">
		<STYLE TYPE="EDITTEXT" VALUELIST="" />
	</FIELD>
	<FIELD NAME="Address Type 1">
		<STYLE TYPE="POPUPLIST" VALUELIST="Address Type List" />
	</FIELD>
```

```
    <FIELD NAME="City 1">
         <STYLE TYPE="EDITTEXT" VALUELIST="" />
    </FIELD>
    <FIELD NAME="State Province 1">
         <STYLE TYPE="EDITTEXT" VALUELIST="" />
    </FIELD>
    <FIELD NAME="Postal Code 1">
         <STYLE TYPE="EDITTEXT" VALUELIST="" />
    </FIELD>
</LAYOUT>
```

4.13 Merge Fields

Single merge fields placed on the layout are listed in the FMPXMLLAYOUT result as EDITTEXT along with fields in the standard format. Multiple merge fields together in a single block may not all be listed in the resulting XML. If multiple merge fields are listed, they may not be in the order in which they appear on the layout. Other variables determine which merge field is used, if any, in the XML result.

Exercise 4.1 Create Merge Fields for FMPXMLLAYOUT

1. Create two new calculated fields:

   ```
   RecCt (Unstored) = Status(CurrentRecordCount)
   FndCt (Unstored) = Status(CurrentFoundCount)
   ```

2. Place the two new fields on any layout as merge fields in one block of text:

   ```
   Found <<FndCt>> of <<RecCt>> Records
   ```

3. Make the same HTTP request to the web published FileMaker Pro and get a result in your browser. Only the first merge field, "FndCt", is returned in the XML, and it is shown as "EDITTEXT" style type:

   ```
   http://localhost/fmpro?-db=Contact%20Management.fp5&-lay=
     Form%20-%20Main%20Address&-format=-fmp_xml&-view
   <!-- result -->
   <FIELD NAME="FndCt">
        <STYLE TYPE="EDITTEXT" VALUELIST="" />
   </FIELD>
   ```

4.14 Value List Information

The final child element of FMPXMLLAYOUT is VALUELISTS. This element is defined to have one child element, VALUELIST (not required), and no attributes.

```
<!ELEMENT VALUELISTS (VALUELIST)*>
```

If there are no fields formatted with value lists, this element may be empty in the XML results.

```
<VALUELISTS />
```

The element VALUELIST has one child element and one required attribute, the name of the value list. The VALUELIST element may be repeated in the XML result for each unique value list on a layout.

```
<!ELEMENT VALUELIST (VALUE)*>
	<!ATTLIST VALUELIST NAME CDATA #REQUIRED>
```

The VALUE element may contain any parsed character data and be repeated in the XML result for each value in the VALUELIST. All of the value list information for this layout is shown in Listing 4.3.

```
<!ELEMENT VALUE (#PCDATA)>
```

Listing 4.3 Value list FMPXMLLAYOUT results

```
<VALUELISTS>
	<VALUELIST NAME="Address Type List">
		<VALUE>Home</VALUE>
		<VALUE>Business</VALUE>
		<VALUE>Home Office</VALUE>
		<VALUE>Vacation</VALUE>
		<VALUE>-</VALUE>
	</VALUELIST>
</VALUELISTS>
```

4.15 Completing the FMPXMLLAYOUT DTD

The FMPXMLLAYOUT definition closes with "]>." The full schema/grammar/DTD is shown in Listing 4.4.

Listing 4.4 FMPXMLLAYOUT Document Type Definition

```
<!DOCTYPE FMPXMLLAYOUT [
	<!ELEMENT FMPXMLLAYOUT (ERRORCODE, PRODUCT, LAYOUT, VALUELISTS)>
		<!ATTLIST FMPXMLLAYOUT
			xmlns CDATA #REQUIRED>
		<!ELEMENT ERRORCODE (#PCDATA)>
		<!ELEMENT PRODUCT EMPTY>
```

```
            <!ATTLIST PRODUCT
                  NAME CDATA #REQUIRED
                  VERSION CDATA #REQUIRED
                  BUILD CDATA #REQUIRED>
      <!ELEMENT LAYOUT (FIELD*)>
            <!ATTLIST LAYOUT
                  NAME CDATA #REQUIRED
                  DATABASE CDATA #REQUIRED>
            <!ELEMENT FIELD (STYLE)>
                  <!ATTLIST FIELD
                        NAME CDATA #REQUIRED>
                  <!ELEMENT STYLE EMPTY>
                        <!ATTLIST STYLE
                              TYPE (POPUPLIST | POPUPMENU | CHECKBOX
                                | RADIOBUTTONS | SCROLLTEXT |
                                SELECTIONLIST | EDITTEXT) #IMPLIED
                              VALUELIST CDATA #IMPLIED>
      <!ELEMENT VALUELISTS (VALUELIST)*>
            <!ELEMENT VALUELIST (VALUE)*>
                  <!ATTLIST VALUELIST
                        NAME CDATA #REQUIRED>
                  <!ELEMENT VALUE (#PCDATA)>
]>
```

4.16 FileMaker Pro Report/Layout Information

Some of the information found in a database layout can be collected using FileMaker Pro built-in design and status functions. Status(CurrentError), FieldNames(Status(CurrentFileName)), Status(CurrentLayoutName), and FieldStyle(database, layout, field) are all example functions of some of the information about a layout. A calculation field or a scripted set field can show the results of these functions. This layout information can be used in various ways in the database or for reports on the structure of the database. These fields could also be used when transforming the XML data with a stylesheet instead of requesting the FMPXMLLAYOUT results.

Some information can be returned using the FMPXMLLAYOUT schema. The way the fields are formatted on the layout may be used to recreate the style type in another display, such as the browser. Value list information is most useful if the XML results are used in a FORM submit field to allow editing of the contents of a field. Value lists are a useful way to restrict data entry. There are several ways to display value lists in the browser. Browser value lists correlate to the formats that FileMaker Pro uses on the layout and are described in Chapter 6.

4.2 FMPXMLRESULT Schema/Grammar

The FMPXMLRESULT is the schema that returns some information about the fields on a layout and the field contents. This grammar is the only format used by FileMaker Pro 6 when importing XML. The example database Contact Management.fp5 will be used with the request to find any record in the database and return the results with the FMPXMLRESULT format. You may make the HTTP request below or export the XML for the fields in Listing 4.5:

```
<!-- HTTP REQUEST-->
http://localhost/fmpro?-db=Contact%20Management.fp5&-lay=
  Form%20-%20Main%20Address&-format=-fmp_xml&-findany
```

Listing 4.5 Export FMPXMLRESULT fields

```
Address Type 1
City 1
Company
Email
First Name
Last Name
Notes
Phone 1
Phone 2
Postal Code 1
State Province 1
Street 1
Title
```

Note: You can make the HTTP request and get container field information, but you cannot export a container field. The Image Data field will not export. The result for the Image Data field from the HTTP request is shown here:

```
<!-- FIELD INFORMATION -->
<FIELD EMPTYOK="YES" MAXREPEAT="1" NAME="Image Data" TYPE="CONTAINER" />
<!-- DATA -->
<DATA>FMPro?-db=Contact Management.fp5&-RecID=24&Image Data=&-img</DATA>
```

The root element in this type of XML document is FMPXMLRESULT and has five child elements: ERRORCODE, PRODUCT, DATABASE, METADATA, and RESULTSET. The attribute xmlns is required. The definition for FMPXMLRESULT begins:

```
<!DOCTYPE FMPXMLRESULT [
<!ELEMENT FMPXMLRESULT (ERRORCODE, PRODUCT, DATABASE, METADATA, RESULTSET)>
	<!ATTLIST FMPXMLRESULT xmlns CDATA #REQUIRED>
	<!ELEMENT ERRORCODE (#PCDATA)>
	<!ELEMENT PRODUCT EMPTY>
		<!ATTLIST PRODUCT
			NAME CDATA #REQUIRED
			VERSION CDATA #REQUIRED
			BUILD CDATA #REQUIRED>
```

Listing 4.6 shows the beginning of the well-formed XML document. The prolog is the same as the FMPXMLLAYOUT result. The xmlns attribute for the root element FMPXMLRESULT has the value "http://www.filemaker.com/fmpxmlresult" and is a unique identifier for this type of document. The first two child elements, ERRORCODE and PRODUCT, are just like the elements in FMPXMLLAYOUT.

Listing 4.6 XML results from -format=-fmp_xml or export as FMPXMLRESULT

```
<?xml version="1.0" encoding="UTF-8" ?>
<FMPXMLRESULT xmlns="http://www.filemaker.com/fmpxmlresult">
	<ERRORCODE>0</ERRORCODE>
	<PRODUCT BUILD="08/09/2002" NAME="FileMaker Pro" VERSION="6.0v3" />
```

4.21 Database Information

The third child element of the FMPXMLRESULT element is DATABASE. The DATABASE element is empty but has five required attributes: the name of the database, the number of records in the database, the name of the layout used in the request (if any), and the date and time formats of the database. The date format and time format are included because of international variations for these kinds of formats.

```
<!ELEMENT DATABASE EMPTY>
	<!ATTLIST DATABASE
		NAME CDATA #REQUIRED
		RECORDS CDATA #REQUIRED
		LAYOUT CDATA #REQUIRED
		DATEFORMAT CDATA #REQUIRED
		TIMEFORMAT CDATA #REQUIRED>
```

The XML result shows how many records are in the database Contact Management.fp5. If you make the HTTP request and specify a layout, it will be listed; otherwise the value for LAYOUT is empty. The date and time formats will be whatever the computer operating system had for the DateTime Control Panel settings when the database was created or cloned. The format of these types of fields on the layout do not change the values.

```
<DATABASE DATEFORMAT="M/d/yyyy" LAYOUT="" NAME="Contact Management.fp5"
  RECORDS="1" TIMEFORMAT="h:mm:ss a" />
```

4.22 Metadata Information

Metadata is data, or information, about the data. The FMPXMLRESULT returns the field information in the METADATA element. This element is empty if there are no fields on the layout (HTTP request):

```
<METADATA />
```

The definition for METADATA contains one child element and no attributes. The child element FIELD may occur zero or more times in the XML result. Listing 4.7 shows the results for the metadata in the Contact Management.fp5 database for those fields in the export or on the layout in an HTTP request.

```
<!ELEMENT METADATA (FIELD)*>
```

The FIELD element is empty and has four required attributes: NAME, TYPE, EMPTYOK, and MAXREPEAT. The type of field is how the field was created in the Define Fields dialog. If the field is a global, calculation, or summary, the field type is the global, calculation, or summary result. The EMPTYOK attribute relates directly to the validation for the named field. The default value for the EMPTYOK attribute is "yes". If the "Not empty" check box is selected under the Validation tab in the Options dialog, this value will be "no". A field defined to be a repeating field will show the maximum number of repetitions as the value for this attribute. MAXREPEAT has a default of "1" for all fields not defined as repeating fields.

```
<!ELEMENT FIELD EMPTY>
     <!ATTLIST FIELD
          NAME CDATA #REQUIRED
          TYPE (TEXT | NUMBER | DATE | TIME | CONTAINER) #REQUIRED
          EMPTYOK (YES | NO) #REQUIRED
          MAXREPEAT CDATA #REQUIRED>
```

Listing 4.7 Metadata in the XML results

```
<METADATA>
     <FIELD EMPTYOK="YES" MAXREPEAT="1" NAME="Address Type 1"
       TYPE="TEXT" />
     <FIELD EMPTYOK="YES" MAXREPEAT="1" NAME="City 1" TYPE="TEXT" />
     <FIELD EMPTYOK="YES" MAXREPEAT="1" NAME="Company" TYPE="TEXT" />
```

```
    <FIELD EMPTYOK="YES" MAXREPEAT="1" NAME="Email" TYPE="TEXT" />
    <FIELD EMPTYOK="YES" MAXREPEAT="1" NAME="First Name" TYPE="TEXT" />
    <FIELD EMPTYOK="YES" MAXREPEAT="1" NAME="Last Name" TYPE="TEXT" />
    <FIELD EMPTYOK="YES" MAXREPEAT="1" NAME="Notes" TYPE="TEXT" />
    <FIELD EMPTYOK="YES" MAXREPEAT="1" NAME="Phone 1" TYPE="TEXT" />
    <FIELD EMPTYOK="YES" MAXREPEAT="1" NAME="Phone 2" TYPE="TEXT" />
    <FIELD EMPTYOK="YES" MAXREPEAT="1" NAME="Postal Code 1"
      TYPE="TEXT" />
    <FIELD EMPTYOK="YES" MAXREPEAT="1" NAME="State Province 1"
      TYPE="TEXT" />
    <FIELD EMPTYOK="YES" MAXREPEAT="1" NAME="Street 1" TYPE="TEXT" />
    <FIELD EMPTYOK="YES" MAXREPEAT="1" NAME="Title" TYPE="TEXT" />
    <FIELD EMPTYOK="YES" MAXREPEAT="1" NAME="FndCt" TYPE="NUMBER" />
    <FIELD EMPTYOK="YES" MAXREPEAT="1" NAME="RecCt" TYPE="NUMBER" />
</METADATA>
```

The names of the fields are listed in the METADATA because the next element, RESULTSET, does not show the names along with the contents of the fields. The order in which the fields are listed in the METADATA is the same order that the fields are listed in the COL elements, shown in Listing 4.8.

4.23 The Resultset (Contents of the Fields)

The last child element of FMPXMLRESULT is RESULTSET. This element has one element and one required attribute. The value of the FOUND attribute is the number of records in the found set. The child element ROW may occur zero or more times in the XML results and will be repeated for each record in the found set:

```
<!ELEMENT RESULTSET (ROW)*>
    <!ATTLIST RESULTSET FOUND CDATA #REQUIRED>
```

The ROW element has one child element, COL, and two required attributes, RECORDID and MODID. The RECORDID is the same as the Status(CurrentRecordID) function and is a unique number created when a new record is created in the database. The number is used when searching for specific records, editing records, and deleting records. The MODID is the same as the Status(CurrentRecordModificationCount) function and changes as the record is modified. The value for the MODID attribute is used to track if a record has changed before submitting data from the web browser. COL is repeated for each field in the METADATA list. The COL element has one child element, DATA, which may be empty if the field is empty. The text between the start and end DATA element markup is the content of each field.

Listing 4.8 Resultset (rows and columns) of data

```
<RESULTSET FOUND="1">
    <ROW MODID="1" RECORDID="1">
        <COL><DATA>A</DATA></COL>
        <COL><DATA>B</DATA></COL>
        <COL><DATA>C</DATA></COL>
        <COL><DATA>D</DATA></COL>
        <COL><DATA>E</DATA></COL>
        <COL><DATA>F</DATA></COL>
        <COL><DATA>G</DATA></COL>
        <COL><DATA>H</DATA></COL>
        <COL><DATA>I</DATA></COL>
        <COL><DATA>J</DATA></COL>
        <COL><DATA>K</DATA></COL>
        <COL><DATA>L</DATA></COL>
        <COL><DATA>M</DATA></COL>
        <COL><DATA>1</DATA></COL>
        <COL><DATA>1</DATA></COL>
    </ROW>
</RESULTSET>
```

4.24 Completing the FMPXMLRESULT DTD

The FMPXMLRESULT definition ends with "]>." The full DTD is shown in Listing 4.9. The advantage for this type of schema is to return the results of rows and columns (records and fields) without needing to know the names of the fields. The same stylesheets can be used for multiple files if the number of columns is the same. The type of field should also match so that the columns can be formatted as needed.

Listing 4.9 FMPXMLRESULT Document Type Definition

```
<!DOCTYPE FMPXMLRESULT [
<!ELEMENT FMPXMLRESULT (ERRORCODE, PRODUCT, DATABASE, METADATA, RESULTSET)>
    <!ATTLIST FMPXMLRESULT xmlns CDATA #REQUIRED>
    <!ELEMENT ERRORCODE (#PCDATA)>
    <!ELEMENT PRODUCT EMPTY>
        <!ATTLIST PRODUCT
            NAME CDATA #REQUIRED
            VERSION CDATA #REQUIRED
            BUILD CDATA #REQUIRED>
    <!ELEMENT DATABASE EMPTY>
        <!ATTLIST DATABASE
            NAME CDATA #REQUIRED
            RECORDS CDATA #REQUIRED
            DATEFORMAT CDATA #REQUIRED
```

```
                TIMEFORMAT CDATA #REQUIRED
                LAYOUT CDATA #REQUIRED>
    <!ELEMENT METADATA (FIELD)*>
          <!ELEMENT FIELD EMPTY>
                <!ATTLIST FIELD
                      NAME CDATA #REQUIRED
                      TYPE (TEXT | NUMBER | DATE | TIME | CONTAINER)
                        #REQUIRED
                      EMPTYOK (YES| NO) #REQUIRED
                      MAXREPEAT CDATA #REQUIRED>
    <!ELEMENT RESULTSET (ROW)*>
          <!ATTLIST RESULTSET FOUND CDATA #REQUIRED>
          <!ELEMENT ROW (COL)*>
                <!ATTLIST ROW
                      RECORDID CDATA #REQUIRED
                      MODID CDATA #REQUIRED>
                <!ELEMENT COL (DATA)*>
                      <!ELEMENT DATA (#PCDATA)>
]>
```

The content of the records and fields on a layout can be returned as well-formed XML with the FMPXMLRESULT schema/grammar. Any style information will be lost in the data returned. The date and time are returned with the date and time format of the database when created or cloned. Number fields are returned as text and may not be formatted as they are on the layout. Container fields will have a link path to retrieve the image for display. The METADATA could be used to label each COL in a stylesheet. The next schema, FMPDSORESULT, returns the name of each field as an element name. There are similarities to FMPXMLRESULT.

4.3 FMPDSORESULT Schema/Grammar

The final Document Type Definition for FileMaker Pro XML results is FMPDSORESULT. DSO is the abbreviation for Data Source Object. This format is used by many XML documents and shows the field or column name with the contents. The same database, Contact Management.fp5, is used for the DSO results. The HTTP request is shown here:

```
http://localhost/fmpro?-db=Contact%20Management.fp5&-lay=Form%20-
  %20Main%20Address&-format=-dso_xml&-findany
```

The FMPDSORESULT definition begins:

```
<!DOCTYPE FMPDSORESULT [
<!ELEMENT FMPDSORESULT (ERRORCODE, DATABASE, LAYOUT, ROW*)>
     <!ATTLIST FMPDSORESULT xmlns CDATA #REQUIRED>
     <!ELEMENT ERRORCODE (#PCDATA)>
     <!ELEMENT DATABASE (#PCDATA)>
```

The root element FMPDSORESULT has four child elements: ERRORCODE, DATABASE, LAYOUT, and ROW, which may be repeated in the XML result zero or more times. The attribute for FMPDSORESULT, xmlns, has the value of "http://www.filemaker.com/fmpdsoresult" in the XML result. The first child element of the root element, ERRORCODE, is the same as in the FMPXMLLAYOUT and FMPXMLRESULT. The element PRODUCT is not used in the DSO results. The DATABASE element is never empty and contains the name of the database between the start and end markup in the XML result. The well-formed XML result has the same prolog and returns:

```
<?xml version="1.0" encoding="UTF-8" ?>
<FMPDSORESULT xmlns="http://www.filemaker.com/fmpdsoresult">
     <ERRORCODE>0</ERRORCODE>
     <DATABASE>Contact Management.fp5</DATABASE>
     <LAYOUT></LAYOUT>
```

4.31 Records (ROWS) and Fields

The last child element of the FMPDSORESULT element is where the records are returned as the ROW element. The field names are the child elements of the ROW. If no layout is specified, all fields are returned. If the layout has no fields on it, the ROW element is empty:

```
     <ROW MODID="1" RECORDID="1">
```

The definition for the ROW element lists the fields on the layout as child elements, and the element has two required attributes, RECORDID and MODID. These attributes serve the same function as the attributes for the ROW in FMPXMLRESULT.

```
<!ELEMENT ROW (FIELD1, FIELD2, ...)>
     <!ATTLIST ROW
               RECORDID CDATA #REQUIRED
               MODID CDATA #REQUIRED>
```

The element names in FMPDSORESULT are the field names in the database, with the following exceptions: spaces ( ) are converted to underscores (_), and the double colons (::) between a relationship name and a related field are converted to a single period (.).

Listing 4.10 shows the results in DSO format for one record in the Contact Management.fp5 database. Container fields return the link path to the image in the database if you use the HTTP request.

Listing 4.10 DSO results for records/rows

```
<ROW MODID="1" RECORDID="1">
     <Address_Type_1>A</Address_Type_1>
     <City_1>B</City_1>
     <Company>C</Company>
     <Email>D</Email>
     <First_Name>E</First_Name>
     <Last_Name>F</Last_Name>
     <Notes>G</Notes>
     <Phone_1>H</Phone_1>
     <Phone_2>I</Phone_2>
     <Postal_Code_1>J</Postal_Code_1>
     <State_Province_1>K</State_Province_1>
     <Street_1>L</Street_1>
     <Title>M</Title>
     <Image_Data>FMPro?-db=Contact Management.fp5&-RecID=
       24&Image Data=&-img</Image_Data>
     <FndCt>1</FndCt>
     <RecCt>1</RecCt>
</ROW>
```

4.32 Related and Repeating Fields

Special considerations are given for repeating fields and related fields (whether in portal or not). See the results with repeating fields in Chapter 2, section 2.23, "Repeating Field Data," and for related fields in Chapter 2, section 2.22, "XML from FileMaker Pro Related Fields." The name of the field is used as the element name, and the element DATA is used for each repeat or related record in the FMPDSORESULT schema:

```
<!ELEMENT FIELD2 (DATA*)>
<!ELEMENT DATA (#PCDATA)>
```

4.33 Completing the FMPDSORESULT DTD

The FMPDSORESULT definition ends with "]>." Listing 4.11 shows the full definition.

Listing 4.11 FMPDSORESULT Document Type Definition

```
<!DOCTYPE FMPDSORESULT [
<!ELEMENT FMPDSORESULT (ERRORCODE, DATABASE, LAYOUT, ROW*)>
      <!ATTLIST FMPDSORESULT xmlns CDATA #REQUIRED>
      <!ELEMENT ERRORCODE (#PCDATA)>
      <!ELEMENT DATABASE (#PCDATA)>
      <!ELEMENT LAYOUT (#PCDATA)>
      <!ELEMENT ROW (FIELD1, FIELD2, ...)>
            <!ATTLIST ROW
                  RECORDID CDATA #REQUIRED
                  MODID CDATA #REQUIRED>
<!-- grammar for a regular field -->
      <!ELEMENT FIELD1 (#PCDATA)>
<!-- grammar for a repeating or related field -->
      <!ELEMENT FIELD2 (DATA*)>
      <!ELEMENT DATA (#PCDATA)>
]>
```

If the names for the fields are needed, the FMPDSORESULT is the schema to use in the XML request. This is the most flexible design for data exchange in which the name is required. The names of these elements (fields) may be needed for processing the data with stylesheets. The DSO result can be used for parsing XML data into the FileMaker Pro database. The next section presents two parsing methods of extracting the DSO formatted XML data.

4.4 A Document Type Definition for Database Design Reports

FileMaker Developer 5.5 has a new report capability. A special version of FileMaker Pro, the Developer application can create design reports of your open databases. There are two formats available for the report. The first report type creates another FileMaker Pro database with information about the fields, layouts, passwords, relationships, scripts, and value lists in your databases. You must have full password access to create the report. The information in the report is the same information that you can obtain by using the design functions in FileMaker Pro. Figure 4.1 shows a sample report created for two related databases. The files used for this example are found in the Time Billing directory in the Templates directory when you install any version of FileMaker Pro.

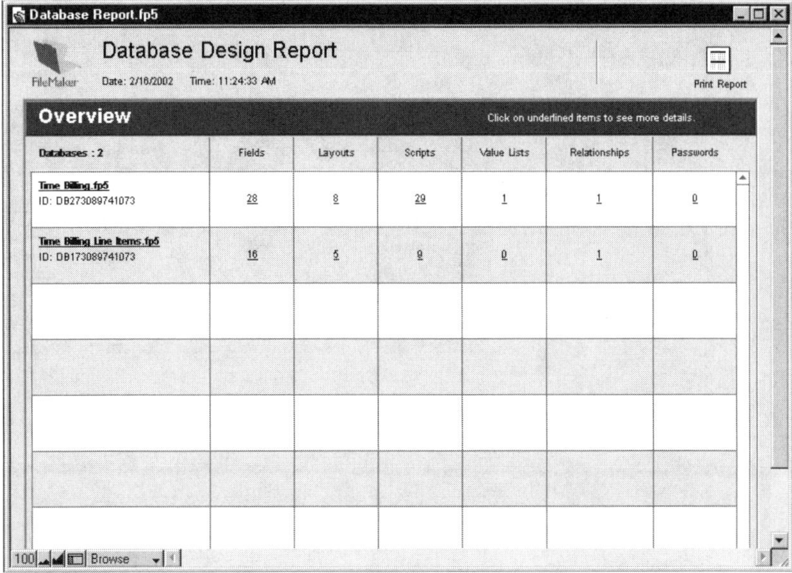

Figure 4.1: Database Design Report overview

The Database Design Report (DDR) is most useful for related files. The links between the files are available in the report. Figure 4.2 has an example of the details for the relationship between the two files. The advantage of using the DDR over using the Design function values is this linking between related files and linking between fields, layouts, value lists, and scripts. You can document your complete database solution and see the relationship for all of the elements in the databases.

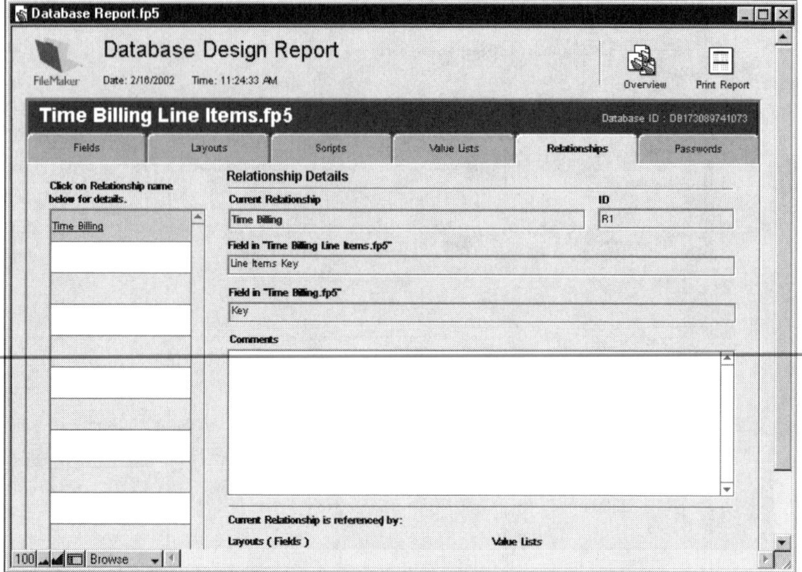

Figure 4.2: Relationship details

To create a DDR, select File, Database Design Report. Figure 4.3 shows the dialog and the open files from the Time Billing templates. The two format options for the report are shown under Report Type. The second option is discussed more fully in this chapter because the report is produced as a well-formed XML document along with the XSL stylesheet to display the report.

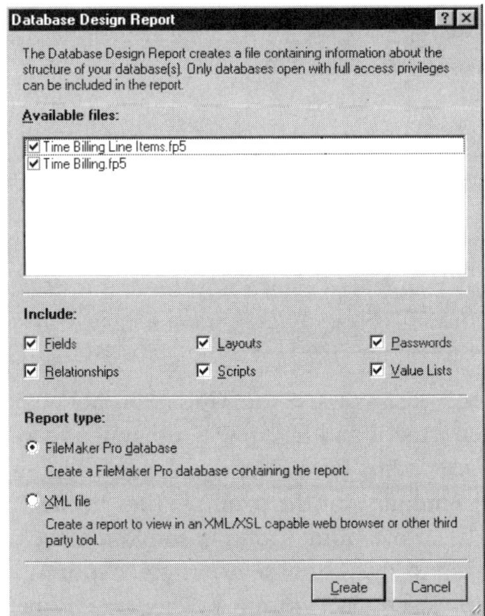

Figure 4.3: Create a Database Design Report

You can read more about the Database Design Report in the FileMaker Pro Developer Help topics "About Database Design Report," "Understanding the FileMaker Pro database report format," "Understanding the XML report format," and "Using Database Design Report."

4.41 Database Design Report with XML and XSL

When you select the XML report type, you are presented with a save dialog, as shown in Figure 4.4. You can name the report anything, but the following examples use the default name Database Report.xml. The Default.xsl stylesheet is included with FileMaker Developer. You can create your own stylesheets to display only selected information. Any XSL document can be selected from the stylesheet pop-up if it is placed in the DDR directory in the FileMaker Developer directory. XSL stylesheets will be discussed in Chapter 7.

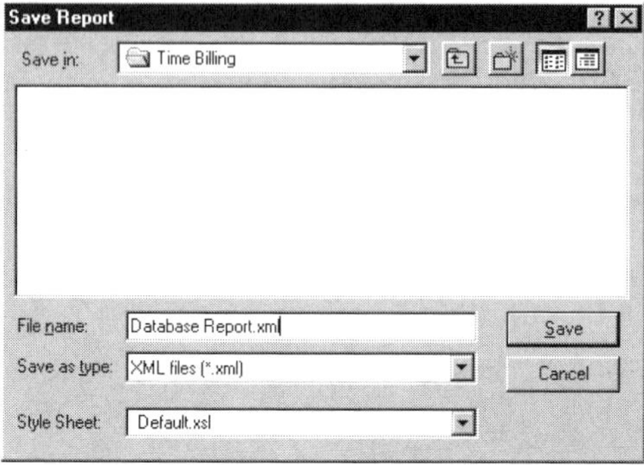

Figure 4.4: Save the Database Design Report

Several text files are created if you use the XML file report type. The first file is Database Report.xml and is the XML document containing the summary of the report items for all the databases in the report. Listing 4.12 shows the summary for the example files in the Time Billing templates folder. The information found in the Summary report is similar to the information in the database overview layout for the Database Design Report as seen in Figure 4.1. The second line in the report is a processing instruction to tell the browser to use the stylesheet DEFAULT.XSL to view the document.

Listing 4.12 Database Report.xml

```
<?xml version="1.0"?>
<?xml-stylesheet type="text/xsl" href="DEFAULT.XSL"?>
<Summary>
	<XMLFileType>Summary</XMLFileType>
	<CreationDate>2/16/2002</CreationDate>
	<CreationTime>12:06:10 PM</CreationTime>
	<File>
		<Name>Time Billing Line Items.fp5</Name>
		<XMLReportFile>Time Billing Line Items_fp5.xml</XMLReportFile>
		<PasswordsCount>0</PasswordsCount>
		<Table>
			<FieldsCount>16</FieldsCount>
		</Table>
		<LayoutsCount>5</LayoutsCount>
		<RelationshipsCount>1</RelationshipsCount>
		<ScriptsCount>9</ScriptsCount>
		<ValueListsCount>0</ValueListsCount>
	</File>
	<File>
		<Name>Time Billing.fp5</Name>
		<XMLReportFile>Time Billing_fp5.xml</XMLReportFile>
		<PasswordsCount>0</PasswordsCount>
```

```
            <Table>
                  <FieldsCount>28</FieldsCount>
            </Table>
            <LayoutsCount>8</LayoutsCount>
            <RelationshipsCount>1</RelationshipsCount>
            <ScriptsCount>29</ScriptsCount>
            <ValueListsCount>1</ValueListsCount>
      </File>
</Summary>
```

A single XML file is created for each open database in the report. The name of the file is the database name and the .xml extension. In the Time Billing example, these two files are Time Billing_fp5.xml and Time Billing Line Items_fp5.xml. The dots in the .fp5 extension on the databases have been changed to an underscore so that the text file has only one extension. The names of these files are used in the Database Report.xml in Listing 4.12, so do not change them after creating the reports.

The final file that is created is the Default.xsl document. The stylesheet document is a copy of the original found in the DDR folder. If you have created and selected a custom XSL stylesheet, a copy of it is placed in the same folder with the Database Report and XML file documents. The default XSL or your custom XSL must be in the same folder with the XML created to view the Database Design Report in the browser.

FileMaker Developer creates the XML and XSL documents and automatically opens a default browser to display the report. The Microsoft Internet Explorer 5 (or greater) web browsers for Windows and Macintosh are recommended for viewing these reports. The XSL in the Database Design Report may not conform to the latest W3C standards, but these differences will be discussed in Chapter 7. You can view the report at any time by opening the Database Report.xml document in your browser. The Default.xsl stylesheet will be used to format the report with hyperlinks between the design elements in the databases.

The XML and XSL documents contain the same links found in the Database Report created as a database. The XML and XSL documents are text and may be opened with any text editor, as well. The XML documents created by the Database Design Report may be used by other applications that can process the XML.

Waves In Motion, http://wmotion.com/analyzer.html, has a commercial product that uses the XML produced by FileMaker Developer. Analyzer enhances the Database Design Report by using the XML and adding references to common errors, broken relationships, broken value lists, and missing items in scripts. Analyzer does not have the ability to link external subscripts.

4.42 XML Output Grammar for Database Design Report

The document "FileMaker Inc. Database Design Report XML Output Grammar" is available at http://www.filemaker.com/downloads/pdf/ddr_grammar.pdf. A revised version is used here to create a DTD for the Database Design Report grammar. Listing 4.12, shows the XML produced for the Database Report. Listing 4.13 shows the XML tree for this report. A Document Type Definition will be created for this XML document in the next section.

Disclaimer: Please remember that this exercise is only used to demonstrate the relationship between an XML document and a "road map of elements and attributes," such as with DTDs, schemas, or grammars. The DTD we will create is not an actual valid document. FileMaker, Inc. has not published any DTD, schema, or grammar for the FileMaker Pro Database Design Report.

The summaries included below are also not actual documents. The structure is based on the document "FileMaker Inc. Database Design Report XML Output Grammar" available in the portable document format on the web site at http://www.filemaker.com/downloads/pdf/ddr_grammar.pdf.

Listing 4.13 Summary XML for the database report

```
<?xml version='1.0' ?>
<?xml-stylesheet type="text/xsl" href="DEFAULT.XSL"?>
<Summary>
      <XMLFileType>
            SUMMARY
      </XMLFileType>
      <CreationDate><!-- creation date of report --></CreationDate>
      <CreationTime><!-- creation time of report --></CreationTime>
      <File><!-- Repeats for each FILE in the report -->
            <Name><!-- the name of the File --></Name>
            <XMLReportFile><!-- XML detail report file name
              --></XMLReportFile>
            <Table>
                  <FieldsCount><!-- number of fields --></FieldsCount>
            </Table>
```

```
            <LayoutsCount><!-- number of layouts --></LayoutsCount>
            <RelationshipsCount><!-- number of relationships
              --></RelationshipsCount>
            <ScriptsCount><!-- number of scripts --></ScriptsCount>
            <ValueListsCount><!-- number of valuelists
              --></ValueListsCount>
            <PasswordsCount><!-- number of Passwords --></PasswordsCount>
      </File>
</Summary>
```

The Summary file type report contains the name of the database files, the report name for the database details, the number of fields, the number of layouts, the number of relationships, the number of value lists, and the number of passwords in each database. Default.xsl uses this data to format the report with hyperlinks to the details. Listing 4.14 shows a sample of the XSL used to display the Database Report.xml. See sections 7.2 and 7.3 for more information about this type of stylesheet.

Listing 4.14 Summary.xsl

```
<?xml version='1.0' ?>
<xsl:stylesheet xmlns:xsl="http://www.w3.org/TR/WD-xsl">
   <xsl:template match="/">
   <html>
   <body>
      <xsl:if match=".[/Summary/XMLFileType = 'Summary']">
         <h2 align="center">FILEMAKER PRO DATABASE DESIGN REPORT</h2>
         <h5 align="center">Creation Date and Time:
            <xsl:value-of select="/Summary/CreationDate" />
            at
            <xsl:value-of select="/Summary/CreationTime" />
         </h5>
      <h2>Report Overview</h2>
      <table cellpadding="3" border="2">
         <tr>
            <td width="150">
               <b>Database</b>
            </td>
            <td align="center" width="100">
               <b>Fields</b>
            </td>
            <td align="center" width="100">
               <b>Layouts</b>
            </td>
            <td align="center" width="100">
               <b>Relationships</b>
            </td>
```

```
        <td align="center" width="100">
            <b>Scripts</b>
        </td>
        <td align="center" width="100">
            <b>Value Lists</b>
        </td>
        <td align="center" width="100">
            <b>Passwords</b>
        </td>
    </tr>
    <xsl:for-each select="/Summary/File">
        <tr>
            <td>
                <a>
                    <xsl:attribute name="HREF">
                        <xsl:value-of select="XMLReportFile" />
                    </xsl:attribute>
                        <xsl:value-of select="Name" />
                </a>
            </td>
            <td align="center">
                <a>
                    <xsl:attribute name="HREF">
                        <xsl:value-of select="XMLReportFile" />
                        #Fields
                    </xsl:attribute>
                    <xsl:value-of select="Table/FieldsCount" />
                </a>
            </td>
            <td align="center">
                <a>
                    <xsl:attribute name="HREF">
                        <xsl:value-of select="XMLReportFile" />
                        #Layouts
                    </xsl:attribute>
                    <xsl:value-of select="LayoutsCount" />
                </a>
            </td>
            <td align="center">
                <a>
                    <xsl:attribute name="HREF">
                        <xsl:value-of select="XMLReportFile" />
                        #Relationships
                    </xsl:attribute>
                    <xsl:value-of select="RelationshipsCount" />
                </a>
            </td>
            <td align="center">
```

```
                <a>
                    <xsl:attribute name="HREF">
                        <xsl:value-of select="XMLReportFile" />
                        #Scripts
                    </xsl:attribute>
                    <xsl:value-of select="ScriptsCount" />
                </a>
            </td>
            <td align="center">
                <a>
                    <xsl:attribute name="HREF">
                        <xsl:value-of select="XMLReportFile" />
                        #ValueLists
                    </xsl:attribute>
                    <xsl:value-of select="ValueListsCount" />
                </a>
            </td>
            <td align="center">
                <a>
                    <xsl:attribute name="HREF">
                        <xsl:value-of select="XMLReportFile" />
                        #Passwords
                    </xsl:attribute>
                    <xsl:value-of select="PasswordsCount" />
                </a>
            </td>
        </tr>
    </xsl:for-each>
  </table>
 </xsl:if>
 </body>
 </html>
 </xsl:template>
</xsl:stylesheet>
```

The XSL processor looks for the elements in the XML document and inserts the values in an HTML page. Figure 4.5 shows the browser display for the report that uses the Summary.xsl in Listing 4.14 and the Database Report.xml in Listing 4.12.

Database Design Report in the Browser

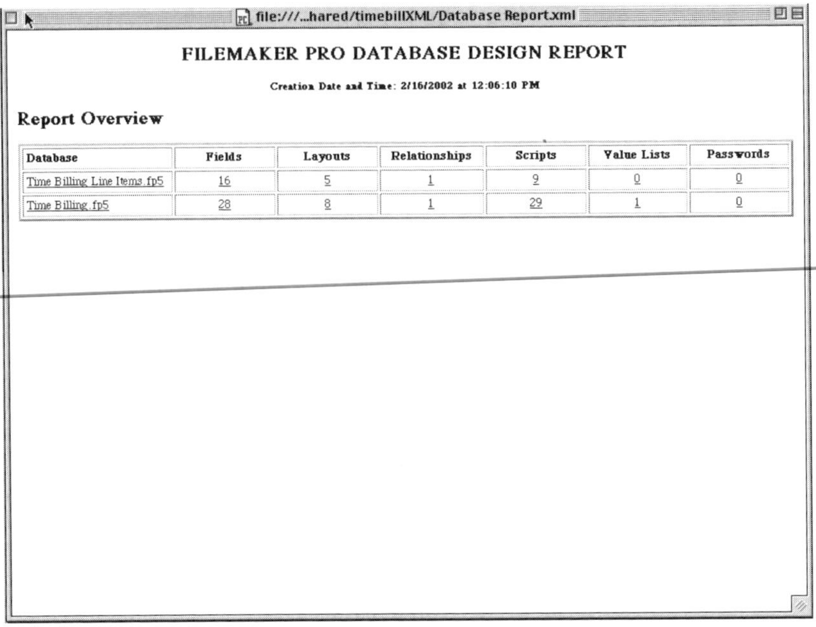

file:///...hared/timebillXML/Database Report.xml

FILEMAKER PRO DATABASE DESIGN REPORT

Creation Date and Time: 2/16/2002 at 12:06:10 PM

Report Overview

Database	Fields	Layouts	Relationships	Scripts	Value Lists	Passwords
Time Billing Line Items.fp5	16	5	1	9	0	0
Time Billing.fp5	28	8	1	29	1	0

Figure 4.5: Document Type Definition for summary

Create the DTD with the declaration for the type of document and the root element Summary. The Summary element has four child elements, one each named XMLFileType, CreationDate, and CreationTime, and one or more File elements.

```
<!DOCTYPE Database Report [
     <!ELEMENT Summary (XMLFileType, CreationDate, CreationTime, File+)>
```

The XMLFileType element is never empty and has the required value "SUMMARY" (uppercase). The W3C recommendations for Element Type Declarations, Section 3.2, "Extensible Markup Language (XML) 1.0 (Second Edition)," http://www.w3.org/TR/2000/REC-xml-20001006, does not provide for required element values. The DTD only shows that parsed character data is used in the contents for this element:

```
          <!ELEMENT XMLFileType (#PCDATA)>
```

The remaining elements for the Database Report document are defined in Listing 4.15. The File element has two required child elements, Name and XMLReportFile. The other child elements for the File element are optional and will be created only if included in the report.

The Database Design Report dialog, shown in Figure 4.3, has check boxes for each item to include.

Listing 4.15 DTD for summary XML report

```
<!DOCTYPE Database Report [
     <!ELEMENT Summary (XMLFileType, CreationDate, CreationTime, File+)>
          <!ELEMENT XMLFileType (#PCDATA)>
          <!ELEMENT CreationDate (#PCDATA)>
          <!ELEMENT CreationTime (#PCDATA)>
          <!ELEMENT File (Name, XMLReportFile, PasswordCount?,
            Table?, LayoutsCount?, RelationshipsCount?, ScriptsCount?,
            ValueListsCount?)>
               <!ELEMENT Name (#PCDATA)>
               <!ELEMENT XMLReportFile (#PCDATA)>
               <!ELEMENT PasswordCount (#PCDATA)>
               <!ELEMENT Table (FieldsCount)>
                    <!ELEMENT FieldsCount (#PCDATA)>
               <!ELEMENT LayoutsCount (#PCDATA)>
               <!ELEMENT RelationshipsCount (#PCDATA)>
               <!ELEMENT ScriptsCount (#PCDATA)>
               <!ELEMENT ValueListsCount (#PCDATA)>
]>
```

The Database Report does not require a DTD to be used by FileMaker. This exercise was included to demonstrate the construction of Document Type Definitions. The limitations of this type of "road map" were demonstrated in the definition for the XMLFileType element. If an element requires a default value, there is no way to include the value in the DTD. The World Wide Web Consortium has proposed using Schema (XSD) to correct this oversight. You can read more about the proposal at http://www.w3.org/XML/Schema.

4.43 Database Design Report File Grammar

When the XML Database Design Report is generated, a text file in XML format is created for each database. The information about the design of each database is written with the Report file type format. The Report file type uses the precise grammar found in the document "FileMaker Inc. Database Design Report XML Output Grammar," available at http://www.filemaker.com/downloads/pdf/ddr_grammar.pdf. A brief version of the Report file type is shown in Listing 4.16. The example shows only some of the main elements for the Report file type. The details will be further expanded later in this section. In the Report file type, the element XMLFileType has the required value "REPORT" (uppercase). This type of XML report has all of the field, relationship, value list, layout, script, and password information for the named database.

You can read the XML produced by the Database Design Report in a text editor. The text is in double-byte format, or UTF-16. Your text editor may not be able to display the text properly. The double-byte format is how many more characters, such as the o-slash, can be used in your FileMaker Pro databases. A very noticeable set of two characters at the beginning of the XML are ASCII 255 (HEX 0xFF) and ASCII 254 (HEX 0xFE). The two characters are the Byte Order Mark (BOM) and tell processors how the double-byte characters are ordered in the Unicode document. Your editor or browser may not be able to display the XML created by the FileMaker Pro Database Design Report. I have found the latest version of the Internet Explorer browser seems to work well on any platform.

Listing 4.16 Report XML for the Database Design Report

```
<?xml version='1.0' ?>
<?xml-stylesheet type="text/xsl" href="DEFAULT.XSL"?>
<File>
	<Name><!-- database name --></Name>
	<XMLFileType>REPORT</XMLFileType>
	<SummaryLink><!-- go back to summary overview --></SummaryLink>
	<CreationDate><!-- creation date of report --></CreationDate>
	<CreationTime><!-- creation time of report --></CreationTime>
	<Table>
		<Name><!-- same as database name for now --></Name>
		<ID>1</ID>
		<FieldCatalog>
			<Field><!-- REPEAT for *each* field --></Field>
		</FieldCatalog>
	</Table>
	<RelationCatalog>
		<Relation><!-- REPEAT for *each* relationship --></Relation>
	</RelationCatalog>
	<ValueListCatalog>
		<ValueList><!-- REPEAT for *each* valuelist --></ValueList>
	</ValueListCatalog>
	<LayoutCatalog>
		<Layout><!-- REPEAT for *each* layout --></Layout>
	</LayoutCatalog>
	<ScriptCatalog>
		<Script><!-- REPEAT for *each* Script in the Database
		  --></Script>
	</ScriptCatalog>
```

```
    <PasswordCatalog>
        <Password><!-- REPEAT for *each* password --></Password>
    </PasswordCatalog>
</File>
```

4.44 Details of the XML Database Design Report

Field Details

The FieldCatalog element has one child element, Field, which is repeated in the report for every field in the database. The information provided for each field can be quite extensive. Listing 4.17 shows the child elements for the element Field: Name, ID, DataType, FieldType, AutoEnterOptions, ValidationOptions, StorageOptions, Calculation, and SummaryOptions. These values may be found in the Define Field dialog. The Database Design Report will contain only those values that apply to a particular type of field. Only summary fields will have a SummaryOptions element, for example, in the report.

Listing 4.17 FieldCatalog elements

```
<FieldCatalog>
    <Field><!-- REPEAT for *each* field -->
        <Name><!-- field name --></Name>
        <ID><!-- field id (same as function) --></ID>
        <DataType><!-- TEXT | NUMBER | DATE | TIME | BINARY_DATA
          | FURIGANA --></DataType>
        <FieldType><!-- EDITABLE | CALCULATED | SUMMARY --></FieldType>
        <AutoEnterOptions>
            <EntryType><!-- CREATION_TIME | CREATION_DATE |
              MODIFICATION_DATE | MODIFICATION_TIME |
              CREATOR_NAME | MODIFIER_NAME | SERIAL_NUMBER |
              PREVIOUS_DATA | CONSTANT_DATA --></EntryType>
            <SerialNumber><!-- only if EntryType is SERIAL_NUMBER
              --></SerialNumber>
            <NextValue><!-- only if EntryType is SERIAL_NUMBER
              --></NextValue>
            <Increment><!-- only if EntryType is SERIAL_NUMBER
              --></Increment>
            <ConstantData><!-- only if EntryType is CONSTANT_DATA
              --></ConstantData>
            <Calculation>
                <AlwaysEvaluate><!-- TRUE | FALSE
                  --></AlwaysEvaluate>
```

```
            <Description>
                <Chunk><!-- REPEAT for *each* chunk
                  (any value) -->
                      <Reference><!-- see _reference_
                        types --></Reference>
                </Chunk>
            </Description>
        </Calculation>
        <Lookup>
            <Reference><!-- see FIELD _reference_ types
              --></Reference>
            <NoMatchCopyOptions><!-- DO_NOT_COPY |
              COPY_NEXT_LOWER | COPY_NEXT_HIGHER |
              USE_CONSTANT --></NoMatchCopyOptions>
            <CopyConstantValue><!-- any Constant Value
              --></CopyConstantValue>
            <CopyEmptyContent><!-- TRUE | FALSE
              --></CopyEmptyContent>
        </Lookup>
        <AllowEditing><!-- TRUE | FALSE --></AllowEditing>
    </AutoEnterOptions>
    <ValidationOptions>
        <StrictDataType><!-- NUMERIC | FOUR_DIGIT_YEAR |
          TIME_OF_DAY --></StrictDataType>
        <NotEmpty><!-- TRUE | FALSE --></NotEmpty>
        <Unique><!-- TRUE | FALSE --></Unique>
        <Existing><!-- TRUE | FALSE --></Existing>
        <ValueList>
            <Reference><!-- see VALUELIST _reference_
              types --></Reference>
        </ValueList>
        <Range>
            <From><!-- any FROM Range Value --></From>
            <To><!-- any TO Range Value --></To>
        </Range>
        <Calculation>
            <AlwaysEvaluate><!-- TRUE | FALSE
              --></AlwaysEvaluate>
            <Description>
                <Chunk><!-- REPEAT for *each* chunk
                  (any value) -->
                      <Reference><!-- see _reference_
                        types --></Reference>
                </Chunk>
            </Description>
        </Calculation>
```

```
        <MaxDataLength><!-- any number 1-64,000
          --></MaxDataLength>
        <StrictValidation><!-- TRUE | FALSE
          --></StrictValidation>
        <ErrorMessage><!-- Display custom message if
          validation fails --></ErrorMessage>
    </ValidationOptions>
    <StorageOptions>
        <Repetitions><!-- any number 1 to 1000, 1 means
          not a repeating field --></Repetitions>
        <Global><!-- TRUE | FALSE --></Global>
        <Unstored><!-- TRUE | FALSE --></Unstored>
        <Indexed><!-- TRUE | FALSE --></Indexed>
        <AutoIndex><!-- TRUE | FALSE --></AutoIndex>
        <IndexLanguage><!-- Catalan | Danish | Dutch |
          English | Finnish | Finnish (v≠w) | German |
          German (ä=a) | Icelandic | Italian | Norwegian |
          Portuguese | Spanish | Spanish (New Style) |
          Swedish | Swedish (v≠w) | Czech/Slovak |
          Hungarian | Polish | Romanian | Croatian | Turkish
          | Russian | Ukrainian | Greek | ASCII
          --></IndexLanguage>
    </StorageOptions>
    <Calculation>
            <AlwaysEvaluate><!-- TRUE | FALSE
              --></AlwaysEvaluate>
            <Description>
                <Chunk><!-- REPEAT for *each* chunk
                  (any value) -->
                    <Reference><!-- see _reference_
                      types --></Reference>
                </Chunk>
            </Description>
    </Calculation>
    <SummaryOptions>
        <Operation><!-- TOTAL | AVERAGE | COUNT | MINIMUM |
          MAXIMUM | STANDARD_DEVIATION | FRACTION_TOTAL
          --></Operation>
        <Reference><!-- see FIELD _reference_ types
          --></Reference>
        <AdditionalOperation><!-- (Total of) RUNNING_TOTAL
          | (Average of) WEIGHTED_AVERAGE | (Count of)
          RUNNING_COUNT | (Standard deviation)
          BY_POPULATION | (Fraction of total) SUB_TOTALED
          --></AdditionalOperation>
        <SortedBy><!-- Summary field, Fraction of total,
          Subtotaled, When sorted by  -->
```

```
                    <Reference><!-- see FIELD _reference_ types
                      --></Reference>
               </SortedBy>
               <WeightedBy><!-- Summary field, Average of,
                 Weighted average, Weighted by -->
               <Reference><!-- see FIELD _reference_ types
                 --></Reference>
               </WeightedBy>
          </SummaryOptions>
     </Field>
</FieldCatalog>
```

Reference Elements

The Reference elements in Listing 4.17 are used whenever another type of FileMaker Pro object is used in the Field Definition. A reference to another field, value list, or relationship might be used to define a field. These references are listed in the report under the Reference element. The child elements for the Reference element vary, but they always have a Type element. The other elements are shown in Listing 4.18.

Listing 4.18 Field Reference elements

```
<Reference>
     <Type>FIELD_REF</Type>
     <Name><!-- field name --></Name>
     <ID><!-- field ID --></ID>
     <TableName><!-- table name that this field is in --></TableName>
     <FileName><!-- name of the database --></FileName>
     <RelationshipName><!-- if a related field is used
       --></RelationshipName>
     <Link><!-- reference used to make a hyperlink in the Report
       --></Link>
</Reference>
```

The TableName element in the Field Reference element above is used because the FieldCatalog element is in a Table element in the File element, as seen in Listing 4.16. Both TableName and FileName are needed in this reference to point to the location of the field being referenced.

The other Reference elements for value lists, relationships, scripts, and layouts are given in the following listings. These have similar child elements:

Listing 4.19 Value List Reference elements

```
<Reference>
     <Type>VALUELIST_REF</Type>
     <Name><!-- value list name --></Name>
     <ID><!-- value list ID --></ID>
     <FileName><!-- name of the database --></FileName>
     <Link><!-- reference used to make a hyperlink in the Report
       --></Link>
</Reference>
```

Listing 4.20 Relationship Reference elements

```
<Reference>
     <Type>RELATIONSHIP_REF</Type>
     <Name><!-- relationship name --></Name>
     <ID><!-- relationship ID --></ID>
     <FileName><!-- name of the database --></FileName>
     <Link><!-- reference used to make a hyperlink in the Report
       --></Link>
</Reference>
```

Listing 4.21 Script Reference elements

```
<Reference>
     <Type>SCRIPT_REF</Type>
     <Name><!-- script name --></Name>
     <ID><!-- script ID --></ID>
     <FileName><!-- name of the database --></FileName>
     <Link><!-- reference used to make a hyperlink in the Report
       --></Link>
</Reference>
```

Listing 4.22 Layout Reference elements

```
<Reference>
     <Type>LAYOUT_REF</Type>
     <Name><!-- layout name --></Name>
     <ID><!-- layout ID --></ID>
     <FileName><!-- name of the database --></FileName>
     <Link><!-- reference used to make a hyperlink in the Report
       --></Link>
</Reference>
```

The file references and function references are in Listings 4.23 and 4.24.

Listing 4.23 File Reference elements

```
<Reference>
     <Type>FILE_REF</Type>
     <Name><!-- file name --></Name>
```

```
    <Link><!-- reference used to make a hyperlink in the Report
      --></Link>
</Reference>
```

Listing 4.24 Function Reference elements

```
<Reference>
    <Type>FUNCTION_REF</Type>
    <Name><!-- function name --></Name>
</Reference>
```

All of the Reference elements may be used in the FieldCatalog, RelationCatalog, ValueListCatalog, LayoutCatalog, and ScriptCatalog. The Reference elements are used to link the other main objects together for the Database Design Report.

Relationship Details

The RelationCatalog has one child element, Relation, which is repeated for every relationship in the database. The child elements for the Relation element are Name, ID, ParentField, ChildField, CascadeDelete, CascadeCreate, and Sorted.

Listing 4.25 RelationCatalog elements

```
<RelationCatalog>
    <Relation><!-- REPEAT for *each* Relationship -->
        <Name><!-- name of Relationship --></Name>
        <ID></ID>
        <ParentField>
            <Reference><!-- see FIELD _reference_types
              --></Reference>
        </ParentField>
        <ChildField>
            <Reference><!-- see FIELD _reference_types
              --></Reference>
        </ChildField>
        <CascadeDelete><!-- TRUE | FALSE --></CascadeDelete>
        <CascadeCreate><!-- TRUE | FALSE --></CascadeCreate>
        <Sorted><!-- TRUE | FALSE --></Sorted>
    </Relation>
</RelationCatalog>
```

The Relation element is repeated in the report for every relationship in the database. The values for these elements can be found in the Define Relationship dialog. The details for sorting the element are restricted to TRUE or FALSE. No other information about the sort for the relationship is provided in the Database Design Report.

Value List Details

The ValueListCatalog has one element, ValueList, if there are any value lists defined. The ValueList element is repeated in the report for every value list in the database. They are Name, ID, Source, CustomList, PrimaryField, SecondaryField, SortSecondaryField, and ValueList. There may be references to fields, files, and other value lists in the Database Design Report.

Listing 4.26 ValueListCatalog elements

```
<ValueListCatalog>
     <ValueList><!-- REPEAT for *each* Value List -->
          <Name><!-- name of Value List --></Name>
          <ID></ID>
          <Source><!-- CUSTOM | LOCAL_FIELD | RELATED_FIELD
            | EXTERNAL_FIELD | EXTERNAL_VALUELIST --></Source>
          <CustomList><!-- list of values if custom --></CustomList>
          <PrimaryField><!-- if local, related or external fields -->
               <Reference><!-- see FIELD _reference_types
                 --></Reference>
          </PrimaryField>
          <SecondaryField><!-- if second field used in value list -->
          <Reference><!-- see FIELD _reference_types --></Reference>
          </SecondaryField>
          <SortSecondaryField><!-- if sorting by second
            field in list: TRUE | FALSE --></SortSecondaryField>
          <ValueList><!-- if external value list -->
               <Reference><!-- see VALUELIST_reference_ types
                 --></Reference>
          </ValueList>
     </ValueList>
</ValueListCatalog>
```

Layout Details

The LayoutCatalog element will contain every layout in the database when the report is created. The Layout element has an Object element, which lists details for the fields and buttons on the named layout. References are made to value lists, script steps, and scripts for the objects on the layout. Details about the layout, such as font, part color, or other layout elements, are not included in the report.

Listing 4.27 LayoutCatalog elements

```
<LayoutCatalog>
    <Layout><!-- REPEAT for *each* layout -->
        <Name><!-- name of layout --></Name>
        <ID></ID>
        <Object><!-- REPEAT for *each* object on this layout -->
            <Name />
            <Type><!-- FIELD | BUTTON | FIELD_AND_BUTTON --></Type>
            <FieldFormat><!-- TEXT_BOX | SCROLLABLE_TEXT_BOX |
              POPUP_LIST | POPUP_MENU | CHECK_BOXES |
              RADIO_BUTTONS  --></FieldFormat>
            <ValueList><!-- if field on layout has value list -->
                <Reference><!-- see VALUELIST_reference_types
                  --></Reference>
            </ValueList>
            <ValueListFormat><!-- POPUP_LIST | POPUP_MENU |
              CHECK_BOXES | RADIO_BUTTONS --></ValueListFormat>
            <Reference><!-- see FIELD _reference_types, if
              object is field --></Reference>
            <AllowEditing><!-- TRUE | FALSE --></AllowEditing>
            <Command><!-- any valid Script Step, if button
              --></Command>
            <Description>
                <Chunk><!-- REPEAT for *each* chunk (any value) -->
                    <Reference><!-- see _reference_ types
                      --></Reference>
                </Chunk>
            </Description>
        </Object>
    </Layout>
</LayoutCatalog>
```

Some of the results from the Time Billing_fp5.xml report are shown in Listing 4.28. This example shows two objects on the Form layout. The first one is a field and the second object is a button.

Listing 4.28 Example report data

```
        <Object>
            <Name>Time Billing Line Items::Date</Name>
            <Type>FIELD</Type>
            <FieldFormat>TEXT_BOX</FieldFormat>
            <Reference>
                <Type>FIELD_REF</Type>
                <Name>Date</Name>
                <ID>67</ID>
                <TableName>Time Billing Line Items.fp5</TableName>
                <FileName>Time Billing Line Items.fp5</FileName>
```

```
                <Link>Time Billing Line Items_fp5.xml</Link>
                <RelationshipName>Time Billing Line
                  Items</RelationshipName>
            </Reference>
      <AllowEditing>TRUE</AllowEditing>
      </Object>
      <Object>
            <Name>List</Name>
            <Type>BUTTON</Type>
      <Command>Perform Script</Command>
            <Description>
            <Chunk> [&quot;</Chunk>
            <Chunk>
                <Reference>
                      <Type>SCRIPT_REF</Type>
                      <Name>Go to List Layout</Name>
                      <ID>34</ID>
                      <FileName>Time Billing.fp5 </FileName>
                      <Link>Time Billing_fp5.xml</Link>
                </Reference>
            </Chunk>
            <Chunk>&quot;]</Chunk>
            </Description>
      </Object>
```

Script Details

The schema for the ScriptCatalog element is simpler but may have many values. The Script element, child of the ScriptCatalog element, is repeated for every script in the database. The Step element is repeated for every step in the Script element. The details in this portion of the Database Design Report are similar to the information found in the Define Scripts dialogs. The ScriptCatalog elements are shown in the following listing:

Listing 4.29 ScriptCatalog elements

```
<ScriptCatalog>
     <Script><!-- REPEAT for *each* Script in the Database -->
          <Name><!-- name of Script --></Name>
          <ID></ID>
          <Step><!-- REPEAT for *each* Step in this Script -->
                <Command><!-- any valid Script Step --></Command>
                <Description>
                      <Chunk><!-- REPEAT for *each* chunk (any value) -->
                            <Reference><!-- see _reference_ types
                              --></Reference>
                      </Chunk>
```

```
            </Description>
        </Step>
    </Script>
</ScriptCatalog>
```

Listing 4.30 shows one script from the Time Billing.xml report. The Chunk element is used to contain script step content that does not change. The Chunk element can also be the parent element for the Reference element, which would contain variable content, such as a field reference. The quote, less than, greater than, and ampersand symbols are automatically converted to the entity equivalents. Read more about the conversion in Chapter 3, section 3.5, "Entities in the DTD."

Listing 4.30 Sample script data

```
    <Script>
        <Name>Open Script</Name>
        <ID>1</ID>
        <Step>
        <Command>Allow User Abort</Command>
            <Description>
                <Chunk> [Off]</Chunk>
            </Description>
        </Step>
        <Step>
        <Command>Set Field</Command>
            <Description>
            <Chunk> [&quot;</Chunk>
            <Chunk>
                <Reference>
                    <Type>FIELD_REF</Type>
                    <Name>Today&apos;s Date</Name>
                    <ID>3</ID>
                    <TableName>Time Billing.fp5</TableName>
                    <FileName>Time Billing.fp5</FileName>
                </Reference>
            </Chunk>
            <Chunk>&quot;, &quot;</Chunk>
            <Chunk>
                <Reference>
                    <Type>FUNCTION_REF</Type>
                    <Name>Status</Name>
                </Reference>
            </Chunk>
            <Chunk>( CurrentDate)</Chunk>
            <Chunk>&quot;]</Chunk>
            </Description>
```

```
        </Step>
        <Step>
        <Command>Go to Record/Request/Page</Command>
            <Description>
            <Chunk> [Last]</Chunk>
            </Description>
        </Step>
        <Step>
        <Command>Perform Script</Command>
            <Description>
            <Chunk> [Sub-scripts, &quot;</Chunk>
            <Chunk>
                <Reference>
                    <Type>SCRIPT_REF</Type>
                    <Name>Clear Sort Indicator</Name>
                    <ID>32</ID>
                    <FileName>Time Billing.fp5</FileName>
                    <Link>Time Billing_fp5.xml</Link>
                </Reference>
            </Chunk>
            <Chunk>&quot;]</Chunk>
            </Description>
        </Step>
    </Script>
```

The script in Listing 4.30 is the same as the following:

Listing 4.31 Script steps for open script

```
Allow User Abort [Off]
Set Field ["Today's Date", "Status(CurrentDate)" ]
Go to Record/Request/Page [Last]
Perform Script[Sub-scripts, "Clear Sort Indicator"]
```

The last script step in Listing 4.31 refers to a subscript. In the XML report, the Reference element provides enough details to allow a link to be made to the subscript in the same file. The XSL stylesheet uses this information to create a hyperlink. If the reference is to an external sub-script, the link is made only to the external file, not directly to the subscript or its name. An example of the external sub-script reference is shown below:

Listing 4.32 External sub-script reference

```
<Step>
    <Command>Perform Script</Command>
    <Description>
        <Chunk> [Sub-scripts, External: &quot;</Chunk>
        <Chunk>
```

```
                    <Reference>
                         <Type>TABLE_REF</Type>
                         <Name>Time Billing Line Items.fp5</Name>
                         <Link>Time Billing Line Items_fp5.xml </Link>
                    </Reference>
               </Chunk>
               <Chunk>&quot;]</Chunk>
          </Description>
     </Step>
```

Password Details

The password information is also in the Database Design Report. This information can only be obtained if the databases are opened with a top-level or master access. None of the design items, such as fields and scripts, can be obtained without this top-level access. You can limit what items are in the report. See Figure 4.3, the dialog for creating the Database Design Report. Should you wish to create the report and not include the passwords, deselect this item in the dialog before creating the report.

Listing 4.33 PasswordCatalog elements

```
<PasswordCatalog>
     <Password><!-- REPEAT for *each* password -->
          <Name><!-- name of password --></Name>
          <Privileges>
               <MasterAccess><!-- TRUE | FALSE --></MasterAccess>
               <BrowseRecords>
                    <!-- TRUE | FALSE -->
               <Description>
                    <Chunk><!-- REPEAT for *each* chunk (any value) -->
                         <Reference><!-- see _reference_ types
                           --></Reference>
                    </Chunk>
               </Description>
               </BrowseRecords>
               <EditRecords>
                    <!-- TRUE | FALSE -->
               <Description>
                    <Chunk><!-- REPEAT for *each* chunk (any value) -->
                         <Reference><!-- see _reference_ types
                           --></Reference>
                    </Chunk>
               </Description>
               </EditRecords>
               <DeleteRecords>
                    <!-- TRUE | FALSE -->
```

```
            <Description>
                <Chunk><!-- REPEAT for *each* chunk (any value) -->
                    <Reference><!-- see _reference_ types
                      --></Reference>
                </Chunk>
            </Description>
            </DeleteRecords>
            <CreateRecords><!-- TRUE | FALSE --></CreateRecords>
            <PrintRecords><!-- TRUE | FALSE --></PrintRecords>
            <ExportRecords><!-- TRUE | FALSE --></ExportRecords>
            <DesignLayouts><!-- TRUE | FALSE --></DesignLayouts>
            <EditScripts><!-- TRUE | FALSE --></EditScripts>
            <DefineValueLists><!-- TRUE | FALSE
              --></DefineValueLists>
            <ChangePassword><!-- TRUE | FALSE --></ChangePassword>
            <Override><!-- (data entry warnings) TRUE | FALSE
              --></Override>
            <IdleDisconnect><!-- TRUE | FALSE --></IdleDisconnect>
            <Menu><!-- NORMAL | EDITING_ONLY | NONE --></Menu>
        </Privileges>
    </Password>
</PasswordCatalog>
```

Listing 4.33 shows the child elements for the PasswordCatalog element. Only one child element, Password, is repeated in the report for every password in the database. The elements for the Password element are similar to the information found in the Define Passwords dialog. The settings in the Define Passwords dialog are used in the Database Design Report. The information found in the Access Privileges dialog is not used in the Database Design Report. The Access Privileges dialog in FileMaker Pro defines the group-level access to layouts and fields.

4.45 FileMaker Pro Document Definitions

The FMPXMLLAYOUT, FMPXMLRESULT, and FMPDSORESULT schema/grammar formats follow the recommendations of the World Wide Web Consortium for writing Document Type Definitions (DTD). The schema/grammar format for the Database Design Report XML output is closer to the style of the more detailed schema documents. All of these types of formats can be used to define particular types of documents. The DTD and schema formats are used to keep a document type standard.

Chapters 3 and 4 have examined the standards for DTDs and FileMaker Pro XML. The next chapter begins to explain how to use the XML in web publishing. A sample was provided in Listing 4.16 to display the Database Design Report in a browser. The stylesheet uses XSL (XML Stylesheet Language) to transform the XML in the report into HTML. Chapter 6 will cover HTML and how it is used to display text in a web browser. Chapter 7 will discuss XSL and how it can be used to transform your FileMaker Pro XML into other kinds of documents.

Chapter 5

XML and FileMaker Pro Web Publishing

Starting with FileMaker Pro 5.0, XML is published by Web Companion, a plug-in that extends the functionality of FileMaker Pro. By issuing particular commands to FileMaker Pro Web Companion, the field names, field content, and some layout information is returned as well-formed and valid XML results.

In this chapter you will learn how to set up FileMaker Pro Unlimited for optimal XML web publishing. A complete overview, with examples, of the XML commands and results used by FileMaker Pro is included here along with considerations for specific field types. Some Claris Dynamic Markup Language (CDML) will be introduced in this chapter, but you will find more about CDML and how it integrates with HTML and XML in Chapter 6. If you are not web publishing your databases on the Internet but are considering using a web published FileMaker Pro database as an XML import source, you should read this chapter.

This chapter is full of options for using FileMaker Pro for XML web publishing and sharing. This chapter begins with "Setting Up Web Companion for XML Requests." If you have already done this successfully and wish to learn about the XML commands and results, jump right to "XML Request Commands for Web Companion." This chapter also covers Web Companion security issues, so you may wish to review those. First, a note about browsers needs to be discussed.

Browser Requirements

Specific browser requirements will be listed by each method of displaying XML with XSL, CSS, JavaScript, or other methods. Generally, Internet Explorer 5 for Windows and Macintosh will work for XML and XSL with FileMaker Pro web publishing. See Chapter 7 to learn how to use XML Stylesheet Language (XSL) to transform XML into HTML. Netscape 6 can be used for Document Object Model (DOM) with JavaScript and will be discussed later. Netscape 6.1 and greater are compliant with XML, XSLT, CSS 1 and 2, and DOM 1 and 2. The Microsoft web site has some updates for Windows and Macintosh versions of Internet Explorer on their web site, and Netscape is available for Macintosh, Windows, and UNIX on the Netscape web site. Some of the wireless devices may use a specific type of browser.

If you get unpredictable results when testing in your browser, you may wish to clear the cache and browser history. For testing purposes, you can set these both to 0 in your browser preferences. Sometimes the browser will remember the last page, even dynamically created ones. Clearing the cache and history forces it to return the true results of your XML request to FileMaker Pro.

5.1 Setting Up Web Companion for XML Requests

Web Companion is a plug-in or, more specifically, an application programming interface (API) used by FileMaker Pro to web publish your databases. The Web Companion API is designed to be both a web server and a Common Gateway Interface (CGI) application. Web Companion has been available since FileMaker Pro 4.0 under various revisions, but only since FileMaker Pro 5.x have the necessary commands for XML publishing been available. You should always use the most recent version of the Web Companion plug-in. This API file is placed in the FileMaker Extensions folder and is called Web Companion on the Macintosh. The Web Companion icon is shown in Figure 5.1. Web Companion is called WEBCOMPN.FMX or webcmpn.fmx and is installed in the SYSTEMS directory of the FileMaker directory if you are using the Windows operating system. The Web Companion will be loaded, as well as the other extensions, when

Web Companion

Figure 5.1: Web Companion plug-in icon

FileMaker Pro is started and it is configured from the Application Preferences, Plug-Ins tab.

5.11 Web Companion as a Web Server

A web server receives requests from a browser when the user types in the location or clicks on a Uniform Resource Locator (URL) link. The web server returns and temporarily transfers formatted text pages, files, movies, graphics, and sounds to your computer. Your browser combines them and translates these into the documents you see on the World Wide Web. There is a two-way communication between the browser and the web server using the platform-independent Hypertext Transfer Protocol (HTTP). Most links you click probably start with "http://." HTTP is the communication and transfer protocol found in the Uniform Resource Locator of the link.

HTTP communication is stateless. A request is made from the browser and sent to the server. After a required file is returned, the connection to the server is broken until another request is made. A typical web page may have multiple requests for text, image, document, or sound files. These connections are sometimes called hits. You can specify in your browser preferences how many multiple simultaneous connections to make (four is the default maximum). After each connection or hit is completed, you are disconnected from the server although you may not think so.

As you design your web-published FileMaker Pro databases, contemplate the statelessness of HTTP. You make a request from the browser that is sent to the web server, in this case, the Web Companion API. The request is processed and a text page and/or images are displayed in the browser and the connection is stopped. You are not connected to Web Companion or FileMaker Pro continuously. You need to plan carefully for the actions of users who will not see changes until the browser window is updated by making a new request or refreshing a web page.

The communication between FileMaker Server hosted files and FileMaker Pro clients is quite different from web-published databases. The only delay in the data exchange from a user's client computer to FileMaker Server is waiting for the user cache (temporary locally stored data) to be written to the server. You can see practically immediately any changes you or another user makes to a database record using a server and clients.

The client-server model has features to prevent more than one user from trying to alter the same piece of information at the same time. This is called record locking and allows all users to see the same record in a multiuser situation but only gives to one user permission to make changes to a record. Because the web is stateless it does *not* provide this protection. When publishing a FileMaker Pro database on the web, you must carefully analyze that you have not assumed record locking will take place. Fortunately, there are some tricks built into FileMaker Pro and the Web Companion commands to check for ownership of a record whether on a network, an intranet, or the Internet. You will read about these tricks and how to maintain state (associate the web user from the last action to the next action) in this chapter.

5.12 Web Companion as CGI

The Common Gateway Interface (CGI) is a standard for interfacing external applications with information servers, such as HTTP or web servers. Hypertext Markup Language was designed to be a static page display mechanism with embedded images and hyperlinks to interconnect various pages. To perform actions such as form processing, image maps, dynamically produced pages, or database interactivity, gateway interfaces were created as an extension to HTML. CGIs are separate applications or scripts that run on a web server and accept commands the web server cannot understand. This is called server-side processing. If the particular commands are acceptable by a Common Gateway Interface, results, often in the form of HTML pages, are returned to the web server to be passed to the browser. Common CGIs are written in a variety of languages, such as Perl, UNIX shell, AppleScript, Python, TCL (Tool Command Language), C/C++, and Visual Basic.

Overview of the Processing Steps for a Web Server and CGI

1. The user enters a location in the browser, clicks a link, or clicks a form submit button.
2. A request is sent to the web server through Hypertext Transfer Protocol (HTTP). This request can also contain hidden information, such as the page from which the request was initiated, a field to search, or the name of an image to apply in the page.
3. The web server processes the request, translating the commands it understands and passing on to the CGI any information it does not understand. Only if the location of the CGI is included in the request can the web server pass along the request. You specify the

location of Web Companion by including "fmpro?" in your links or form actions.

4. The CGI accepts the information it needs from the request and communicates with any resources necessary to process the request, such as a database or file server.
5. If the request is sent to FileMaker Pro, the CGI (Web Companion) tells FileMaker Pro to perform actions as if the user had manually entered them or performed a FileMaker Pro script. These actions will create new records, edit fields, delete records, and find and sort records. CGI requests to FileMaker Pro in CDML or XML can be actions, replacement text, or variables.
6. Any actions performed will return a result, so the Web Companion CGI passes the results, even errors, back to the web server. This is returned to the web server as HTML, which the web server understands.
7. The Web Companion web server sends the HTML results back to the browser along with any associated files, images, or sound and breaks the connection.
8. The CGI portion of the Web Companion API performs the translation of the unique commands sent to it. These commands are either XML and/or a proprietary set of commands called Claris Dynamic Markup Language (CDML). Some of the commands are actions to create new records or save and return variables like the current database. Some of the CDML commands are replacement text, for example, returning field contents, controlling flow, or providing today's date. The commands for XML publishing are similar and use many of the same names as CDML. You will read more about CDML and FileMaker Pro XML commands in this chapter and in Chapter 6.

Now that you know what Web Companion is and a little about how it works as a web server and a Common Gateway Interface, you are ready to continue the setup of FileMaker Pro for web publishing. If you have not already done so, verify that the Web Companion plug-in is in the proper location of your FileMaker Pro directory: WEBCOMPN.FMX is in the SYSTEM directory for Windows; Web Companion is in the FileMaker Extensions folder for Macintosh.

Web Companion can also be used as an Asynchronous Common Gateway Interface (ACGI). Asynchronous means both connections can communicate without waiting for a reply. Web Companion can communicate asynchronously with another web server. The advantages of

"Alias-of-FMP-as-an-acgi" addressed in Appendix B: Resources are speed, caching, control of MIME mappings, use of other CGIs, and security features.

5.13 Static or Persistent Server Address

Web Companion does not require that you be using TCP/IP as the network protocol TCP/IP in FileMaker Pro, but TCP/IP networking must be set up correctly on the machine. This setting is found in Edit, Preferences, Application, General tab. You may need to restart FileMaker Pro if you change this setting. If you cannot choose TCP/IP, verify that the TCP/IP extension is in the same folder as Web Companion. You may also need to install a network card and/or driver and check your network settings for your computer. You can read more about FileMaker Pro networks in the document *A Guide to Networking FileMaker Pro Solutions*, referenced on p. 166. Section 5.15, "Standalone Considerations," may help you set up some of the settings for network or standalone web publishing.

Figure 5.2: TCP/IP plug-in icon

TCP/IP (Transmission Control Protocol/Internet Protocol) is used for sending data around the Internet and networks as small chunks called packets. Used together, TCP maintains the connection between two systems and tracks the packets so that they are sent and reassembled correctly and IP delivers the data by routing the packets from the computer to a local network and on to the Internet.

The address you assign your computer or server so that other systems may identify it is the IP address. This number must be unique and composed of four segments separated by "." (dot). Each segment is a number from 0 to 255, reflecting the maximum decimal digits that correspond to the hexadecimal numbers 00 to FF or the binary digits (bits) 00000000 to 11111111 in a byte (any single ASCII character).

For another computer to access the data on your server or a web server, it must know the location. As an HTTP request, the location can be formatted in a URL such as: http://192.0.0.10/ or as a name of a particular domain: http://www.mydomain.com/. The domain name is convenient to humans, but the servers and TCP/IP are looking for the number. Domain Name System (DNS), a network of servers with a list of domain names and corresponding IP addresses, will resolve this name to the correct number and pass the information along. It also allows you to change the IP address of www.mydomain.com, for example, to work transparently without you having to pass the new IP address to everyone.

Web publishing, including XML publishing, with FileMaker Pro requires that the databases are open on a system with an address that can be found by other computers. FileMaker Pro Help recommends a static IP address. Whether you host databases for a network, a browser accessed intranet, or the Internet, carefully consider the security concerns when these files are available. For security reasons, you may have the files hosted only at times when they can otherwise be regulated. Regardless of when your files are available, you need to provide the location to the user. A unique and static IP address is more convenient for sharing your databases. Your server may also have a domain name that can resolve to an IP address.

Warning: ISPs (internet service providers) can offer to you a unique and static IP address. However, they may *not* have the equipment or software necessary to host FileMaker Pro files. You may need to co-locate (provide your own servers at an ISP) or have a persistent connection to the Internet from your own location. You may also find hosting companies that provide this service.

5.14 FileMaker Pro Products for XML Publishing

A single copy of the standard FileMaker Pro application can be used as a small network host or a web publisher. As a web-publishing application, FileMaker Pro 5, 5.5 (FMP5), and FileMaker Pro 6 support connections to Web Companion for ten users' IP addresses in a 12-hour consecutive period. Under no circumstances should this machine also be used as a client while it is hosting databases.

For development and testing or only a very small number of users, you will be able to web publish well-formed and valid XML documents with standard FileMaker Pro 6. For more efficient web publishing, place your files on FileMaker Server and open with the Host dialog. The databases are enabled for web sharing before being placed on a networked computer with FileMaker Server. Any FileMaker Pro application, except runtime versions, enabled for web publishing can produce XML from an HTTP request, even if it is part of the network. The XML export and import work with FileMaker Pro and not FileMaker Server. This gives each person the ability to work with XML.

FileMaker Developer (FMD) installs an expanded version of FileMaker Pro that includes script debugging and Database Design Report. It also contains additional items that may assist you in web-enabling your databases. You get the FileMaker Developer Tool, Design Tools sample files, External FileMaker API files, and the Developer's Guide. These additional items assist you with renaming files and maintaining relationships across multiple related files. Examples and usage of JDBC and XML is included with FileMaker Developer. Other features of FMD are beneficial to developers working with network or web publishing of files and include: creating a Kiosk mode so that the user does not see some of the standard operating system and application elements or interface, ODBC support, renaming files while maintaining the relationships in multiple files, examples, and artwork. The new Database Design Report gives you a listing of the fields, scripts, layouts, relationships, value lists, and passwords. The report options are used to create a new database, add to an existing database, or create an XML/XSL report summary or full report. These options were explored in Chapter 4.

FileMaker Pro Unlimited (FMU) is a special version of the standard FileMaker Pro application that allows an unlimited number of IP connections for web publishing from FileMaker Pro. The FileMaker Pro Unlimited install also includes the Web Server Connector (WSC). The WSC is a Java servlet that extends the functionality of Web Companion by working with some existing web servers. If you are using a middleware application, CGI, or application server, FMU can be used to facilitate the integration of your applications and web servers with FileMaker Pro. Web Companion does not have built-in support for Secure Socket Layer (SSL) and server-side includes (SSI), so the Web Server Connector can be used as a plug-in by your web server and take advantage of these features.

Using multiple FileMaker Pro Unlimited sets, you can set up a Redundant Array of Inexpensive Computers (RAIC) and the Web Server Connector to process requests and distribute the load. If you are serving the same databases on each computer in the RAIC and one goes down, the WSC will forward the request to another. See the FileMaker Pro Unlimited Administrator's Guide for more information about FileMaker Pro Unlimited and about using the Web Server Connector Java servlet. FileMaker Pro Unlimited will also be used with middleware with FileMaker Pro for web publishing.

Using Middleware with FileMaker Pro Unlimited

Any application that can make an HTTP request to FileMaker Pro can be used to create, edit, and delete records. For example, the web application server ColdFusion, by Macromedia, can make a request and create a new record. The first example that follows shows the hypertext link, followed by the equivalent FORM request. You can see in the last example how ColdFusion <cfhttp> can send the same information to FileMaker Pro:

1. HTTP request:

```
fmpro?-db=Xtests.fp5&-lay=web&firstname=Joe&lastname=Brown&-format=
  -dso_xml&-new
```

2. FORM request:

```
<form action="fmpro" method="post">
    <input name="-db" type="hidden" value="Xtest.fp5" />
    <input name="-lay" type="FormField" value="web" />
    <input name="firstname" type="hidden" value="Joe" />
    <input name="lastname" type="hidden" value="Brown" />
    <input name="-format" type="hidden" value="-dso_xml" />
    <input name="-new" type="submit" value="" />
</form>
```

3. ColdFusion request to create a new record in FileMaker:

```
<cfhttp url="hostname/fmpro" method="post">
    <cfhttpparam name="-db" type="FormField" value="Xtest.fp5">
    <cfhttpparam name="-lay" type="FormField" value="web">
    <cfhttpparam name="firstname" type="FormField" value="Joe">
    <cfhttpparam name="lastname" type="FormField" value="Brown">
    <cfhttpparam name="-format" type="FormField" value="-dso_xml">
    <cfhttpparam name="-new" type="FormField" value="">
</cfhttp>
```

FileMaker Server (FMS) is a special database engine application that is optimized for serving FileMaker Pro files over a network. It cannot directly create, open, or edit FileMaker Pro files, but it shares them as a host and takes care of some of the housekeeping necessary to rotate client users in and out of the files. FMS increases the speed of operations and allows up to 250 users to access the files.

FileMaker Server cannot web publish files directly, as this function is performed by the Web Companion. The FileMaker Pro Web Companion plug-in works with FileMaker Pro, FileMaker Pro Unlimited, and FileMaker Developer only. However, I strongly recommend that all databases to be web published be placed on a computer and hosted with FileMaker Server. FileMaker Server can greatly stabilize the workload.

Database files can be enabled for Web Companion sharing and set to Multi-User (see “Sharing Databases for Web Companion” in section 5.17) before being opened by FileMaker Server. FileMaker Pro or FileMaker Pro Unlimited then opens them remotely. The Web

Companion, as a part of these client applications, becomes the web publisher. Using FileMaker Server is not required but strongly recommended for production systems. This arrangement is not a requirement but can improve the web/network experience.

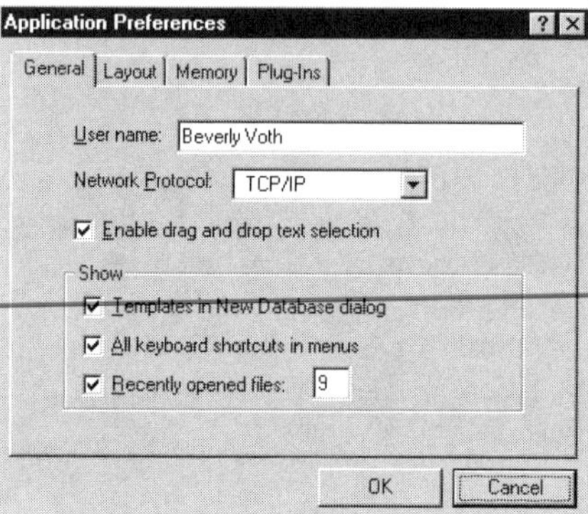

Figure 5.3: Setting network protocol for FileMaker Pro

For additional information about setting up a FileMaker Pro network, consult the document *A Guide to Networking FileMaker Pro Solutions* by Wim Decorte and Anne Verrinder. This guide is a thorough explanation of how to set up TCP/IP as your network on both the Windows and Macintosh OS. The document covers:

- IP addresses and subnet masks
- Finding and pinging your IP address
- Sharing databases on a network
- Memory considerations
- A tutorial on opening hosted databases and creating an opener database file
- A review of the products and how peer-to-peer and client-server models differ
- How to monitor with server administration and server event logs
- The techniques and need for backups of your databases

This document is available for download from www.wordware.com/fmxml, the book's web site, www.moonbow.com/xml, and from Kim Jordan at http://www.pair.com/kjordan/NetworkingGuide.pdf.

Another useful guide is the TechInfo document from FileMaker, Inc., http://www.filemaker.com/support/techinfo.html, TechInfo #101295, "Optimizing Network Performance for Shared Databases." Among this document's recommendations:

- Use a fast network connection
- Use TCP/IP protocol
- Locate your databases on the host computer
- Host the databases on a computer running only FileMaker Pro
- Host your databases with FileMaker Pro Server (a.k.a. FileMaker Server)
- Optimize the host computer
- Optimize the guest computers
- Optimize connecting as a guest
- Optimize the databases

In summary, Web Companion is used for XML publishing, and FileMaker Server cannot directly perform this task. The Web Companion API is only available in FileMaker Pro, FileMaker Developer, and FileMaker Unlimited. Files set to Multi-User and sharing for Web Companion and hosted on the FileMaker Server are available for web serving, too. Files for web publishing must be placed on the same machine with FileMaker Server and opened through Hosts on a client machine with FileMaker Pro or FileMaker Pro Unlimited. There are several options for hosting files over a network and web publishing the same databases. See "FileMaker Unlimited," section 5.18.

5.15 Standalone Considerations for Testing

You can set up your computer to test web publishing from FileMaker Pro without being connected to the Internet or a network. Standalone testing allows you to be the web publisher and the client (browser) all on the same computer. If you already have TCP/IP set up on your computer, you do not need to change it. Review the final paragraphs of this section, "Finish TCP/IP Setup for All Systems," for hints on how to use this method. The following recommendations are from the FileMaker Pro Help topic, "Testing the Web Companion without a network connection," with minor revisions.

Macintosh OS 8.x, 9.x Open Transport TCP/IP Configuration

Important: Follow the instructions and duplicate an existing configuration, make the changes, and save them. You can safely return to your current settings when needed.

1. Open the TCP/IP control panel. This dialog is shown in Figure 5.4.

2. Under the File menu, select **Configurations**.
3. Click on any configuration to highlight it and then click on the **Duplicate** button.
4. Give this new configuration a name, such as **Web Companion Testing**.
5. If prompted to make these new settings active, click the **Make Active** button.
6. Enter the following values in the new configuration:
   - Connect via: **AppleTalk (MacIP)**
   - Configure: **Using MacIP Manually**
   - MacIP server zone: <current AppleTalk zone>
   - IP Address: **192.0.0.10**
   - Router address: (leave blank)
   - Name server addr: (leave blank)
   - Implicit Search Path: Starting domain name: (leave blank)
   - Ending domain name: (leave blank)
   - Additional Search domains: (leave blank)

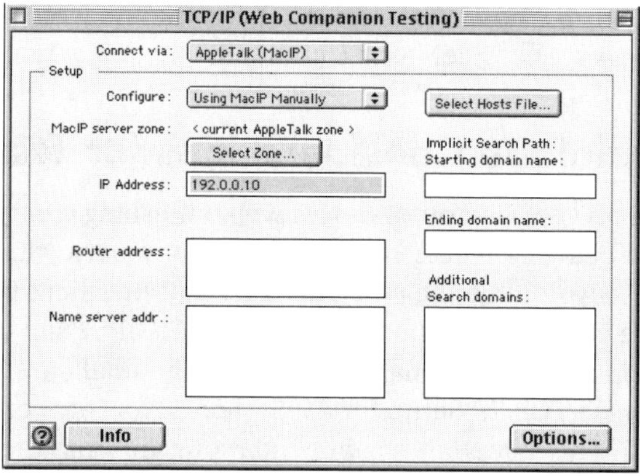

Figure 5.4: TCP/IP control panel (Macintosh OS 9.1)

7. Close the TCP/IP control panel. If asked to save your settings, click **Yes**.
8. To revert to your previous settings, open the TCP/IP control panel, press **command+K**, or choose **File**, **Configurations**, and make the original TCP/IP configuration active.

Setting TCP/IP on Windows 95, 98, NT, Me, and 2000

Important: Following these instructions will remove any network connection currently in place on your Windows PC. If your PC is already connected to a network or to an ISP, please make a careful note of how your Windows PC was originally configured before making these changes.

1. Open the Network control panel (in the Control Panel directory). The dialog for setting TCP/IP on NT is shown in Figure 5.4.
2. If you have any network adapter, network clients, or network protocols installed, remove them.
3. Click the **Add** button. Then, double-click on the **Adapter** item in the menu.
4. Select **Microsoft** from the list of manufacturers. From the right-hand menu, select **Dial-Up Adapter**, and click **OK**.
5. In the Network control panel again, click the **Add** button. Then, double-click on the **Protocol** item in the menu.
6. Scroll down the list of manufacturers until you reach **Microsoft**. Select it. Then, from the right-hand menu, select **TCP/IP**, and click **OK**.
7. In the list displayed in the Network control panel, you should see both a Dial-Up Adapter and the TCP/IP protocol. If you see anything else, such as an IPX/SPX or NetBEUI protocol, remove it.

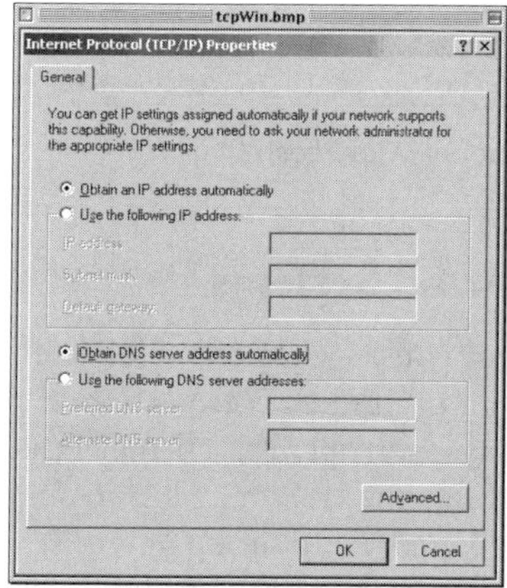

Figure 5.5: TCP/IP control panel (Windows NT)

8. Double-click the TCP/IP protocol to edit its properties. Enter **10.10.10.10** as the IP address, disable WINS and DNS services, and enter **10.10.10.1** as the gateway. Click **OK**.
9. Click **OK** and restart your computer.

Setting TCP/IP on Macintosh OS X

1. Choose **System Preferences**, **Network**. The dialog for Macintosh OS X is shown in Figure 5.6.
2. From the Location: pop-up, select **New Location**.
3. In the Name your new Location dialog, enter **Web Companion Testing**.
4. Select **Built-in Ethernet** from the Configure pop-up (this may vary depending on your network).
5. Select the **TCP/IP** tab and enter the following information:

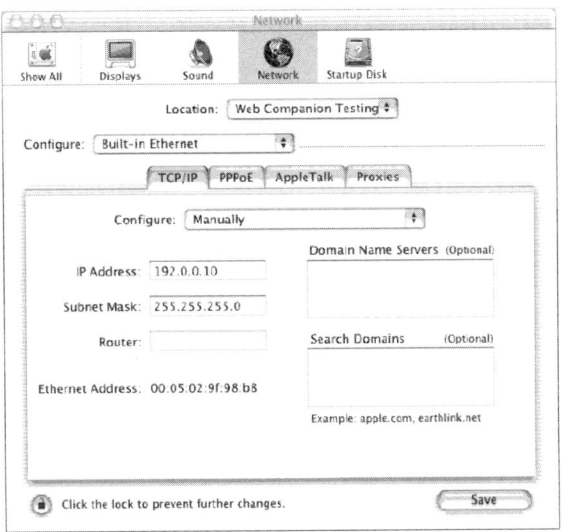

Figure 5.6: TCP/IP control panel (Macintosh OS X)

Finish TCP/IP Setup for All Systems

You are now ready to use your computer to test FileMaker Pro web publishing without an Internet or Ethernet connection. If you changed your TCP/IP settings, you may interrupt your current Internet or Ethernet connections (including email). Remember to change your TCP/IP settings back when needed. Only set up a new TCP/IP configuration if you do not have a network to test your files. A simple network of two computers using an Ethernet crossover cable may be preferable to disrupting your existing network access or Internet configurations.

You must choose TCP/IP as your network protocol in FileMaker Pro under the General tab in the Edit, Preferences, Application dialog.

After you restart FileMaker Pro, you can use the Web Companion for instant web publishing, custom web publishing, JDBC publishing, or XML publishing. You access the web server by entering the IP address you created as your "domain" in the URL: http://192.0.0.10/ or http://10.10.10.10/. You may also access the Web Companion with the default loopback IP address of http://127.0.0.1/. The loopback address may be called with the default server name: http://localhost/. If the defaults do not work, try the IP address of your machine.

5.16 Web Companion Setup

After you have TCP/IP set correctly on your computer through a network or for standalone testing, you are ready to configure the Web Companion plug-in for publishing. The important items of which to be mindful are the TCP/IP extension, the Web Companion plug-in, the Web folder (located in the FileMaker Pro folder), and the Web Security folder. The Web Security folder contains the Web Fields_.fp5, Web Users_.fp5, and Web Security_.fp5 databases, along with sample web pages for remote administration and the guide, "Web Security.pdf." Another step to web publishing is enabling particular databases. The next section in this chapter, "Sharing Databases for Web Companion," covers where to place your files (databases and web files). Web security is discussed in section 5.41, "Security with Web Companion."

Open a FileMaker Pro application and choose Edit, Preferences, Application and then the Plug-Ins tab. In Windows FileMaker, Figure 5.7 is the Application Preferences dialog for selecting plug-ins. Enable the Web Companion plug-in if it is not already checked. You can enable the Web Companion plug-in without any databases open. If you launch the application and cancel the Open File dialog or the New Database dialog, you have access to the plug-ins and can configure the Web Companion.

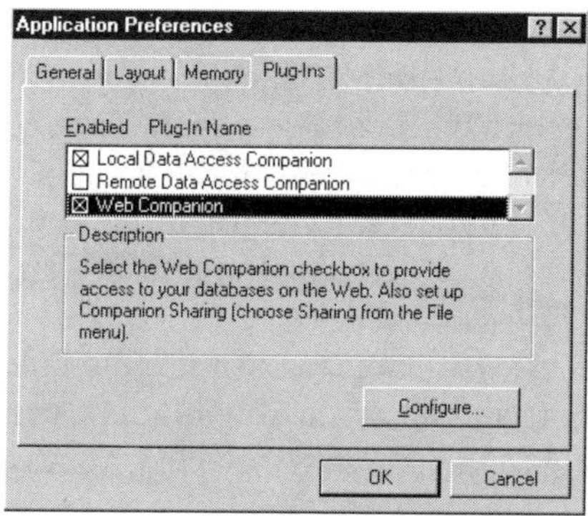

Figure 5.7: Application Preferences Plug-Ins tab

The menus have been changed slightly for Macintosh OS X. The Preferences are now listed under the second menu, FileMaker Pro (File is the third menu). Choose FileMaker Pro, Preferences, Application and then the Plug-Ins tab. The configuration is the same, only the location of the menu has changed.

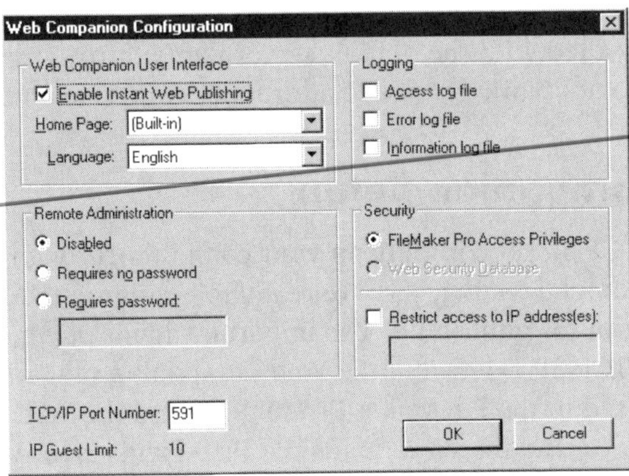

Figure 5.8: Web Companion Configuration dialog

Look at the Web Companion Configuration dialog in Figure 5.8. It may be beneficial for you to understand what it does as it will be used for XML publishing. If you have left the Application Preferences Plug-Ins dialog, return there by choosing Edit, Preferences, Application and the Plug-Ins tab. Highlight the Web Companion plug-in; if it is enabled (checked) you will see information in the Description box and the Configure button. Click the Configure button to view the Web Companion Configuration dialog.

The Web Companion user interface is available for setting up Instant Web Publishing (IWP) and is used by custom web publishing. You can use IWP as a test to see if your setup is working correctly, so leave Enable Instant Web Publishing checked for now. Also, you can select a default home page to be viewed in your web browser if a particular database is web published. Built-in is the default home page for Instant Web Publishing and available only if Enable Instant Web Publishing is checked. If you do not have a database open for web sharing and Enable Instant Web Publishing is unchecked, the home page pop-up will be blank. A list of web pages in the top level of the Web folder will be listed here if you have a database open and shared using Web Companion.

The Language pop-up is also available here. It is quite unique, as it changes the interface elements and onscreen help of the instant web published database according to the language selected. Your choices for language are Dutch, English, French, German, Italian, Spanish, and Swedish. The Display parameter is used by the CDML tags [FMP-CurrentAction], [FMP-FindOpItem], and [FMP-SortOrderItem]. It can be a source of confusion and possible errors if the language is accidentally changed. If you get unpredictable results, you might want to check this setting. It has no apparent effect on XML publishing and does not change the language of your field names and field contents.

Logging gives you three check boxes to select. The Access log file option, if checked, records every request to Web Companion from a web browser by creating and maintaining the file access.log in your FileMaker Pro folder.

For each request, this access log file lists:

- The remote IP address or hostname
- The rfc931 required by UNIX systems for determining the identity of a user of a particular TCP connection with the Authentication Server Protocol
- The authenticated user name
- The date and time of the request
- The request from the user as sent by clicking a link or submitting a form
- The HTTP status of the request. For example, if you go to a web site and the page is moved or no longer exists, you may receive a notice stating "404 Not found." This is the HTTP status for that request. This is also called the Server Response Code.
- The size of the document (web page, graphic image, or other type of file) returned to the browser

The error log file (error.log) is also created and stored in the FileMaker Pro folder if you have selected this option. This file lists the date and time with the error number and description of any unusual errors. Common errors are not reported to this file. There is no definitive list of errors considered common by Web Companion. You should remember this does not list all errors encountered. The access.log (above) provides all information, including errors.

The information log file (info.log) is placed in the FileMaker Pro folder and accepts any information you have specifically placed there with a custom CDML request [FMP-Log: _your text here_]. The date and time of the request is logged.

Remote Administration is used to access the Web folder from another location. Your options are Disabled, Requires no password, and Requires password with a field to specify the password. The Web folder is located in the FileMaker Pro folder of the machine, which is used for web publishing. External files, such as images, can be placed in the Web folder. You can use HTTP Put and Get to exchange files, and you do not need direct access to the machine. Remote Administration access also allows you to administer the Web Security databases remotely. If you will be using the Web folder for any reason, it is advisable to set the configuration to Requires password and specify a password or to disable remote access.

Security gives you some options to allow or deny access to your web-published databases. Web Companion security is not the only precaution you should implement. If you already have passwords enabled in your databases and different groups and access features (browse, create, and edit), you use the same access for your web published databases. Any permission not granted by password is denied to the user through web published files. Your current passwords and groups are used if you select FileMaker Pro Access Privileges. If you have the Web Security databases open, you will see the option Web Security Database; otherwise, this option is disabled. The "Security with Web Companion" section later in this chapter will explain where these files should go and how to use them.

Another security option is Restrict access to IP address(es). Here you can specify a single IP address, a list of addresses separated by commas, or a range of addresses. The range is really a single address with an asterisk replacing one segment of the four-part IP address (123.456.78.*). See section 5.13, "Static or Persistent Server Address," for IP address information. Only those IP addresses listed are allowed to access your databases. This feature can be especially beneficial to databases hosted on an intranet (internal network), but it can be used for any web publishing where this needs to be restricted.

The default TCP/IP port number is 80. Port number 80 is a specific designation for the Hypertext Transfer Protocol (HTTP). Assigning a port allows TCP to know the endpoint of a connection. The port number may be registered or generally reserved for common usage. Port 80 is used by HTTP and may be used by your web server if you are using one. You may specify any port number in the Web Companion Configuration dialog, but if it is not 80, you must use it in the URL (Internet address) when accessing your web-published database. If you assign port 123, for example, you would use http://my-domain.com:123/the/rest/. Since the default port number is 80, you need not specify it in the URL: http://mydomain.com/the/rest/.

If you must use a port other than 80, FileMaker Pro Help suggests, "FileMaker, Inc. has registered port number 591 with the Internet

Assigned Numbers Authority (IANA) for use with FileMaker Pro Web Companion."

Warning: If you just pick some other port, especially ports below 1023, some part of your computer may stop working and/or FileMaker may act strange when you try to give it mail or FTP traffic.

The first time you select the Web Companion plug-in after you install FileMaker Pro on Macintosh OS X, you will be instructed to specify a port number. Mac OS X reserves all ports 0 to 1023 for security reasons. You may use port 80 or port 591 for Web Companion on Mac OS X, but you must set this up. If you do not change this when you first install, you must reinstall FileMaker Pro to reset the port. If you choose to use port 1024 or higher, specify this in the Web Companion Configuration dialog and use it in your URL.

IP Guest Limit is the number of IP addresses allowed access to your web-published databases in a concurrent 12-hour period. If you have FileMaker Pro 5, 5.5, or 6, this will be set automatically to 10. If you have FileMaker Pro Unlimited, this is automatically set to Unlimited. If you have installed FileMaker Pro Unlimited and see 10 in this location, try reinstalling. The IP Guest Limit does not affect the number of connections you may have set up if you use FileMaker Server 5. This setting only affects web publishing.

5.17 Sharing Databases for Web Companion

This section discusses where to put your FileMaker Pro databases and any web files or documents (including XML or XSL files). It is important to think about security while doing this setup. If you do not password protect the files, anyone on the network can change the files! Any database set to sharing with Web Companion is available for data extraction and possibly data corruption or deletion. Whatever password access you allow or limit in your databases also works for web-published databases.

Databases

If your databases are currently being hosted with FileMaker Server, close them on the server, move them if necessary to a computer with FileMaker Pro 6, and open them off the network. Open your database and set it to Single User to make the changes. Choose Sharing from the File menu, and select the Single User button under FileMaker Network

Sharing. Then under Companion Sharing, select Web Companion. If you will be placing this file back on FileMaker Server, you may leave it as Single User if you have FMS set to share single-user files or change it to Multi-User or Multi-User (Hidden). Figure 5.9 shows the sharing dialog and the Multi-User (Hidden) option selected. It may or may not be necessary to set to Single User before sharing with Web Companion. However, I have found this to be helpful. Make your other sharing options after enabling Web Companion.

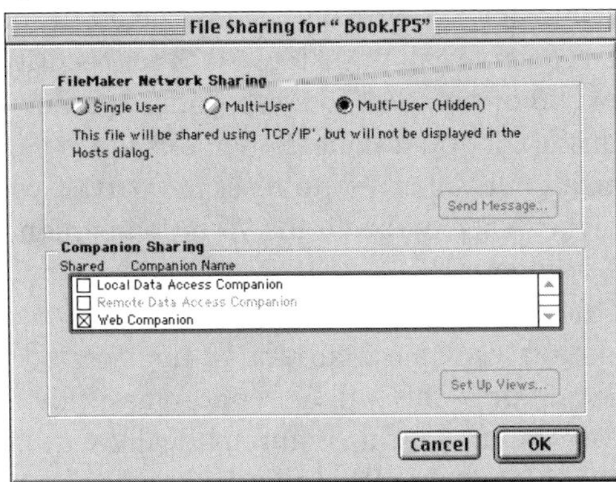

Figure 5.9: File Sharing dialog

Databases may be placed in the Web folder, but they also are more accessible this way. It is much more secure if you leave databases outside of the Web folder. However, if you will be using Remote Administration in the Web Companion Configuration dialog, files need to be in this folder. You may use an alias or shortcut to the actual file, as long as this is placed in the Web folder.

The FileMaker Pro Developer's Guide, p. 6-18, suggests: "For better security, place your databases in subfolders within the Web folder. This way, unauthorized users will not know the rest of the path even if they gain access to the Web folder."

Do not place your Web Security database in the Web folder. Do not enable the Web Security database sharing with Web Companion. If you have Web Security databases open, Web Companion will use them.

Databases may be placed on a server and opened with FileMaker Server. Access to the databases is via the Hosts button. FileMaker Server does not web publish, as this is a function of the Web Companion plug-in. Launch FileMaker Pro or FileMaker Pro Unlimited with Web Companion enabled and open the databases by selecting File, Open and clicking the Hosts button in FileMaker Pro. New in FileMaker Pro 5.5 and 6 is Open Remote under the File menu.

Databases hosted by FileMaker Server will be available for web publishing but not for control through Remote Administration.

Text Pages

FileMaker Pro Web Companion is looking in the Web folder when you specify the URL http://localhost/ or http://127.0.0.1, the IP address, or the domain name of your database web publisher for all files called directly. These text files may be HTML files (.htm or .html), JavaScript files (.js), include files (small reusable code of any type: .inc or .txt), cascading stylesheets (.css), and .xml and .xsl files. XML and XSL files for import and export should not be placed in the Web folder.

All of your web pages can be placed in the Web folder of the FileMaker folder. You can place them there as aliases (Macintosh) or shortcuts (Windows) for greater security. You may place them in subfolders in the Web folder, but remember to include the subfolder name in your path to the file. You can also have text documents on other servers, but each must be called with the full path to the document. Since any file placed in the Web folder is now accessible, secure documents may need to be placed on another server that provides directory security (login with username and password). The new folder, cdml_format_files with FileMaker Pro 6, should be where you place CDML files for added security. See the document folder_info.htm installed in the cdml_format_files folder for more information.

Always provide a default file in every directory to help prevent listing of the files in any directory. This file can be a link back to your main page. The file is a simple HTML file called default.htm, default.html, index.html, or index.htm. The "Security Blankets" section later in this chapter gives some examples of default files that you can use.

Images

Image files can be placed in the Web folder, a subfolder, or multiple subfolders of the Web folder. Images may also be located on another web server. If you will be exchanging images with any frequency, images on an FTP-capable server is advisable. Specifying their location publishes images. This location can be dynamically placed on a web page if the path is a field in the database. Images that change can simply be uploaded to the same location, and the database need not even be revised if the file name is the same. Static images such as a site logo can also be used with a field reference or listed on the page requesting it. Remember to use full paths for images located on another server.

Include the default HTML file, even in Image folders. Your link to images may be http://mydomain.com/images/ and users could enter this in a browser. The default file directs the user back to your main page rather than allowing these files to be listed.

Consider the browser that will be displaying these images. Optimize them for the smallest possible size and provide alternative images for wireless devices. Give all images an "alt" attribute (name of the image) for browsers that do not display images.

Other Files

You may have other files available for download, such as Adobe's Portable Document Format (PDF). Browser preferences can be set to display these files or download them. If in doubt, compress them for convenient download. Binary files compressed with Aladdin Stuff-it, available at http://www.aladdin-sys.com, WinZip, available at http://www.winzip.com, or similar applications can be placed in the Web folder or any location, as long as the path to the file is available. If you have binary files, provide multiple options for download. Consider platform and browsers by compressing the files for any user.

5.18 FileMaker Pro Unlimited

FileMaker Pro Unlimited and the *FileMaker Pro 6 Unlimited Administrator's Guide* (included with installation) suggest eight configurations for using Web Server Connector. You can read more details on how to set these up with various servers in the guide. These configurations are:

- FileMaker Pro Unlimited on a single machine
- FileMaker Pro Unlimited, the FileMaker Web Server Connector, and web server software on a single machine
- FileMaker Pro Unlimited on one machine, the FileMaker Web Server Connector on another machine
- RAIC with multiple copies of the same database
- RAIC with multiple, different databases
- RAIC using FileMaker Server as a back-end host
- RAIC using FileMaker Pro as a back-end host
- FileMaker Pro Unlimited with middleware

RAIC is defined as a Redundant Array of Inexpensive Computers. Web Server Connector can switch among the servers in an RAIC. Computers running OS X cannot serve as an RAIC machine.

Middleware is defined as another application that can query FileMaker Pro through Web Companion or the Web Server Connector. Some applications that are considered middleware are Lasso, Cold Fusion, Tango/Witango, Perl, PHP, Java, and Flash.

The Web Server Connector (WSC) is a Java servlet. A servlet is a Java component that is a platform-independent method for building web-based applications, without the performance limitations of CGI programs. The *FileMaker Pro 6 Unlimited Administrator's Guide*, included with FileMaker Pro Unlimited, says, "A servlet is a Java-based web server extension that is an alternative to traditional, platform-specific CGIs."

The minimum requirements for using WSC on Windows 95, 98, NT, or later is with Java Runtime Environment (JRE) 1.1.8. Mac OS Runtime Java (MRJ) 2.1.4 is needed for use with Macintosh OS 8.6 or later. Using Web Server Connector with a version of FileMaker Pro other than Unlimited will produce an error. For all three platforms (Windows, Mac OS X Server, and Red Hat Linux), the version of JDBC driver needs to be JDK/JRE 1.1.8 to 1.3 compliant. The latest Java Runtime Environment software is available on the Sun site, http://www.java.sun.com.

The advantage of using the Web Server Connector is the ability to use FileMaker Pro Unlimited with another web server. FileMaker Pro Web Server Connector works with a wide variety of other web servers. See http://www.filemaker.com/ for the latest versions for web publishing FileMaker Pro.

Web Server Connector works with FileMaker Pro Unlimited and Web Companion to provide additional functions. Some of these functions are a part of the WSC, such as configuring an RAIC to share the load of database serving on the web. It can redirect a request to another machine if the Web Companion is not responding on any machine. Web Companion does not have built-in support for secure web serving. The Web Server Connector can be used to work with any of the supported web servers that have Secure Socket Layer (SSL) or server-side includes (SSI).

Secure Socket Layer is a protocol similar to HTTP. A program is between the HTTP and TCP protocols to send encrypted data. A key is provided on both ends so the data can be sent securely. Links to secure servers often use https:// at the beginning of the link. The browser may change to reflect a secure site. Sometimes a key is displayed and/or there is a blue border around the page on a secure site. Web Companion can send messages to and receive messages from a secure site but does not encrypt the data itself. Encryption is the function of the SSL.

Server-side includes are common on some web servers. A command is sent to the server, interpreted, and returns a value, such as the current date. In the format similar to a comment, <!--#command parameter(s)="argument"-->, the server processes the command. They function more like XML processing instructions than comments. If the web server does not understand the command, however, it is ignored like a comment. Some commands will allow you to include a file, execute an external program, return the date of the server, the document name, or the date the document was last modified, for example.

Chapter 7, "Using the Web Server Connector as host," of *The FileMaker Web Server Connector Administrator's Guide*, found in FileMaker Pro Unlimited, has details for configuring the WSC. The setup is done through your browser. You can open the configuration file remotely by entering the URL http://yourIPorDomain/FMPro?config or by pointing to the file FileMaker WSC Admin on your hard drive. You have three options on the first page: Configure by Host, Configure by Database, or Configure Administration Account. This home page is shown in Figure 5.10.

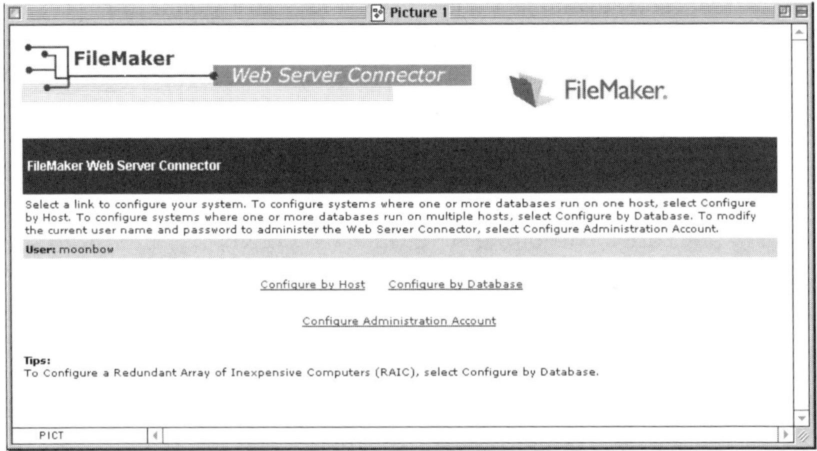

Figure 5.10: FileMaker Web Server Connector Admin

In addition to the log files you can generate with the Web Companion, the Web Server Connector (WSC) produces two other log files,

FMWSC.log and FMWSCNative.log. These files contain the date and time of server start and close events for each server and any errors that the servlet encounters. Together, the WSC and WC log files can list problems with the servers or individual files on the servers.

5.2 XML Request Commands for Web Companion

A request is sent to FileMaker and Web Companion from the browser as an HTTP request. HTTP has many methods for a request. Post and get are the most common and the get method of a hyperlink is used in this section. The post method is more common with form submission and will be discussed in section 6.5, "Using the Form Element to Make HTTP Requests." A request made to Web Companion must be formatted as other HTTP requests. The location of the server may be included in a hyperlink, followed by a port number (if any) and the location of the CGI. The initial query is to Web Companion itself. It asks the web server to find the CGI with "fmpro?". All other information after the question mark (?) is the request commands processed by the Web Companion CGI. Each additional piece of the request is separated with the ampersand character (&) and name-value pairs or other CGI commands. These calls to Web Companion are shown here:

```
fmpro?
fmpro?doThis&doThat&anotherRequest&action
```

You should remember that the request must be URL-encoded (ready for HTTP request). If you have any database names or layout names with spaces, for example, they must be converted or they may cause errors. The space character may be changed to "+" or "%20." You can use the External("Web-ToHTTP", parameter) function in a script or calculation to make the conversion for you. An example script step is included:

```
Set Field [ myfilename, [External("Web-ToHTTP", Status(CurrentFileName) ]
```

5.21 Database and Layout

A request is placed to a specific database and layout. Example requests are shown in Listing 5.1. When you make a web request for a layout, FileMaker Pro navigates to an open file and to a particular layout, as with a Go to Layout[] Script step. Any fields residing on the named layout in that database are accessible to the request. FileMaker Pro does not need to physically open the layout but has access to just those fields. The command for specifying the correct database is the parameter -db, and the command for layout is the parameter -lay.

Listing 5.1 Database and layout requests

```
-db=Xtests.fp5
-lay=web
-db=Xtests.fp5&-lay=web
fmpro?-db=Xtests.fp5&-lay=web& ...
```

Naming Suggestions

Web Companion will produce well-formed and valid XML from your database. Well-formed XML does not like spaces in element names. Web Companion will convert these to an underscore (_). If your database is named Invoice Items.FP5, it will be converted to Invoice_ Items.FP5. The same will apply to layout names, field names, script names, value list names, and relationship names. The FileMaker Pro Help topic, "Designing cross-platform databases," suggests that filenames should not contain these characters: quotation mark ("), slash (/), backslash (<), colon (:), asterisk (*), question mark (?), greater than or less than (> or <), or vertical bar, also called a pipe character (|). XML uses greater than, less than, and slash symbols (>, < and /) for tags, so these should not be used in any names in your database.

5.22 Actions

Every request needs an action to be fulfilled by Web Companion. These perform the equivalent of menu commands or script steps in FileMaker Pro databases. Common actions on the web or in the database are Create a New Record, Find a Record, Edit a Record, and Delete a Record. Privileges for any of these actions depend upon the permission set for them in the Password dialog of the database or through the Web Security files.

"Name=value" pairs are often appended to the request to create and edit records or used as search criteria to find a record. The name is the name of the field in the database, and the value is whatever will appear in the field upon action completion. At least one name=value is required for a new or edit action. In addition, deleting or editing a record requires a special parameter, -recid (RecordID), to verify that the action is performed upon the correct record. The following are some examples:

```
firstname=Joe&lastname=Brown&-recid=5846
company=Procter+&amp;+Gamble&date=03/05/97
```

Create New Records

-new—This creates a new record in the database. Any fields specified in the request are populated and your defined auto-enter fields are triggered. The RecordID (-recid) and any field data are returned by this action and can be used in the next action. Equivalent to the New Record/Request script step or menu command, it creates the new record and places all your named fields with the values supplied in the request. The result is a well-formed and valid XML document containing the fields on the layout, the contents, and the RecordID. If you do not specify a -format, no record will be created and you may get a browser error.

Listing 5.2 New Record requests and result

```
fmpro?-db=Xtests.fp5&firstname=Joe&lastname=Brown&-new
fmpro?-db=Xtests.fp5&-lay=web&firstname=Joe&lastname=Brown&-format=
  -dso_xml&-new
<?xml version="1.0" encoding="UTF-8" ?>
<FMPDSORESULT xmlns="http://www.filemaker.com/fmpdsoresult">
<ERRORCODE>0</ERRORCODE>
<DATABASE>Xtests.fp5</DATABASE>
<LAYOUT>web</LAYOUT>
<ROW MODID="1" RECORDID="36488">
    <firstname>Joe</firstname>
    <lastname>Brown</lastname>
    <RecordID>36488</RecordID>
</ROW>
</FMPDSORESULT>
```

It is important to note that the fields on the layout are what drives the response from WC. If you add or delete fields to the layout or change layouts, you can get different records back from FileMaker. As an exercise, duplicate the layout "web," name it "dweb," change the fields that appear on it, and then modify your request to call dweb instead of web. For extra credit, change the format parameter to use the fmpxmlresult DTD. (Hint: It's called fmp_xml.)

Duplicate Records

-dup—Duplicating a record is similar to creating a new record. A new RecordID is created for this record and auto-enter fields are populated, but all other data is copied from the specified record you are duplicating. Supply a -recid for the record you want to duplicate. The results returned will be for the new record. If you supply field values, these will not be entered into the new record. Duplicate creates the new record with the same data but changes the internal RecordID. Use this step to return a new record, which may be edited.

```
fmpro?-db=Xtests.fp5&-lay=web&-recid=234&-format=-dso_xml&-dup
```

Edit Records

-edit—Requires the parameter -recid to know which record to update. You can get the -recid from a -new or -find. Just like -new, any fields specified in the request are updated. All other fields retain their original data. Any field that would auto-enter upon modification will do so unless you supply a value. A sample request to edit is shown in Listing 5.3. There is no specific equivalent in the database, as any record is updated by entering new information in any field and exiting the record. The XML returned by this action is the record designated by the -recid, with all the fields on the specified layout. Like the -new action, this returned record can be used in the next action.

Listing 5.3 Edit requests and result

```
fmpro?-db=Xtests.FP5&-lay=web&-format=-dso_xml&firstname=Jane&lastname=
  Doe&-recid=36488&-edit
<?xml version="1.0" encoding="UTF-8" ?>
<FMPDSORESULT xmlns="http://www.filemaker.com/fmpdsoresult">
<ERRORCODE>0</ERRORCODE>
<DATABASE>Xtests.fp5</DATABASE>
<LAYOUT>web</LAYOUT>
<ROW MODID="2" RECORDID="36488">
    <firstname>Jane</firstname>
    <lastname>Doe</lastname>
    <RecordID>36488</RecordID>
</ROW>
</FMPDSORESULT>
```

Delete Records

-delete—Requires the parameter -recid to delete the correct record. This is equivalent to the Delete Record script step or menu command. Listing 5.4 shows some -delete requests. If you do not specify a layout in this request, you will get all the field data back from the default layout. XML is not returned with this action, and the record is removed from the database. Perform another action after -delete to return to the record or records needed. If you specify a layout, you will get back the current record as it was before deleting with only those fields on that layout. Consider this distinction and the possibilities. You could save the record even as you delete it. This may be advantageous if you need to log the delete action or provide a "rollback" if the transaction should not be completed.

Listing 5.4 Delete requests and results

```
fmpro?-db=Xtests.fp5&-format=-dso_xml&-recid=36488&-delete
fmpro?-db=Xtests.fp5&-format=-dso_xml&-lay=web&-recid=36488&-delete
<?xml version="1.0" encoding="UTF-8" ?>
<FMPDSORESULT xmlns="http://www.filemaker.com/fmpdsoresult">
<ERRORCODE>0</ERRORCODE>
<DATABASE>Xtests.fp5</DATABASE>
<LAYOUT>web</LAYOUT>
<ROW MODID="2" RECORDID="36486">
    <firstname>Jane</firstname>
    <lastname>Doe</lastname>
    <RecordID>36486</RecordID>
</ROW>
</FMPDSORESULT>
```

Find Records

-find—Like the database, you place the search criteria into appropriate fields. This is accomplished through Web Companion by appending name=value pairs to the request or using the -recid. The internal record ID is returned along with any found records and can be used for subsequent actions. The attribute <RECORDID> is in every <ROW> element regardless of the action. The -find action performs the combined script steps as Enter Find Mode[], Set Field [name, value], and Perform Find [].

You can also find all records by using -findall. This action does not require any name=value pairs or record IDs. It simply returns all records in the named database and is equivalent to Show All Records.

Another option is -findany. It will randomly return a record from the current database. While this does not have a direct command or single script step equivalent, random records could be used to supply a parameter result, such as a dynamic picture for a catalog "special."

These find requests return the results depending on the type of request and the number of records that match the criteria. -find with the parameter -recid or the -findany request will return only one record (or none). If no records are found, you get an error code of 401 just as you would in the database. Listing 5.5 shows some example find requests and example results of requests.

Listing 5.5 Find Records requests and results

```
<!-- requests -->
fmpro?-db=Xtests.fp5&-lay=web&-recid=36488&-find
fmpro?-db=people.fp5&-lay=web&-findall
fmpro?-db=Xtests.fp5&-lay=web&firstname=Joe&lastname=Brown&-find
fmpro?-db=Xtests.fp5&-lay=web&-findany
<!-- nothing found (ERROR= 401) result -->
<?xml version="1.0" encoding="UTF-8" ?>
<FMPDSORESULT xmlns="http://www.filemaker.com/fmpdsoresult">
<ERRORCODE>401</ERRORCODE>
<DATABASE>Xtests.fp5</DATABASE>
<LAYOUT>web</LAYOUT>
</FMPDSORESULT>
<!-- all records returned -->
<?xml version="1.0"?>
<FMPDSORESULT xmlns="http://www.filemaker.com/fmpdsoresult">
<ERRORCODE>0</ERRORCODE>
<DATABASE>people.fp5</DATABASE>
<LAYOUT>cgi</LAYOUT>
<ROW MODID="3" RECORDID="1">
    <Name>Dave Samud</Name>
    <Title>Web Administrator</Title>
    <Phone>555 555-1212</Phone>
    <Picture>FMPro?-DB=people.fp5&amp;-RecID=1&amp;
        Picture=&amp;-Img</Picture>
</ROW>
<ROW MODID="1" RECORDID="2">
    <Name>Robert Siwel</Name>
    <Title>Web Designer</Title>
    <Phone>555 555-1212</Phone>
    <Picture>FMPro?-DB=people.fp5&amp;-RecID=2&amp;
        Picture=&amp;-Img</Picture>
</ROW>
</FMPDSORESULT>
```

The following actions are for accessing other information about or controlling your database other than record and field contents. All data is returned in well-formed and valid XML and could be used with your stylesheets or as a report of the database information.

Layout Request

-view—This command is used by Web Companion and the -format parameter to return the layout information. An example request for layout information is shown in Listing 5.6. You can use this layout information to format your results. For example, if the database and layout has a field formatted as a check box, this is returned in the request using -view. -db, -lay, and -format are required with this action.

Listing 5.6 View Layout Information request and result

```
fmpro?-db=Xtests.fp5&-lay=web&-format=-fmp_xml&-view
<?xml version="1.0" encoding="UTF-8" ?>
<FMPXMLLAYOUT xmlns="http://www.filemaker.com/fmpxmllayout">
<ERRORCODE>0</ERRORCODE>
<PRODUCT BUILD="5/4/2002" NAME="FileMaker Pro Web Companion"
     VERSION="6.0v1" />
<LAYOUT DATABASE="xtests.fp5" NAME="web">
     <FIELD NAME="firstname">
          <STYLE TYPE="EDITTEXT" VALUELIST="" />
     </FIELD>
     <FIELD NAME="lastname">
          <STYLE TYPE="EDITTEXT" VALUELIST="" />
     </FIELD>
     <FIELD NAME="RecordID">
          <STYLE TYPE="EDITTEXT" VALUELIST="" />
     </FIELD>
</LAYOUT>
<VALUELISTS />
</FMPXMLLAYOUT>
```

Database Names Request

-dbnames—To return a list of all open databases with Web Companion enabled, use this command. Listing 5.7 shows the results of the request for the open databases. This is equivalent to the design function request DatabaseNames, but only databases shared by Web Companion are returned in this XML list. The parameter -format is required with this action. The XML data returned gives you a lot of information about the open databases.

Listing 5.7 Request for database names and result

```
fmpro?-format=-fmp_xml&-dbnames
<?xml version="1.0" encoding="UTF-8" ?>
<FMPXMLRESULT xmlns="http://www.filemaker.com/fmpxmlresult">
<ERRORCODE>0</ERRORCODE>
<PRODUCT BUILD="5/4/2002" NAME="FileMaker Pro Web Companion" VERSION=
  "6.0v1" />
<DATABASE DATEFORMAT="" LAYOUT="" NAME="DBNAMES" RECORDS="1"
  TIMEFORMAT="" />
<METADATA>
     <FIELD EMPTYOK="NO" MAXREPEAT="1" NAME="DATABASE_NAME" TYPE="TEXT" />
</METADATA>
```

```
<RESULTSET FOUND="1">
<ROW MODID="0" RECORDID="0">
     <COL><DATA>Xtests.FP5</DATA>
</COL>
</ROW>
</RESULTSET>
</FMPXMLRESULT>
```

Layout Names Request

-layoutnames—When you specify a particular database in this request, all the layouts for that database are returned. This is equivalent to the design function LayoutNames (dbname). The database name and -format needs to be specified with this action. Listing 5.8 shows the XML returned by a request for the layout name in the Xtests database.

Listing 5.8 Request for layout names and result

```
fmpro?-db=Xtests.fp5&-format=-fmp_xml&-layoutnames
<?xml version="1.0" encoding="UTF-8" ?>
<FMPXMLRESULT xmlns="http://www.filemaker.com/fmpxmlresult">
<ERRORCODE>0</ERRORCODE>
<PRODUCT BUILD="5/4/2002" NAME="FileMaker Pro Web Companion" VERSION=
  "6.0v1" />
<DATABASE DATEFORMAT="M/d/yyyy" LAYOUT="" NAME="xtests.fp5" RECORDS="23"
  TIMEFORMAT="h:mm:ss a" />
<METADATA>
     <FIELD EMPTYOK="NO" MAXREPEAT="1" NAME="LAYOUT_NAME" TYPE="TEXT" />
</METADATA>
<RESULTSET FOUND="23">
<ROW MODID="0" RECORDID="0">
     <COL>
     <DATA>About</DATA>
     </COL>
</ROW>
<ROW MODID="0" RECORDID="0">
     <COL>
     <DATA>Form View</DATA>
     </COL>
</ROW>
<ROW MODID="0" RECORDID="0">
     <COL>
          <DATA>web</DATA>
     </COL>
</ROW>
<ROW MODID="0" RECORDID="0">
     <COL>
     <DATA>webForm</DATA>
```

```
        </COL>
</ROW>
<ROW MODID="0" RECORDID="0">
        <COL>
        <DATA>webList</DATA>
        </COL>
</ROW>
</RESULTSET>
</FMPXMLRESULT>
```

Script Names Request

-scriptnames—Equivalent to the design function ScriptNames (dbname), this command will return the list of all the scripts in the named database. Listing 5.9 shows that only the database name, result format, and the action need to be specified in this request.

Listing 5.9 Request for script names and result

```
fmpro?-db=Xtests.fp5&-format=-fmp_xml&-scriptnames
<?xml version="1.0" encoding="UTF-8" ?>
<FMPXMLRESULT xmlns="http://www.filemaker.com/fmpxmlresult">
<ERRORCODE>0</ERRORCODE>
<PRODUCT BUILD="5/4/2002" NAME="FileMaker Pro Web Companion" VERSION=
  "6.0v1" />
<DATABASE DATEFORMAT="" LAYOUT="" NAME="SCRIPTNAMES" RECORDS="48"
  TIMEFORMAT="" />
<METADATA>
        <FIELD EMPTYOK="NO" MAXREPEAT="1" NAME="SCRIPT_NAME" TYPE="TEXT" />
</METADATA>
<RESULTSET FOUND="48">
<ROW MODID="0" RECORDID="0">
        <COL>
        <DATA>New Request</DATA>
        </COL>
</ROW>
<ROW MODID="0" RECORDID="0">
        <COL>
        <DATA>openURL</DATA>
        </COL>
</ROW>
<ROW MODID="0" RECORDID="0">
        <COL>
        <DATA>Edit Request</DATA>
        </COL>
</ROW>
<ROW MODID="0" RECORDID="0">
        <COL>
```

```
            <DATA>Delete Request</DATA>
      </COL>
</ROW>
<ROW MODID="0" RECORDID="0">
      <COL>
      <DATA>Find Request by ID</DATA>
      </COL>
</ROW>
<ROW MODID="0" RECORDID="0">
      <COL>
      <DATA>Find Request by Field</DATA>
      </COL>
</ROW>
</RESULTSET>
</FMPXMLRESULT>
```

Open or Close Databases Command

-dbopen and -dbclose—These two commands are used to control which databases are available to the web users. Any file opened or closed by these commands must reside in the Web folder of the FileMaker Pro folder and have the Web Companion enabled. Specify Remote Administration in the Web Companion Configuration dialog for FileMaker Pro. The parameter -password is optional but advisable for remote administration. These two commands are shown below:

```
fmpro?-db=Xtests.fp5&-format=-fmp_xml&-dbopen
fmpro?-db=Xtests.fp5&-format=-dso_xml&password=master&-dbopen
fmpro?-db=Xtests.fp5&-format=-fmp_xml&-dbclose
```

Warning: Placing any file in the Web folder may have security implications. If you must use this feature, provide a password for your database. Do not enable the Try default password option in the Edit, Preferences, Document Preferences dialog.

Request for Image in a Container Field

-img—This command is used specifically with images placed in a container field in the database. FileMaker Pro will produce a link pattern to the image and provide the -img action for you. Images may be in a container field or stored with a field referencing the path to the images. The -img action is used only with stored images.

The XML created for the container field Picture is shown in the following code. Using this information and one of the stylesheet methods, you can web publish the container field to a web page. The text created has to be converted to HTML encoding, so that the "&" shows as

"&", but the character is converted back if this field is used as a link to display the graphic.

```
<Picture>FMPro?-DB=people.fp5&amp;-RecID=1&amp;Picture=&amp;-Img</Picture>
<Picture>FMPro?-DB=people.fp5&amp;-RecID=2&amp;Picture=&amp;-Img</Picture>
```

Actions are used singly and not together. One action at a time can be performed. Careful design may be needed to produce desired results from web-published FileMaker Pro and XML. Actions equate to simple steps on the databases themselves. Using scripts we can perform multiple steps, but these may not be appealing for the web-published data. Using these actions, you can manipulate the information in your database through a web page interface. The actions rarely perform alone and require different parameters to act upon.

5.23 Parameters

Parameters are similar to actions because they begin with the "-" sign. However, they use the name=value notation, requiring a value. These parameters could also be called variables. The value of the parameter depends on how it is used. The first two parameters, -db and -lay, have already been discussed.

Database Parameter

-db—This parameter is required by all actions except -dbnames. The full name of the database file (including extension) needs to be provided. Case may or may not matter, so use the exact name of the file. You can determine the current database name with the function Status(CurrentFileName). You can also use the Design functions to determine all open database names. If the -db is not set up for sharing with Web Companion, you will get results with the error number 973. See section 5.5, "Error Codes for XML," for more errors you may get with XML publishing.

Layout Parameter

-lay—The layout name is optional with -find, -findall, and -findany but required to return the list of fields when used with the -view action. -lay also is required for -edit and -new requests if you need to access related fields.

A default layout named "Layout 0" (zero) is similar to the Define Fields dialog. It contains all the fields in the current database and will be used if no layout is specified. To use related data, you must specify the layout where these related fields are displayed or create calculated fields based on the relationship. On the layout, you can place related fields in or out of a portal. Single related fields are treated as if they were the first record in the related file. For all the related records, a portal should be displayed on the layout with those fields required by the request.

XML Format Parameter

-format—When using Web Companion and CDML, -format is used to designate a particular HTML-formatted page used to display the results of the HTTP request. New in FileMaker Pro, this parameter is used to specify which well-formed and valid XML document to return. How it is used depends upon the results you want. There are four format types, and they are combined with the actions to return five different types of XML: FMPDSORESULT, FMPDSORESULT with DTD, FMPXMLRESULT, with DTD, FMPXMLRESULT, and FMPXMLLAYOUT. The DTD formats were discussed more fully in Chapter 4.

-dso_xml is used to return the field names as the tag names and is the easiest to work with for specific data reading and writing: <fieldname>field contents</fieldname>. The root of the XML document is <FMPDSORESULT></FMPDSORESULT>. DSO is the acronym for Data Source Object. A sample request to FileMaker Pro is shown in Listing 5.10. -dso_xml differs from -fmp_xml by using the field names as the names of the element tags.

Listing 5.10 Request for FMPDSORESULT

```
fmpro?-db=Xtests.FP5&-lay=web&-format=-dso_xml&-recid=36489&-find
<?xml version="1.0" encoding="UTF-8" ?>
<FMPDSORESULT xmlns="http://www.filemaker.com/fmpdsoresult">
<ERRORCODE>0</ERRORCODE>
<DATABASE>xtests.fp5</DATABASE>
<LAYOUT>web</LAYOUT>
<ROW MODID="0" RECORDID="36489">
      <firstname>Sue</firstname>
      <lastname>Smythe</lastname>
</ROW>
</FMPDSORESULT>
```

-fmp_xml is more generic and perhaps allows greater flexibility for formatting the results. The root element of the XML results returned is <FMPXMLRESULT></FMPXMLRESULT>. The field names are returned near the beginning of the document and found in the element <METADATA></METADATA>. By including the METADATA, some of the layout information for each field is also returned. Listing 5.11 shows a request for the data in Xtest.fp5 with fmp_xml results.

Listing 5.11 Request for FMPXMLRESULT

```
fmpro?-db=Xtests.FP5&-lay=web&-format=-fmp_xml&-recid=36489&-find
<?xml version="1.0" encoding="UTF-8" ?>
<FMPXMLRESULT xmlns="http://www.filemaker.com/fmpxmlresult">
<ERRORCODE>0</ERRORCODE>
<PRODUCT BUILD="5/4/2002" NAME="FileMaker Pro Web Companion" VERSION=
  "6.0v1" />
<DATABASE DATEFORMAT="M/d/yyyy" LAYOUT="web" NAME="xtests.fp5" RECORDS="4"
  TIMEFORMAT="h:mm:ss a" />
<METADATA>
      <FIELD EMPTYOK="YES" MAXREPEAT="1" NAME="firstname" TYPE="TEXT" />
      <FIELD EMPTYOK="YES" MAXREPEAT="1" NAME="lastname" TYPE="TEXT" />
      <FIELD EMPTYOK="YES" MAXREPEAT="1" NAME="RecordID" TYPE="NUMBER" />
</METADATA>
<RESULTSET FOUND="1">
<ROW MODID="0" RECORDID="36489">
      <COL>
      <DATA>Sue</DATA>
      </COL>
      <COL>
      <DATA>Smythe</DATA>
      </COL>
      <COL>
      <DATA>36489</DATA>
      </COL>
</ROW>
</RESULTSET>
</FMPXMLRESULT>
```

-dso_xml_dtd is used to return the DTD for this format. If you do not specify a layout or find any particular record, all the fields on the default layout will be returned. The same request as Listing 5.11 is issued but this time asking for the Document Type Definition to be returned.

Listing 5.12 Request for FMPDSORESULT with DTD

```
fmpro?-db=Xtests.FP5&-lay=web&-format=-dso_xml_dtd&-recid=36489&-find
<?xml version="1.0" encoding="UTF-8" ?>
<!DOCTYPE FMPDSORESULT (View Source for full doctype...)>
<FMPDSORESULT>
<ERRORCODE>0</ERRORCODE>
<DATABASE>xtests.fp5</DATABASE>
<LAYOUT>web</LAYOUT>
```

```
<ROW MODID="0" RECORDID="36489">
      <firstname>Sue</firstname>
      <lastname>Smythe</lastname>
      <RecordID>36489</RecordID>
</ROW>
</FMPDSORESULT>
```

Notice the new line added to the XML returned, "<!DOCTYPE FMPDSORESULT (View Source for full doctype...)>." Showing the browser source code reveals the full doctype for the request in Listing 5.12. The DTD in Listing 5.13 tells the document what elements and attributes it can contain and is why the document is valid XML. The element names are specific to the fields on the named layout.

Listing 5.13 DTD for FMPDSORESULT request

```
<!DOCTYPE FMPDSORESULT [
<!ELEMENT FMPDSORESULT (ERRORCODE, DATABASE, LAYOUT, ROW*)>
      <!ELEMENT ERRORCODE (#PCDATA)>
      <!ELEMENT DATABASE (#PCDATA)>
      <!ELEMENT LAYOUT (#PCDATA)>
      <!ELEMENT ROW (firstname,lastname,RecordID)>
            <!ATTLIST ROW RECORDID CDATA #REQUIRED MODID CDATA #REQUIRED>
            <!ELEMENT firstname (#PCDATA)>
            <!ELEMENT lastname (#PCDATA)>
            <!ELEMENT RecordID (#PCDATA)>
]>
```

-fmp_xml_dtd includes the DTD for the particular XML document returned when an action is performed. Similar to the DTD for FMPDSORESULT, Listing 5.14 shows the Document Type Definition for an FMPXMLRESULT request.

Listing 5.14 DTD for FMPXMLRESULT request

```
<!DOCTYPE FMPXMLRESULT [
<!ELEMENT FMPXMLRESULT (ERRORCODE,PRODUCT,DATABASE,METADATA,RESULTSET)>
      <!ELEMENT ERRORCODE (#PCDATA)>
      <!ELEMENT PRODUCT EMPTY>
            <!ATTLIST PRODUCT NAME CDATA #REQUIRED VERSION CDATA #REQUIRED
              BUILD CDATA #REQUIRED>
      <!ELEMENT DATABASE EMPTY>
            <!ATTLIST DATABASE NAME CDATA #REQUIRED RECORDS CDATA #REQUIRED
              DATEFORMAT CDATA #REQUIRED TIMEFORMAT CDATA #REQUIRED LAYOUT
              CDATA #REQUIRED>
      <!ELEMENT METADATA (FIELD)*>
      <!ELEMENT FIELD EMPTY>
            <!ATTLIST FIELD NAME CDATA #REQUIRED TYPE (TEXT|NUMBER|DATE|
              TIME|CONTAINER) #REQUIRED EMPTYOK (YES|NO) #REQUIRED
```

```
            MAXREPEAT CDATA #REQUIRED>
    <!ELEMENT RESULTSET (ROW)*>
        <!ATTLIST RESULTSET FOUND CDATA #REQUIRED>
        <!ELEMENT ROW (COL)*>
            <!ATTLIST ROW RECORDID CDATA #REQUIRED MODID CDATA
              #REQUIRED>
            <!ELEMENT COL (DATA)*>
                <!ELEMENT DATA (#PCDATA)>
]>
```

-fmp_xml when used with the action -view will produce another kind of document containing the layout information. The database name, layout name -format=-fmp_xml is needed to return the document type. The root of this document is <FMPXMLLAYOUT></FMPXML-LAYOUT>. Listing 5.15 shows the request and results for the layout information of the "web" layout in the Xtests.fp5 database. Just changing the action to -view results in the FMPXMLLAYOUT.

Listing 5.15 Request for FMPXMLLAYOUT and result

```
fmpro?-db=Xtests.fp5&-lay=web&-format=-fmp_xml&-view
<?xml version="1.0" encoding="UTF-8" ?>
<FMPXMLLAYOUT xmlns="http://www.filemaker.com/fmpxmllayout">
<ERRORCODE>0 </ERRORCODE>
<PRODUCT BUILD="5/4/2002" NAME="FileMaker Pro Web Companion"
  VERSION="6.0v1" />
<LAYOUT DATABASE="xtests.fp5" NAME="web">
    <FIELD NAME="firstname">    <STYLE TYPE="EDITTEXT" VALUELIST="" />
    </FIELD>
    <FIELD NAME="lastname">
    <STYLE TYPE="EDITTEXT" VALUELIST="" />
    </FIELD>
    <FIELD NAME="RecordID">
    <STYLE TYPE="EDITTEXT" VALUELIST="" />
    </FIELD>
</LAYOUT>
<VALUELISTS />
</FMPXMLLAYOUT>
```

RecordID Parameter

-recid—This parameter is required with -edit and -delete actions to act upon a specific record. When used with the -find action, it will return a specific record if it exists in the named database. FileMaker Pro automatically assigns this ID to each record as it is created. It is always unique in any given database. The number assigned is not sequential, so it is rarely used for an invoice number or relationship key. In the database this can be determined by creating an unstored calculation: RecordID=Status(CurrentRecordID). The value of this parameter is returned in the XML results in the record element: <ROW RECORDID="" MODID="">. Here are some sample requests using -recid:

```
fmpro?-db=Xtests.FP5&-lay=web&-format=-dso_xml&firstname=
  Jane&lastname=Doe&-recid=36488&-edit
fmpro?-db=Xtests.fp5&-format=-dso_xml&-lay=web&-recid=36488&-delete
fmpro?-db=Xtests.fp5&-lay=web&-recid=36488&-find
```

Record Modification Count Parameter

-modid—Introduced in FileMaker Pro 5, the count status of a particular record is updated every time the record is modified. This function in the database is Status (CurrentRecordModificationCount). When a record is returned to the browser, the value of the parameter is in the record element: <ROW RECORDID="" MODID="">. -modid is used by the -edit action, optionally, to determine if the information is to be edited or not.

This function is most important when using the web for record editing. When using peer-to-peer or client-server networking, the database only allows one user in a record with edit privileges. This is called record locking. Other users can view the record but cannot modify it until the "owner" exits that record. In contrast, the stateless HTTP protocol used by Web Companion for editing the database sends the request for a record and disconnects from the database. By noting the MODID when a record is returned to the browser, you can determine if another user has modified it and decide whether to continue or notify the web user of the new state.

Parameters for Using Stylesheets

-styletype and -stylehref—These two parameters are used together to point to the type and name (or location) of the stylesheet used to format the results of the XML request. FileMaker Pro uses XSL and CSS stylesheets with this parameter. While other means can be used to format your XML results, these files placed in the Web folder are read by the parameter. Depending on your browser capabilities, the stylesheet will display the data with formatting, such as font and location on the browser window. XSL stylesheets and Cascading Style Sheets (CSS+) are discussed in Chapter 7. The two parameters for a stylesheet are as follows:

```
-styletype=text/xsl&stylehref=Xtests.xsl
-styletype=text/css&stylehref=Xtests.css
```

Password Parameter for -dbopen Request

-password—This optional parameter is used with the -dbopen action. If the database has a password, you can use the parameter to specify which password to use when opening the database.

```
fmpro?-db=Xtests.fp5&-password=a1b2c3&-dbopen
```

Find Request Parameters

The following parameters work with the -find action to alter the found set with operators, number of records, sorting, and scripts to perform.

Logical Operator for Multiple Find Requests

-lop—This logical operator is used when making multiple find requests. The choices are AND (find this and that) and OR (find this or that), with the default value of AND if you do not specify this parameter. AND finds will combine the name=value pairs to match all of the values in their associated fields. OR will search for the values in any record and return any of the matches, much like using multiple find requests. The following examples show the requests for XML and equivalent scripted finds in the database.

In the examples, Listing 5.16 shows an AND request to two different fields. Listing 5.17 shows an equivalent scripted AND request to the database. The logical operator (-lop) is used in Listing 5.18 to find two values in the same field. The scripted equivalent is shown in Listing 5.19. And finally, the OR request is shown in Listing 5.20, with a scripted version in Listing 5.21.

Listing 5.16 AND request with XML results

```
fmpro?-db=Xtests.fp5&-lay=web&firstname=Joe&lastname=Brown&-find
<?xml version="1.0" encoding="UTF-8" ?>
<FMPDSORESULT xmlns="http://www.filemaker.com/fmpdsoresult">
<ERRORCODE>0</ERRORCODE>
<DATABASE>xtests.fp5</DATABASE>
<LAYOUT>web</LAYOUT>
<ROW MODID="0" RECORDID="36490">
     <firstname>Joe</firstname>
     <lastname>Brown</lastname>
     <RecordID>36490</RecordID>
</ROW>
</FMPDSORESULT>
```

Listing 5.17 Scripted AND find for multiple fields

```
Enter Find Mode []
Set Field [ firstname, "Joe" ]
Set Field [ lastname, "Brown" ]
Perform Find []
```

Listing 5.18 AND request using LOP with XML results

```
fmpro?-db=Xtests.fp5&-lay=web&customer=Joe&-lop=and&customer=Brown&-find
<?xml version="1.0" encoding="UTF-8" ?>
<FMPDSORESULT xmlns="http://www.filemaker.com/fmpdsoresult">
<ERRORCODE>0</ERRORCODE>
<DATABASE>xtests.fp5</DATABASE>
<LAYOUT>web</LAYOUT>
<ROW MODID="0" RECORDID="36490">
	<customer>Joe Brown</customer>
</ROW>
<ROW MODID="0" RECORDID="36490">
	<customer>Brownly, Joel</customer>
</ROW>
</FMPDSORESULT>
```

Listing 5.19 Scripted AND find for single field

```
Enter Find Mode []
Set Field [ customer, "Joe Brown" ]
Perform Find []
```

Listing 5.20 OR request with XML results

```
fmpro?-db=Xtests.fp5&-lay=web&firstname=Joe&-lop=or&lastname=Brown&-find
<?xml version="1.0" encoding="UTF-8" ?>
<FMPDSORESULT xmlns="http://www.filemaker.com/fmpdsoresult">
<ERRORCODE>0</ERRORCODE>
<DATABASE>xtests.fp5</DATABASE>
<LAYOUT>web</LAYOUT>
<ROW MODID="0" RECORDID="36490">
	<firstname>Joe</firstname>
	<lastname>Jones</lastname>
	<RecordID>36490</RecordID>
</ROW>
<ROW MODID="0" RECORDID="36490">
	<firstname>Elmer</firstname>
	<lastname>Brown</lastname>
	<RecordID>36532</RecordID>
</ROW>
</FMPDSORESULT>
```

Listing 5.21 Scripted OR finds

```
Enter Find Mode []
Set Field [ firstname, "Joe" ]
New Record/Request
Set Field [ lastname, "Brown" ]
Perform Find []
```

Comparison Operator for Each Find Request

-op—The comparison operator is similar to the symbols used by FileMaker Pro when making a find request. The default search operator is "begins with." FileMaker will select words that begin with the pattern of the search criteria. For the multiple words in the search criteria, the -op parameter is applied to the beginning of the search phrase, but all words are used in the search. The default operator for the remaining words is "begins with." This parameter is appended to the first word of the search string (before, after, or both).

Table 5.1 FileMaker Pro symbols and comparison operators

Symbol	-op (Operator)	Searches
(none--default)	(none--begins with)	search
(wildcard, zero or more characters)	bw (begins with)	search*
	ew (ends with)	*search
*	(no equivalent -op)	sear*ch
"" (literal)	cn (contains)	"search"
@ (wildcard, one character)	(no equivalent -op)	se@r@ch
? (invalid date or time)	(no equivalent -op)	?
! (duplicates)	(no equivalent -op)	!
// (today's date)	(no equivalent -op)	//
... (ranges)	(no equivalent -op)	a...g
.. (same as ...)		a..g
= (exact match)	eq (equals)	=search
= (with omit)	neq (not equals)	= (omit)
<> (same as = with omit)		
≠ (same as = with omit)		
== (field content match)	(no equivalent -op)	==search
< (less than)	lt (less than)	<search
<= (less than or equal)	lte (less than or equal)	<=search
≤ (same as <=)		<=search
> (greater than)	gt (greater than)	>search

Symbol	-op (Operator)	Searches
>= (greater than or equal)	gte (great than or equal)	>=search
≥ (same as >=)		>=search

All of these searches can be performed over the web if the user enters the symbols. The -op is a convenient way to present the user of those operators with an equivalent without using the symbols, which may not encode properly in the request. When a request is made with the -op and the find criteria, Web Companion converts the appropriate symbol after the request is submitted. Several requests are listed below, followed by an example of a pop-up menu for specifying the -op for the field myField.

Request for first name, but not Joe:

```
-op=neq&firstname=Joe
```

Request for cost below $5,000:

```
-op=lt&cost=5000
```

Request for literal (full phrase) “scraped knee”:

```
-op=cn&injury=scraped+knee
```

Listing 5.22 Creating an options request in HTML

```
<select name='-op'>
     <option value="bw" selected> begins with </option>
     <option value="eq"> equals </option>
     <option value="cn"> contains </option>
     <option value="ew"> ends with </option>
     <option value="gt"> greater than </option>
     <option value="gte"> greater than or equal </option>
     <option value="lt"> less than </option>
     <option value="lte"> less than or equal </option>
     <option value="neq"> does not equal <option>
</select> <input type="text" name="myField" value="" />
```

You can use the select method before every field to which you want to apply a comparison operator. Web Companion will perform the appropriate conversion when the data is submitted. Not every value needs to be used in a selection process. For example, if your field searched is a number field, such as the cost request above, you may only wish to provide the number comparison operators: =, <, <=, >, >=, and <>. An example of this is found in Listing 5.23.

Listing 5.23 The cost request

```
<select name='-op'>
      <option value="eq"> = </option>
      <option value="gt"> &gt; </option>
      <option value="gte"> &gt;= </option>
      <option value="lt"> &lt; </option>
      <option value="lte"> &lt;= </option>
      <option value="neq"> &lt;&gt; <option>
</select> <input type="text" name="cost" value="" />
```

You can specify some of the other find options that may not be available by direct -op equivalent. A form field used to submit the find request will combine all the values if a particular field name is used more than once. When the input type is hidden, you can effectively control what is submitted. This method is useful for a login request for user name and password or other situations where you need an exact field content match and not merely a "begins with" search. Listing 5.24 shows how to use these hidden fields with the input fields.

Listing 5.24 Sample login request

```
<form method="post" action="fmpro">
      <input type="hidden" name="-op" value="bw" />
      <input type="hidden" name="user" value="==" />
      User Name: <input type="text" name="user" value="" size="30" /><br />
      <input type="hidden" name="-op" value="bw" />
      <input type="hidden" name="pass" value="==" />
      Password: <input type="password" name="pass" value="" size="30" />
</form>
```

Tip: You can see any search if you submit a request on the web and then perform a manual or scripted Modify Last Find. This is probably not wise to do with "live data" but you can test this with samples.

Parameter for Returning a Maximum Number of Records

-max—The default maximum number of records returned by Web Companion in any find request is 25. This number probably has significance because displaying a list of more than 25 items on a web page can take some time. Depending on the layout of the data records, the perceived time to the user may be too long. If you do not include the -max parameter, up to the default number will be returned. You can set this parameter to include a limited number of records or use the keyword all to return all records. Any number, 1 to 2,147,483,647, can be used as the value of this parameter. The -max parameter is often used with the -skip parameter. The examples below and Listing 5.25 show how to provide for a limited set of values for the -max parameter.

```
-max=all
-max=1
-max=10
```

Listing 5.25 Giving the user a choice for -max

```
<select name="-max">
      <option value="5">5</option>
      <option value="10">10</option>
      <option value="15">15</option>
      <option value="25">35</option>
      <option value="all">All</option>
</select>
```

Starting Record Number Parameter

-skip—This parameter is set with the number of records to skip before displaying and is used with the -max parameter. Together, these parameters allow the user to see all the records a small amount at a time. If this parameter is not specified, the default record is the first record of the found set. The skip value is often used in a next or previous link. Examples with -max and -skip are shown below.

```
-max=5&-skip=5
-max=5&-skip=10
-max=5&-skip=15
-max=5&-skip=20
```

Sorting Parameters

-sortfield—You can use more than one field for a sort and they will be equivalent to specifying the same fields in the Sort Records dialog. The last -sortfield is sorted first, followed by the next and so on, until the sort is complete. The sort is performed after the action (usually -find).

-sortorder—The default sort order is Ascending, but you can specify Ascend (or Ascending), Descend (or Descending), or Custom. The custom sort uses the value list of the field being sorted if it is displayed as a value list on the layout. This parameter and value must follow the -sortfield to which it applies and multiple sorts can be requested. Example find actions with the sorting parameters are shown here:

```
-sortfield=lastname&-sortfield=firstname&-findall
-sortfield=date&-sortorder=descend&-findall
```

```
-sortfield=company&-sortorder=ascend&-sortfield=date&-sortorder=
  descend&-findall
-lay=web&-sortfield=sizes&-sortorder=custom&-findall
```

Script Parameters

Scripts are triggered by specifying the -script parameter and the name of the script as the value of the parameter. An action is required and usually a script is performed with the -find action. However, -new, -edit, and -delete actions can also use a -script parameter. The actual script should not conflict with the action just performed, although it might depend on your script steps. Any script requiring user interaction (clicking a button, entering data, or dismissing a dialog) may not function correctly when called through the Web Companion.

-script—You can specify a script to be performed after the -find action and sort of the found set.

-script.prefind—If you wish a script to run before the -find action, use this parameter and specify the name of the script.

-script.presort—A script normally runs after the find and the sort, but you may specify a script to run before the sort and after the find.

Any sort specified with the action -find is performed after the find. Any -script specified is performed after the find and sort. The two special -script options -script.prefind and -script.presort are performed just as their names say, before the find or before the sort, respectively. The following list will help you remember the precedence of these actions and parameters:

-script.prefind
find
-script.presort
sort
-script

5.24 Creating the XML Requests

These request actions and parameters will be used throughout this chapter and in section 6.5. You can create these requests by typing them into a browser. Any database referenced will need to be web enabled (sharing with Web Companion). Instructions for this are included above in section 5.1, "Setting Up Web Companion for XML Requests." Rather than creating these requests manually, you may choose to do the exercise below. The file shown in Figure 5.11 will create your requests.

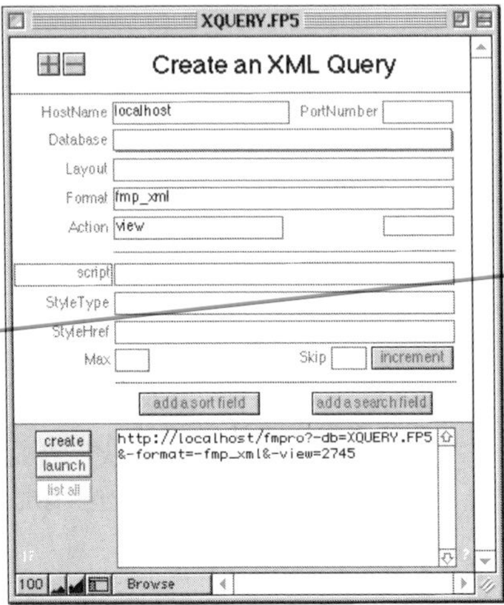

Figure 5.11: XQUERY.FP5

Exercise 5.1 Creating XML Requests

You can download the database XQUERY.FP5 from the companion web sites: www.wordware.com/fmxml and www.moonbow.com/xml. This file uses the design functions to determine open databases and retrieve the layout, script, and field names for creating XML queries. The queries are properly formatted HTTP requests for the get method.

When performing any of the actions, use only backup copies of your files, as they will be changed! You must also have password privileges for full access to open the file and get the information.

Web Companion must be enabled in the XQUERY.FP5 file for the scripts that convert field contents with the External("Web-ToHTTP") function. In addition, launching the request that you create requires Web Companion sharing on any database referenced.

1. Open the file XQUERY.FP5 with FileMaker Pro.
2. Open copies of any file for which you want to create a query. If a password is required, enter a password that allows export privileges.
3. Verify that the FileMaker Pro application has Web Companion enabled with **Edit**, **Preferences**, **Application**, **Plug-Ins**. Instant Web publishing need not be enabled, but take notice of the port used in the Configuration dialog.

4. Verify that all open files (including XQUERY.FP5) have Web Companion enabled with **File**, **Sharing**.
5. Create your requests by entering data into the fields provided in XQUERY.FP5. The instructions on the following page explain how the fields and buttons can be used to create the HTTP request. Some fields are buttons to trigger the design function scripts. These buttons over the fields populate the value list of the field. You may need to click a field twice to trigger the update script.
6. Complete the calculation for the request by clicking on the **Calc** button. Any changes to Database or Layout will clear this calculation field so that the correct information will be included in the calculated request.
7. Copy the resulting text and paste it into your browser or click the **launch** button to perform the Open URL script. If you have your browser set to automatically launch with the Open URL script step, you will see the results of the request.
8. Any error message will be displayed in the tags <ERRORCODE>0 </ERRORCODE> of the resulting XML. Any error other than 0 (zero) will equate to FileMaker Pro's error codes.
9. Internet Explorer should display a tree-like structure of the well-formed and valid XML results. Netscape 6 will display the contents, but viewing the source will reveal the XML.

If your browser does not launch, check the FileMaker Pro Help for the topic "Open URL script step." Try setting the maximum number of records to a low number (5) so that your browser does not take a long time to show the results. Also, pick a layout with few fields for the initial tests.

Along with clearing the cache and history in the browser, the author usually includes a random number at the end of any action. Actions such as -view=1298, -find=510, and -edit=9 ensure that the request will be unique each time and trick the browser into loading the new results.

The XQUERY.FP5 database (see the following Note) will assist you in creating HTTP hyperlink requests for XML results. You can also use it to create HTTP hyperlink requests for CDML. Context help is available by clicking the [?] buttons.

Note: "XQUERY.FP5" is not to be confused with "Xquery," the XML language used to make SQL-like queries to XML documents and sources. See http://www.w3.org/ for more information about the proposals for the XML Query Language.

Instructions

1. Create a NEW query. Use the button on the layout, rather than manually duplicating or creating a new record.
2. Choose a HOST. This is the IP address or domain where the databases to be web published are located. You can try "localhost" or the default loopback "127.0.0.1" if you are testing the databases and browser on the same machine. You may need to specify the IP address of your local machine rather than using "localhost" or the loopback IP.
3. Choose a PORT (optional). If you have set up Web Companion to use a port other than the default of 80, you must set this field.
4. Refresh the list of open databases by clicking the "refresh" icon (circular arrows). This will populate a value list for choosing a database for the query. This will also clear the layouts, scripts, and fields when you refresh. All databases for web publishing should already be set to Sharing with Web Companion.
5. Choose a DATABASE name.
6. Refresh the LAYOUTS to select one that is in the chosen database. (optional) A layout that is not specified will give you *all* of the fields in the chosen database. If you want to use related fields, you *must* specify a layout with these fields upon it.
7. Choose a FORMAT. If you want to make an HTTP request for CDML, you can enter an HTML/CDML page name. All CDML pages must be in the Web folder or, beginning with 6.0, the cdml_format_files folder. If you want to make an HTTP request for XML results, choose one of the predefined values in the pop-up. "-format=-fmp_xml" will give you layout information if your action is "-view," for example.
8. Choose an ACTION.
    a. Some actions require a "-recid" to be set and some are optional. The label will appear when this field is to be used. The find action can specify a record ID for searching for a specific record. You can use "-recid" as a search field in the Add a Search Field dialog.

Tip: Create a calculated field in all your databases with RecID=Status(CurrentRecordID) to use this value in an HTTP request.

9. Chose a script type, refresh the scripts, and choose a SCRIPT name (optional).
   a. Script types are: -script, -script.prefind, and -script.presort.
   b. Use scripts very carefully with web-enabled databases! If you can, try to perform the same results with multiple HTTP requests.
10. Choose a STYLE TYPE and STYLE HREF (XML only).
    a. The style type can be XSL (XML Stylesheet Language) or CSS (Cascading Style Sheet).
    b. The "href" is the hypertext link to the location of the stylesheet. The link can be an absolute path to another server or a relative link. Stylesheets should be placed in the Web folder.
11. Choose the MAXimum number of records to return in a find request. By default, 25 records will be returned if you do not specify a value.
12. Choose the SKIP # if you do not want to start the result on the first record. The [INCREMENT] button will add the MAX to SKIP each time it is clicked (optional, but only works with MAX).
13. To ADD SORT FIELDS or ADD SEARCH FIELDS, click on those buttons. If a chosen layout has no fields, clear the layout field or chose a layout with fields.
    a. After you choose a SORT FIELD, you can choose a SORT ORDER (optional). Add or remove sort fields in the order you want them to sort.
    b. Choose a FIELD NAME and enter the VALUE (optional) for that field. New or edit actions will enter this value and the find action will search for it. You can also choose an OPERATOR and LOGICAL OPERATOR.
    c. Go back to the main query screen by clicking the [BACK] button or clicking anywhere above the list of fields.
14. Click the [CALC] button to refresh the HTTP request. A random value will be appended to the action. This is used to force a unique request to browsers that may be caching pages.

15. LAUNCH will open your primary browser and send the HTTP request. You may select the request and paste into any browser or use the request with any application that can use it.
16. You can LIST ALL the requests to see what they look like.

5.25 Creating or Editing Related Records

To create a related record, you use the relationship name, a double colon (::), and the field name. A new related record must have ".0" appended to each field name in the related record. You can add a new related record to an existing parent record, one at a time. Rather than use the action -new, you are adding new related records but not new records, so we use the action -edit. To edit the parent record, you must specify the record ID parameter (-recid). Listing 5.26 shows the results of the request to add a related record on the webForm layout. The file Company.FP5 from Chapter 2 is used for these examples. The entire record with the added related record is returned in the request.

```
http://localhost/fmpro?-db=COMPANY.FP5&-lay=webForm&-format=-dso_
  xml&-recID=5&-edit=1675&CoID::Department.0=department&CoID::
  EmployeeID.0=6&CoID::EmployeeName.0=name
```

Listing 5.26 Result of adding a new related record

```
<?xml version="1.0" encoding="UTF8" ?>
<FMPDSORESULT xmlns="http://www.filemaker.com/fmpdsoresult">
<ERRORCODE>0</ERRORCODE>
<DATABASE>COMPANY.FP5</DATABASE>
<LAYOUT>webForm</LAYOUT>
<ROW MODID="3" RECORDID="5">
<CompanyID>2</CompanyID>
<CompanyName>Herbson's Pices</CompanyName>
<CoID.EmployeeID>
      <DATA>5</DATA>
      <DATA>6</DATA>
      <DATA>7</DATA>
      <DATA>6</DATA>
</CoID.EmployeeID>
<CoID.EmployeeName>
      <DATA>Rosemary Thyme</DATA>
      <DATA>Elvis Parsley</DATA>
      <DATA />
      <DATA>name?</DATA>
</CoID.EmployeeName>
<CoID.EmployeePhXt>
      <DATA>3256</DATA>
```

```
        <DATA />
        <DATA />
        <DATA />
</CoID.EmployeePhXt>
<CoID.Department>
        <DATA>Seasons</DATA>
        <DATA>Pickles</DATA>
        <DATA>Chutney</DATA>
        <DATA>department</DATA>
</CoID.Department>
</ROW>
</FMPDSORESULT>
```

To edit an existing related record, use the same format except that the .n extension is the related record number. This related record number is the portal row of a sorted relationship. You can edit multiple rows by specifying the correct portal row number with the fields to be edited. This request edits the related record, created in Listing 5.26, to add the employee's phone extension and edit the name.

```
http://localhost/fmpro?-db=COMPANY.FP5&-lay=webForm&-format=-dso_xml&
  -recID=5&-edit=4852&CoID::EmployeePhXt.4=9874&CoID::EmployeeName.4=
  Hot%20Pepper
```

Listing 5.27 Result of editing a portal row

```
<?xml version="1.0" encoding="UTF8" ?>
<FMPDSORESULT xmlns="http://www.filemaker.com/fmpdsoresult">
<ERRORCODE>0</ERRORCODE>
<DATABASE>COMPANY.FP5</DATABASE>
<LAYOUT>webForm</LAYOUT>
<ROW MODID="3" RECORDID="5">
<CompanyID>2</CompanyID>
<CompanyName>Herbson's Pices</CompanyName>
<CoID.EmployeeID>
        <DATA>5</DATA>
        <DATA>6</DATA>
        <DATA>7</DATA>
        <DATA>6</DATA>
</CoID.EmployeeID>
<CoID.EmployeeName>
        <DATA>Rosemary Thyme</DATA>
        <DATA>Elvis Parsley</DATA>
        <DATA />
        <DATA>Hot Pepper</DATA>
</CoID.EmployeeName>
<CoID.EmployeePhXt>
        <DATA>3256</DATA>
        <DATA />
```

```
      <DATA />
      <DATA>9874</DATA>
</CoID.EmployeePhXt>
<CoID.Department>
      <DATA>Seasons</DATA>
      <DATA>Pickles</DATA>
      <DATA>Chutney</DATA>
      <DATA>department</DATA>
</CoID.Department>
</ROW>
</FMPDSORESULT>
```

Deleting Related Records

Related records can be created or edited from a parent record by appending the correct extension to the end of the field name. ".0" will create a new related record and ".n" (the number of the portal row) will edit the related record. The correct action for creating or editing related records is -edit. The use of the -delete action on related records is different. If you allow the deletion of related records in the Define Relationship dialog, all related records will be deleted along with the parent record. The check box When deleting a record in this file, also delete related records must be selected. The -delete action on a parent file requires the Record ID of the parent record:

```
http://localhost/fmpro?-db=COMPANIES.FP5&-recid=5&-delete=457
```

You can also create, edit, or delete the related records directly by calling the related database directly and specifying the key field CompanyID, for example. If the record is a new record, the correct action is -new:

```
http://localhost/fmpro?-db=EMPLOYEES.FP5&-lay=webForm&-format=
  -dso_xml&-new=1675&CompanyID=2&Department=department&
  EmployeeID&EmployeeName=name
```

The results will be the EMPLOYEES.FP5 database and the one new record you created. You can use the key field CompanyID to perform another action and return you to the COMPANY.FP5 database. This is an additional step, so the editing of related records from the parent record may be preferable. Use the same methods to edit or delete a record.

5.26 Repeating Field Data

Repeating fields use the same format as related fields. This means that creating and editing repeating fields uses the ".n" extension on the field name. The command to edit data in a repeat could be: "&repeat1.1=this%20is%20line%20one". This is similar to the script step to change data in a particular repeat number: Set Field ["repeat1"-1, "this is line one". Clearing a single repeat would use this extension, too, but clearing the field with no extension, such as "&repeat1=", clears all of the repeats in that field. The code below shows some of these requests:

```
http://localhost/fmpro?-db=MAIN.FP5&-lay=web&-format=-fmp_xml&-findall
http://localhost/fmpro?-db=MAIN.FP5&-format=-dso_xml&repeat1.1=
  this%20is%20line%20one&-edit
http://localhost/fmpro?-db=MAIN.FP5&-format=-fmp_xml&-op=cn&-repeat2=
  one&find
http://localhost/fmpro?-db=MAIN.FP5&-format=-dso_xml&repeat1=&-edit
```

The results of an HTTP request to a web-published FileMaker Pro database is similar to the export of repeating fields. The results of the above requests are not included here. The request for -format=-fmp_xml and -format=-fmp_dso will produce different results for repeating fields. The result is similar for either request and uses the DATA element around each repeat, whether there is data or not. See Chapters 2 and 4 for more information about repeating fields and XML.

5.3 Performing Scripts on Web-Published Databases

If you grant permission to perform a -script with an action, there are some serious considerations listed here. Script steps that pause and wait for response will not display a dialog or button through the web browsers. Script steps that are meant to display a dialog and await data entry will not display through the web browser. If the Perform without dialog option is selected, some script steps may work in web-published databases. Script steps that perform file- or machine-specific actions may be useful to web-published databases but provide unpredictable results if not thoroughly tested. Tables 5.2 through 5.5 group some of the script steps by interaction requirements and provide additional suggestions for their use or non-use. Heed the advice for securing your scripts if you must use them. You can read more about script security in the “Script Security” section later in this chapter.

Table 5.2 Script steps that pause or require dialog response

Pause/Resume Script []	Break your script steps into separate actions and get a response from the browser through a link or form submission.
Enter Browse Mode [Pause]	This may be helpful from the database perspective to restore it to a state that is helpful to web publishing. If this script step is used, do not select the Pause option.
Enter Find Mode [Pause]	Use a web form to allow entry of search criteria and use the action -find in the submit button.
Enter Preview Mode [Pause]	You could have a separate web display page for printing. Instruct the user to print manually with the browser commands.
Insert From Index []	Do not use this script step, because it must pause to allow the index of a field to be displayed.
Insert Movie []	Do not use this script step, as it displays the Mac OS Open dialog box to select a Quick Time movie.
Insert Quick Time []	Do not use this script step, as it displays the Windows Open dialog box to select a Quick Time movie.
Insert Picture []	Do not use this script step, because it displays the Open file dialog box.
Insert Object []	This script step may work on Windows if all the parameters are preconfigured.
Change Password []	Use a login and registration process to track passwords. This script step uses a dialog box that does not display on the web.
Recover []	This is a file-level script step that can cause severe damage. Do not use it in any script.
Spelling	Do not use any of the spelling script steps, as they may require a dialog box. These steps are Check Selection, Check Record, Check Found Set, Correct Word, Spelling Options, Select Dictionaries, and Edit User Dictionary.
Preferences and developer dialogs	There should be no need to use these script steps in web-published databases. Each of these use a dialog, which does not display in the web browser: Open Application Preferences, Open Document Preferences, Open Define Relationships, Open Define Value Lists, Open ScriptMaker, and Open Sharing.
Show Message []	This script step is often used as a branch to different actions based upon the buttons selected. You can provide these choices with HTML forms or links.

The following table contains script steps that may perform as expected if you have selected the Perform without dialog option when you created the script. Additional comments are also included to assist with performing these actions from a web browser.

Table 5.3 Script steps that require "Perform without dialog"

Sort []	Web Companion includes two parameters for use with an action. -sortfield and -sortorder are discussed in the "Sorting Parameters" section in this chapter. However, if this script step does not require user response, it can safely be used with web-published databases.
Print Script steps	Print Setup (Windows), Page Setup (Mac OS), and Print [] all could require user response. If you enable the "Perform without dialog," where would this report be printed? If you have a printer connected to your computer serving web-published databases, it might function as expected. Test this before relying upon this script step in web-published databases.
Revert Record/ Request []	The stateless nature of the World Wide Web practically negates the need for this script step. Transactions are not complete until the user submits a form or follows another link.
Delete All Records []	Used wisely, with security measures and avoiding a dialog, this script step may be necessary to remove a found set of records from a web-published database. The -delete action in Web Companion only works with whichever record ID (-recid) is specified in the request.
Replace []	Dangerous, at best, on a networked system, this script could take exceeding long for the web user if requested.
Relookup []	This may not function as expected if used with web-published databases.
Dial Phone []	This will send a signal through the serial/phone port to dial the number. When the script is executed on the computer serving as a web publisher, it will show a dialog pausing even with Perform without dialog selected.
Open URL []	Sending an Open URL request by script may not reconnect back to web-published database pages. Rather than relying upon this script step, use a field in the database with the URL and format the resulting web page to contain the field contents in an anchor or a link. See the "Hyperlinks and Anchors" section of Chapter 6 for more information about anchors and links.
Import/Export Records []	This script step works off the local machine, not the server, if you are web publishing the databases. This may be advantageous to web-published databases if you have file control with a plug-in. The path to an exported file can be used in a hyperlink to allow the user to download the file. The path must be relative to the page with the link or an absolute path. Use this set with great care. Remember that the database must have export permission to return XML results.
Execute SQL []	SQL requests may display a password dialog to ODBC data source if this has *not* been previously saved.

Send Mail []	This script will use the email client on the web publisher machine if one is available. The -mailto parameter is not available with XML publishing. Use the mailto: protocol of the user's browser to send email.
Insert Current User Name []	The user name is taken from the system that is web publishing the database. It will be the same for all users. The External ("Web-ClientName", 0) function can be used to enter the web user if a password browser login has been used.
Allow Toolbars []	This script step has no effect on web-published databases
Toggle Window []	The database window will toggle, but the step does not affect the browser window.

Table 5.4 File actions requiring passwords or not allowed

New []	This script step will create a new database, and may display a dialog box. No interaction can be implemented by the web users, so do not use this script step when web publishing databases.
Open []	This step may display a dialog box requesting the location of the file to open but may be used to open a closed database.
Open Hosts []	This script step may display a dialog box to choose a file from the server. Do not use with web-published databases, but use the Open [] step, above, to open specified databases.
Close []	This may be used with web-published databases. If the file to close is *not* specified, this step will close the current file.
Save a Copy As []	This script step may display a dialog box but may be used carefully with web-published databases.
Exit Application	Windows command to quit FileMaker Pro.
Quit Application	Macintosh command to quit FileMaker Pro.

Table 5.5 Undesired events with these script steps

Beep	This may be performed, but the sound will be produced on the web publisher machine and not in the user's browser.
Speak []	This will be performed on the web publisher machine and not in the user's browser.
Send Apple Event (Mac OS) []	Platform-specific steps may not work as desired when requested in a -script called in an XML request.
Perform AppleScript (Mac OS) []	Platform-specific steps may not work as desired when requested in a -script called in an XML request.
Send DDE Execute (Windows) []	Platform-specific steps may not work as desired when requested in a -script called in an XML request.
Send Message (Windows) []	Platform-specific steps may not work as desired when requested in a -script called in an XML request.

Navigation	(Go to Field, Go to Layout, Go to Record, Go to Related Record) The navigation script steps may perform unpredictably when requested from a web user. Since the interface is the web browser, these steps may not be needed. The request may not complete before the next web user makes a request and halts the current script. Use the XML parameters and requests to perform any of these actions.

5.31 Script Steps to Avoid in Web Publishing

- Go to Layout can be replaced with the -lay value in the XML request.
- Do not ask for a response to any dialog, such as Show Message[]. The web user will not see these and the database may freeze waiting for a reply. Check out DialogMagic at http://www.nmci.com/ for a plug-in method of dismissing dialog boxes.
- Do not provide any scripts or script steps that may be developer commands (Open Define Fields or Toggle Window[Show]). Any script can be performed in an XML request. Avoid using these script steps in web-published databases for security reasons.
- Use extreme caution when creating, editing, or deleting records or field data in script steps. These actions can all be performed with XML requests.
- Avoid performing finds with scripts. Most of these can be accomplished with the -find action. See the section, "Script Parameters," in this chapter for information on when a scripted find is performed in relation to the -find action.
- Do not allow any pauses in any script steps!
- Many script steps can be used safely with the XML request. Test the results with many users to see if they work as predicted. Try to revise the way these steps could be performed with the XML actions and parameters rather than with a script.

5.4 Security on the Web

The security of your web-published databases is very important, so those considerations will be discussed here. You have several options for setting security on your databases through Web Companion. You can use passwords and associated access privileges to control access to databases published on the web. You can use the Web Security database to control access to your web-published databases.

These options are set in the Web Companion Configuration dialog. The Web Security database option is not available until you have that database open. The configuration dialog is part of the FileMaker Pro application and is available by choosing Edit, Preferences, Application and selecting the Plug-Ins tab. Select the Web Companion plug-in and click on the Configure button. The configuration dialog is shown in Figure 5.12. If you cannot configure Web Companion, go back and check the setup of TCP/IP and other suggestions listed earlier in section 5.16, "Web Companion Setup."

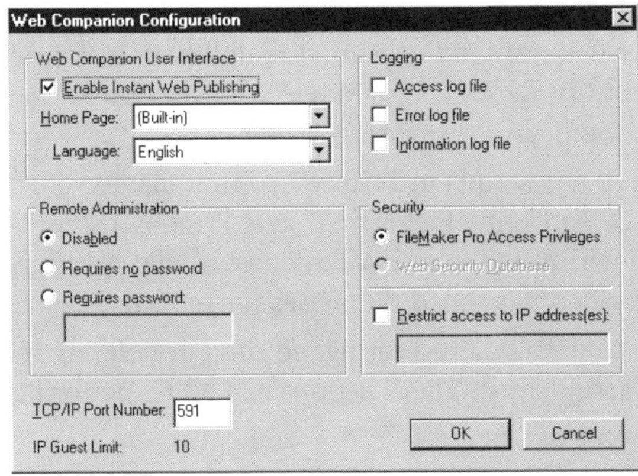

Figure 5.12: Web Companion Configuration dialog

Password access and the Web Security Database provide the same protection with a few exceptions. Both have password protection, field security, record security, and allow the creating, viewing, editing, and deleting of records. Script calls are either allowed or disallowed by the Web Security Database but restricted by privileges if FileMaker Pro access privileges are used. Additional features for the Web Security Database are user name verification, finding in a specific field, and remote administration.

5.41 Security with Web Companion

The document Web Security.pdf, found in the Web Security folder of the FileMaker Pro folder, is a useful document discussing access privileges vs. Web Security Database, field-level and record-level security with the Web Companion plug-in, the Web Security Database, and general web security tips. This document is titled "Using the Web Security Database" in FileMaker Pro. An updated version of this document is installed with FileMaker Pro 5.5 or FileMaker Pro 6 and is titled "Securing data on the Web." The main difference is the record-level access available in FileMaker Pro 5.5 and greater security in FileMaker Pro 6.

Get the latest version of FileMaker Pro to ensure that security issues have been optimized. You may be able to update the Web Companion plug-in for your particular version by itself. Check the FileMaker, Inc. web site for updates, http://www.filemaker.com/support/updaters.html. Also, check for specific Web Companion reports on the following web site: http://www.filemaker.com/support/webcompanion.html.

5.42 Security vs. Security Blanket

There are methods that are secure, and there are methods that give the user a good sense of comfort but are not really secure. Both are discussed here. Do not discount the user experience of a security blanket. A cover is still a cover and few may attempt to lift it. The look of your web pages can be enhanced with the security blanket methods as well. Hiding some of the coding or HTTP requests can be less confusing to the user. Use both methods wisely to enhance the experience for both yourself and your users.

Security Blankets

Some of the methods for providing a security blanket are to place a default page in all web folders, use frames to hide the HTTP requests, redirect back to a main page with JavaScript, and use forms to hide the HTTP requests. Other methods for providing a security blanket are to prevent search engine robots from indexing pages and to prevent or clear browser caching of pages. There may also be other methods that are not more secure but merely provide a sense of security.

Place a Default Page in Web Folders

The Web folder, found in the FileMaker Pro folder, is the default location for files used by Web Companion. The default folder can have subfolders and still be used by Web Companion. You can also use other folders in different directories and on different servers. All folders whose permissions allow read have contents available. Pages and files available for read can also be copied to another computer. A directory or folder without a default page may list all the files in that directory, but including a default page in all folders will prevent this. The topic

"About creating a custom home page," found in FileMaker Help, discusses a default page when using Instant Web publishing, but the advice is valid for any web-published databases.

If the Web folder does not have any files, add one called index.html, index.htm, default.html, or default.htm and select it in the Home Page pop-up of the Web Companion Configuration dialog. This file can be very simple and include only base information along with a link back to the main page of your web site. By default, if no page is specified when linking to a site, one of these files will be used. This prevents users from seeing a list of your files in any folder where your index or default page resides. A simple default page is shown in Listing 5.28. You can also create a redirect, as shown in Listing 5.29, back to your main page. If the browser does not support the redirect, include the link.

Listing 5.28 Sample default.htm

```
<html>
<head>
<title>MyDomain</title>
</head>
<body>
Please return to the <a href="http://www.mydomain.com/mainpage.htm">
      main page</a>.
</body>
</html>
```

Listing 5.29 Sample redirect for default.htm

```
<html>
<head>
<title>MyDomain</title>
<meta http-equiv="refresh" content="0;URL=http://www.mydomain.com/
  mainpage.htm"/>
</head>
<body>
If your browser does not directly go there, click here to return to
  the <a href="http://www.mydomain.com/mainpage.htm">main page</a>.
</body>
</html>
```

Use a Frameset and Frames to Hide HTTP Requests

Creating a web site with frames can hide the full request to a database. The user goes to a main page the first time. This page, in Listing 5.30, sets up the frames, and all subsequent pages will be displayed within a frame or multiple frames. The user only sees the first link, to the main page, in the browser location field. If you want to go outside this frame, to another site for instance, make a link or form call with TARGET="_top". This is only a security blanket, because the browser also allows the user to open any frame in a new window or view the source for the main window or any frame.

Listing 5.30 Request to a database in a frame page

```
<!DOCTYPE html PUBLIC "-//W3C//DTD XHTML 1.0 Frameset//EN"
"http://www.w3.org/TR/2000/REC-xhtml1-20000126/DTD/xhtml1-frameset.dtd">
<html xmlns="http://www.w3.org/1999/xhtml" xml:lang="en" lang="en">
<head>
<meta http-equiv="content-type" content="text/html; charset=utf-8" />
<title>Framed</title>
</head>
<frameset rows="100%,*">
<frame src="http://yourDomain.com/fmpro?-db=MyDatabase&-lay=web&-format=
  -dso_xml&-view" name="main" marginheight="0" marginwidth="0" scrolling=
  "auto" />
<frame name="none" marginheight="0" marginwidth="0" scrolling="no"
  noresize="noresize" />
</frameset>
</html>
```

Redirect Back to Main Page with JavaScript

This tip from Lynda LaCour, at Lylac Inc., uses a JavaScript object that gets called when any page is opened. The JavaScript method onload() can be placed in the <BODY> element of the page and will be triggered as the page loads in the browser. If every page includes this onload event and is opened outside of the intended frame, it will take the user immediately back to a main file and frameset. Listing 5.31 shows the main page with a frameset. The user is taken to this page if he tries to view a page outside of the frameset. Include this JavaScript on every page in your web site except the main page:

```
<BODY onload="if(parent.frames.length==0)top.location='index.html';">
```

Listing 5.31 index.html

```
<HTML>
<HEAD>
<TITLE>Main Page</TITLE>
</HEAD>
<FRAMESET ROWS="135,100%" FRAMEBORDER=1>
<FRAME SRC="NTOP.HTM" NAME=thetop NORESIZE MARGINWIDTH=0 MARGINHEIGHT=0
  FRAMEBORDER=0>
<FRAME SRC="FMPro?-db=myDatabase&-lay=cgi&-format=-dso_xml&-findall"
```

```
  NAME=thebottom MARGINWIDTH=0 MARGINHEIGHT=0 FRAMEBORDER=0>
</FRAMESET>
</HTML>
```

Use Forms to Hide the Request

Most of the HTTP requests we have used thus far are links using the get method. Form requests can also use the get HTTP method, but the post method is more commonly used. More about forms will be discussed in Chapter 6, "Using HTML and XHTML to Format Web Pages." The form requests are hidden in the browser location field with the post method. This is a security blanket, as the request can still be found in the source of the page. Listing 5.32 is a page containing a form request to "MyDatabase." All of the fields are hidden, and the user will only see the Submit button. The link equivalent is:

```
<a href="fmpro?-db=MyDatabase&-lay=web&-format=-dso_xml&-findany">
  Show Me!</a>
```

Listing 5.32 Request to database using a form

```
<!DOCTYPE html PUBLIC "-//W3C//DTD XHTML 1.0 Transitional//EN"
  "http://www.w3.org/TR/2000/REC-xhtml1-20000126/DTD/xhtml1-
  transitional.dtd">
<html lang="en">
<head>
<meta http-equiv="content-type" content="text/html; charset=utf-8">
<title>Formed</title>
</head>
<body>
<form action="fmpro" method="post" target="main">
      <input type="hidden" name="-db" value="MyDatabase" />
      <input type="hidden" name="-lay" value="web" />
      <input type="hidden" name="-format" value="-dso_xml" />
      <input type="submit" name="-findany" value="Show Me!" />
</form>
</body>
</html>
```

Hide from Robots

Search engines may send out requests to index web pages so that they can be easily listed. This is accomplished with a special program called an indexing robot (or bot). No harm is done unless you do not wish a page to be listed forever. Dynamic pages may or may not be included for indexing. Many robots look for a special page, called robots.txt, in your web directory. If this file exists, it may specify whether a particular directory is to be indexed.

```
Disallow: /myPages/
```

Include a meta tag in the head portion of your document to specify whether that particular page is to be indexed or not. In addition, a page may be indexed, but you may not want any links within it followed:

```
<HEAD>
    <META NAME="robots" CONTENT="index, nofollow" />
</HEAD>
```

These rules may or may not be used by any given robot, so even the security blanket does not cover you well. Add these elements if you wish, as they may provide some coverage, but do not rely upon them.

No Cache and Expire Cache

Two other meta tags, which should be sent as the hidden part of any HTTP request, could be included in the head but may be ignored. The first one instructs browsers to expire the page from the browsers' memory after a certain date and time. Dates are to be listed in GMT format. The second meta tag tells browsers not to cache the page. If the user presses the Back button in the browser, the page may be still available but will not be saved if he returns to the same page later. The code below shows both of these meta tags. Browsers do not always comply with these requests, so your results may vary. As with the robot exclusion, use the caching meta tags, but do not rely upon them for security or security blanket coverage.

```
<HEAD>
    <META HTTP-EQUIV="pragma" CONTENT="no-cache" />
    <META HTTP-EQUIV="expires" CONTENT="dayname, day Month year
      hour:minute:second GMT" />
</HEAD>
```

Security

Better security can be provided by the use of FileMaker Pro passwords along with browser login. Web Companion can be configured to disable Instant Web Publishing and to allow only access from specific IP addresses. Web servers can be configured with permissions to various directories and pages to add another layer of security. FileMaker Pro's network protocol can be limited and the passwords can provide record-level access. If scripts are used with web-published databases, they can be made more secure by the way they are designed. Two FileMaker Pro plug-ins, the Troi-Coding plug-in and the Crypto Toolbox plug-in, can encrypt data that need to be shared but secure.

FileMaker Pro Passwords and the Web

Your first line of defense is to use FileMaker Pro's passwords for web-published data. You can specify the access privileges for a database in the Define Passwords dialog. Choose File, Access Privileges, Passwords to open the dialog shown in Figure 5.13 or 5.14. One password must be designated to allow all access privileges if you plan to set up additional passwords to restrict privileges. Select the Access the entire file check box and type a master password in the Password field. Passwords are not case sensitive, may be up to 31 characters long, and should have at least six characters in a mix of letters and numbers. Using nonalphanumeric characters may produce unpredictable results in cross-platform usage or when databases are web enabled.

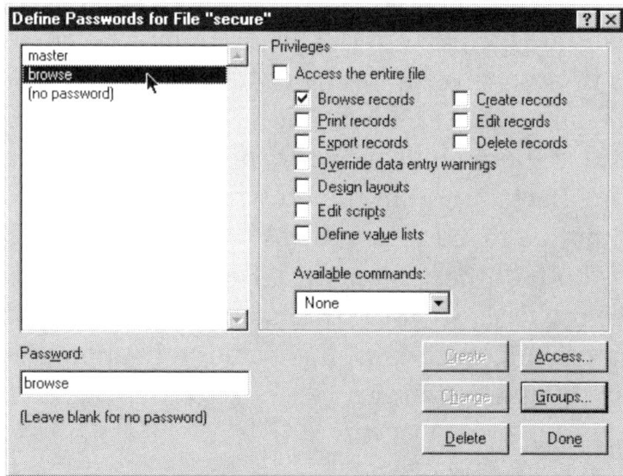

Figure 5.13: Define Passwords dialog, Windows

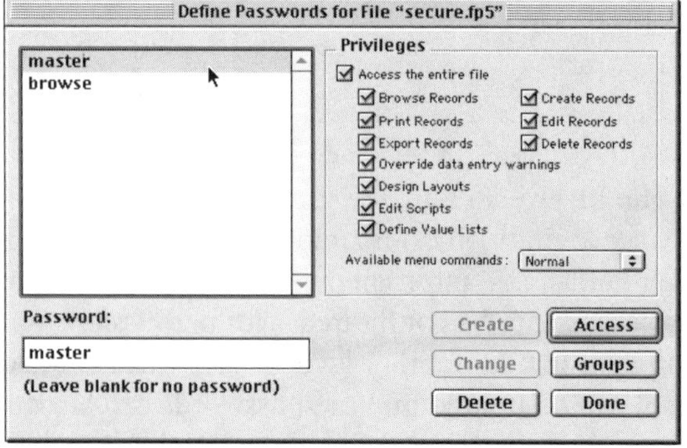

Figure 5.14: Define Passwords dialog, Macintosh

If you need to restrict browsing, editing, deleting, or creating records, uncheck each appropriate check box for all records and create a new password. New in FileMaker Pro 5.5 and FileMaker Pro 6 is record-level access. Select the pop-up menu next to Browse records, Edit records, or Delete records and specify a calculation to limit access. A user restricted to browsing, editing, or deleting only records according to a validation has the same restrictions for web-published databases.

The following documents in FileMaker Pro Help can assist you in setting passwords and access privileges: "Defining and changing passwords" and "General notes about passwords." Notes about limiting access on a record-by-record basis in Help gives some examples and tips on using this feature.

Record-level access is available in FileMaker Pro 5.5 and greater. Any database created using these record-level limitations may be opened with FileMaker Pro 5.0 but will have restrictions. If Browse records is limited or removed in FileMaker Pro 5.5, the database cannot be opened with FileMaker Pro 5.0 with that password. The user cannot delete or edit records when the database is opened with FileMaker Pro 5.0 if Delete records or Edit record (respectively) have restrictions set with FileMaker Pro 5.5. You can open a database with a full access password in FileMaker Pro 5.0, but it will remove any restrictions set with FileMaker Pro 5.5 if you change any of those passwords.

Browser Login Required

If you use passwords or the Web Security database, your user may be asked to enter the password from the browser page. A base web page that does not perform a database action will not display a login dialog, but the first page to perform a database request and return results from an action will trigger the browser login dialog to appear. Figure 5.15 shows this dialog in Netscape 6. The user must complete the login before the action will proceed. This login may specify the database name and the domain name and ask for a user name and password. Incorrect entry will return an error, which you can use to branch to an error display page. After the first request for a database, the user will not be asked to log in again during that browser session. If another file has a different password, the browser dialog will appear again.

Sometimes the password may be saved in the browser preferences. The login dialog for Internet Explorer is shown in Figure 5.16. The check box for saving this password is in the dialog. Unfortunately, you will not have control over your users' selection of this option. You may wish to caution them against it in any opening pages before they log in. If a password has been saved, it can be deleted from the browser preferences. Security can be compromised if the password is saved and another user has access to the browser on that machine. The login will still be requested with the first database action, but the browser will supply the saved user name and password.

Figure 5.15: Web login on Macintosh, Netscape 6

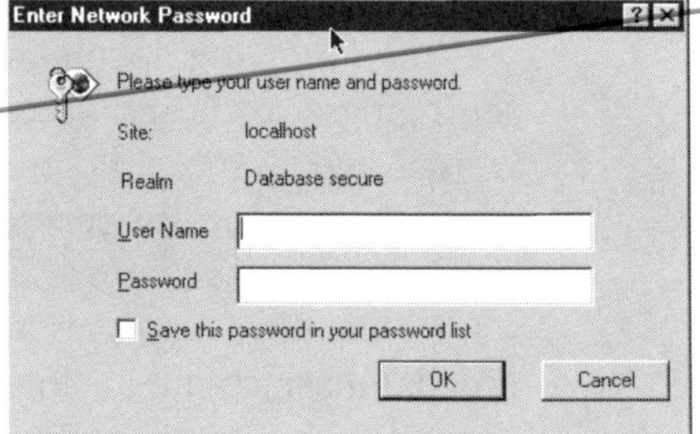

Figure 5.16: Web login on Windows, Internet Explorer 5

The browser asks for a user name and password. The user name need not be completed for the password to be checked in your database. The values for both of these fields are maintained as long as the user is in your site. Any password entered for one database will apply to any other database with the same password. You are asked for the password once if it is the same for every file accessed. The access privileges apply to the highest level for that particular password. If the user leaves your site and returns, he likely will not be asked to enter the password again. He may have to quit the browser and go to your site again to be asked to login. If you set default passwords in your databases, your users will not be asked for a password in the browser.

The user name that is entered in the browser dialog can be used with record-level access. See "Record-level Access" later in this chapter for how you can check this value. The user name is persistent until the user leaves the web site or quits the browser.

Set Permissions on Directories

On some web servers, you can set the directory permission to be read or write only. These can also have passwords set. On UNIX and NT directories, privileges to directories can be read, write, and executable. These privileges can be set to allow owner, group, and all access. Each access can have different privileges. Generally, files and folders inside a protected directory inherit the same protection. This may also need to be specified. Passwords can be set upon these directories. Consult your server documentation for setting up permissions and passwords for UNIX and NT directories. If you are using AppleShare IP or Macintosh OS X, consult the documentation for setting directory permission and passwords.

Permission to access the Web folder is set by the Web Companion plug-in. If you have a database set to sharing with Web Companion, any files within the Web folder are available on the machine with that database. This folder is your root directory used by Web Companion to access files. You can place aliases to these files in the Web folder rather than the files themselves, but they will still be available for access. Any file, including images, shown on a web page can be saved or downloaded. Source can be viewed, revealing information you may not want seen. These files are protected only if you have IP address filtering set in the Web Companion Configuration dialog.

Never store databases in the Web folder. If you must use remote administration, set a password on any databases in this folder. -dbopen and -dbclose only work on databases located in the Web folder.

Disable Instant Web Publishing

If you are no longer testing Web Companion setup, uncheck Enable Instant Web Publishing in the Web Companion Configuration dialog. If Instant Web Publishing is enabled, any file set to sharing with Web Companion will be available simply by addressing it in the browser. Sample calls to web sites with databases are shown below. Any passwords and group access settings you have implemented will also apply to Instant Web-published databases. Disabling Instant Web Publishing just adds another layer of prevention by not making them available to Instant Web Publishing.

```
<http://www.mydomain.com/>
<http://localhost/>
<http://127.0.0.1:591/>
<http://123.123.123.123/>
```

Set Databases to Multi-User (Hidden) Sharing

Your databases set to sharing with Web Companion may also be available for access through the TCP/IP network protocol. With a fast enough connection, a database can be directly accessed when the Hosts button is selected in the Open File dialog of FileMaker Pro. Figure 5.17 shows this dialog. You can save the entered address by checking Permanently add entry to Hosts list. The next time you select the Host button, this IP address or domain name will be listed. If your network settings in Application Preferences are TCP/IP and the files have Multi-User or Multi-User (Hidden) sharing set, they may be available for direct access.

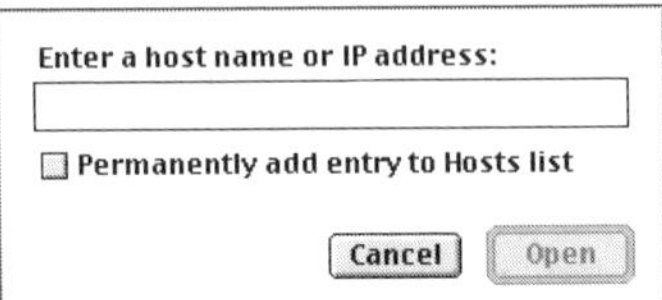

Figure 5.17: Specify host address to open remote databases

You will want to prevent files from being seen in the Host dialog for security. If you specify the filename with the underscore (_) and select Multi-User in the File Sharing dialog, your database may still be available through TCP/IP. Selecting Multi-User (Hidden) will hide this file in the Host dialog even if your host name or IP number is used. The FileMaker Network Sharing dialog is shown in Figure 5.18. If you use Filemaker Server to host the databases, it can open files set as Single User, Multi-User, or Multi-User (Hidden). Single User files can only be hosted by FileMaker Server if you have enabled Allow FileMaker Server to host Single User files. This option is a part of Server and only available there.

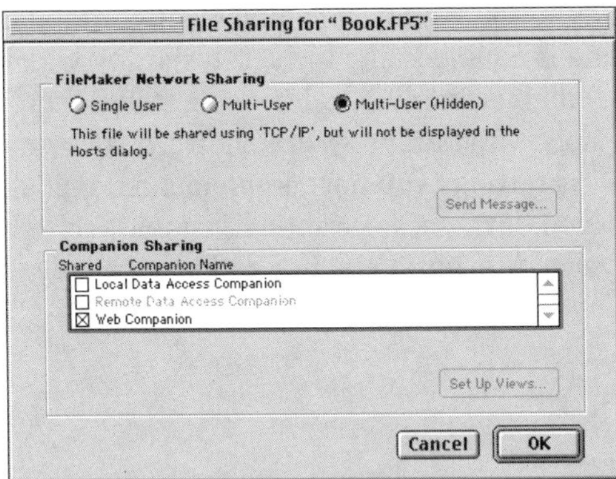

Figure 5.18: Network sharing

"Securing data on the web," the PDF document found in the Web Security folder of the FileMaker Pro folder, states: "It is not necessary to enable FileMaker Pro Multi-User sharing or OS-level file sharing to share Filemaker Pro databases over the Web. It is not necessary to specify TCP/IP as the Network Protocol in FileMaker Pro application preferences. Enable these technologies only if you need them for other types of network access."

If you have Enable Instant Web Publishing unchecked, no database will be listed on a default page, whether you use the underscore in the filename or not. However, they will all be available for Web Companion to use for custom web publishing, including XML publishing, if you have set them for sharing with Web Companion.

You can also prevent databases from being listed on the built-in home page with Instant Web Publishing if they have an underscore (_) as the last character of the filename, excluding the extension. "SECURE_.FP5", "DONTSHOW_", or "nolist_.fp5" are examples of how to use this underscore character.

Including the underscore does *not* provide additional security. These files simply will not be listed on the default home page for Instant Web Publishing if it is enabled. You can still use these files for custom web publishing by using the full name, including underscore.

Export Privileges Required for Web Publishing

Web Companion requires shared files to have export privileges. Any file shared for web publishing needs to be opened by a password that allows export. Therefore, at least one password other than your master password should have Export Records checked. Files opened by a password without export privileges will produce an error when web published. Be aware, though, that files with export privileges can also allow a user to export data if they have access to your database through TCP/IP.

Remember that files with export privileges can be accessed if you do not include a password! Export privileges provide a means to web publish your data. They also provide a means to export your data.

If you specify related fields on a layout of a shared database and the related file does not have export privileges, those fields are still available for web publishing. If no layout or Layout 0 is specified for web publishing, none of these related fields are available. However, anyone having access to your files can export *any* field that is related, whether it is on a layout or not.

Do not include secure data, even in related files. Any available data is, well, available! Related fields can be exported from any database with a relationship. If a database allows export, a related file need not have export privileges to be accessed! A related field on a layout is available, even if the related database does not have export privileges or does not have Web Companion sharing enabled.

Exercise 5.2 *Create a Browse-only Password*

This exercise will set up a file for web publishing with very basic privileges. The user will be able to view the data and search for specific data but will not be able to create, edit, or delete any records. It is assumed that you have Web Companion enabled in FileMaker Pro and you are using self-testing. If you have the files on a network, change all references of "localhost" to the IP address or domain name of your web publishing server. If you require a port number, add that to the address, too.

1. Create a new database called **BROWSE_.FP5**.
2. Create three fields: ItemID (number), ItemName (text), and ItemDescription (text). These fields may be typical in a catalog or products file. Items for viewing should only be changed by a user with an administrative-level password. Web users will want to search and see the results.
3. Create a layout called **web** and place the three fields on this layout. See the FileMaker Pro Help topic, "Placing and removing fields on a layout" if you need assistance. The format of the fields, and the font, size, and color do not matter. You will only be extracting the field names and contents with XML results, so the layout can (and should) be very basic.
4. Create three to five new records and enter data into these fields.
5. Create a master password, "master," and a default password, "user," by selecting **File**, **Access Privileges**, **Passwords**. Passwords should follow the guidelines above and include a mix of letters and numbers. Simple passwords are included in these examples for convenience.
6. Select these privileges for "user": **Browse Records** and **Export Records**. Also set the available menu commands to **None**. The browser does not see these menu commands, but should the database be opened through a network, this hides the menu commands, including Export.
7. Set the default password to "user" by selecting **Edit**, **Preferences**, **Document**. Check **Try default password** and type **user** into the box. This will not ask for a password when the file is opened. You will be asked to enter a password in the browser, however.
8. Launch your browser and enter this URL: **http://localhost/fmpro?-db=BROWSE%5f.FP5&-lay=web&-format=-dso_xml&-findall**. Notice that the underscore (_) is changed to (encoded as) "%5f". -db=BROWSE_.FP5 will also work.
9. You will be asked to enter a user name and password. Enter **user** for both and continue. The results will be similar to the following:

```
<?xml version="1.0" encoding="UTF-8" ?>
<FMPDSORESULT xmlns="http://www.filemaker.com/fmpdsoresult">
<ERRORCODE>0</ERRORCODE>
<DATABASE>browse_.fp5</DATABASE>
<LAYOUT>web</LAYOUT>
<ROW MODID="1" RECORDID="36492">
      <ItemID>1234</ItemID>
      <ItemName>Red Ball</ItemName>
      <ItemDescription>Bouncy ball, soft enough for baby to
        hold.</ItemDescription>
</ROW>
<ROW MODID="2" RECORDID="36493">
      <ItemID>1235</ItemID>
      <ItemName>Paper Airplane Kit</ItemName>
      <ItemDescription>Book with patterns for folding different paper
        airplanes.</ItemDescription>
</ROW>
<ROW MODID="1" RECORDID="36494">
      <ItemID>1236</ItemID>
      <ItemName>Teddy Bear</ItemName>
      <ItemDescription>Cuddly, stuffed bear with t-shirt.
        </ItemDescription>
</ROW>
</FMPDSORESULT>
```

10. Remove "&-lay=web" from the URL and see what results you get. If you have created any other fields, these will be listed, as well as the three on our web layout. When you do not specify a layout, the default Layout 0 (or all the fields in this database) is available.
11. Close this file and open it again while holding down the Shift key on Windows or the Option key on Macintosh. When you are asked for a password, type the word **master** in the dialog.
12. Quit your browser to clear your user login and then relaunch it. Enter the same URL as above (with or without the layout specified). Even with the database opened by the main password with all access privileges, you are asked to enter a password in the browser. If you use the master password, you have all privileges. If you use the user password, you only have browse and find privileges.
13. Create a new blank password with the same privileges as the user password. Change the Document Preferences to auto-enter the blank password (clear this field).
14. Close the BROWSE_.FP5 database and open it again. You will not be asked for a password to open this file. You have set the blank password to be entered for you.

15. Quit your browser again to clear the login and relaunch. When you enter the same URL, you will not be asked for a password. If you try to perform any action other than to view or find, you will be asked to enter a user name and password for the browser login.

The lowest level password setting is the blank password with Browse, Export privileges, and limited menu commands. If you use this password as auto-enter in your Document Preferences, the user will not be asked for a password if the file is web published and the action is to browse or find. If no layout is specified, *all* fields and their contents in the file are available to the user.

Warning: The "browse-only" access level still allows scripts to be performed! If you want data to be available for searching and viewing only, do not include any scripts in the file with this password. Scripts will perform based upon privileges set. For example, if you do not allow delete privileges, that script step cannot be performed.

The document "TechInfo #107663" found at http://www.filemaker.com/support/techinfo.html states that using a (no password) can compromise your security. If you must use this so that your user does not have to log in, create it as the first password in the Define Passwords dialog. See "FileMaker Pro Passwords and the Web" earlier in this chapter for information about creating passwords. Check for the latest version of FileMaker Pro, as this may be fixed in a future revision.

Record-level Access

New in FileMaker Pro 5.5 and FileMaker Pro 6 is record-level access for browsing, editing, and deleting. This access is set in the Define Fields dialog and uses a Boolean calculation to determine if a record is to be displayed or not. A find request for records will omit any record that has a false result in the calculation. Any valid calculation can be used to check a user login, access group, or date, for example.

If you request a browser login, the user name entered in that dialog can be used to identify a set of records. The browser remembers the login name until the user quits the browser. Web Companion can recall the name and place it in a field. It can also test for the presence of that login name when searching, viewing, editing, or deleting records. Create a field called webUser and have it auto-enter this value. If you check for this field in your requests, the user will be prevented from seeing records that do not match the login name.

```
External("Web-ClientName", 0)
```

For more examples using record-level access, see the FileMaker Pro Help topic, "Notes about limiting access on a record-by-record basis." Web Companion usage of record-level access is also covered in "Securing data on the web." This document is installed in the Web Security folder with FileMaker Pro, and reminds you that global fields, unstored calculations, and summary fields may still be displayed. Record-level access will not include restricted data in a summary field.

Assign Groups

Assign groups in FileMaker Pro and use the function Status (CurrentGroups) at the beginning of your script to decide whether to proceed or not. Create your passwords before creating groups, as they are closely tied together. Use the database created in Exercise 5.2 to add group access in Exercise 5.3. This file should have (no password) as the default password. The database will open automatically and no browser login will be requested. Remember that this password only allows browsing and finding records. We want to limit the fields available even if no layout is specified and the request is to find all records.

Exercise 5.3 *Assign Access Groups to Web-Published Databases*

1. Open the Browse_.fp5 database, created in Exercise 5.2, with the Option key (Macintosh) or Shift key (Windows) held down. This will bring up the password dialog. You need to enter the master password to change group access settings.
2. Open the Define Groups dialog by selecting **File**, **Access Privileges**, **Groups**.
3. Enter **none** into the Group Name field and click the **Access** button. This dialog is where you select the passwords and fields that are assigned to each group. The access privileges can be set to Accessible, Not accessible, and Read only.
4. Note here that layouts can be selected for access but will be ignored by web-published databases. If you share a database on a network as well as web published, you can change these.
5. Select the group you just created, **none**. When it is selected, you choose the passwords assigned to it. Leave the master password and (no password) to Accessible, but click on the circle beside user password until it is grayed (Not accessible).

6. Set all the fields to **Not accessible**, except for the fields ItemDescription, ItemID, and ItemName. Set these fields to **Read only**. You may not have any fields except these three, so just set them to Read only.
7. Save the group settings and click on **Done** to close the Define Groups dialog.
8. Close the file and let the default (no password) access open the file.
9. Web publish the database with this -findall command:

```
http://localhost/fmpro?-db=BROWSE_.FP5&-format=-dso_xml&-findall=1137
```

You will see only those fields with read-only permission.

If you change the action to -new, you will be asked to enter a user name and password in the browser dialog. This is because you only have browse and search permission with (no password) and have limited field access with groups.

Field-level access can be set with groups to add security to password access. If you create several groups, you can add permissions or restrictions based upon the password entered. We used the none group to restrict the field access. If we requested a -new action as above and entered the password master into the browser login, we would have been granted full access to all fields and all actions.

5.43 Script Security

Several script security tips are listed here:

- If you must maintain scripts within your web-published databases, you can use conditional tests to verify the level of access. The function Status(CurrentGroups) will return a list of all the groups attached to the password used to log in. Use this test in an opening script step:

```
If [ PatternCount(Status(CurrentGroups), "AccessibleGroupName") ]
.. proceed with script...
End If
```

- Do not allow any Go to Layout scripts. Layouts can be changed in an HTTP request on the web with the -lay parameter.
- Do not allow developer action scripts. Files may have developer scripts to unlock status, for example. If you must include these, provide a check for a password and group access before proceeding.

- Scripts that change or delete data can be called from another database or from an HTTP request if the password allows these privileges.
- Any database with an auto-enter or blank (none) password can be compromised by not setting low-level access.
- Do not use scripts with dialogs requesting response. Regardless of access privileges, these dialogs are not displayed in the browser and will cause FileMaker Pro to halt processing.

5.44 Final XML Web Publishing Thought

Security is a big issue and you should read the Web Security documents from FileMaker. You should set up your networks for the optimum in security to make them as secure as possible. You can also find white papers about security on the FileMaker web site, http://www.filemaker.com. Use encryption, as described here, to transmit your data over the Internet. Whether you make HTTP requests to FileMaker Pro or web publish your databases, consider some of the advice given here.

5.5 Error Codes for XML

The error code returned in the XML result is found in the element <ERRORCODE>, one level down from the root element in the XML document, whether you web publish XML or use export and import of XML. This number corresponds to the FileMaker Pro error codes found in Appendix B of the *FileMaker Unlimited Administrator's Guide* or in the Help topic "Status (CurrentError) function." Not all the codes are given in Table 5.6 but those specifically found in web publishing or XML export and import with FileMaker Pro. You may also receive errors in a dialog from the XML parser and XSL processor when you export and import XML.

Table 5.6 Specific error codes

Code	Explanation
0	This means no error. You want this to be your result.
4	"Command is unknown" is a catchall error. Check your web publishing setup first, then look for spelling errors in database names, layout names, etc.

Code	Explanation
5	"Command is invalid" can mean many things. A common error when web publishing, error 5 can be the result of an incorrect password or the database is not open.
101	"Record is missing" may be returned if a particular -recid does not exist in a -find or -edit request.
102	"Field is missing" is also a common web publishing error. Especially found if the field called in a CDML -format page or in a stylesheet is not on the layout. Related fields only need to be on a layout once and not necessarily in a portal for web publishing.
104	"Script is missing" may let you know that you have misspelled a -script name when web publishing.
105	"Layout is missing" could be returned if you specify a layout (-lay) that is spelled incorrectly. The layout is not used with XML import or export.
301	"Record is in use by another user" is a rare error when web publishing your database unless you also allow users to access the same files on a network.
306	"Record modification ID does not match" will be returned it you are trying to -edit a record and use the MODID attribute to prevent overwriting another user's changes. This is similar to error 301, except the web user gets the data in a stateless environment. This is the only way to verify the change correctly. This error is no longer listed in FileMaker Pro 6 Help.
400	"Find criteria is empty" may not be an error that you see, as a null or empty value is acceptable in a CGI request. You may simply get no results returned with a -find, -findall, or -findany action.
401	"No records match the request" is the error you may get if the find criteria are empty or no results are returned.
409	The "Import order is invalid" error may occur if you have changed field names or the fields in your scripted import.
410	"Export order is invalid." As with error 409, this most likely will occur if the fields have changed since the scripted export was created.
411	"Cannot perform delete because related records cannot be deleted" is an error that may be returned when you use the -delete action in an HTTP request if the relationship allows deleting, but the related records have a password disallowing deletion.
500 – 511	These are field validation errors and may not occur if you create records through an HTTP request or import XML.
700	"File is of the wrong file type for import." You can import XML only with the FMPXMLRESULT grammar. You probably will get a dialog rather than see this error in any XML.
714	"Password privileges do not allow the operation" error may return a browser dialog rather than the error code when you web publish.
717	"There is not enough XML/XSL information to proceed with the import or export." You may receive this generic error code and you may also see a dialog with specific information about the error in the XML or XSL documents.

Code	Explanation
718	"Error in parsing XML file (from Xerces)." If the XML for import is not in the proper FMPXMLRESULT grammar, the Xerces parser cannot continue.
719	"Error in transforming XML using XSL (from Xalan)." You may also see a dialog specifiying the error in the XSL document and where it occurs (line number). These dialogs may help you determine the necessary changes to your XSL document.
720	"Error when exporting; intended document format does not support repeating fields" may be an error that is not seen with XML export or web publishing with XML. FileMaker Pro will display the element <COL> with a <DATA> element for all the repeats of a field, regardless of the number of repeats shown on a layout or the last repeat with contents.
721	"Unknown error occurred in the parser or the transformer" is a generic error, but you may also get more information in a dialog.
800	"Unable to create file on disk" may be the error you get when you try to export and have insufficient disk space, for example.
950	"Adding repeating related fields is not supported" is an error in design and may not show in the web-published results.
951	"An unexpected error occurred" is very generic and difficult to pinpoint. The error could be in the HTTP request, in the display of the results, or in the sharing of the database.
971	"The user name is invalid" may be returned if the incorrect user ID is entered in the browser login or if the user name for the database is not set correctly.
972	"The password is invalid" may be shown in a browser dialog rather than returned as an error code.
973	"The database is invalid" may be the error code returned if the database has not been set to sharing with Web Companion.
974	"Permission denied" may be returned if the login fails or the CMDL -format pages are not available.
975	"The field has restricted access" may be the error code shown when the field on a layout has restrictions set in the Password dialog or the record level prevents creation, modification, or deletion of the field's contents.
976	"Security is disabled" may be returned if the configuration for Web Companion has been changed.
977	"Invalid client IP address" is the error presented if you have restricted the access to a range of IP addresses in the configuration for Web Companion.
978	"The number of allowed guests has been exceeded." This error is returned if FileMaker Pro Unlimited is not used and more than 10 unique IP addresses make HTTP requests over a 12-hour period.

5.51 JavaScript Errors

In addition to the FileMaker Pro errors, Web Companion may return these server errors. You may get a page with the error listed rather than returned in your XML results.

Table 5.7 JavaScript error codes

Code	Explanation
OK	No error.
Bad Request	The server could not process your request due to a syntax error.
403A Forbidden	You do not have authorization to access this server.
403B User Limit Exceeded	The maximum number of licensed users are connected. Try again later.
Not Found	The requested URL "xyz" was not found on this server. (This is the same as web server error "File not found.")
Internal Server Error	An internal server error has occurred.
Not Implemented	The server does not support the functionality required to fulfill this request.
HTTP Version Not Supported	The server does not support the HTTP protocol version that was used in the request message.

When encountering errors, check the error code list first and carefully check the request made. The errorcode element results can be used in a stylesheet to return the error message rather than a cryptic code.

Chapter 6

Using HTML and XHTML to Format Web Pages

Hypertext Markup Language (HTML) was developed by Tim Berners-Lee at CERN (the European Laboratory for Particle Physics), http://cern.web.cern.ch/CERN/WorldWideWeb/WWWandCERN.html. Many variations of HTML have been developed to accommodate various browsers and devices. Compact Hypertext Markup Language (cHTML), Handheld Device Markup Language (HDML), and i-mode are subsets of the original HTML and are designed for wireless personal digital assistants, cellular phones, and pagers. Dynamic Hypertext Markup Language (DHTML) is a combination of HTML, JavaScript, and Cascading Style Sheets (CSS) because HTML alone may be insufficient for dynamic web publishing. "XHTML™ 1.0: The Extensible Hypertext Markup Language (Second Edition)" has been made a recommendation by the World Wide Web Consortium to revise HTML 4.0 documents to work as XML 1.0, http://www.w3.org/TR/xhtml1.

HTML provides a means of displaying and accessing information on the World Wide Web. Web pages may also be viewed in a browser without the user being connected to the Internet. The use of this form of document for information exchange has become more common. Modern email clients may send and receive HTML-formatted messages. HTML is one of the methods of transforming XML into a browser document. Even if you do not plan to web publish XML, you may still find this chapter useful for these reasons.

HTML uses Hypertext Transfer Protocol, URIs, fragments, and a tag-based language to display the items located by the URI and requested by the HTTP protocol. HTML is also based on Standard Generalized Markup Language (SGML). The elements and attributes are similar to XML, however the empty elements in HTML do not always adhere to the strict rules of XML. Therefore, XHTML converts some of these elements for compliance with XML. All the elements shown here will be in XHTML format with a description of the original HTML form, if necessary. Browsers may be forgiving in allowing attributes to be unquoted, but all of the attributes will be quoted here for conformance with XHTML.

When designing HTML documents, the W3C recommends these considerations: 1) separate the structure and presentation; 2) design for universal access—this means for Braille, text readers, and language differences; and 3) design for the fastest load and rendering of the pages—especially if target users are using dial-up connections.

While this chapter is not a comprehensive HTML or XHTML reference, it provides you with an overview for using HTML with FileMaker Pro and XML. HTML can be used to present the results of a request to Web Companion. The <form> element and its associated elements can be used to submit information to your databases to find records, create new records, and edit and delete records. The two documents that may help you the most with details about HTML and XHTML are "HTML 4.01 Specification," http://www.w3.org/TR/html401, and "1.0: The Extensible Hypertext Markup Language XHTML," found at http://www.w3.org/TR/xhtml1.

The element and attributes names in this chapter are listed as uppercase (<ELEMENT ATTRIBUTE="">) and as lowercase (<element attribute="">). Often HTML is written in uppercase to distinguish the elements from the XML elements, which are lowercase. However, XHTML should use lowercase for the HTML elements and attributes. If you use element names in uppercase, lowercase, or mixed case, remember to be consistent in the XML document. Be especially consistent in the case of the start tag and the end tag for the same element. XML is case sensitive.

6.1 HTML Document Structure

The proper HTML document begins with a prolog just like an XML document. This prolog consists of the Document Type Declaration and comes in three versions. Each of these may limit or increase the usage of particular markup. Original versions of HTML used some markup that has become deprecated (outdated or revised) or obsolete. Any of these deprecated elements used in this chapter are so noted. The three !DOCTYPEs are:

- <!DOCTYPE HTML PUBLIC "-//W3C//DTD HTML 4.01//EN" "http://www.w3.org/TR/html4/strict.dtd">

  This declaration is for very strict pages with no deprecated elements and attributes or framesets.

- <!DOCTYPE HTML PUBLIC "-//W3C//DTD HTML 4.01 Transitional//EN" "http://www.w3.org/TR/html4/loose.dtd">

  This declaration contains all the elements and attributes from the strict declaration and includes the use of deprecated markup. Most of these deprecated elements are for the styling of text in the HTML document.

- <!DOCTYPE HTML PUBLIC "-//W3C//DTD HTML 4.01 Frameset//EN" "http://www.w3.org/TR/html4/frameset.dtd">

  This is the most common markup. It uses all of the transitional elements and includes framesets and frames.

XHTML has similar Document Type Declarations:

- <!DOCTYPE html PUBLIC "-//W3C//DTD XHTML 1.0 Strict//EN" "http://www.w3.org/TR/xhtml1/DTD/xhtml1-strict.dtd">
- <!DOCTYPE html PUBLIC "-//W3C//DTD XHTML 1.0 Transitional//EN" "http://www.w3.org/TR/xhtml1/DTD/xhtml1-transitional.dtd">
- <!DOCTYPE html PUBLIC "-//W3C//DTD XHTML 1.0 Frameset//EN" "http://www.w3.org/TR/xhtml1/DTD/xhtml1-frameset.dtd">

HTML and XHTML documents must have a root element to make them well formed. This root element may have attributes to further define the document. Browsers may render the page differently based upon these attributes. The version attribute specifies the version listed in the DOCTYPE. The lang attribute can list the base language of the page. The dir attribute works with the lang attribute to specify the direction of the language as it is read natively. The values of the dir attributes can be left to right (LTR) or right to left (RTL). The <dir> element has been deprecated.

```
<html version="4.01" lang="EN" dir="LTR|RTL">
<!-- comments are the same in HTML as in XML -->
</html>
```

6.2 The HEAD Element

Basic HTML documents have two elements, <head> and <body>. The <head> portion of this type of document can define the document and contain information about it that may not be displayed in the browser. Search engines often use the contents of the markup in the <head>. Also contained in the <head> element are references to other documents and objects that may be used in the document but not contained in the <body>. The following shows the basic elements of the <head> element:

```
<head>
<title></title>
<meta />
<link></link>
<base />
</head>
```

6.21 The TITLE Element

The <title> is the page header in the browser window. This element is required in all HTML documents. This markup has a start tag and end tag and is never empty. The <title> in the <head> element is different from "title" attribute, often used within other elements.

```
<title>This is my document!</title>
```

6.22 The META Element

The <meta> element has many attributes and provides information about the document. The name attribute is used to specify values such as keywords, author, copyright, and date. Search engines that index your web page may use the name attribute. Other values for the name attribute are: author-corporate, author-email, author-personal, description, generator, htdig-email, htdig-email-subject, htdig-keywords, htdig-noindex, htdig-notification-date, publisher-email, and robots. Instead of name, the http-equiv attribute is used to send a message to the browser with values such as expires, refresh, and Content-Type. Other http-equiv values are: cache-control, content-language, content-script-type, content-style-type, PICS-Label, pragma, vary, and set-cookie. The attribute content is required and used with the name or http-equiv attributes. The <meta> element is always empty, as seen in Listing 6.1, so include the space and slash characters (/) at the end of the element to make it XHTML compliant.

Listing 6.1 META element examples

```
<meta name="keywords" content="HTML, XML, XHTML" />
<meta name="author" content="Beverly Voth" />
<meta name="copyright" content="2001" />
<meta name="date" content="2002-01-01" />
<!-- to force the browser to reload a page -->
<meta http-equiv="expires" content="" />
<!-- to redirect the browser to another page -->
<!-- the content specifies the seconds to wait before going to the URL -->
<meta http-equiv="refresh" content="5;URL=theNextPage.html" />
<meta http-equiv="Content-Type" content="" />
```

The document "HTML 4.01 Specification W3C Recommendation 24 December 1999," http://www.w3.org/TR/1999/REC-html401-19991224, states in section 4.3 that the Content-Type for an HTML document is text/html. It is strongly recommended that charset is included.

```
<meta http-equiv="Content-Type" content="text/html; charset=Latin-1" />
```

6.23 The LINK Element Can Replace STYLE and SCRIPT

In HTML, you can specify stylesheets and JavaScript. These elements can be placed within the <head> element or the <body> element. The first example below shows the placement and format of these elements. If an external document is used, then the source of the document is provided instead of the code shown in the second example below.

```
<!-- EXAMPLE ONE -->
<head>
<style type="text/css">
     <!-- list your Cascading Style Sheets description here -->
</style>
<script type="text/javascript">
     <!-- list your JavaScript here -->
</script>
</head>
<!-- EXAMPLE TWO -->
<head>
     <style type="text/css" src="myStyles.css" />
     <script type="text/javascript" src="myJavaScript.js" />
</head>
```

If you include the <style> and <script> elements within your XHTML document, you must make them CDATA (character data). Characters such as "<," ">," and "&" are used by XML and XHTML. If you include them in your stylesheet or JavaScript references, the XML processors and browsers may process them incorrectly. The code below shows the correct method of formatting in XHTML.

```
<script type="text/javascript">
<![CDATA[
... unescaped script content ...
]]>
</script>
```

Using external references to stylesheets and JavaScript is a very good way to separate the content from the presentation of your document. Since the HTML, XHTML, and XML documents may be displayed on various devices, a separate stylesheet may be used for each device.

STYLE and SCRIPT in external documents can also be replaced with the single element LINK. This element is always empty and always placed within the <head> element. The attributes for the <link> are described in Table 6.1. An advantage of using <link> is the ability to include more than stylesheets and external script documents.

Table 6.1 LINK attributes

rel	The relationship from this page to others. The values of rel can be Alternate, Stylesheet, Start, Next, Prev, Contents, Index, Glossary, Copyright, Chapter, Section, Subsection, Appendix, Help, and Bookmark. An example of <link> attributes is shown below:
	`<head>`
	`    <title>Page 2</title>`
	`    <link rel="Index" href="index.html" />`
	`    <link rel="Prev" href="page1.html" />`
	`    <link rel="Next" href="page3.html" />`
	`</head>`

type	The content type of the document. Some of the values for the type attribute can be any of the MIME types such as text/css, text/javascript, or application/msword.
href	The location of the referenced document.

Other attributes for the <link> element are rev (reversed link to this document), id, class, lang (language), dir (direction of language), title, style, src (location of stylesheet document), onfocus, onblur, onclick, ondblclick, onmousedown, onmouseup, onmouseover, onmouseout, onkeypress, onkeydown, onkeyup, target (used with href if using windows and frames), tabindex (tab order), accesskey, media (such as screen, TV, print, Braille), and charset. You can read more about some of these attributes as they apply to other elements listed here.

6.24 The BASE Element

The final element in the <head> element is the <base> element. <base> is a way to specify the location of the particular document containing the BASE element. This element is also used by any internal references by the current document to external sources. Rather than include a full path to each reference (absolute path), you can include the relative path to the <base> path of the document. This resolves possible confusion with these relative resources. The sample code for this element is shown below. <base> should be listed in the <head> element and above any relative paths, including any that might be in <style>, <script>, <meta>, and <link>.

```
<head>
    <base href="http://mydomain.com/anotherFolder/thisDocument.html"
      target="_top" />
    <link rel="Next" href="page3.html" />
</head>
```

6.3 The Main BODY of the HTML Document

The document that you see in a web browser or on a mobile telephone is formatted by the elements in the <body>. The BODY element contains several attributes and is never empty if you want something to display. Some of these elements have been deprecated (are no longer used) but are listed for reference.

Table 6.2 BODY attributes

background	An image resource or path to an image to be displayed behind all other items on the page. The image will be displayed with a tiling effect. It will first appear in the upper-left corner and repeat down and to the right. If you make the image sufficiently wide, this effect will not be shown unless the user scrolls past the first repeat. It is also possible to create a small image with repeating patterns that appear to be one big graphic. This attribute has been deprecated for use with XHTML and XML, so use stylesheets to specify a background image.

bgcolor	The background color of the body of the web page. By default, the browser may display white or gray if no background color is specified in this element. This attribute is a solid color and does not have the tiling effect of background. Both attributes may be used, but the background may completely obscure a bgcolor. It may still be useful if an image cannot be found. While not deprecated, this attribute may also be specified in a stylesheet.
text	The color of the text on the page, also called the foreground color. If you use a bgcolor of black, you would specify white or another light color for the text, for example. This attribute is also deprecated and often specified in a stylesheet. The default foreground color or the text of the page is black if you do not specify one.
link	Hypertext links have a default of blue underline if you place them in a web page. Once they have been selected and visited, they change color. Your browser can override the defaults, or you can specify the color (or none) by using this deprecated attribute. vlink is the color of visited links and alink is the color of the selected links. These attributes can work together or separately with link, and all have been deprecated.

Other attributes for <body> are id (*must* be unique in any document), class, lang, title, style, onload, onunload, onclick, ondblclick, onmousedown, onmouseover, onmouseup, onmousemove, onmouseout, onkeypress, onkeydown, and onkeyup. The most common attribute is the onload attribute. As the document loads into the window of the browser, the <body> element can perform a script. An example usage for preloading images for animation effects is shown in the code below. This is calling the script preloadImageJS for the two images next.gif and prev.gif including the relative path to these images.

```
<body onload="preloadImageJS('images/nav/next.gif','images/nav/prev.gif')">
```

The <body> element contains the elements that compose the page. These are text, tables, lists, blocks, anchors, images, objects, and forms. Each of these elements will be described in this chapter.

6.31 Text

Text is not specifically an element by name, but the text of the document can be contained in other elements. Some of these elements are methods of formatting the text within the <body> of the document. The <body> element is an HTML element that can contain content and other elements. It is perfectly legal to have a document of all text, although your results may not be as you intended, such as in the following example.

```
<body>
Here is the text of this document.
Even though there are returns between the
lines, the browser will render only the text
and ignore the extra white space.

The blank line above, for example, will not display as a blank line.
Only the width of the window may make the text wrap and appear as
separate lines.
</body>
```

Here is the text of this document: Even though there are returns between the lines, the browser will render only the text and ignore the extra white space. The blank line above, for example, will not display as a blank line. Only the width of the window may make the text wrap and appear as separate lines.

To display the text as we intended, we can use the block element <div> and the inline element <span> to group the text. An advantage of doing this is to later apply stylesheets to these groups. Use the id and class attributes to identify these elements within the document. Examples of these elements are shown in Listing 6.2. Typically, <div> will be used where a line break would occur, although it does not provide the means to insert a break character.

Other attributes for <div> and <span> are lang, dir, title, style (for specific style of this element), align (left, right, or center), onclick, ondblclick, onmousedown, onmouseup, onmouseover, onmousemove, onmouseout, onkeypress, onkeydown, and onkeyup.

The align attribute has been deprecated in favor of assigning this with a stylesheet rather than within the element. However, it is common to still include this attribute. The default alignment of text within any element is to the left. If you do not specify align or choose align="right" or align="center", the text will display starting on the left. Keep in mind the use of the lang and dir attributes along with this attribute. The language and direction (RTL, or right to left) will not be changed but the text margin will be on the left by default.

Listing 6.2 Grouping text

```
<body>
<div id="1">
<span id="3">
Here is the text of this document.
</span>
<span id="4">
Even though there are returns between the
```

```
lines, the browser will render only the text
and ignore the extra white space.
</span>
</div>
<br />
<br />
<div id="2">
<span id="5">
The blank line above, for example, will not display as a blank line.
Only the width of the window may make the text wrap and appear as
separate lines.
</span>
</div>
</body>
```

Separating this text into divisions and spans only improves the look if you include the linebreak (<br />). But with the unique id attribute for each element, you can change the look of the text by applying fonts, colors, and text sizes to each ID. External stylesheets can apply different font values for each ID, depending on the device that will be displaying the text.

The linebreak is always an empty element in XHMTL and is used to force the browser to insert a return. This linebreak character is the carriage return, linefeed, or a combination of carriage return and linefeed, depending upon the platform displaying the text. The BR character does not insert a blank line but returns to the default left margin of the text. This element can contain the attributes id, class, title, style, and clear. The clear attribute can be used to assure that text flowing around another object begins again after the object is completely rendered.

Text can also be grouped with the paragraph element, <p>, which is never an empty element. How the text content in a paragraph is rendered in the browsers may be variable, but the paragraph element typically provides a blank line after the text. Sometimes the <p> element is used to align the text to the left, right, or center. Rather than the <p> element, use the <div> and <span> elements to group your text and rely upon stylesheets to format the text.

To visually separate text or other objects, the element <hr> (horizontal rule) is used. The attributes for <hr> that have been deprecated in favor of using stylesheet controls are align, noshade, size (height in pixels or percent), and width (in pixels or percent). The standard way the <hr> is rendered is a two-tone line. If the attribute noshade is set, the <hr> is rendered as a solid color. The other attributes of the horizontal rule element are id, class, lang, dir, title, style, onclick, ondblclick, onmousedown, onmouseup, onmouseover, onmousemove, onmouseout, onkeypress, onkeydown, and onkeyup.

Specialized types of text are headings, addresses, quotations, structured text, and preformatted text and are described below.

Headings

The <hx> element can display differently in various browsers but always includes a new line after the heading. The original purpose of headings was to emphasize more important sections of a document. There are six values for the "x" and this element is never empty. The attributes of <hx> are id, class, lang, dir, title, style, align, onclick, ondblclick, onmousedown, onmouseup, onmouseover, onmousemove, onmouseout, onkeypress, onkeydown, and onkeyup. Search engines may use these elements to outline your document. The lowest number in the <hx> element is for the most important topics of the document. The example code below displays in Internet Explorer 5.0, Macintosh as in Figure 6.1:

```
<body>
<h1>Chapter 1</h1>
<h2>Sub-Chapter</h2>
<h3>Topic</h3>
<h4>Sub-Topic</h4>
<h5>Extra Information</h5>
<h6>Final Heading Type</h6>
</body>
```

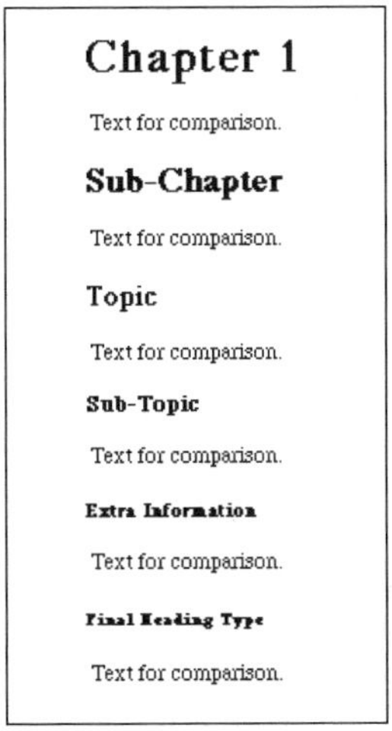

Figure 6.1: Head elements in a browser

Addresses

The <address> element is a convenient place to list contact information. This may be rendered as italic or emphasis font in the web browser. The <address> element may also be used by the search engines and should be used for specific and consistent information about the owner or host of the web site. The attributes for <address> are id, class, lang, dir, title, style, align, onclick, ondblclick, onmousedown, onmouseup, onmouseover, onmousemove, onmouseout, onkeypress, onkeydown, and onkeyup. An example of the <address> element is provided below.

```
<address>
Your Name<br />
Your Company<br />
yourwebsite.com
</address>
```

Quotations

Double quotes (") and single quotes or apostrophes (') are used in the HTML, XHTML, and XML markup. To specify a section of text as a quotation, two special elements, <blockquote> and <q>, are used rather than displaying the text with the quote characters. Longer quotations are displayed using <blockquote> and may be rendered as indented text on the left and right margins. Shorter quotes displayed with <q> may be rendered with quote marks automatically by the browser and may be nested for quotes within quotes. If you wish to indicate these quote characters specifically, use the entities " (") and ' ('), but do not use them in the <blockquote> or <q> contents.

An example of <blockquote> and <q> is shown in Listing 6.3. These two elements are never empty and may have attributes. A special attribute of <blockquote> or <q>, cite, is used to specify the source of the document as a URI. These elements have the attributes id, class, lang, dir, title, style, onclick, ondblclick, onmousedown, onmouseup, onmouseover, onmousemove, onmouseout, onkeypress, onkeydown, and onkeyup.

Listing 6.3 Quotations in the HTML document

```
<body>
Quotations:
<blockquote>
Now is the winter of our discontent. All good boys do fine. One potato,
two potato, three potato, four.
```

```
</blockquote>
<q>
Now is the winter of our discontent.
</q>
</body>
```

The above displays as:

```
    Now is the winter of our discontent. All good boys do fine. One
    potato, two potato, three potato, four.
    "Now is the winter of our discontent."
```

Structured Text

Although a goal of XML and HTML is to separate the formatting from the text of the document, some structure can be applied to text to make it stand out in the document. The use of structured text can also give the document standards, which can be used to search for key words or phrases in the document. Listing 6.4 shows the code for EM, STRONG, DFN, CODE, SAMP, KBD, VAR, CITE, ABBR, ACRONYM, SUB, and SUP. The rendering of these format elements may be different in various browsers and may be ignored in hand-held devices. Carefully consider the result if these elements are nested within each other or with other elements. A subscript and superscript structure should never be used for the same text, for example. The structure elements are never empty and may contain attributes.

Listing 6.4 Structured text elements

```
<em>For emphasis</em>
<strong>Stronger emphasis</strong>
<dfn>defining instance of the enclosed term</dfn>
<code>fragment of computer code</code>
<samp>sample output</samp>
<kbd>text to be entered from the keyboard by the user</kbd>
<var>variable or program argument</var>
<cite>citation or reference</cite>
<abbr>abbreviation</abbr>
<acronym>acronym</acronym>
subscript: H<sub>2</sub>O is the chemical abbreviation for water
superscript: the Area of a circle can be found with π<sup>2</sup>
```

The attributes of these elements are id, class, lang, dir, title, style, onclick, ondblclick, onmousedown, onmouseup, onmouseover, onmousemove, onmouseout, onkeypress, onkeydown, and onkeyup.

The following structured text elements have been deprecated as style attributes, and stylesheets should be used to replace them.

```
<b>bold</b>
<i>italic</i>
<u>underline</u>
```

Preformatted Text

Another way to present text that keeps the white space for multiple spaces and returns is to use the <pre> element. The width attribute has been deprecated, but it was used to maintain a length in characters of the preformatted text. This attribute should no longer be used. The rendering of the text in this element may be monospaced font to keep the spacing the same for each letter. In this way, a simple table can be displayed with white space padding between the columns. This element also has the attributes id, class, lang, dir, title, style, onclick, ondblclick, onmousedown, onmouseup, onmouseover, onmousemove, onmouseout, onkeypress, onkeydown, and onkeyup. While other elements can be within the <pre> element, it should not contain other <pre> elements, or <img> (images), <object>, <sub>, or <sup> elements. The following listing shows a sample of this type of text.

Listing 6.5 Preformatted text code and result

```
<pre>Now is the winter of our discontent.
All good boys do fine.
One potato,     two potato,     three potato,     four.
</pre>
```

This displays as:

```
Now is the winter of our discontent.
All good boys do fine.
One potato,     two potato,     three potato,     four.
```

The PRE element is rarely used. Tables and stylesheets are more often used to place the text in precise locations.

6.32 Listed Items in HTML

An outline can be included in HTML and XHTML by using list elements. There are unordered lists or bulleted lists (<ul>), ordered lists or numbered lists (<ol>), and definition lists (<dl>). Two other list types, <menu> and <dir> (directory), have been deprecated.

The unordered list <ul> displays, by default, the bullet or disc before every list item (<li>). The type attribute for <ul> could previously specify disc, square, or circle. This attribute has been deprecated in favor of using stylesheets. Unordered lists can be nested as seen in Listing 6.6 and Figure 6.2.

Listing 6.6 Unordered list

```
<ul>
    <li>item one</li>
    <li>item two
        <ul>
            <li>sub-item one</li>
            <li>sub-item two</li>
        </ul>
    </li>
    <li>item three</li>
</ul>
```

Unordered Lists

- item one
- item two
  - sub-item one
  - sub-item two
- item three

Figure 6.2: Unordered lists

Ordered lists are similar to an outline document and can have the type attributes "1" (numeric), "a" (lowercase alphabet), "A" (uppercase alphabet), "i" (small Roman numeral), and "I" (large Roman numeral). The type attribute for ordered lists has also been deprecated. Listing 6.7 shows the code of a numbered list and an outline, which are shown in Figure 6.3. If ordered lists are nested, each level may indent when rendered.

Listing 6.7 Ordered lists

```
<div>Ordered Lists
    <ol type="1">
        <li>line one</li>
        <li>line two</li>
        <li>line three</li>
    </ol>
</div>
<div>Outline
    <ol type="I">
        <li>Part one
            <ol type="A">
                <li>Section one</li>
                <li>Section two
                    <ol type="a">
                        <li>subsection one</li>
                        <li>subsection two</li>
```

```
                    </ol>
                </li>
            </ol>
        </li>
        <li>Part two</li>
    </ol>
</div>
```

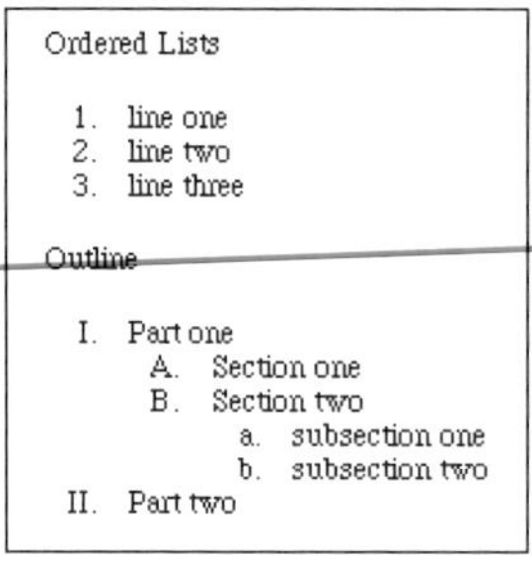

```
Ordered Lists

  1. line one
  2. line two
  3. line three

Outline

  I. Part one
       A. Section one
       B. Section two
            a. subsection one
            b. subsection two
  II. Part two
```

Figure 6.3: Ordered lists

Definition lists (<dl>) use the elements <dt> (definition term) and <dd> (definition). This kind of list might be used to display a glossary of terms. The code for a definition list and the result is shown in Listing 6.8.

Listing 6.8 Definition lists

```
<div>Glossary
    <dl>
        <dt>HTML</dt>
        <dd>Hypertext Markup Language</dd>
        <dt>XHTML</dt>
        <dd>Extensible Hypertext Markup Language</dd>
        <dt>XML</dt>
        <dd>Extensible Markup Language</dd>
    </dl>
</div>
```

```
Glossary

   HTML
       Hypertext Markup Language
   XHTML
       Extensible Hypertext Markup Language
   XML
       Extensible Markup Language
```

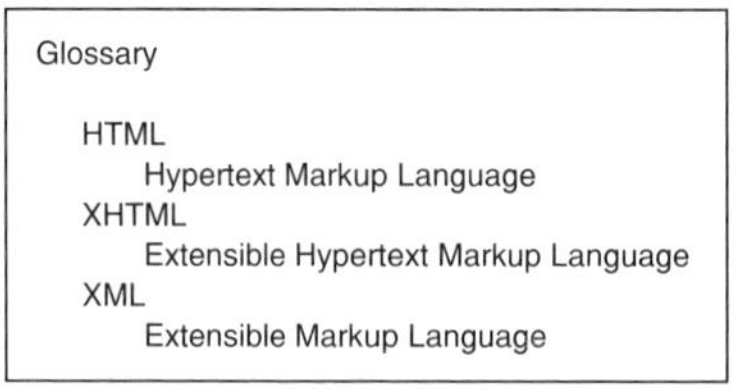

Figure 6.4

Unordered lists, ordered lists, and definition lists may have the attributes id, class, lang, dir, title, style, onclick, ondblclick, onmousedown, onmouseup, onmouseover, onmousemove, onmouseout, onkeypress, onkeydown, and onkeyup.

6.33 Presentation of the Web Page with the TABLE Element

The <table> element is often used to place text and images within rows and columns. The table has greater flexibility than using the <pre> element. The <table> has the elements <caption> (title for the table), <tr> (table row), and <td> (table definition or cell). The rows can be grouped with the elements <thead> (table header), <tfoot> (table footer), and <tbody> (main table rows). The columns of the table can be grouped with the elements <colgroup> and <col>. A simple table is shown in Listing 6.9 and Figure 6.5.

You should not attempt to simulate desktop publishing by using tables to place objects in a browser window. Stylesheet commands, which set the position of objects, may be better suited for this and give more control.

The document "Request For Comment (RFC) 1942," found at http://www.faqs.org/rfcs/rfc1942.html, states, "The (table) model is designed to work well with associated style sheets but does not require them. It also supports rendering to Braille, or speech, and exchange of tabular data with databases and spreadsheets." The latest version of the HTML 4.01 specification, http://www.w3.org/TR/html401, "11.1 Introduction to tables," states, "The HTML table model allows authors to arrange data—text, preformatted text, images, links, forms, form fields, other tables, etc.—into rows and columns of cells." The <table> element and its associated subelements are designed to group information for display on various devices. Depending upon the complexity of the table, such as a table within a table, the result may or may not be desirable. Great caution should be taken to test the results on the devices that will be displaying these tables.

Some browsers will wait until a table is fully loaded from the server before drawing it on the web page. Large and complex tables may take much longer to render. Group the design of a web page into smaller tables rather than complex nested tables.

Listing 6.9 Simple table

```
<body>
<table summary="This is the test table">
      <caption>Test Table</caption>
      <tr>
            <td>_Row_1_Cell_1_</td>
            <td>_Row_1_Cell_2_</td>
      </tr>
```

```
    <tr>
        <td>_Row_2_Cell_1_</td>
        <td>_Row_2_Cell_2_</td>
    </tr>
    <tr>
        <td>_Row_3_Cell_1_</td>
        <td>_Row_3_Cell_2_</td>
    </tr>
</table>
</body>
```

Test Table

_Row_1_Cell_1_	_Row_1_Cell_2_
_Row_2_Cell_1_	_Row_2_Cell_2_
_Row_3_Cell_1_	_Row_3_Cell_2_

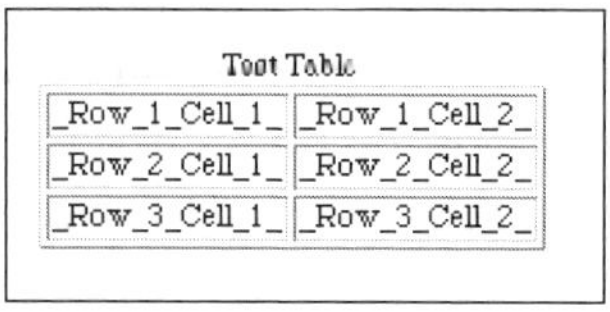

Figure 6.5: Simple table in a browser

TABLE Attributes

The summary attribute describes the table. Screen readers or Braille readers may use this attribute to explain the structure of the table. The summary is not a required attribute for the TABLE element.

The outline of the table is set by the border attribute. This attribute previously was always on by default and 1 pixel wide, unless you specified <table border="0">. Current specifications add frame and rules attributes to work with the border size. The frame is the outside border and the rules are the borders between rows and cells. External or internal stylesheets can control the <table> attributes, rather than including the styles in the element. In some browsers, the border color can be controlled.

The frame attribute may contain one of these values:

void	The border has no sides and is the default value.
above	Only the top of the border is rendered.
below	The bottom side only is rendered.
hsides	The top and bottom border sides are rendered.
vsides	The right and left sides are rendered.
lhs	The left-hand border is rendered.
rhs	The right-hand border is rendered.
box	All four sides are rendered, same as frame="border".
border	All four sides are rendered.

The rules attribute may contain one of these values:

none	No rules. This is the default value.
groups	Rules will appear between row groups.
rows	Rules will appear between rows only.
cols	Rules will appear between columns only.
all	Rules will appear between all rows and columns.

The element and its default attributes, <table border="0" frame= "void" rules="none">, will produce a table with no border around the items in the table. This may be the most flexible for various devices. The value "0" for border implies that there is no frame or rules, so these values need not be specified. A border of 1 or more pixels assumes that frame="border" and rules="all" unless otherwise specified.

The width attribute may have the value in pixels or a percentage. Using precise pixels does not allow the table to adjust for a variety of screen resolutions but may be desirable when placing text and graphics in precise locations on the screen. When you use percentage rather than pixels, the table will adjust to the viewer's choice of width and font preferences. The instruction <table width="50%"> will be drawn half the width of the screen. Do not mix pixels and percentages, as some browsers do not render the table width properly.

To save the viewer from scrolling to see the full table, consider designing a maximum width of 540 pixels. If the screen resolution is 72 pixels per inch, 540 pixels equates to 7½ inches. On a web page designed for printing or viewing at 640x480 screen size, 540 pixels is the best width for the table. If, however, you are reasonably sure that your viewers have monitors set to 800 or greater screen widths, you may safely design a table at a greater pixel width.

The align attribute has been deprecated if you are using strict XHTML but may be used to allow the flow of text around the <table> object. The values for align are "left", "right", and "center". Text will flow around the <table> only with the "left" or "right" alignment. These values can also be set with a stylesheet. An example of this is shown in Listing 6.10 and Figure 6.6.

Listing 6.10 Text flow around a table

```
<table border="1" align="right" width="200">
    <tr>
        <td>_Row_1_Cell_1_</td>
        <td>_Row_1_Cell_2_</td>
```

```
	</tr>
	<tr>
		<td>_Row_2_Cell_1_</td>
		<td>_Row_2_Cell_2_</td>
	</tr>
	<tr>
		<td>_Row_3_Cell_1_</td>
		<td>_Row_3_Cell_2_</td>
	</tr>
</table>The element and its default attributes, &lt;table border="0"
frame="void" rules="none"&gt;, will produce a table with no border around
the items in the table. This may be the most flexible for various devices.
The value "0" for border implies that there is no frame or rules, so these
values need not be specified. A border of 1 or more pixel assumes that
frame=border and rules=all, unless otherwise specified.
```

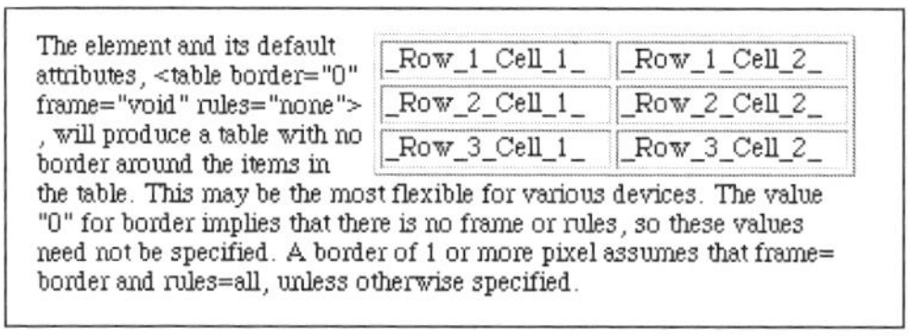

_Row_1_Cell_1_	_Row_1_Cell_2_
_Row_2_Cell_1_	_Row_2_Cell_2_
_Row_3_Cell_1_	_Row_3_Cell_2_

The element and its default attributes, <table border="0" frame="void" rules="none">, will produce a table with no border around the items in the table. This may be the most flexible for various devices. The value "0" for border implies that there is no frame or rules, so these values need not be specified. A border of 1 or more pixel assumes that frame= border and rules=all, unless otherwise specified.

Figure 6.6: Text flowing around a table in a browser

Two more <table> attributes, cellpadding and cellspacing, are independent of the table border attributes. The values can be specified in pixels or a percentage. The cellpadding places white space around all sides of the contents of all cells in the tables. This keeps text, for example, away from the sides of the cell. Cellspacing is the width of the border around each cell or between cells. These values are considered when rendering a fixed-width table. If cellpadding and cellspacing are not specified, the browser may assign a default. Include these attributes and values if you want to control how the table is rendered in the browser.

The attribute bgcolor (color of the table borders, rows, and cells) can be assigned with a stylesheet or included in the table definition. If individual colors are assigned to rows or cells, these will override the background color of the table. The border color may be determined by the table bgcolor. You can set the table bgcolor to one value and each cell bgcolor to another value. Tables can also have the attributes id, class, lang, dir, title, style, onclick, ondblclick, onmousedown, onmouseup, onmouseover, onmousemove, onmouseout, onkeypress, onkeydown, and onkeyup.

TABLE Rows

The attributes for the table row (<tr>) will be used for the table cells (<td>) unless specified for each cell. The attributes for <tr> are bgcolor, align, char, charoff, valign, id, class, lang, dir, title, style, onclick, ondblclick, onmousedown, onmouseup, onmouseover, onmousemove, onmouseout, onkeypress, onkeydown, and onkeyup. Rows can be grouped with the elements <thead>, <tfoot>, and <tbody>. The HTML 4.01 specification describes these grouping elements as the ability to scroll the "table bodies independently of the table head and foot." This would also add the head and foot information to long tables that need to be printed on multiple pages. Tables using these group elements can have multiple <tbody> elements, but they are listed after <thead> and <tfoot>. An example table is shown in Listing 6.11 and Figure 6.7. The display of the <tbody> is between the <thead> and <tfoot>, even though the code lists the TBODY element after the THEAD and TFOOT elements.

Listing 6.11 Table with header and footer

```
<table border="1">
	<caption>Table with header and footer </caption>
	<thead>
		<tr>
			<th>column one </th>
			<th>column two </th>
		</tr>
	</thead>
	<tfoot>
		<tr>
			<td>end one </td>
			<td>end two </td>
		</tr>
	</tfoot>
	<tbody>
		<tr>
			<td>_Row_1_Cell_1_ </td>
			<td>_Row_1_Cell_2_ </td>
		</tr>
		<tr>
			<td>_Row_2_Cell_1_ </td>
			<td>_Row_2_Cell_2_ </td>
		</tr>
	</tbody>
</table>
```

Table with header and footer

column one	column two
_Row_1_Cell_1_	_Row_1_Cell_2_
_Row_2_Cell_1_	_Row_2_Cell_2_
end one	end two

Figure 6.7: Table headers and footers in a browser

The Table Cell

Text or graphics are contained in table cells. A special table cell, <th>, can be used to specify a heading label. The <th> can be used for column labels or row labels. While not a requirement for tables, the <th> element can be used to distinguish it from the normal table cell. By default, the browser may render the <th> as centered and bolded text. Stylesheets can be used to override the default settings.

The <td> has one of two special attributes, rowspan and colspan, that are used to allow the text or images to be rendered over more than one cell without the borders between these cells. An example table with rows and columns spanning is shown in Listing 6.12 and Figure 6.8. A table cell with rowspan="2" will be drawn the depth of two cells. A table cell with colspan="2" will be drawn with the width of two cells. With the careful use of both of these attributes, you can display your web contents in unique ways.

Listing 6.12 Table rows and columns with span

```
<table border="1">
      <tr>
            <td rowspan="2">_Row_1_Cell_1_</td>
            <td rowspan="2"></td>
            <td colspan="3">_Row_1_Cell_3_</td>
      </tr>
      <tr>
            <td colspan="3">_Row_2_Cell_3_</td>
      </tr>
      <tr>
            <td>_Row_3_Cell_1_</td>
            <td>_Row_3_Cell_2_</td>
            <td>_Row_3_Cell_3_</td>
            <td>_Row_3_Cell_4_</td>
            <td>_Row_3_Cell_5_</td>
      </tr>
      <tr>
            <td>_Row_4_Cell_1_</td>
            <td>_Row_4_Cell_2_</td>
            <td>_Row_4_Cell_3_</td>
```

```
            <td>_Row_4_Cell_4_</td>
            <td>_Row_4_Cell_5_</td>
      </tr>
</table>
```

_Row_1_Cell_1_		_Row_1_Cell_3_		
		_Row_2_Cell_3_		
_Row_3_Cell_1_	_Row_3_Cell_2_	_Row_3_Cell_3_	_Row_3_Cell_4_	_Row_3_Cell_5_
_Row_4_Cell_1_	_Row_4_Cell_2_	_Row_4_Cell_3_	_Row_4_Cell_4_	_Row_4_Cell_5_

Figure 6.8: Table row and cell span in a browser

The attributes nowrap, width, and height have been deprecated from the <td> and <th> elements. If these are not specified, the table can be rendered more loosely. They can be set by stylesheet if necessary. The attributes align and valign (vertically align) are used to place the cell contents within the cell. The attribute align can have the values "left", "right", "center", "justify", or "char". The values for the attribute valign are "top", "middle", "bottom", or "baseline". The text of a cell can be further defined by using the char attribute. When char="." is used with align="char", the text is aligned on the decimal point of numbers. The <td> attribute charoff is the offset (in pixels) for the first text character in the cell. This attribute is a handy way to display an indented paragraph. The alignment may render differently in your browser. Other attributes for the <td> element are bgcolor, id, class, lang, dir, title, style, onclick, ondblclick, onmousedown, onmouseup, onmouseover, onmousemove, onmouseout, onkeypress, onkeydown, and onkeyup.

Table Within a Table

The table within a table can further refine the alignment of elements on the web page. Although Cascading Style Sheets could also be used for precise placement of elements, the table can use stylesheet commands to change the look of the original document. An example of a nested table, or table within a table, is shown in Listing 6.13 and Figure 6.9. Use the table within the table carefully and remember that the display of any table on a smaller device, such as the mobile phone, may be prohibitive. A stylesheet can accommodate the difference in displays by changing the table structure.

Listing 6.13 Nested tables

```
<table border="1">
      <tr>
            <td>
                  <table border="1">
```

```
                <tr>
                    <td>_Row_1_Cell_1_</td>
                    <td>_Row_1_Cell_2_</td>
                </tr>
                <tr>
                    <td>_Row_2_Cell_1_</td>
                    <td>_Row_2_Cell_2_</td>
                </tr>
                <tr>
                    <td>_Row_3_Cell_1_</td>
                    <td>_Row_3_Cell_2_</td>
                </tr>
            </table>
        </td>
        <td>_Row_1_Cell_2_</td>
        <td>_Row_1_Cell_3_</td>
    </tr>
    <tr>
        <td>_Row_2_Cell_1_</td>
        <td>_Row_2_Cell_2_</td>
        <td>_Row_2_Cell_3_</td>
    </tr>
</table>
```

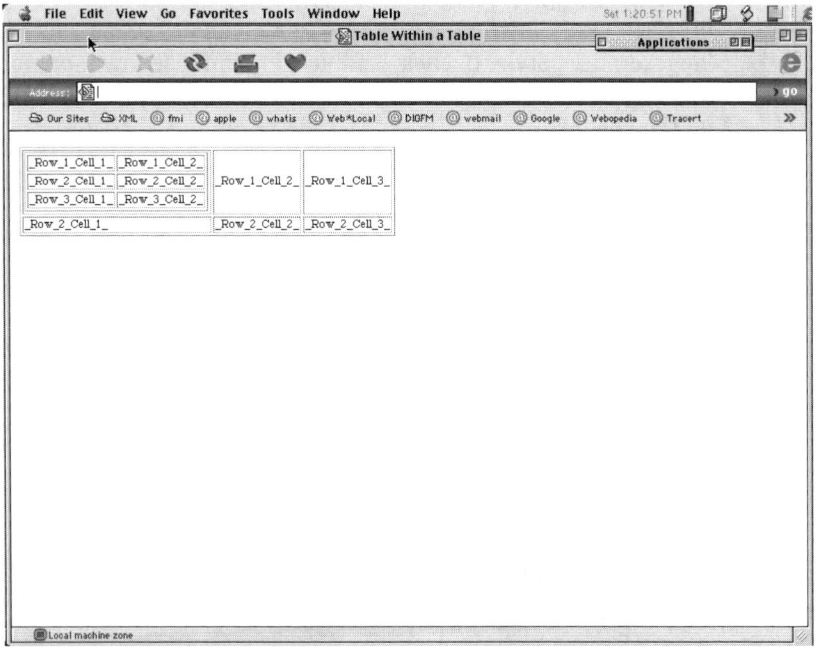

Figure 6.9: Nested tables in a browser

6.34 Hyperlinks and Anchors

Web pages are highly distinguishable from other text documents with the addition of hyperlinks. Navigating from page to page puts the control into the hands of the user. Any page can be connected to multiple other pages. The CGI requests to Web Companion can be hyperlinks. The requests can return precise results or variable results controlled by the user.

The standard hyperlink uses the anchor element <a>. The primary attribute for the <a> element is the href, or hyperlink reference, with the value being the location of the linked document. The anchor element may, alternatively, have a name attribute. This name is an anchor to a location on the current page. Hyperlinks can use the anchor to navigate to a precise location on a page. The location is a fragment of the page. Examples of anchors and hyperlinks are shown in Listing 6.14. Even if the anchor element is empty, as when it uses the name attribute, it uses the start tag and end tag.

Listing 6.14 Anchor element

```
<a name="placeholder1"></a>
<!-- some content here -->
<!-- a link to this anchor will jump here -->
<a name="placeholder2"></a>
<!-- Web Companion request as a hyperlink -->
<a href="fmpro?-db=myfile.fp5&-lay=web&-format=-fmp_xml&id=123&-find>FIND
  123</a>
<!-- more page content -->
<div>
This is a link to the first <a href="#placeholder1">anchor</a> on this
  page.<br />
This is a link to <a href="page2#placeholder3">another page</a> and anchor.
</div>
<!-- a link to a larger image from a thumbnail -->
<a href="bigImage.jpeg"><img src="smallImage.jpeg" border="2" /></a>
```

The hyperlink can have other attributes, such as title, charset, lang, dir, type, rel, rev, shape, coords, tabindex, accesskey, id, class, target, style, onfocus, onblur, onclick, ondblclick, onmousedown, onmouseup, onmouseover, onmousemove, onmouseout, onkeypress, onkeydown, and onkeyup. The most common attribute for the <a> element may be the onclick call to a scripted event. An anchor element that uses the onclick attribute may not go to another location but may perform an action that loads another image. The next section defines the attributes that are used to perform an action.

Images can be hyperlinks by including the <a> element around the <img> element. By default, a border may appear around the hyperlinked image unless you specify the border value to be "0". The last line of Listing 6.14 shows a hyperlink around a small image. The link will display the larger image on a new page. A single image may have multiple hyperlinks by specifying a shape and the coordinates of the <area> element of the <map> element. See “Image Maps” in section 6.35.

Attributes for Script Calls

Links and anchors often have attributes with JavaScript or other event calls. But most objects on a web page can use these events. Read the full specifications for each object to see what attributes may be used. The following script attributes are defined in section 18.2.3 of the “HTML 4.01 Specification,” http://www.w3.org/TR/html401. These events may be handled with JavaScript or other scripts, including Cascading Style Sheet changes.

onload	The onload event occurs when the user agent finishes loading a window or all frames within a FRAMESET. This attribute may be used with BODY and FRAMESET elements.
onunload	The onunload event occurs when the user agent removes a document from a window or frame. This attribute may be used with BODY and FRAMESET elements.
onclick	The onclick event occurs when the pointing device button is clicked over an element. This attribute may be used with most elements.
ondblclick	The ondblclick event occurs when the pointing device button is double-clicked over an element. This attribute may be used with most elements.
onmousedown	The onmousedown event occurs when the pointing device button is pressed over an element. This attribute may be used with most elements.
onmouseup	The onmouseup event occurs when the pointing device button is released over an element. This attribute may be used with most elements.
onmouseover	The onmouseover event occurs when the pointing device is moved onto an element. This attribute may be used with most elements.
onmousemove	The onmousemove event occurs when the pointing device is moved while it is over an element. This attribute may be used with most elements.
onmouseout	The onmouseout event occurs when the pointing device is moved away from an element. This attribute may be used with most elements.

onfocus	The onfocus event occurs when an element receives focus either by the pointing device or by tabbing navigation. This attribute may be used with the following elements: A, AREA, LABEL, INPUT, SELECT, TEXTAREA, and BUTTON.
onblur	The onblur event occurs when an element loses focus either by the pointing device or by tabbing navigation. It may be used with the same elements as onfocus.
onkeypress	The onkeypress event occurs when a key is pressed and released over an element. This attribute may be used with most elements.
onkeydown	The onkeydown event occurs when a key is pressed down over an element. This attribute may be used with most elements.
onkeyup	The onkeyup event occurs when a key is released over an element. This attribute may be used with most elements.
onsubmit	The onsubmit event occurs when a form is submitted. It only applies to the FORM element.
onreset	The onreset event occurs when a form is reset. It only applies to the FORM element.
onselect	The onselect event occurs when a user selects some text in a text field. This attribute may be used with the INPUT and TEXTAREA elements.
onchange	The onchange event occurs when a control loses the input focus and its value has been modified since gaining focus. This attribute applies to the following elements: INPUT, SELECT, and TEXTAREA.

6.35 Images and Objects

Objects are the images, sounds, and applets that previously were included as separate elements in the HTML page. Images can be single graphic elements or image maps with multiple "hot spots" to be processed for further actions. Both the <img> element and <object> element can be used to display these graphic elements. Smaller devices may not render images and objects.

The <img> (image) element is always empty (no content) and has one required attribute, src. This src attribute is the location or source of the image. The image can be various file types, but common images shown on the web are .gif (Graphics Interchange Format), .jpeg or .jpg (Joint Photographic Experts Group), and .png (Portable Network Graphics). The source of this image can be the full absolute path to the image located on any server or the partial relative path to the image from the page on which it will be displayed.

Use the .gif format for images that have large sections of a single color, and use the .jpeg format for images that have a larger range of colors. Both formats use a compression algorithm, which allows the images to be displayed quickly in a web browser.

The alt attribute is beneficial for text-only browsers and screen readers, as the text of this attribute is displayed or spoken when an image cannot be viewed or displayed on the web page. The text of the alt attribute should be helpful in describing any missing image, as well. Well-formed XHTML documents use the alt attribute in the <img> element.

If a small clear image is used for padding space, alt=" " (single space) is often used. For bullet images, alt="*" is often used.

Another attribute for the <img> element is border, which is shown if border is specified or image is a hypertext link. The attribute longdesc is the location of a fuller description of the image than should be specified by the alt attribute. The name attribute may be used for scripting. The attributes id and class may be used in stylesheets to specify some of the values that previously were attributes. The deprecated attributes for the <img> element are width and height (size of the image), align (placement of image in relationship to any text that may flow around it), and hspace and vspace (the pixels or percentage of white space around the image). Some of these attributes are used in the code below:

```
<img src="butterfly.gif" border="0" alt="Monarch Butterfly" width="30
  height="58" align="center" />
<img id="234" name="btrfly1" src="http://www.mysite.com/images/
  butterfly.gif" alt="Monarch Butterfly" />
```

Additional attributes for the <img> element are lang, dir, title, and style. Images can use the script calls onclick, ondblclick, onmousedown, onmouseup, onmouseover, onmousemove, onmouseout, onkeypress, onkeydown, and onkeyup. Two more attributes for the image element are usemap, for classifying the image as a client-side image map, and ismap, for classifying the image as a server-side image map. The Web Companion server is not designed to process server-side image maps, so the client-side image map example is used in this chapter.

Image Maps

A single image can contain multiple hyperlinks by specifying the shape and coordinates in an image map. The server-side image map uses different elements and attributes and requires a server that can process the map. The browsers can render client-side image maps.

The <img> attribute usemap has the same value as the name of the <map> element. The image map is the name of the map and a list of the coordinates for the shapes rectangle, circle, and polygon (many-sided shape). A single graphic can be mapped with these coordinates and actions assigned to each defined shape. The <map> element contains the <area> elements, which define the shapes and can be located anywhere on the web page. A "default" shape is used to cover any of the image coordinates that are not specified by other shapes.

The rectangle shape is defined with these four coordinates: left, top, right, and bottom ("x1", "y1", "x2", "y2"). The center point of the shape and the radius size defines the circle: "cx", "cy", "cr". The polygon is composed of multiple pairs of "x" and "y" coordinates. The first set of coordinates and the last set are the same coordinates to close the polygon. A rectangle could also be defined with these four coordinates: x1, y1, x2, y2, x3, y3, and x4, y4 and back to starting point: x1, y1. An example image with its associated map is listed here.

```
<img src="stateMap.gif" alt="State Map" usemap="mystate" />
<map name="mystate">
     <area shape="default" />
     <area shape="rect" coords="10, 15, 50, 82" href="ourTown.html"/>
     <area shape="circle" coords="100, 100, 22" href="theCapital.html"/>
<!-- this is a triangle -->
     <area shape="poly" coords="120, 40, 160, 200, 80, 160, 120, 40"
       onmouseover="javascript:blink()" />
</map>
```

Each of the <area> elements can have these additional attributes: alt (text to be displayed for the shape), tabindex (the number of the <area> in the tab order for the page), accesskey, onfocus, and onblur.

Objects

The image can also be displayed with the <object> element. This element is more flexible for including images, sounds, and applets. Examples of the OBJECT element are shown in Listing 6.15. You can read more about HTML objects in section 13 of the "HTML 4.01 Specification," http://www.w3.org/TR/1999/REC-html401-19991224.

Listing 6.15 Image and object examples

```
<img src="butterfly.gif" border="0" alt="Monarch Butterfly" width="30
  height="58" align="center" />
<!-- as an object: -->
<object classID="butterfly.gif">
     <param name="width" value="30" valuetype="data" />
     <param name="height" value="58" valuetype="data" />
     <param name="border" value="0" valuetype="data" />
     Monarch Butterfly
</object>
```

```
<object codetype="application/java" classid="java:flight.class"
  width="400" height="200">
     Java applet to display an animation.
</object>
```

6.36 FRAME Your Web Pages

Frames in web pages are often misunderstood, misused, and sometimes a blessing in disguise. All web pages are displayed in a window. The <frameset> and <frame> elements can be used to divide a window into subsections. If the <frameset> is used in a web page, the <body> element is redundant and not needed in the page. When the window and each frame are given a name attribute, that name can be used with the target attribute in hyperlinks and form submissions. Listing 6.16 shows example target attributes.

Four target values can be used instead of a frame or window name. The "_top" value sends the new page to the current window and removes all frames. The "_self" value for the target attribute will send the page to the frame in which the <a> or <form> is displayed. The "_blank" target value will open a new window and display the new page there without closing the current window. When frames are inside other frames, as you will see shortly, the "_parent" value for the target will display the new page in the frame or window that is the parent of the current frame. Window or frame names are used in the target requests listed below.

Listing 6.16 Target attributes

```
<a href="newpage.html" target="_top">New Page</a>
<a href="frametop.htm" target="header">Change the Header</a>
<a href="fmpro?-db=thisTest.fp5&-lay=web&-format=-fmp_xml&-findany"
  target="ListView">Find Random</a>
<a href="miniPage.htm" target="_blank">Quick Mini Page</a>
<form action="fmpro" method="post" target="Main">
     <!-- additional information here -->
     <input type="hidden" name="-db" value="thisTest.fp5" />
     <input type="hidden" name="-lay" value="web" />
     <input type="hidden" name="-format" value="-fmp_xml" />
     <input type="hidden" name="-findany" value="" />
     <input type="submit" name="-findany" value="Find Random" />
</form>
```

Set up a window for subdivision by defining a <frameset>. A <frameset> can be composed of multiple rows or columns, and a <frameset> can be inside another <frameset>. The rows or cols attributes are a comma-separated list with the pixel width or percent of the space for each frame. If the width of a defined row or column is the wildcard character (*), the frameset divides the remaining space. A frameset with percent values will adjust to the size of the space as the window is resized manually. Other attributes for <frameset> and <frame> elements are id, class, style, onload, and onunload.

After the <frameset> is declared, an empty <frame> element is defined for each row or column in the <frameset>. Other pages use the name attribute for the <frame> element wherever a reference to a target is used. The src attribute is the page or image or other element to be displayed in the FRAME and may be empty. A frame width or height can be resized by the user unless you specify the attribute noresize="noresize". By default a <frame> will have a border, but you can remove it with the attribute frameborder="0". The scrolling attribute can have the values "auto" to add a scroll bar automatically if needed, "no" to prevent a scroll bar at the side or bottom from being added, or "yes" to implicitly render a scroll bar. The <frame> may be rendered away from the left and top margins of the window. Use the attributes marginwidth="0" and marginheight="0" to place the frame to the left, right, top, and bottom of the window or the next <frame>.

The following examples in Listings 6.17, 6.18, and 6.19 show simple <frameset> and <frame> definitions. A more complex example in Listing 6.20, frame.htm, uses multiple frames but references pages containing framesets. The more complex example allows greater flexibility for replacing the contents of frames.

Listing 6.17 Frameset with rows

```
<frameset rows="100,*,100">
      <frame src="top.gif" name="header" frameborder="0" scrolling="no"
        noresize="noresize" />
      <frame src="mainpage.html" name="main" />
      <frame src="bottom.gif" name="footer" frameborder="0" scrolling="no"
        noresize="noresize" />
</frameset>
```

Listing 6.18 Frameset with columns

```
<frameset cols="100,*,100">
      <frame src="left.html" name="menu" frameborder="0" scrolling="yes"
        noresize="noresize" />
      <frame src="mainpage.html" name="main" />
      <frame src="" name="ads" frameborder="0" scrolling="yes"
        noresize="noresize" />
</frameset>
```

Listing 6.19 Framesets with rows and columns

```
<frameset cols="100,*">
     <frame src="left.html" name="menu" frameborder="0" scrolling="yes"
       noresize="noresize" />
     <frameset rows="100,*">
          <frame src="top.gif" name="header" frameborder="0"
            scrolling="no" noresize="noresize" />
          <frame src="mainpage.html" name="main" />
     </frameset>
</frameset>
```

If the browser is very old, a <noframes> element may be used to display alternate content in the page. The transitional and frameset DTDs will support the <noframes> element. This element is never empty if it is used and may contain the attributes id, class, lang, dir, title, style, onclick, ondblclick, onmousedown, onmouseup, onmouseover, onmousemove, onmouseout, onkeypress, onkeydown, and onkeyup.

Frames can be used to hide any links followed from a page. The <title> from the first frameset is used as the title in the browser. The location field in the browser will contain the original link instead of the links to each additional page within the FRAMESET. Each page within a frame can be opened in a new browser window and the source code for each page can be viewed. This is a *not* a security feature, merely a way to temporarily hide information.

Frames Using Frameset Pages

The key to this exercise is creating pages with a <frameset>, which can load additional pages. Reference an outer frame by name and use a page with a frameset as the source. Then the contents of each frame can be replaced. Create each of the pages, placing them in a folder, and open Listing 6.20, frame.html, in your browser.

Listing 6.20 frame.html

```
<!DOCTYPE html PUBLIC "-//W3C//DTD XHTML 1.0 Frameset//EN"
     "http://www.w3.org/TR/2000/REC-xhtml1-20000126/DTD/
       xhtml1-frameset.dtd">
<html xmlns="http://www.w3.org/1999/xhtml" xml:lang="en" lang="en">
<head>
     <meta http-equiv="content-type" content="text/html; charset=utf-8" />
     <title>FRAMES DEMO - Home Page</title>
</head>
<frameset cols="25%,75%">
     <frame src="A.html" name="A" noresize="noresize" scrolling="no"
       marginwidth="0" marginheight="0" frameborder="0" />
```

```
    <frame src="B.html" name="B" marginwidth="0" marginheight="0"
      frameborder="0" />
    <noframes>Sample text if no frames....</noframes>
</frameset>
</html>
```

Listing 6.21 loads into the left side or navigation bar of the window (frame "A"). The page A.html contains links that target the right side of the window (frame "B"). Each link loads a different page or frameset into frame "B."

Listing 6.21 A.html

```
<!DOCTYPE html PUBLIC "-//W3C//DTD XHTML 1.0 Transitional//EN"
     "http://www.w3.org/TR/2000/REC-xhtml1-20000126/DTD/
       xhtml1-transitional.dtd">
<html xmlns="http://www.w3.org/1999/xhtml" xml:lang="en" lang="en">
<head>
     <meta http-equiv="content-type" content="text/html; charset=utf-8" />
     <title>FRAMES DEMO - Menu Bar</title>
</head>
<body bgcolor="#99FFFF">
<p>INDEX</p>
<p><a href="B.html" target="B">Home</a></p>
<p><a href="CD1.html" target="B">Page One</a></p>
<p><a href="CD2.html" target="B">Page Two</a></p>
</body>
</html>
```

Listing 6.22, B.html, is a single page that loads into frame "B" but may be viewed separately by opening it directly in the browser.

Listing 6.22 B.html

```
<!DOCTYPE html PUBLIC "-//W3C//DTD XHTML 1.0 Transitional//EN"
     "http://www.w3.org/TR/2000/REC-xhtml1-20000126/DTD/
       xhtml1-transitional.dtd">
<html xmlns="http://www.w3.org/1999/xhtml" xml:lang="en" lang="en">
<head>
     <meta http-equiv="content-type" content="text/html; charset=utf-8" />
     <title>FRAMES DEMO - Main Page</title>
</head>
<body bgcolor="#FFFFFF">
<h1 align="center">Welcome to <br />a demonstration <br />of Frames</h1>
<p align="center">Click on one of the links to go to that page.</p>
</body>
</Html>
```

The following listing, 6.23, CD1.html, will be loaded into frame "B" when the link "Page One" is clicked in page A.html. CD1.html is a frameset page with two frames ("C" and "D") and it loads two other pages, C1.html and D1.html.

Listing 6.23 CD1.html

```
<!DOCTYPE html PUBLIC "-//W3C//DTD XHTML 1.0 Frameset//EN"
    "http://www.w3.org/TR/2000/REC-xhtml1-20000126/DTD/
      xhtml1-frameset.dtd">
<html xmlns="http://www.w3.org/1999/xhtml" xml:lang="en" lang="en">
<head>
    <meta http-equiv="content-type" content="text/html; charset=utf-8" />
    <title>FRAMES DEMO - Document one frame</title>
</head>
<frameset rows="15%,85%">
    <frame src="C1.html" name="C" noresize="noresize" scrolling="no"
      marginwidth="0" marginheight="0" frameborder="0" />
    <frame src="D1.html" name="D" marginwidth="0" marginheight="0"
      frameborder="0" />
</frameset>
</html>
```

CD2.html in Listing 6.24 is also a frameset page. It redefines frames "C" and "D." The pages C2.html and D2.html are opened as two frames within the "B" frame. If this frameset page is opened in a new browser window, it merely creates the new frames "C" and "D" and loads the page.

Listing 6.24 CD2.html

```
<!DOCTYPE html PUBLIC "-//W3C//DTD XHTML 1.0 Frameset//EN"
    "http://www.w3.org/TR/2000/REC-xhtml1-20000126/DTD/
      xhtml1-frameset.dtd">
<html xmlns="http://www.w3.org/1999/xhtml" xml:lang="en" lang="en">
<head>
    <meta http-equiv="content-type" content="text/html; charset=utf-8" />
    <title>FRAMES DEMO - Document two frame</title>
</head>
<frameset rows="15%,85%">
    <frame src="C2.html" name="C" noresize="noresize" scrolling="no"
      marginwidth="0" marginheight="0" frameborder="0" />
    <frame src="D2.html" name="D" marginwidth="0" marginheight="0"
      frameborder="0" />
</frameset>
</html>
```

Listing 6.25, C1.html, is a plain page that may be used as a title or banner location. It gets loaded into frame “C” when frameset page CD1.html is loaded into frame “B.”

Listing 6.25 C1.html

```
<!DOCTYPE html PUBLIC "-//W3C//DTD XHTML 1.0 Transitional//EN"
      "http://www.w3.org/TR/2000/REC-xhtml1-20000126/DTD/
        xhtml1-transitional.dtd">
<html xmlns="http://www.w3.org/1999/xhtml" xml:lang="en" lang="en">
<head>
      <meta http-equiv="content-type" content="text/html; charset=utf-8" />
      <title>FRAMES DEMO - Title 1</title>
</head>
<body>
<h2 align="center">This is page one!</h2>
</body>
</html>
```

The following code for Listing 6.26, D1.html, has a hyperlink to open a plain document. Even though the D1.html page is loaded into frame “C,” the link can target frame “B,” which is the parent of frames “C” and “D.” Clicking the link will open the new page in the parent frame. If CD1.html is opened in the browser and not called by the link in A.html, the link in page D1.html will open in a new window named “B.”

Listing 6.26 D1.html

```
<!DOCTYPE html PUBLIC "-//W3C//DTD XHTML 1.0 Transitional//EN"
      "http://www.w3.org/TR/2000/REC-xhtml1-20000126/DTD/
        xhtml1-transitional.dtd">
<html xmlns="http://www.w3.org/1999/xhtml" xml:lang="en" lang="en">
<head>
      <meta http-equiv="content-type" content="text/html; charset=utf-8" />
      <title>FRAMES DEMO - Document 1</title>
</head>
<body>
<p>This is the text for Document one. You can see that the title is above.
  </p>
<p>If you have any links in this document, be sure to set the targets so
  that the link shows up in the correct frame or no frames. </p>
<p>Go to <a href="Plain.html" target="B">plain document</a> <b>in </b>this
  &quot;frame&quot;</p>
<p>This is dummy text to show that this frame does have scroll bars.
  -repeat this text - This is dummy text to show that this frame does have
  scroll bars.</p>
<p>This is dummy text to show that this frame does have scroll bars.
```

```
  -repeat this text - This is dummy text to show that this frame does have
  scroll bars. </p>
</body>
</html>
```

The next listing, 6.27 C2.html, is similar to Listing 6.25, C1.html. Both of these pages are loaded into the "C" frame, which is inside the "B" frame.

Listing 6.27 C2.html

```
<!DOCTYPE html PUBLIC "-//W3C//DTD XHTML 1.0 Transitional//EN"
      "http://www.w3.org/TR/2000/REC-xhtml1-20000126/DTD/
        xhtml1-transitional.dtd">
<html xmlns="http://www.w3.org/1999/xhtml" xml:lang="en" lang="en">
<head>
      <meta http-equiv="content-type" content="text/html; charset=utf-8" />
      <title>FRAMES DEMO - Title 2</title>
</head>
<body bgcolor="#CCCCFF">
<h2 align="center">This is page two!</h2>
</body>
</html>
```

Page D2.html in Listing 6.28 is loaded into frame "D" when frameset page CD2.html is loaded into frame "B." This page has a link that targets a new page to be loaded outside all frames and framesets. TARGET="_top" will load the new page in the parent window.

Listing 6.28 D2.html

```
<!DOCTYPE html PUBLIC "-//W3C//DTD XHTML 1.0 Transitional//EN"
      "http://www.w3.org/TR/2000/REC-xhtml1-20000126/DTD/
        xhtml1-transitional.dtd">
<html xmlns="http://www.w3.org/1999/xhtml" xml:lang="en" lang="en">
<head>
      <meta http-equiv="content-type" content="text/html; charset=utf-8" />
      <title>FRAMES DEMO - Document 2</title>
</head>
<body>
<p>This is the text for Document one. You can see that the title is above.
  </p>
<p>If you have any links in this document, be sure to set the targets so
  that the link shows up in the correct frame or no frames. </p>
<p>Go to <a href="Plain.html" target="_top">plain document</a> <b>out</b>
  of all frames. </P>
```

```
<p>This is dummy text to show that this frame does have scroll bars. -
  repeat this text - This is dummy text to show that this frame does have
  scroll bars. </p>
<p>This is dummy text to show that this frame does have scroll bars. -
  repeat this text - This is dummy text to show that this frame does have
  scroll bars. </p>
</body>
</html>
```

The simple page in Listing 6.29 is loaded into whichever frame is targeted by the link.

Listing 6.29 Plain.html

```
<!DOCTYPE html PUBLIC "-//W3C//DTD XHTML 1.0 Transitional//EN"
     "http://www.w3.org/TR/2000/REC-xhtml1-20000126/DTD/
       xhtml1-transitional.dtd">
<html xmlns="http://www.w3.org/1999/xhtml" xml:lang="en" lang="en">
<head>
     <meta http-equiv="content-type" content="text/html; charset=utf-8" />
     <title>Plain</title>
</head>
<body>
<h3 align="center">Plain page that stays within the frame....</h3>
<h3 align="center">Or NOT!</h3>
<h3 align="center">Click the Back button on your browser to return.</h3>
</body>
</html>
```

Frames can be nested and links will open new pages in the same frame or in another frame or window. If you use FRAMESET pages and FRAME elements, remember to target all hyperlinks to other sites to the "_top" of the window. If you forget to go outside of your frameset and you open another site containing frames, you may get very unpredictable results.

6.4 Deprecated HTML Elements

The following elements used for formatting text should no longer be used. If you are displaying on older browsers that cannot interpret stylesheet languages, you may have to use them. Older HTML code may also contain these elements. The following elements have been deprecated:

<applet>	This element loads Java applets. Use the <object> element.
<basefont>	This element occurs in the <head> element and sets the font size of the document. It may be overridden by individual <font> elements in the document. Use stylesheets.
<center>	This element may be used to center text, tables, and images. Use stylesheets or as the attribute align="center" in other elements.
<dir>	List type element
<font>	Along with the common attributes (face, color, and size), this element changed the style of the text. Use stylesheets.
<isindex>	This element allows a single line input. Use <form> and <input type="text">.
<listing>	A type of text format
<menu>	A list type format
<s>, <strike>	Strikethrough font style. Use stylesheets.

In addition, the font styles big, small, b (bold), and i (italic) can be set with stylesheets. The attributes for size, bgcolor, color, and align may all be controlled with stylesheets. The attributes of the <body> element, such as alink, vlink, link, and text, can all be set with a stylesheet. Many other elements and attributes have been deprecated. If you use the elements found in XHTML Basic, you will have greater flexibility in choice of display devices. XHTML Basic is discussed later in this chapter.

6.5 Using the FORM Element to Make HTTP Requests

The <form> element occurs within the body element but is included here to define how this element can be used with Web Companion to make HTTP requests. In section 5.2, "XML Request Commands for Web Companion," all of the requests were made with direct commands in the browser. In section 6.34, "Hyperlinks and Anchors," the anchor or hyperlink is used to send the request. The <form> children elements are <input>, <textarea>, <button>, <select>, and <option>.

The main attributes of <form> are action and method. The action attribute is the URL to the CGI, in this case Web Companion, and is required to have a value. The value for the Web Companion action is the root path to the Web folder. When the value of the action attribute is specified as "fmpro", "FMPRO", or "Fmpro", Web Companion can process the request. The action can also be a JavaScript call. The method attribute can be "get" or "post", with "get" as the default if no method is specified.

```
<form action="fmpro" method="post" target="_top">
<!-- other form elements here -->
</form>
```

If you use a <form> with <table> elements, the <form> elements must be around the <table> elements or entirely within a cell. You must not intersperse the form elements <input>, <select>, <textarea>, or <button> between table rows or cells (<tr> and <td>).

Another attribute for the <form> element is enctype. The value of this is the ContentType of the document being submitted. The default value is "application/x-www-form-urlencoded" if you do not specify an enctype. This attribute can be used with the <input type="file"> to upload attachments with the form submitted. The Web Companion is not designed to allow file uploads. Files can be uploaded with File Transfer Protocol (FTP) and a field submitted with the path to the file. Your action must be to another CGI or application server.

```
<form action="cgiCall" method="post" enctype="multipart/form-data">
<input type="file">
</form>
```

The other attributes for the <form> element are target, accept, accept-charset, name, id, class, lang, dir, style, title, onsubmit, onreset, onclick, ondblclick, onmousedown, onmouseover, onmousemove, onmouseout, onkeypress, onkeydown, and onkeyup.

6.51 Input Text

The most common <form> element for entering text is the <input> element. The <input> element has the type attribute to specify the element details. These types can be text for standard field entry and password for standard text entry with an asterisk to hide the entry.

The type="password" setting does not encrypt the entry; it only replaces every character with an asterisk, and the transmission of the entry is not secure. These two input types have a name attribute to specify where the data is to be stored. The value attribute is where the actual entry is made. If the value is not empty, typing over the contents can change it when the form is submitted. The size attribute is the number of characters to be displayed in the INPUT element. The maxlength attribute limits the number of characters that can be entered into the <input> field. The <input> element is always empty, as seen in the examples below:

```
<input type="text" name="firstName" value="Joe" size="30" />
<input type="text" name="state" value="" size="5" maxlength="2" />
<input type="password" name="userPass" value="Login here" size="20" />
```

Other <input> types are "checkbox" and "radio". These two <input> types are similar to the value list formats found in FileMaker Pro. The FileMaker Pro Help topic "Formatting fields to use a value list" can help you understand these two types of text formats in FileMaker Pro and in the browser. The check box allows more than one selection to be entered into the same field and is often rendered as a small square in the browser. The radio button is mutually exclusive; selecting one will deselect the other values for the same field. The radio button type may render as a small circle in the browser. Examples of these two <input> types are shown in Listing 6.30. You must specify a label for each element or the user will not know what is being checked. The checked attribute makes the default selection(s) for these elements.

Listing 6.30 Check boxes vs. radio buttons

```
<!-- any or all of these values may be selected -->
<input type="checkbox" name="choices" value="1" /> One<br />
<input type="checkbox" name="choices" value="2" checked="checked" />
  Two<br />
<input type="checkbox" name="choices" value="3" /> Three<br />
<input type="checkbox" name="choices" value="4" checked="checked" />
  Four<br />
<!-- only one of these values may be selected -->
<input type="radio" name="choices" value="1" checked="checked" /> One<br />
<input type="radio" name="choices" value="2" /> Two<br />
<input type="radio" name="choices" value="3" /> Three<br />
<input type="radio" name="choices" value="4" /> Four<br />
```

Multiline text is entered with the <textarea> element. This element has the attributes rows and cols to specify the visible number of lines of text (rows) and the number of characters (cols) for the width of the text area. This element is never empty and has the start and end tags. The <textarea> element does not use the value attribute to display the default content of the field. The text between the two tags is the actual content of the <textarea>.

```
<textarea rows="3" cols="40">This text will be displayed in a TEXTAREA
  box.</textarea>
```

By default, a scroll bar is rendered for this type of text input field in the browser. Other attributes for the <textarea> element are name, id, class, lang, dir, title, style, readonly, disabled, tabindex, onfocus, onblur, onselect, onchange, onclick, ondblclick, onmousedown, onmouseup, onmouseover, onmousemove, onmouseout, onkeypress, onkeydown, and onkeyup.

Select Menus

The <select> element allows the user to choose values in a pop-up menu or drop-down list. Specifying the attribute size renders the menu or list. If the size attribute has a value of more than 1, the list is rendered; otherwise the menu is rendered. More than one value can be selected in the list if the attribute multiple is set. The <select> element is never empty and contains the <option> element to display the choices. The attribute name specifies the field that will be populated by the value of the option selected.

The <option> element has the attribute value, which contains the value of the <select> element when the option is chosen. The <option> element may be empty but must contain the attribute label if the displayed text is to be different from the text of the value. The <option> tag may have a start and end tag with the text of the label between them. To display the text of any value by default, the attribute selected is set in the OPTION element.

Other attributes for the <select> and <option> elements are name, id, class, lang, dir, title, style, readonly, disabled, tabindex, onclick, ondblclick, onmousedown, onmouseup, onmouseover, onmousemove, onmouseout, onkeypress, onkeydown, and onkeyup. Examples of the <select> and <option> elements are shown in Listing 6.31.

Listing 6.31 SELECT and OPTION elements

```
<select name="color">
     <option value="Blue" />
     <option value="Red" selected="selected" />
     <option value="Green" />
     <option value="P" label="Purple" />
</select><br />
Choose your sizes: <select name="sizes" size="5">
     <option value="S">Small</option>
     <option value="M">Medium</option>
     <option value="L">Large</option>
     <option value="XL">Xtra Large</option>
</select>
```

Hidden Text

The INPUT element can be used to pass along hidden text when the form is submitted. Many times this is the name of the database (-db), the name of the layout (-lay), the format (-fmp_xml), and anything else you want to pass. The <input> element has the type attribute, which has a value of "hidden". This hides the name and value from being seen if the form is submitted with the "post" method. Examples of the hidden input element are shown in Listing 6.32.

The contents for an INPUT type="hidden" can be seen in the source code for the HTML document. This form element is *not* secure.

Listing 6.32 Hidden INPUT type

```
<input type="hidden" name="-db" value="myDatabase.fp5" />
<input type="hidden" name="-lay" value="web" />
<input type="hidden" name="-format" value="-dso_xml" />
<input type="hidden" name="-recid" value="12345" />
<input type="hidden" name="userName" value="Beverly Voth" />
```

The hidden input type can also be used to force an "empty" value when submitting data to Web Companion. This value is necessary for value list fields. Sometimes clearing all the values from check boxes, for example, does not clear them in the database when the form is submitted. Use the same name as the values list in the hidden input. An example of this usage is seen here:

```
I would like more information about: <br />
<input type="hidden" name="product" value="" />
<input type="checkbox" name="product" value="FMP" /> FileMaker Pro<br />
<input type="checkbox" name="product" value="FMD" /> FileMaker
  Developer<br />
<input type="checkbox" name="product" value="FMS" /> FileMaker Server<br />
<input type="checkbox" name="product" value="FMU" /> FileMaker
  Unlimited<br />
<input type="checkbox" name="product" value="FMM" /> FileMaker Mobile<br />
```

If the action is repeated with a hidden empty value, the form can be submitted when the user presses Return or Enter from the keyboard, instead of clicking the submit button with the mouse.

```
<input type="hidden" name="-find" value="" />
<input type="submit" name="-find" value=" FIND " />
```

6.52 Submitting the Form

The form must be submitted to CGI for processing. Until the user clicks the submit button or presses Return or Enter, the information just sits in the fields on the web page with the form. The INPUT element can have a type attribute with the value "submit". This tells the browser to send the data in the fields to the action value of the FORM element. The possible values for the name attribute of the submit input are seen in Listing 6.33. The value attribute is the text that will be displayed in the button when it is rendered in the browser.

Listing 6.33 Submit XML actions

```
<!-- CREATE A NEW RECORD -->
<input type="hidden" name="-new" value="" />
<input type="submit" name="-new" value=" ADD " />
<!-- EDIT A RECORD -->
<input type="hidden" name="-edit" value="" />
<input type="submit" name="-edit" value="Update" />
<!-- DELETE A RECORD -->
<input type="hidden" name="-delete" value="" />
<input type="submit" name="-delete" value="Delete!" />
<!-- FIND A RECORD -->
<input type="hidden" name="-find" value="" />
<input type="submit" name="-find" value=" BEGIN SEARCH " />
<!-- FIND ALL RECORDS -->
<input type="hidden" name="-findall" value="" />
<input type="submit" name="-findall" value="Show All Records" />
```

To clear the fields or reset to predefined values on the form, use the INPUT type attribute value of reset:

```
<input type="reset" name="reset" value="Clear the fields" />
```

A FORM may also be submitted by including a BUTTON element instead of the INPUT type. This method has more options than input type="submit" because an image can be used along with content. The attribute type can be one of three values: submit (default if no type is specified), reset, and button. The name attribute functions the same as the submit input. The value attribute is not used to label the button, but the content is used. This element is never empty and must contain an image or text:

```
<button type="submit" name="-find" value="">FIND <img src="findbutton.gif"
  border="0" /></button>
```

Image maps may not be used with the BUTTON element. The BUTTON element must not contain the other FORM elements.

The last value for the type attribute for the <button> element will perform any client-side script that is a part of the button. It is not used to submit a form. The attributes for the event calls are listed in the "Attributes for Script Calls" section earlier in this chapter. If the script is JavaScript, it must be declared on the same page as the BUTTON or referenced with the <link> element in the <head> element.

```
<button type="button" name="showMe" value="showMe" onclick=
  "doThisScript">SHOW ME!</button>
```

Other attributes for the <button> element are disabled, tabindex, accesskey, onfocus, onblur, id, class, title, lang, dir, style, onclick, ondblclick, onmousedown, onmouseover, onmousemove, and onmouseout.

You can read more about HTML elements in "HTML 4.01 Specification," http://www.w3.org/TR/html401, and "1.0: The Extensible Hypertext Markup Language XHTML," found at http://www.w3.org/TR/xhtml1.

6.53 Using Forms for XML Requests

The CGI requests in section 5.2, "XML Request Commands for Web Companion," were all made with the hyperlinks or direct inclusion in the browser address bar. Another method of sending information to Web Companion from a browser is the <form> element and associated elements. The attributes for the <form> element are method and action. Use the value "post" for the method in most cases. The action value is to Web Companion itself: "fmpro". If you are using a <frameset>, you can include the <form> attribute target with the value of the named window or frame. The following example is a basic <form> with hidden fields for some of the request values and is equivalent to the hyperlink "fmpro?-db=Xtests.fp5&-lay=web&-findall."

```
<form method="post" action="fmpro">
     <input type="hidden" name="-db" value="Xtexts.fp5" />
     <input type="hidden" name="-lay" value="web" />
     <input type="submit" name="-findall" value="Find All" />
</Form>
```

6.54 Fields in Your Database and FORM Elements

The other actions and XML commands will be covered shortly, but first we will discuss the fields in your database. The <input> element is most often used for adding data to your fields. The name attribute is the name of your field. This field must be on the layout or you will receive the error, "102 Field is missing." An advantage of using the <form> and <input> elements, instead of the hyperlink, is that field names (the value of the name attribute) are enclosed in quotes and field names with spaces can be used. Examples of the <input> element are listed below. The <input type="text"> is the standard method of passing data to a CGI. The type of field such as number, date, and time are also "text" in the browser but are entered correctly when passed to your FileMaker Pro database.

```
<input type="text" name="First Name" value="" size="30" />
<input type="text" name="zipcode" value="" size="10" maxlength="10" />
<input type="text" name="age" value="" size="5" />
<input type="text" name="OrderDate" value="" size="20" />
```

The check boxes, radio buttons, select pop-up lists, and menus can be used with the fields on your layout. The name attribute is the name of your field. Examples of these are shown in the following examples. Multiple input statements will be used with the same field name for checkboxes and radio buttons.

```
<!-- checkboxes: the field in the database is "colors" -->
Choose your colors:<br />
<input type="checkbox" name="colors" value="blue" /> Blue<br />
<input type="checkbox" name="colors" value="red" /> Red<br />
<input type="checkbox" name="colors" value="green" /> Green<br />
Choose your colors:
_ Blue
_ Red
_ Green
<!-- radio buttons: the field in the database is "fish" -->
Do you like to fish? <input type="radio" name="fish" value="yes" /> Yes
  <input type="radio" name="fish" value="no" checked="checked" /> No<br />
Do you like to fish? () Yes () No
<!-- select menu: the field in the database is "state" -->
<select name="state">
      <option value="" selected>- State -</option>
      <option value="AL">Alabama</option>
```

```
	<option value="AK">Alaska</option>
...
	<option value="WA">Washington</option>
</select>
```

Value list items may not clear if you uncheck or unselect all of the values. Add a hidden empty input to submit a clear command to the field. Use the same name as the field.

```
<input type="hidden" name="colors" value="" />
<input type="checkbox" name="colors" value="blue" />Blue
```

Text areas can also be used for input. If the field has contents, it is displayed between the start and end tags. For new data entry, remember to leave *no* content between the tags. If a return is inserted between the start and end tags for the <textarea> element, it may be interpreted as a space when the form is displayed in the browser or submitted for processing. You may have a space in the field in a search request, for example, and get unexpected results.

```
<textarea name="scrollableField" rows="10" cols="150"></textarea>
```

6.55 Actions

The <form> is generally submitted to the database with the submit button. This <input> element is where you place your action, such as find, edit, or delete. Include a hidden empty value for the same action to allow the browser to submit when the user presses the Enter key instead of clicking the button. The label for the button is taken from the value attribute. Example actions used to submit the forms are shown in the listings below. These are equivalent to the hyperlink actions in Chapter 2 and the results will be the same.

Listing 6.34 New record requests

```
<form method="post" action="fmpro">
	<input type="hidden" name="-db" value="Xtests.fp5" />
	<input type="hidden" name="-lay" value="web" />
	<input type="hidden" name="-format" value="-dso_xml" />
	First Name: <input type="text" name="firstname" value="Joe" /><br />
	Last Name: <input type="text" name="lastname" value="Brown" /><br />
	<input type="hidden" name="-new" value="" />
	<input type="submit" name="-new" value="New Record" />
</Form>
```

Listing 6.35 Duplicate records

```
<form method="post" action="fmpro">
     <input type="hidden" name="-db" value="Xtests.fp5" />
     <input type="hidden" name="-lay" value="web" />
     <input type="hidden" name="-format" value="-dso_xml" />
     <input type="hidden" name="-recid" value="1234" />
     <input type="hidden" name="-dup" value="" />
     <input type="submit" name="-dup" value="Duplicate Record" />
</form>
```

Listing 6.36 Edit records

```
<form method="post" action="fmpro">
     <input type="hidden" name="-db" value="Xtests.fp5" />
     <input type="hidden" name="-lay" value="web" />
     <input type="hidden" name="-format" value="-dso_xml" />
     <input type="hidden" name="-recid" value="36488" />
     First Name: <input type="text" name="firstname" value="Jane" /><br />
     Last Name: <input type="text" name="lastname" value="Doe" /><br />
     <input type="hidden" name="-edit" value="" />
     <input type="submit" name="-edit" value="Update Record" />
</form>
```

Listing 6.37 Delete records

```
<form method="post" action="fmpro">
     <input type="hidden" name="-db" value="Xtests.fp5" />
     <input type="hidden" name="-lay" value="web" />
     <input type="hidden" name="-format" value="-dso_xml" />
     <input type="hidden" name="-recid" value="36488" />
     <input type="hidden" name="-delete" value="" />
     <input type="submit" name="-delete" value="Delete Record" />
</form>
```

Listing 6.38 Find records with AND logical operator

```
<form method="post" action="fmpro">
     <input type="hidden" name="-db" value="Xtests.fp5" />
     <input type="hidden" name="-lay" value="web" />
     <input type="hidden" name="-format" value="-dso_xml" />
     First Name: <input type="text" name="firstname" value="Joe" />
     <input type="hidden" name="-lop" value="and" /> <br />
     Last Name: <input type="text" name="lastname" value="Brown" />
       <br />
     <input type="hidden" name="-find" value="" />
     <input type="submit" name="-find" value="Find Records" />
</Form>
```

Listing 6.39 Find records with -recid, -findany, or -findall

```
<!-- find only this record -->
     <input type="text" name="-recid" value="36488" /> <br />
     <input type="hidden" name="-find" value="" />
     <input type="submit" name="-find" value="Find Record" />
</form>

<!-- find any record -->
     <input type="hidden" name="-findany" value="" />
     <input type="submit" name="-findany" value="Random" />
</form>

<!-- find all records -->
     <input type="hidden" name="-findall" value="" />
     <input type="submit" name="-findall" value="All Records" />
</form>
```

Listing 6.40 View layout information request

```
<form method="post" action="fmpro">
     <input type="hidden" name="-db" value="Xtests.fp5" />
     <input type="hidden" name="-lay" value="web" />
     <input type="hidden" name="-format" value="-fmp_xml" />
     <input type="hidden" name="-view" value="" />
     <input type="submit" name="-view" value="Layout Info" />
</form>
```

The action requests for database names (-dbnames), layout names (-layoutnames), script names (-scriptnames), open database (-dbopen), and close database (-dbclose) follow the same format. Use the hidden field with the same name to allow browsers to submit upon pressing the Enter key.

6.56 Parameters in Forms

The parameters, like database (-db) and layout (-lay), can be hidden fields or can be input types to allow the user a choice. If you will be processing the results with a stylesheet, do not make the format (-format) a choice. The other parameters, such as operator (-op) or logical operator (-lop), more commonly may be user choices when performing a find.

The -recid parameter is required with -edit, -dup, and -delete actions and is optional with the -find action. The value of the -recid parameter will be returned in the XML result with all actions that return records. The user will rarely see this value, so it will be submitted as a hidden <input> element:

```
<input type="hidden" name="-recid" value="123456" />
```

The -modid (record modification count) is also returned with these records, but it is automatically set by FileMaker Pro. The -modid should not be set with a hyperlink or <form> <input> method.

Stylesheets may be specified by the user or set as hidden fields:

```
<input type="hidden" name="styletype" value="text/xsl" />
<input type="hidden" name="stylehref" value="Xtests.xsl" />
```

Logical operators may be hidden or input. To allow only specified values, use radio buttons or a pop-up menu. The logical operator (-lop) is placed between fields to specify the kind of find.

```
First Name: <input type="text" name="firstname" value="Joe" />
 <select name="-lop">
     <option value="and" selected="selected">AND</option>
     <option value="or">OR<option>
</select> <br />
Last Name: <input type="text" name="lastname" value="Brown" /> <br />
```

Comparison operators are often presented in a selection popup, too. Listing 5.22 shows an example of this selection type.

Your users may want to choose the number of records returned. The -max parameter can be an <input> element or <select>. The example showing this is in Listing 5.25.

Sorting can be by particular fields and sort order. Often this is by user choice. The following code shows these choices in the <form> elements <select> and <input type="radio">.

```
Sort by: <select name="-sortfield">
     <option value="firstname">First Name</option>
     <option value="lastname" selected="selected">Last Name</option>
     <option value="company">Company</option>
     <option value="invoiceNum">Invoice Number</option>
     <option value="invoiceDate">Invoice Date</option>
</select> <input type="radio" name="-sortorder" value="ascend" /> Ascending
  <input type="radio" name="-sortorder" value="descend" /> Descending<br />
```

Scripts are rarely a user choice but may be specified by the <input> element in a <form>.

```
<input type="hidden" name="-script" value="emailMe" />
```

The FORM elements are used to submit data and action commands to a FileMaker Pro database. The result returned depends upon the input submit name (the XML action command). If a -new, -delete, or -edit action is used, the single record is returned. If a -find, -findany, or -findall action is used, the result is the found set of records. A stylesheet may be called to display the XML results by using a hidden type INPUT element.

6.6 Claris Dynamic Markup Language

The Claris Dynamic Markup Language (CDML) is the basis for many of the CGI calls to Web Companion. There are additional commands in CDML that perform conditional actions, email from the browser, and replace the CDML elements with common HTML elements and attributes. The command set for CDML is limited and it is a proprietary language. The XML produced with the command set is sufficient to submit and retrieve field contents from a database. XML can be used with XSL, JavaScript, or other processing methods to format the results.

CDML is similar to a mail merge formatted page within a word processor. As Web Companion CGI encounters the proprietary language, it returns the information in the fields. XML processing by Web Companion is more like an export of the field contents with an export of the metadata about the fields. The raw data needs further processing but has more options for processing. Both methods use similar commands for the actions to interact with the database. XML and CDML requests cannot be mixed on the same page, but both XML and CDML may be used in the same web site.

The most notable difference between CDML and XML calls to Web Companion is the -format parameter. In CDML, this value is used to go to the next web page to display the results. In XML, the -format parameter is used to specify the schema to return the results. It is the diverse usage of the -format parameter that prevents CDML and XML from being displayed on the same page.

The intent of this section is not to teach you how to use CDML. The similarities may be made apparent as XML Stylesheet Language (XSL) is discussed in Chapter 7. You can download the "CDML Reference" and "CDML Tool" documents from FileMaker, Inc. at http://www.filemaker.com/downloads/. These are also available when you install FileMaker Pro Unlimited or FileMaker Developer. There are many other resources for learning CDML. These resources are listed in Appendix B.

6.61 Languages Related to HTML

i-mode

A subset of XHMTL that is used by many "smart phones" in Japan is called i-mode. The subset uses the same elements, but the content design should be altered to accommodate the small display. NTT DoCoMo, Inc., http://www.nttdocomo.com/home.html (click on i-mode), recommends displaying only 8 full-width Japanese characters (or 16 half-width characters). The screen displays approximately six lines at a time. A limited graphic can be used in the .gif format with a maximum size of 94 x 72 pixels. The elements that may be used when writing for i-mode are:

<!-- -->	(comment)
<html>	(root element)
<head>	(header information: title, base)
<title>	(title of the document)
<base>	(base URL)
<body>	(main content)
<div>	(text block)
<h>	(heading text)
<p>	(paragraph)
 	(linebreak)
<pre>	(preformatted text)
<blockquote>	(quoted text)
<a>	(anchor/hyperlink)
<img>	(image)
<hr>	(horizontal rule)
<dl><dt><dd>	(definition list)
<ul>	(unordered list: li)
<ol>	(ordered list: li)
<li>	(list item)
<form>	(form submission)
<input>	(text, hidden, submit, password types)
<select>	(selection list: option)
<option>	(option for selection list)
<textarea>	(multiline text field)

The command set is limited and input is accomplished with fields and selection lists only. There are no <table> elements, and frames are not allowed. There are no text formatting elements or script calls. The design of the content is meant for small devices, so each page should only have 2 to 5 Kb of data, including graphics.

FileMaker, Inc. has announced a new version of FileMaker Mobile. FileMaker Mobile for i-mode is only being released in Japan, and the software will convert the database content to i-mode format. No design may be necessary, but if you plan to create custom pages, follow the above guidelines.

Compact HTML (cHTML) and XHTML Basic

Another subset of XHTML is also designed for smaller devices. Compact HTML allows for basic text, simple forms, images, and hyperlinks. Unlike i-mode, cHTML does allow tables and object support. The document "XHTML Basic," http://www.w3.org/TR/xhtml-basic is a recommendation for using these compact versions of HTML and XHTML. Some of these recommendations are listed below:

- Stylesheets are supported with the <link> element and should be external documents.
- Scripts are not supported as these may require events that interact with an operating system. The XHTML Basic documents may be viewed on multiple devices and may not support script events.
- Fonts are likely to be dependent upon the device. No formatting should be included in an XHTML Basic document. Stylesheets may be used for separate devices.
- Input may not occur on all devices, but basic forms may be included in XHTML Basic documents. The input buffer size may be limited on smaller devices.
- Simple tables may be included. The recommendations for tables in the document "Web Content Accessibility Guidelines 1.0," http://www.w3.org/TR/WAI-WEBCONTENT, should be followed.
- Frames should not ever be used when designing for multiple devices.

The XHTML Basic document must begin:

```
<!DOCTYPE html PUBLIC "-//W3C//DTD XHTML Basic 1.0//EN"
     "http://www.w3.org/TR/xhtml-basic/xhtml-basic10.dtd">
<html xmlns="http://www.w3.org/1999/xhtml">
```

The elements are similar to i-mode and the HTML elements in this chapter. The basic structure of the document uses head, title, meta, base, and body elements. Hyperlinks use the a (anchor) element. Text can be displayed with abbr, acronym, address, blockquote and q (quote), cite, code, dfn, em, h1...h6, kbd, samp, strong, var, div and span, pre, p (paragraph), and br (linebreak). Images can be displayed with img or object. Basic tables use the elements caption, table, tr, th, and td. Lists can be displayed as definition lists (dl, dt, and dd), unordered lists (ul and li), or ordered lists (ol and li). Basic forms use the elements form, input, label, textarea, select, and option.

Back to Basics

HTML started as a smaller set of elements and evolved to include tables, frames, and other multimedia content. Each browser may have had separated elements that would not get interpreted by the other browsers. In a LYNX browser, a common means of reading HTML text, many of these elements were prohibitive. Some elements are confusing to screen readers and simply too complex for mobile devices. A trend to separate the data and presentation begins with XML. However, the XML can use XHTML to display the content in a pleasing format. XML Stylesheet Language (XSL) can use commands to transform XHTML and XML into web pages. XSL is discussed in the next chapter.

Chapter 7

Extensible Stylesheet Language (XSL) and FileMaker Pro

An XML document can contain the data and metadata of fields and field contents from many sources. FileMaker Pro produces well-formed XML, which can be transformed into Hypertext Markup Language (HTML), Wireless Markup Language (WML), text, or other formats specific to various devices, including another XML document. Transformation for different devices from the same XML source document can be accomplished with the use of stylesheets.

The XML transformation process occurs by different methods. The most common method uses an Extensible Stylesheet Language (XSL) document embedded with commands to read the XML document tree and produce XML, HTML, WML, or other formats. Browsers that can read both XML and XSL documents will perform the transformation as a client-side process. In the second method, servers can be used to process the XML with stylesheets and transform XML into other formats. The results are sent to the client as transformed text, most commonly in HTML format. The third method to transform XML uses applications to convert the data into formats usable by other devices. This chapter discusses the transformation of the XML produced by FileMaker Pro with the use of XSL stylesheets. The stylesheets may be used with

FileMaker Pro 6 export or import, or with web-published XML from FileMaker Pro.

The document "Extensible Stylesheet Language (XSL) Version 1.0," http://www.w3.org/TR/xsl/, states that XSL is a language used for transforming XML as well as formatting the output. Formatting may be applied to different devices in unique ways. XSL encompasses the XSLT (Transformation) markup and the Formatting Objects markup (FO) along with the XPath and XPointer expressions for resolving the location of the elements and attributes to be transformed or formatted. It is beyond the scope of this chapter to cover all of the formatting capabilities of XSL.

The XSL commands listed here will be a general set in the XSLT 1.0 standard, which may also be usable by common web browsers to transform XML into HTML. The Xalan processor built into FileMaker Pro for use with import and export supports XSLT 1.0 and XPath 1.0. The document "XSL Transformations (XSLT) Version 1.0" found at http://www.w3.org/TR/xslt contains the XSLT 1.0 standards, and the document "XML Path Language (XPath) Version 1.0" found at http://www.w3.org/TR/xpath contains the XPath 1.0 standards. This chapter will further explain the XPath functions as they are used with XSLT and FileMaker Pro 6.

7.1 XSL is XML

XSL documents are written with rules and recommendations that follow the structure of well-formed and valid XML documents. If you open an XSL document with a text editor, you will see the familiar tree-like structure of XML with start, end, and empty markup tags. The transformations that are performed by the Extensible Stylesheet Language can be used to create XML documents, as well as other document formats.

The XSL document begins with the XML prolog:

```
<?xml version="1.0" ?>
```

The root element for the XSL document is <xsl:stylesheet>. This root element has the attribute "xmlns," for XML namespace. The value for the xmlns attribute has caused some controversy. An early adoption of XSL by Microsoft for use in the Internet Explorer browser uses the xmlns "http://www.w3.org/TR/WD-xsl." The current standard set by the World Wide Web Consortium uses the namespace "http://www.w3.org/1999/XSL/Transform." The version that you use will depend on the browser that is used to display the stylesheet. The examples in this chapter will use all the namespace declarations and qualify the browser type and version used with each. For XML import and export in FileMaker Pro, use the most current namespace declaration, "http://www.w3.org/1999/XSL/Transform."

```
<!-- current namespace declaration -->
<xsl:stylesheet xmlns:xsl="http://www.w3.org/1999/XSL/Transform">
<!-- old namespace declaration -->
<xsl:stylesheet xmlns:xsl="http://www.w3.org/TR/WD-xsl">
```

The element xsl:stylesheet can have the attributes xmlns, id, extension-element-prefixes, exclude-result-prefixes, and version. Version is the only required attribute. An alternate root element name, xsl:transform, performs the same as xsl:stylesheet.

```
<xsl:stylesheet version="1.0"
      xmlns:xsl="http://www.w3.org/1999/XSL/Transform">
... or ...
<xsl:transform version="1.0"
      xmlns:xsl="http://www.w3.org/1999/XSL/Transform">
```

The attribute exclude-result-prefixes can list the elements that should not copy over the namespace prefix from the source XML to the resulting XML. You may use this when you are transforming the FMPXMLRESULT and simply changing the field names. An example showing the usage of this attribute is found in Listing 2.12 when the xsl:copy-of element is used.

```
<xsl:stylesheet version="1.0" xmlns:xsl="http://www.w3.org/1999/XSL/
  Transform" xmlns:fmp="http://www.filemaker.com/fmpxmlresult"
  exclude-result-prefixes="fmp">
```

7.11 Namespace Declarations

The namespace value is written as a Uniform Resource Identifier (URI). The namespace declaration looks like a hypertext link to a valid location on the Internet. The URI does not always go to a location, but it does identify a unique name. Some namespace URIs may be valid hypertext references with the XML Schema or DTD documents at that location. The document "Namespaces in XML," found at http://www.w3.org/TR/REC-xml-names, defines the namespaces. The namespace declaration serves as a reference to the elements and attributes used in the document and binds them with the unique reference.

Elements without namespace prefixes may use the namespace of the parent elements, including the root element. Browsers may accept the HTML markup without a namespace declaration and use the default unique identifier for HTML. For example, the HTML document may contain HTML markup without specifying the namespace. By declaring the namespace at the beginning of the document a shortcut to the resource can be used or the default can be assumed, as in Listing 7.2.

Listing 7.1 HTML elements with namespaces

```
<!-- HTML elements with namespace -->
<html:html xmlns:html="http://www.w3.org/TR/xhmtl1/strict">
<html:head>
<html:title>Document Name</html:title>
      </html:head>
      <html:body>
            <!-- content here -->
      </html:body>
</html:html>
```

Listing 7.2 HTML elements without namespaces

```
<!-- HTML elements with default namespace -->
<html xmlns:html="http://www.w3.org/TR/xhmtl1/strict">
<head>
<title>Document Name</title>
      </head>
      <body>
            <!-- content here -->
      </body>
</html>
```

The above examples are greatly exaggerated but serve to introduce the concept of namespace declarations to identify the elements in an XML document. The namespace declarations for multiple sources provide a means to associate the elements with the correct source. The example in Listing 7.3 shows the declarations and associations for multiple XML element sources.

Listing 7.3 Namespace usage

```
<?xml version="1.0" encoding="UTF-8" ?>
<xsl:stylesheet xmlns:xsl="http://www.w3.org/1999/XSL/Transform"
      xmlns:html="http://www.w3.org/TR/REC-html4.0"
      xmlns:fm="http://www.filemaker.com/fmpxmlresult"
      xmlns:sql="http://sql.yourdomain.com/myquery">
<xsl:template match="/">
            <html:p>This is from a FileMaker Pro result:
```

```
            <xsl:value-of select="//fm:ROW/fm:COL/fm:DATA" />
                <html:br/>
                This is from an SQL query: <xsl:value-of
                  select="//sql:ROW/sql:COL/sql:DATA" />
          </html:p>
</xsl:template>
</xsl:stylesheet>
```

The multiple declarations allow us to use the same element names from multiple sources. The "//ROW/COL/DATA" elements in Listing 7.3 could easily confuse the processor if we had not appended the prefix to them. The use of the prefix binds the element to a unique namespace in the XML document.

The namespace is copied to the resulting document except in the following circumstances:

- The xsl: namespace in the xsl:stylesheet element is never copied.
- Namespace prefixes listed with the xsl:stylesheet attributes extension-element-prefixes and extension-result-prefixes are not copied to the result document.

7.12 Namespaces in FileMaker Pro 6

The XML that results from a query to a web-published FileMaker Pro database with the -format parameter includes the namespace declaration. Each of the three schema types has a different namespace:

- -format=-fmp_xml&-view

  <FMPXMLLAYOUT xmlns="http://www.filemaker.com/fmpxmllayout">
- -format=-fmp_xml&-find

  <FMPXMLRESULT xmlns="http://www.filemaker.com/fmpxmlresult">
- -format=-fmp_dso&-find

  <FMPDSORESULT xmlns="http://www.filemaker.com/fmpdsoresult">

Database Design Reports and Namespaces

The document Default.xsl is included with FileMaker Pro Developer 5.5 for displaying the XML produced by the Database Design Report. This document uses the older namespace version xsl:stylesheet xmlns:xsl="http://www.w3.org/TR/WD-xsl". You may change the declaration to the newer version if you have a browser that is compliant with the World Wide Web Consortium recommendations. The XSL and XPath standards may be different when you use the older namespace, so merely changing the namespace declaration may not render the report correctly in the browser. Differences in XSL namespace and XPath usage will be noted in this chapter.

Example XML Files in FileMaker Pro

The example files, which are included with FileMaker Pro Developer 5.0 and FileMaker Pro Unlimited 6, use the older namespace in the people_form.xsl:

```
<?xml version="1.0"?>
<xsl:stylesheet
     xmlns:xsl="http://www.w3.org/TR/WD-xsl"
     xmlns:fm="http://www.filemaker.com/fmpdsoresult">
```

The examples also use JavaScript and the Document Object Model (DOM) to present the XML published by Web Companion. Only the Windows version of Internet Explorer 5 or greater will work properly with the examples. The JavaScript calls ActiveX, which only works on the Windows operating system.

```
var xmlDocument = new ActiveXObject("Microsoft.XMLDOM");
```

You may get unpredictable results using these examples.

7.13 Stylesheet Instruction in XML Documents

The XML information for a database file in the Database Design Report contains the prolog <?xml version="1.0"?>. The second line in the report is a processing instruction specifying the stylesheet to be used with the document:

```
<?xml-stylesheet type="text/xsl" href="Default.xsl"?>
```

The processing instruction xml-stylesheet has six attributes. The type attribute is required. If the stylesheet is XSL, the type attribute will have the value "text/xsl". The Cascading Style Sheet has a type attribute value of "text/css". The href attribute is also required in the xml-stylesheet processing instruction. The href attribute may be a relative or absolute URI path to the stylesheet document. Just like the hyperlink reference in HTML, this URI is not a namespace declaration, but the real location to the document. The href can be a fragment path, thus allowing the stylesheet to be a part of the XML document:

Listing 7.4 XML with embedded XSL

```
<?xml version="1.0" ?>
<?xml-stylesheet type="text/xsl" href="#RefName" ?>
<abc>
      <xsl:stylesheet id="RefName" version="1.0"
                  xmlns:xsl="http://www.w3.org/1999/XSL/Transform"
                  xmlns:fo="http://www.w3.org/1999/XSL/Format">
            <xsl:template match="/"
                  <xsl:apply-templates />
            </xsl:template
            <xsl:template match="def">
                  <fo:block>
                        <xsl:value-of select="." />
                  </fo:block>
            </xsl:template>
      </xsl:stylesheet>
      <def>some content</def>
</abc>
```

The stylesheet processing instruction has optional attributes that are not used by FileMaker Pro. The title, media, charset, and alternate attributes may be used with the XSL processing instruction in other applications.

7.14 Stylesheet Processing Instruction from HTTP Requests

When you issue an XML request to FileMaker Pro Web Companion, you can specify a stylesheet to be used with the result. There are two parameters used to bind the result to the stylesheet. These parameters are -styletype and -stylehref and are the two required attributes for the xml-stylesheet processing instruction. If the stylesheet is placed in the Web folder, Web Companion will find it and use it to transform the XML result. The request for an XSL document is:

```
http://localhost/fmpro?-db=myDB.FP5&-format=-fmp_dso&-styletype=text/
  xsl&-stylehref=Default.xsl&-findany
```

The xml-stylesheet processing instruction is automatically added to the prolog of the result:

```
<?xml version="1.0" encoding="UTF-8" ?>
<?xml-stylesheet type="text/xsl" href="Default.xsl"?>
<FMPDSORESULT xmlns="http://www.filemaker.com/fmpdsoresult">
<ERRORCODE>0</ERRORCODE>
```

```
<DATABASE>myDB.FP5</DATABASE>
     <LAYOUT />
...
```

7.2 Top-level Elements in XSL

The Extensible Stylesheet Language is a transformation and formatting language that uses specific child elements to transform an XML document. Some of these elements may only be used at the topmost level in the XSL document. These top-level elements are listed here:

Import—The element <xsl:import> is an empty element and has one attribute, href. The value of the href attribute is a URI pointing to the location of another stylesheet to be imported into the calling stylesheet. This element may not work in all browsers but shows the ability to make modular stylesheets and import as needed. Multiple stylesheets may be imported. Care must be taken when using imported stylesheets; the rules of the imported stylesheet take precedence over the internal rules.

```
<xsl:import href="anotherTemplate.xsl" />
```

Include—Like the <xsl:import> element, the top-level element <xsl:include> has one attribute, href, and is an empty element. However, it differs from the <xsl:import> element because a copy of an external stylesheet is placed in the document. The precedence of the rules for an included stylesheet is the same as the internal document rules. This element may not function properly, depending upon the browser.

```
<xsl:include href="anotherRule.xsl" />
```

Strip Space—This top-level element, <xsl:strip-space elements= "listOfElements" />, may not work in all browsers. The value for the elements attribute is a space-delimited list of elements in the document that need to explicitly have white space removed. White space is spaces, horizontal tabs, carriage returns, and linefeeds. Table 1.2 shows the white space characters. Listing 7.5 shows the XSL used with a FileMaker Pro 6 export. The return as the final character in some of the fields was converted to LF (linefeed) but was not stripped from the result. The use of the function normalize-space() will remove this character, as shown in this chapter.

```
<xsl:strip-space elements="DATA" />
```

Listing 7.5 stripSpace.xsl

```
<?xml version="1.0" encoding="UTF-8" ?>
<xsl:stylesheet version="1.0" xmlns:xsl="http://www.w3.org/1999/XSL/
  Transform" xmlns:fm="http://www.filemaker.com/fmpxmlresult" >
<xsl:strip-space elements="fm:DATA" />
<xsl:template match="/">
<xsl:copy-of select="fm:FMPXMLRESULT" />
</xsl:template>
</xsl:stylesheet>
```

Preserve Space—The empty element <xsl:preserve-space elements="listOfElements" /> works just the opposite of the strip-space element. The space-delimited list of elements in the attribute will have all white space preserved. This element may not process correctly in all browsers.

```
<xsl:preserve-space elements="bigField valueList" />
```

Key—Elements in the XML document may have unique identifiers. Elements may also cross-reference each other. The <xsl:key> element has the required attributes name (the name of the key), match (a pattern or node containing the key), and use (an expression, the value of the key). This element may be used by the XSLT function key(keyName, object).

For example, the ROW element in the FMPXMLRESULT and the FMPDSORESULT both use the attributes MODID and RECORDID. The MODID may help tell you what records have changed since you last retrieved the data. The RECORDID is the unique identifier for each record in a database. The key for each ROW (record) could be the RECORDID. Set the key in your XSL top-level elements. Some examples are shown here:

```
<xsl:key name="recID" match="//ROW" use="@RECORDID" />
<xsl:key name="unique" match="//ROW use="attribute::RECORDID" />
```

Once the key is declared, it can be used throughout the document. The following example uses the key with a static or predetermined value. This value could be obtained dynamically, as the stylesheet processes the XML from the top down. A good example for using the xsl:key and the key() function can be found in the stylesheet subsummary.xsl. This document is found in the FileMaker Pro 6 folder FileMaker Examples\XML Examples\Export.

```
key('recID', '12345')
key('unique', '342')
```

Decimal Format—When numbers are used in an XSL stylesheet, there are defaults for how the number is formatted in the result, but these may be changed with the <xsl:decimal-format> top-level element. Multiple formats may be declared, so the first required attribute is name. The other attributes have these defaults: decimal-separator (the period character), grouping-separator (the comma character), infinity (a string "infinity", may be "8"), minus-sign, NaN (the string "NaN" for not a number), percent (the % character), per-mille (‰ or #x2030), zero-digit (0), digit (#), and pattern-separator (;).

This format is used by the function format-number(number, pattern, decimal-formatName).

```
<xsl:decimal-format name="phone" digit="x" />
<xsl:value-of select="format-number(NumberField, "(xxx) xxx-xxxx",
  phone) />
```

Namespace Alias—The default output of the result tree uses the namespaces in the source tree. If, for example, you want a template to use namespace declaration for the result tree and do not want to confuse the XSL processor, use this top-level element. The attribute stylesheet-prefix has the value of the prefix name or "#default". The attribute result-prefix has the value of the prefix name or "#default". Remember that the namespaces used in a document must be unique.

```
<xsl:stylesheet
      xmlns:fmp="http://www.filemaker.com/fmpxmlresult"
      xmlns:fm2="http://www.filemaker.com/fmpxmlresult2">
<xsl:namespace-alias stylesheet-prefix="fm2" result-prefix="fmp" />
```

The result tree will use the correct namespace if you use the alias in the XSL document.

Attribute Sets—Sometimes an XSL document will use a standard set of attributes for the result element. For example, you may wish to use the same text style attributes, but want to avoid entering them multiple times in the XSL stylesheet. Or maybe you want to have a convenient way to change an attribute set at the beginning of the document and have the styles apply throughout the document without a find and replace routine. The top-level element <xsl:attribute-set> may be used multiple times in the XSL document to create many sets. The required attribute for this element, name, is the name of the set. The element has another attribute that allows it to use other attribute sets, use-attribute-sets. You can specify a white space-separated list of other sets. The element can have a child element <xsl:attribute>. When you use the attribute use-attribute-sets with <xsl:element>, <xsl:copy>, or <xsl:attribute-set>, it will apply the attributes to those elements as if you entered them manually.

```
<xsl:attribute-set name="myStyles">
     <xsl:attribute name="font">Arial, Helvetica,
       Sans-Serif</xsl:attribute>
     <xsl:attribute name="size">12</xsl:attribute>
</xsl:attribute-set>
<xsl:element name="p" use-attribute-sets="myStyles"></xsl:element>
```

This XSL element is useful for creating FIELD elements in the METADATA element if you import XML. The FIELD elements all have the attributes EMPTYOK, MAXREPEAT, NAME, and TYPE. The NAME attribute element will be different for every field, but the other attributes may be the same and have no impact on the import. The example below creates an attribute set for the FIELD element:

```
<xsl:attribute-set name="fields">
     <xsl:attribute name="EMPTYOK">YES</xsl:attribute>
     <xsl:attribute name="MAXREPEAT">1</xsl:attribute>
     <xsl:attribute name="TYPE">TEXT</xsl:attribute>
</xsl:attribute-set>
```

Variables—Two XSL elements can be used to pass variables. They can be used as top-level elements or within the templates. Only top-level declarations can be used throughout the document. <xsl:variable> has the attributes name (required) and select (value of the variable). The variable is used by using the "$" symbol before the variable name in any expression. The <xsl:param> element allows a default value to be used if none is supplied. The <xsl:param> element also has two attributes, name and select.

Variables may be passed to templates with the <xsl:with-param> element in apply-templates, call-template. The <xsl:with-param> element has the same two attributes for all variables, name and select. The <xsl:with-param> element is never used as a top-level element. The value within the curly braces ({ and }) is evaluated before further processing.

```
<xsl:variable name="myVar" select="Literal" />
<xsl:param name="myParam" select="default" />
<xsl:value-of select="{$myVar}" />
<xsl:apply-templates>
     <xsl:with-param name="sendThis" />
</xsl:apply-templates>
```

Output—The result tree can be formatted correctly using the top-level element <xsl:output>. This element is always empty but may be used multiple times in the top of the XSL document. The attribute method values may be "xml", "html", or "text". The final device for output may treat each of these methods differently. An attribute version="1.0" is included for forward compatibility. The encoding of the result document may be specified with the encoding attribute. The value of encoding is a string with the charset found in RFC2278 or begins with "x-". By default the result tree may be encoded as UTF-16 or Unicode. You can read about these language encodings in section 1.42, "Unicode vs. ASCII."

Other attributes for <xsl:output> are omit-xml-declaration (values may be "yes" or "no"), standalone (values may be "yes" or "no"), doctype-public (value may be a string with the name of the public doctype), and doctype-system (value may be a string with the name of the internal doctype). The attribute indent will format the result tree with indented child elements if this value is "yes" and media-type is the value of the MIME content type of the result. If method="text", the attribute media-type may have the value "text/plain".

```
<xsl:output method="html" version ="1.0" encoding="us-ascii"
  indent="yes" />
```

The attribute cdata-section-elements lists the elements in the document that need to be CDATA in the output. CDATA allows entities to be passed from the source to the result without parsing. For example, you may have HTML within a field and need to pass the code as raw text without converting the "<" to "<" or ">" to ">".

Templates—The final top-level element, <xsl:template>, deserves its own section in this chapter (see the following). The XSL stylesheet is template-based and may have internal templates or external templates (inserted with <xsl:import> and <xsl:include> elements).

7.21 XSL Templates

After all the other top-level elements are declared, the basic stylesheet uses the element <xsl:template> to set up rules for using or not using the elements from the source document. The <xsl:template> element has the attribute match to test for a section of the XML. Usually, the match value is an XPath expression or pattern. Since every document has a root, the XPath shortcut "/" can be used as the match for any document where the elements are unknown. Once a match is made, the contents of the template are used to find more rules, display the result of the match, or return literal text to the result tree. All the other XSL elements are used within the templates. The variables <xsl:variable> and <xsl:param> may also be used within a template.

```
<xsl:template match="/">
     Every well-formed XML document has a root.<br />
     This basic template will display for every
     document.
</xsl:template>
```

The template rule is recursive and will match every pattern or XPath within the current node. For example, the FMPXMLRESULT grammar will return a ROW element for every record in a found set. Any template rule for match="fm:ROW" will apply to all the records (or ROW elements) in the XML document. You can further specify the match with predicates in the XPath express that indicate a match for a ROW with a unique ID, an attribute value, or the position in the document.

```
     <!-- first record only -->
<xsl:template match="fm:ROW[1]">
     <!-- only the record with the ID of 3758 -->
<xsl:template match="fm:ROW/@RECORDID=3758">
     <!-- the last record -->
<xsl:template match="fm:ROW[last()]">
```

The <xsl:template> element can also be used to set up a named template. Templates may be called as needed in an XSL document. The attribute name has the unique name of a template. Rules are set up inside the named template just as for the match template. The element <xsl:call-template name="UniqueName" /> can be used anywhere in the XSL document to branch to the named template.

XSL templates are very similar to FileMaker Pro scripts. You can even have subscripts in other documents! The top-level elements <xsl:include> and <xsl:import> are used to bring in the template rules from other sources.

```
<xsl:call-template name="myRules" />
<xsl:template name="myRules">
     When you call this template, it will bring its
     rules with it.
</xsl:template>
```

XSL templates are also like a FileMaker Pro layout. If you have layout with the view set to list, you only place the fields, layout labels, graphics, and other elements in the body part. These elements are repeated for every record in the found set. The values in the fields may change, but the rules for applying the values and the rules for displaying the elements are the same for each record. Form View layouts also "repeat" because you do not have to create a layout for each record. You do not need to use every field on every layout. The XSL template does the same for each match, only setting rules for the elements it contains. You can combine the templates to view only the data you need, just like the fields on the layout.

Default Templates—Many XSL processors, including browsers, have built-in templates. These may be implied and are not necessary to explicitly declare. When the <xsl:template match="*|/"> is used, for any element (*) or the root element (/), the default rule is to apply any other templates in the XSL stylesheet.

```
<xsl:template match="*|/">
     <xsl:apply-templates />
</xsl:template>
```

The use of the empty element <xsl:apply-templates /> is implied. If a rule is not within a template, the XSL processor should look for more templates. However, <xsl:apply-templates> should be used to make the XSL document more easily understood by all processors.

Some other default templates are for modes, attributes, processing instructions, and comment elements. The default match for any element or the root with a particular mode passes on to apply any other templates for the same mode. The template that matches any text node or any attribute (@*) will default to use the value of the text node or the attribute. Processors often ignore the processing instructions and comments if there are no template rules set up for them. These defaults are shown below:

```
<!-- for modes -->
     <xsl:template match="*|/" mode="myMode">
          <xsl:apply-templates mode="myMode" />
     </xsl:template>
<!-- for attributes -->
     <xsl:template match="text()|@*">
          <xsl:value-of select="." />
     </xsl:template>
<!-- p.i. and comments -->
     <xsl:template match="processing-instruction()|comment()" />
```

Template Mode—The mode attribute can be used to allow an element to be processed multiple times in a stylesheet. Otherwise, the source tree is processed once for every element in the XML document. The mode attribute is only used with the match attribute and is declared in the <xsl:template> element and the <xsl:apply-templates> element.

Apply Other Templates—The default rule is to continue processing an XML document until all matches have been made. This element, <xsl:apply-templates />, is implied but should be included if conditional branching is used. The attribute select is used to name a particular XPath of the document to be processed. The mode attribute can also be used with the <xsl:apply-templates> element. Both attributes are optional and if none is included, the processor continues to search for other templates. The <xsl:apply-templates> element can be empty or may contain the elements <xsl:sort> or <xsl:with-param>.

```
<xsl:apply-templates />
<xsl:apply-templates>
     <xsl:sort />
</xsl:apply-templates>
<xsl:apply-templates select="fm:ROW" />
```

Use a Named Template—The branch to a named template uses the <xsl:call-templates> element. The required attribute for this element is name and has the value of the named template for the branch. This element can be empty or use the <xsl:with-param> child element between the start and end tags.

```
<xsl:call-template name="myRules">
     <xsl:with-param />
</xsl:call-template>
<xsl:call-template name="yourRules" />
```

Pass Parameters to Templates—The element <xsl:with-param> can be used with the <xsl:apply-templates> and <xsl:call-template> elements, as shown above. This element has two attributes, the name of the parameter and the select attribute, which is the value of the parameter to pass. The name of the parameter matches a declared <xsl:param> element in the top level or within the same template.

```
<xsl:param name="myDefault">abc</xsl:param>
<xsl:apply-templates>
     <xsl:with-param name="myDefault">def</xsl:with-param>
</xsl:apply-templates>
<!-- this has just changed the default value for the parameter
  "myDefault" -->
<!-- had none been specified, the original parameter would have been
  used -->
```

Apply Imported Templates—Another way to change the rules for a template is to use the top-level <xsl:apply-imports> element. This element is always empty and has no attributes or child elements. It is used only inside a stylesheet that has at least one <xsl:import> element.

Templates use other XSL elements to process the source tree and transform it into the result tree. These elements are fully explained in the W3C document “XSL Transformations (XSLT), Version 1.0,” http://www.w3.org/TR/xslt. Brief examples of the more common elements are presented in the following section.

7.3 Other XSL/XSLT Elements

7.31 Repeating Elements

The template can be used to set a rule for every element in the source tree. Another element can be used within the template to repeat a rule. This element is <xsl:for-each> and is never an empty element. The only attribute for this element is select, which has the value of an XPath expression. The <xsl:sort> element can be used with <xsl:for-each> to sort the source elements before returning to the results tree. Literal text, other elements, and rules can be used between the start and end elements of this <xsl:for-each> element just as for the templates. The following template will return all the field names from the FMPXMLRESULT grammar:

```
<xsl:template match="fm:FMPXMLRESULT/fm:METADATA">
     <xsl:for-each select="fm:FIELD">
          FieldName: <xsl:value-of select="@NAME" /><br />
     </xsl:for-each>
</xsl:template>
```

7.32 Sorting the Source Document

FileMaker Pro can presort before exporting or web publishing the XML results, but sometimes that is not sufficient for the resulting output. Two XSL elements, <xsl:apply-templates> and <xsl:for-each>, can use a child element, <xsl:sort>, to presort the selected elements. Otherwise, no sorting is done to the document and all rules are applied to the elements as they occur in the document.

Multiple <xsl:sort> elements can be used, just as multiple fields in FileMaker Pro can be used in a sort. This element has several attributes to specify the type of sort. The first attribute, select, can use child elements of the current node or even attributes as the key for sorting. The lang attribute is used to specify the language used for the sort. The data-type attribute has a value of "text" or "number" for the sort. The default sort order is "ascending" by uppercase, followed by lowercase. You can change these attributes or explicitly declare them. For example, order="ascending" or "descending" or case-order="upper-first" or "lower-first".

```
<xsl:sort select="fm:lastName" order="descending" data-type="text" />
<xsl:sort select="fm:firstName" />
```

7.33 XSLT Elements for Text

Several elements are used to copy the source elements, the value of particular elements, literal text, or the value of comments. These elements are the most used to display the text content of the XML document. By default, the string value of any element (even those with children elements) is the concatenation of all the string values for all children elements. To be specific on what is returned to the result tree, including the value of attributes or XPath expressions, use these elements.

Element and Attribute Values—The <xsl:value-of> element is used to return the string value of an element and its descendants, if any. Any XPath expression may be used as the value for the single attribute select including any attribute name in any element. The other attribute, disable-output-escaping, has the value of "yes" or "no" and is used to return raw data or encode entities. The <xsl:value-of> element is always empty and has no child elements. If a node with child elements is used for the value of the select attribute, the result string will be a concatenation of the string values of the element and all its descendants.

```
<!-- show the value "5" -->
<xsl:value-of select="2+3" />
<!-- show the contents of the 3rd row, 2nd column, DATA element -->
<xsl:value-of select="fm:ROW[3]/fm:COL[2]/:fm:DATA" />
<!-- show the value of the NAME attribute for the Database -->
<xsl:value-of select="/fm:DATABASE[@NAME]" />
```

Text—Sometimes you need to include white space characters and do not want them ignored by the processors. You can also use the element <xsl:text> to display any literal values that may be parsed into entities, such as ">" or "<." New lines (carriage return and/or linefeeds) can be added between the start and end elements. See the following examples. This element is never empty and has one attribute. Use the attribute disable-output-escaping with the value of "yes" to prevent the literal contents from being parsed. This element can contain any parsed character data.

```
<!-- add three spaces here -->
<xsl:text>   </xsl:text>
<!-- here's a new line: -->
```

```
<xsl:text>
</xsl:text>
<!-- this will produce the correct characters "<?" -->
<xsl:text disable-output-escaping="yes">&lt;?</xsl:text>
```

Copy and Copy Of—You can use the source XML elements in the result XML. The element <xsl:copy> will copy the current element and its text value to the result document. The attributes and children elements may not be copied. This is called a shallow copy. The <xsl:copy> element may be empty or have other template elements. The attribute use-attribute-sets allows you to apply a particular set of attributes to the copy.

```
<xsl:for-each select="fm:ROW">
    <xsl:copy />
</xsl:for-each>
```

If you want to use a deeper copy, the empty element <xsl:copy-of> can be used. The copy-of element is similar to the value-of element, but the result is not converted to a string. The required attribute select has an XPath expression for the value. The example below will place the element <DATA> and its text value into the result XML document.

```
<xsl:copy-of select="fm:DATA" />
```

Comments—You can add comments to the result XML with the use of the <xsl:comment> element. Whatever you place between the start and end tags will be in the resulting comment. The comment is inserted between "<!--" and "-->" when it is placed in the result document.

```
<xsl:comment>
    This text will be my comment.
</xsl:comment>
<!--This text will be my comment.-->
```

Literal Text and Elements—You can add literal text to the result document by simply adding it to the template. Other elements, such as the HTML tags, can also be used in the template. The text and elements will be placed in the result XML. The example below inserts the literal text and a small HTML table into the result for each row/record in the found set.

```
<xsl:template match="fm:ROW[1]">
Hey! I found a Record. Let's create a table:<br />
<table>
    <tr>
        <td>Table!</td>
```

```
    </tr>
</table>
</xsl:template>
```

This is an easy way to start building a template for repeating elements. First, display some text for the first occurrence of the expression to let you know you have made the correct match. Then change the literal to something dynamic, based upon a value of the match. Finally, remove the predicate "[1]" so that each repeat will be displayed:

```
<table>
<xsl:template match="fm:ROW">
    <tr>
        <td>Hey! I found a Record. Let's create another row,
          if any:</td>
    </tr>
</xsl:template>
</table>
```

7.34 Conditional Tests

FileMaker Pro has several script steps and functions to test the value of something (field or literal) and then proceed when the correct (or true) condition is met. The FileMaker Pro logical functions are If(test, trueResult, falseResult), Case(test1, result1, test2, result2, ..., Default-Result), Choose(NumericValueTest, result0, result1, ... resultN), IsEmpty(test), and IsValid(test). XSL has just two conditional elements, and the XPath expressions can be used to test for an empty value.

If—The element <xsl:if> has one required attribute, test. The template rules and literal text or elements between the start and end tags are used in the result only if the test is true. The test can be any XPath expression. This element can test for an empty value by using the text() function of an element. The test must resolve to a Boolean true. There is no "else" or "elseif" tests or "false" result to the test. The next element, <xsl:choose>, can be used for more than one test. You can nest a choose inside an if should you need to test the existence before proceeding, as seen in Listing 7.6. The example below tests for a value in a field.

```
<xsl:if test="fm:DATA/text()">
    Ah ha! This has the data: <xsl:value-of select="." />
</xsl:if>
```

Choose—The <xsl:choose> element is similar to the FileMaker Pro Case() function. This element is never empty but must have at least one child element, <xsl:when>. The "when" element is like the

<xsl:if> element because it has the test attribute and only a Boolean "true" will process the template between the start and end tags. You may have multiple <xsl:when> tests in the <xsl:choose> element. You may nest other conditional statements inside the <xsl:when> element.

Just like FileMaker Pro's Case() function, the <xsl:choose> element has an optional child element, <xsl:otherwise>. There is no attribute for the <xsl:otherwise> element, but it is never empty if it is used in the <xsl:choose> conditional tests. The example below uses the <xsl:if> and <xsl:choose> elements:

Listing 7.6 Conditional XSL

```
<!-- is there an attribute "Color"? -->
<xsl:if test="@Color">
<!-- if there is then output the HEX value -->
      <xsl:choose>
            <xsl:when test="@Color = red">#FF0000</xsl:when>
            <xsl:when test="@Color = blue">#0000FF</xsl:when>
            <xsl:when test="@Color = green">#00FF00</xsl:when>
            <xsl:otherwise>#000000</xsl:otherwise>
      </xsl:choose>
</xsl:if>
```

7.35 Add Elements and Attributes

You can add elements by simply including them in the template for the result document. Most HTML elements are added this way. You can use the <xsl:copy> and <xsl:copy-of> elements to make replicas of elements from the source to the result. You can also use the XSL element <xsl:element> to create new elements in the result document.

This tag is most often used to transform an attribute into an element. For example, the FMPDSORESULT grammar and the FMPXMLRESULT grammar have the repeating element ROW for each record in the found set. Within the ROW element are the two attributes modid and recordid. Should you need to make these attributes into an element you could use the example below. The element <xsl:element> has one required attribute, name, and two optional attributes, namespace and use-attribute-sets.

```
<!-- This tag in the XML source: -->
<xsl:element name="ModID">
      <xsl:value-of select="fm:ROW/@MODID" />
</xsl:element>
```

```
<!-- becomes in the XML result: -->
<ModID>2</ModID>
```

Attributes may be added to created elements or copied elements by using the use-attribute-sets attribute with <xsl:element> and <xsl:copy>. Attributes may also be explicitly added to elements, such as HTML elements in the template source. XSL has an element for adding attributes called <xsl:attribute>. This element has one required attribute, name, which is the name of the attribute. The attribute namespace is optional for the <xsl:attribute> element. The <xsl:attribute> element may be used to transform an element in the source to an attribute in the result document.

Multiple <xsl:attribute> elements may be added to a single element. You can use attribute-sets or list all of the attributes for a single element. The created attributes will be applied to the nearest element in the source to become an element with those attributes in the result. The value of the attribute is the XPath expression or literal text between the start and end tags. Two examples are shown below. Listing 7.7 creates a hyperlink with one attribute for the href and the text for the link between the start and end tags. Listing 7.8 creates an image element, <img />, with three attributes. Even though the element is empty, the attributes are added to it.

Listing 7.7 Creating a hyperlink with a field value

```
<a>
     <xsl:attribute name="href">
          <xsl:value-of select="fm:link" />
     </xsl:attribute>
     <xsl:attribute name="target">
          <xsl:text>_top</xsl:text>
     </xsl:attribute>
     <xsl:value-of select="fm:text" />
</a>
<!-- becomes in the result: -->
<a href="mylink.html" target="_top">My Text<a>
```

Listing 7.8 Displaying an image with path name field

```
<img />
     <xsl:attribute name="src">
          <xsl:value-of select="fm:PictNamePath" />
     </xsl:attribute>
     <xsl:attribute name="width">
          <xsl:value-of select="fm:PictWidth" />
     </xsl:attribute>
     <xsl:attribute name="height">
```

```
            <xsl:value-of select="fm:PictHeight" />
      </xsl:attribute>
<!-- becomes in the result: -->
<img src="images/MyPict.gif" width="100" height="75" />
```

The <xsl:attribute> element may also be used to display images in container fields in FileMaker Pro. The image may be in the database or a reference to the image. The FMPXMLRESULT grammar and the FMPDSORESULT grammar both will return the image as a linked source. The -img parameter on the element value tells Web Companion to make the connection to the database, grab the image in the field on a given record, and return it as a JPEG.

```
<!-- FMPDSORESULT for container field "Pict" -->
<Pict>FMPro?db=Products.fp5&RecID=16&Pict=&-img<Pict>
<!-- use this in a stylesheet: -->
<xsl:element name="img" />
      <xsl:attribute name="src">
            <xsl:value-of select="fm:Pict" />
      </xsl:attribute>
```

Using <xsl:element> and <xsl:attribute> allows you the freedom to transform elements and attributes into attributes and elements. Also, because the XSL elements are not nested, the XSL processors can set multiple attributes to a single element.

7.4 XPath Functions

XSL uses the XPath notations as listed in Chapter 1. This section lists some of the XPath 1.0 functions with descriptions that include similarities to FileMaker Pro functions. Example usage of the XPath functions with the XSL element <xsl:value-of> is presented. Not all XPath functions may be properly supported by the web browsers, so test them carefully. The functions are:

last()—This function has a numeric result. Most often used in the predicate of the XPath expression, this function returns the string-value of the last element: <xsl:value-of select="fm:ROW[last()]" />. This function is similar to the FileMaker Pro function last(repeatingOrRelatedField).

position()—This function has a numeric result. This function is also used in the XPath predicate. It returns the numeric position of the current node as the template goes through all the elements in document order. More similar to the FileMaker Pro function Status(CurrentRecordNumber), this XPath function uses particular fields/elements and the position of a child element in a parent element.

```
<!-- return the position of the DATA element -->
<xsl:value-of select="fm:DATA[position()]" />
<!-- test the current position against a value -->
<xsl:if test="fm:DATA[position()=2]">
```

count(node-set)—This function has a numeric result. This XPath function is similar to the FileMaker Pro functions Status(CurrentFoundCount), Status(CurrentRecordCount), or Count(RepeatingOrRelatedField).

```
<xsl:value-of select="count(fm:ROW)" />
```

id(uniqueIDNum)—This function has a node-set result. Elements that have a unique ID can be selected by a special attribute, ID. This function returns the nodes with a match.

```
<!-- return the value of any element with the unique ID of "abc" -->
<xsl:value-of select=id('abc') />
```

The ID attribute is not used with FMPXMLRESULT or FMPDSORESULT. However, each ROW (record) does have a unique ID with the attribute RECORDID. You can use this attribute value to find a particular record. Often the key() function is used with the unique identifiers.

```
<xsl:value-of select="fm:ROW/@recordid=3894" />
```

local-name(node-set)—This function has a string result. This function returns the name of the current element without the namespace URI, if any. The parameter node-set is optional. The FileMaker Pro function Status(CurrentFieldName) is similar to the XPath function local-name().

```
<!-- return the value "FirstName" or the name of the element -->
<xsl:value-of select="local-name(fm:FirstName)" />
```

namespace-uri(node-set)—This function has a string result. Related to the previous function, this XPath function returns the string of the namespace URI associated with an element. Namespaces are more fully described in sections 7.11 and 7.12. Elements may have a namespace attribute (ns, xmlns), which binds it to that element and all its child elements and attributes.

There is no FileMaker Pro equivalent, but if you imaged each field bound to layouts, the layout would be the location of the field. That way, a field formatted on a layout is unique from the same field on another layout formatted a different way.

name(node-set)—This function has a string result. This XPath function is related to the last two functions. An element with a local name and a namespace would be the expanded name of the element. The parameter node-set is optional in this function, so the current node is implied if the parameter is empty. Since the FMPXMLRESULT and FMPDSORESULT do not have namespace attributes, this function would return the name of the current node in an XSL document.

```
<!-- return the name of the element and the namepace URI.-->
<xsl:value-of select="name(FirstName)" />
```

The name() and local-name() XPath functions can be used with FMPDSORESULT and FMPXMLRESULT to return the list of field names used in the XML result. FMPDSORESULT has the field names as the element names, and FMPXMLRESULT has the field names in the attribute of the children of the <METADATA> element.

```
<!-- return the list of fields with FMPDSORESULT -->
<!-- put this code snippet inside an HTML page
<xsl:for-each select="fm:ROW[1]/*">
     <xsl:value-of select="name()" /><br />
</xsl:for-each>
<!-- return the list of fields with FMPXMLRESULT -->
<xsl:for-each select="fm:METADATA/fm:FIELD">
     <xsl:value-of select="@NAME" /><br />
</xsl:for-each>
```

string(object)—This function has a string result. This XPath function is used to convert other object types, such as numbers and booleans, to string types. There is no exact function in FileMaker Pro, although the functions NumToText(), DateToText(), and TimeToText() might be similar.

```
<xsl:value-of select="string('123') />
```

concat(string, string, ...)—This function has a string result. A comma-delimited list of values and literals can be used to combine strings. Variables may also be used in this XPath function. FileMaker Pro allows concatenation in the Specify Calculation dialog with the "&" symbol and by using merge fields on a layout.

```
<!-- similar to "firstname" & ' ' & "lastname" in a calculation -->
<!-- or "<fname> <lname>" in a merge field -->
<xsl:value-of select="concat($fname, ' ', $lname)" />
```

starts-with(string, text)—This function returns a Boolean result. This function returns "true" if the text string is at the beginning of the first parameter string.

Exact(Left(string, Length(text)), text) is a FileMaker Pro function that is similar. The Exact() function is used in this example because the XPath function is case-sensitive.

contains(string, text)—This function returns a Boolean result. The FileMaker Pro function PatternCount(string, text) > 1 is similar to this XPath function.

substring-before(string, text)—This function has a substring result. This XPath function returns the substring of the string that precedes the first occurrence of the text string in the first parameter string, or the empty string if the string does not contain the text. The FileMaker Pro functions Left(), Middle(), Right(), Position(), and PatternCount() are often used to extract substrings of text from strings. A similar calculation would be Left("abcde", Position("abcde", "cd", 1, 1) -1).

```
<xsl:value-of select="substring-before('abcde', 'cd') />
<!-- returns "ab" -->
```

substring-after(string, text)—This function has a substring result. This function returns the substring of the string that follows the first occurrence of the text string in the first parameter string, or the empty string if the string does not contain the text. The function substring-after('abcde', 'cd') returns "e." In FileMaker Pro, this could be Right("abcde", Length("abcde") – (Position("abcde", "cd", 1, 1) + 1)).

substring(string, start, length)—This function has a string result. The XPath function returns the substring of a string starting with the position specified by start with length specified in the third parameter. <xsl:value-of select-"substring('abcde', 1, 2)" /> returns "ab." The third parameter is optional and if not specified, is assumed to be the end of the string. This is equivalent to the function Middle(text, start, size) in FileMaker Pro.

string-length(string)—This function returns a number. The FileMaker Pro function Length() is similar to this XPath function, which returns the number of characters in the string.

normalize-space(string)—This function returns a string. This XPath function will strip leading and trailing white space. White space is made up of spaces, tabs, carriage returns, and linefeeds. Multiple instances of white space between other characters in the string are reduced to one white space. The FileMaker Pro function Trim() will strip leading and trailing spaces only but does not remove tabs, carriage returns, linefeeds, or reduce multiple white space characters.

```
<xsl:value-of select="normalize-space('abc
  def  ')" />
<!-- return 'abc def' -->
```

translate(string, findText, replaceText)—This function returns the string with occurrences of characters in the findText string replaced by the character at the corresponding position in the replaceText string. This function is similar to the FileMaker Pro Substitute(string, find, replace) function, but the string gets translated using any of the characters in replaceText as the pattern(s) to replace the character patterns in findText. The first character in findText is found in the string and replaced by the first character in replaceText, etc.

```
<xsl:value-of select='Translate("abcda", "ab", "CD")' />
<!-- returns "CDcdC" -->
```

boolean(object)—This function is a Boolean conversion. Any function in FileMaker Pro that returns Boolean results is equivalent to this XPath function.

not(boolean)—This function is a Boolean. This function returns the negative of the previous test. True becomes false and false becomes true. The logical operator not performs a similar function in FileMaker Pro calculations.

true()—This function is a Boolean. This XPath function simply returns the Boolean results of "true". It is used to compare other XPath expressions.

false()—This function is a Boolean and returns the Boolean value "false" when this XPath expression is used.

lang(string)—This function is a Boolean. Sometime the language of a particular element is tested against the language of the XML document. The Boolean "true" is returned if the languages match. You may find an element defined as <p xml:lang="en"> for example. The lang("en") function would return true when tested against this "p" element.

number(object)—This function is a number conversion. The FileMaker Pro function TextToNum() is equivalent to this XPath function.

sum(node-set)—This function has a numeric result. This adds the numeric values of a set of elements and returns the sum. The Sum(repeatingOrRelatedField) function in FileMaker Pro performs similarly.

floor(number)—This function returns an integer. A number value is reduced to the largest integer that is not greater than the number. The FileMaker Pro function Int(1.8) returns "1," as would "floor(1.8)".

ceiling(number)—This function returns an integer. A number is rounded up to the next higher integer, dropping the decimal portion of a number. There is no similar function in FileMaker Pro, but Int(1.8) +1 would be the same as ceiling(1.8) or the integer "2."

round(number)—This function has a numeric result. This XPath function will return the closest integer (up or down) to the argument. The FileMaker Pro function Round(number, precision) is more specific and returns whole numbers, not just integers.

7.41 Additional XSL Functions

There are several other functions in the "XSL Transformations (XSLT), Version 1.0 Recommendation," http://www.w3.org/TR/xslt. XSL uses both XPath and XSLT functions. These additions in the XSLT document are listed below.

Extension functions may be created and used by XSL processors. These functions are processor dependent and may not work for all XSL processors. A prefix is declared and the function called: prefix:function(). A common usage in the Xalan processor is to include JavaScript. The elements <xalan:component> and <xalan:script> contain the JavaScript. The processor must be properly configured to use the JavaScript. See http://www.apache.org/ for more information about the Xalan processor.

```
<xalan:component prefix="" elements="" functions="">
      <xalan:script lang="javascript">
            function xyz {
                  (your javascript here)
            }
      </xalan:script>
</xalan:component>
```

document()—The standard method of transforming XML is to use the stylesheet processing instruction inside the XML document. See section 7.13, "Stylesheet Instruction in XML Documents" and section 7.14, "Stylesheet Processing Instruction from HTTP Requests."

```
<?xml-stylesheet type="text/xsl" href="Default.xsl"?>
```

To include other external XSL stylesheets, the elements <xsl:include> and <xsl:import> can be used in the stylesheet. But to include another XML document, the XSL function document(object, node-set) is used. The second parameter, node-set, is optional and may be the element to retrieve. The first object is the URI (location) of the XML source to be included in the current document.

```
<xsl:variable name="mydoc" select="document(fmpro?-db=myfile.FP5&amp;
  -lay=web&amp;-format=-fmp_xml&amp;-view)" />
```

Since all documents use the "/" root, this symbol should not be used in templates when reading multiple XML documents.

Multiple XML exports from FileMaker Pro can be used with your stylesheet. This is most useful when you have related data and need to structure the result document without the relationship names. Export the child data and use the stylesheet with the parent export to bring in the child data.

When more than one XML document is used with the stylesheet, it is very important to maintain distinct namespace prefixes for the elements. The XSL element <xsl:namespace-alias> would be helpful if the source is more than one FMPXMLRESULT or FMPDSORESULT document. You can read about namespace-alias in section 7.2.

This may be a better way to use a database with related values. When a portal has too many rows, it is difficult to limit the number of rows in the output. It is also difficult to format the portal rows easily with XSL. One solution can be to use the related file for the XML request and simply show the first occurrence of any parent file fields.

7.5 XSL and HTML

An XSL stylesheet can be used to transform XML into HTML, a more common method of web delivery. The HTML markup must conform to the XHTML standards. See Chapter 6 for more information about HTML as well-formed XML tags. In addition, Cascading Style Sheets (CSS) may be used in the HTML to provide the formatting. The preferred method of CSS inclusion is with the XHTML <link> element:

```
<link rel="stylesheet" type="text/css" href="myStyles.css" />
```

The table row <tr> is generally a repeated element and may be dynamically produced by the XSL elements <xsl:template> or <xsl:for-each>. Furthermore, the table cell element <td> may be dynamically produced by using the templates for field elements. Listing 7.9 shows a simple table produced with the FMPDSORESULT. You can see more XSL examples in the FileMaker Examples folder included with FileMaker Pro 6 and in the XSLT library on the web site http://www.filemaker.com/xml/xslt_library.html.

Listing 7.9 Dynamic table

```
<xsl:template match="/">
     <table border="1" cellpadding="3" cellspacing="2">
          <xsl:for-each select="fmp:ROW">
          <tr>
               <xsl:for-each select="./*">
<!-- get all children and display the results -->
               <td>
                    <xsl:value-of select="." />
               </td>
               </xsl:for-each>
          </tr>
          </xsl:for-each>
     </table>
</xsl:template>
```

7.6 FileMaker Pro Value Lists and XSL

The FMPXMLRESULT with the -view action can return the value lists used for a field on a layout if you make an HTTP request. You can use the results to create a dynamic value list with XSL. The template will match the name of a list. The XML is shown below, followed by the XSL stylesheet to transform it into HTML.

Listing 7.10 Value list in XML

```
<VALUELIST NAME="list">
<VALUE>one</VALUE>
<VALUE>two</VALUE>
<VALUE>three</VALUE>
<VALUE>four</VALUE>
<VALUE>longword</VALUE>
<VALUE>five</VALUE>
<VALUE>six</VALUE>
<VALUE>longerwordhere</VALUE>
</VALUELIST>
```

Listing 7.11 XSL to use value list

```
<xsl:template match="fm:VALUELIST/@NAME=list">
     <select name="myfield">
          <option value="">-choose-</option>
     <xsl:for-each select="fm:VALUE">
```

```
            <option>
                  <xsl:attribute name="value">
                        <xsl:value-of select="." />
                  </xsl:attribute>
                  <xsl:value-of select="." />
            </option>
      </xsl:for-each>
      </select>
</xsl:template>
```

Listing 7.12 HTML select list

```
<select name="myfield">
      <option value="">-choose-</option>
      <option value="one">one</option>
      <option value="two">two</option>
      <option value="three">three</option>
      <option value="four">four</option>
      <option value="longword">longword</option>
      <option value="five">five</option>
      <option value="six">six</option>
      <option value="longerwordhere">longerwordhere</option>
</select>
```

Listing 7.13 XSL to create check boxes

```
<xsl:template match="fm:VALUELIST/@NAME=list">
      <xsl:for-each select="fm:VALUE">
            <input type="checkbox" name="myfield" />
                  <xsl:attribute name="value">
                        <xsl:value-of select="." />
                  </xsl:attribute>
                  <xsl:text> </xsl:text>
                  <xsl:value-of select="." /><br />
      </xsl:for-each>
</xsl:template>
```

You can create dynamic value lists based on the returned field contents, as well. For example, you may return a found set of records with FMPXMLRESULT and use the first field (fm:COL[1]) in each record (fm:ROW) as the value for the pop-up list, but the second field (fm:COL[2]) is the displayed text. Create your value list with XSL:

Listing 7.14 Value list with found set

```
<xsl:template match="fm:RESULTSET">
      <select name="myfield">
            <option value="">-choose-</option>
      <xsl:for-each select="fm:ROW">
            <option>
```

```
                <xsl:attribute name="value">
                    <xsl:value-of select="fm:COL[1]" />
                </xsl:attribute>
                <xsl:value-of select="fm:COL[2]" />
            </option>
        </xsl:for-each>
        </select>
</xsl:template>
```

7.7 Browsers and XSL

The latest web browsers are more compliant with the World Wide Web Consortium standards for XML 1.0, XPath 1.0, XSLT 1.0, CSS 1.0, JavaScript, HTML 4.0 (and XHTML), and DOM. There are changes being made to each of these standards (see http://www.w3.org), but at least there are currently more choices for the use of XML in web pages. Since the very core recommendation for XML is to be machine and platform independent, the newest browsers are providing the means for processing XML more easily.

7.8 Cascading Style Sheets (CSS) and XML

HTML can be enhanced by allowing stylesheets to handle font sizes, colors, and placement of text and graphics. The mechanism for attaching a CSS stylesheet to an HTML document is to include it inside the document with <style> tags. For compliance with XHTML standards, the preferred method is to call an external stylesheet with the <link /> tag. We will explore the latter method in this section. Because XHTML can use CSS, XML and XSL can also use these terms to format documents. However, browsers are the most frequent method of displaying any document with Cascading Style Sheets.

Browser compliance with CSS 1.0 is fairly common, but the set of allowable terms is more limited than with CSS 2.0. Test your browser with these examples. The more complete set of terms are very similar to the XSL formatting objects. You can read about CSS at the World Wide Web Consortium web site at http://www.w3.org/. Your browser preferences can be changed to use your own stylesheets or ignore any supplied stylesheets.

You can create Cascading Style Sheets in any text editor. Some of the more popular HTML editors may have shortcuts and assistance for creating them. There are two main ways to set a style and use it. The first way to create a style is to name an element and describe how to display it. The second way is to create a class and then include its name in any element to use that style. This is somewhat similar to setting up XSL templates to handle XML elements. We will show both methods here.

7.81 A Simple Rollover Effect

To show CSS in action, we will create two styles, on and off, and use them with text. The event to change the style is included in the element.

Create a new text file and call it roll.css. Creat the first class, on, and add a period to the beginning of the class name. This signifies that the name of the style is not the name of an element found in your document. How you want any object with this class to be displayed is entered between the curly braces, "{" and "}." For the "on" state, we have chosen our font size to be 16 pts. The next style we want to apply to the text is to make it underlined and blue. Add the class "off" as in Listing 7.15 and save the stylesheet.

Listing 7.15 roll.css

```
.on   {
      font-size: 16;
      text-decoration: underline;
      color: blue;
      }

.off  {
      font-size: 16;
      text-decoration: none;
      color: red;
      }
```

Create a new HTML file and call it CSSrollover.htm. This will be a small document with one text line. Within the <head> element, we will place the <link> element to call the stylesheet roll.css. Type some text within a <div> element. We've chosen to place our rollover "effect" on the text "RED." The styles are set as a default by calling the class "off." Then two events are tested as the mouse is over the text and out of the text. Each of these events will change the class of the text. As the class changes, the stylesheet uses the correct style. Save the HTML document and place it in the same directory as the stylesheet roll.css. Open the HTML document in your browser. Move your mouse over the "RED" text and see what happens!

Listing 7.16 CSSrollover.htm

```
<!DOCTYPE html PUBLIC "-//W3C//DTD XHTML 1.0 Transitional//EN"
     "http://www.w3.org/TR/2000/REC-xhtml1-20000126/DTD/
       xhtml1-transitional.dtd">
<html xmlns="http://www.w3.org/1999/xhtml" xml:lang="en" lang="en">
<head>
     <meta http-equiv="content-type" content="text/html; charset=utf-8" />
     <title>CSS rollover</title>
     <link rel="Stylesheet" href="roll.css" type="text/css" />
</head>
<body>
<div>This text is <span class="off"  onMouseOver = "this.className ='on';"
  onMouseOut = "this.className = 'off';">RED</span> until you place your
  mouse over it!</div>
</body>
</html>
```

7.82 Common CSS Terms

We used the font-size, text-decoration, and color Cascading Style Sheet terms to define our styles for the previous example. Some of the more common terms are listed and defined here. You can find a complete set of CSS 1.0 terms at http://www.w3.org/TR/REC-CSS1.

Your document's font can be set with the deprecated HTML element <font> or with the font CSS terms. The font-family, for example, defines the typeface to use. Because of the variety of cross-platform font styles, the name of any family may not render exactly the same. You can specify several families and the browser or processor will pick the one that matches as closely as possible from the list. An example for setting the font within the <body> of an HTML document is shown here:

```
body { font-family: Arial, Helvetica, Sans-serif }
```

The usage of the word "cascading" for this type of stylesheet can be demonstrated with the above style setting. The <body> element in an HTML document has several child elements. Each of these children will inherit the styles of the parent (body) element. The style is said to "cascade" down.

The font-style can be normal (default), italic, or oblique. The following example will make all of the text on the page italic (slanted) if the browser supports the style.

```
body { font-family: Sans-serif; font-style: italic; }
```

The font-weight: bold term is similar to the <b> element in HTML. The use of the stylesheet allows a single change to many elements that may use that style. The following example uses the class "b1" to be { font-weight: bold } and "b2" to be { font-weight: bold; color: red; }. If you decide later that all bold words should be in red, you can add it to the "b1" style and every occurrence of class "b1" and class "b2" will display the color.

```
<p>This text has a few <b>BOLD</b> words. Every instance of the <b>BOLD</b>
element must be changed if you decide you really wanted to have the <font
color="red">BOLD</font> words in a different style.</p>
<p>This text has a few <span class="b1">BOLD</span> words. Every instance
of the <span class="b1">BOLD</span> element must be changed if you decide
you really wanted to have the <span class="b2">BOLD</span> words in a
different style.</p>
```

The font-size can be shown as point size, relative size, length, or percentage. This CSS term is similar to the HTML <font size="3">. The advantage of using the CSS method to set the font size is that as with the above example, you can make document-wide changes simply by changing the style one time.

The font term can be used when you want to show the family, weight, and size within one style.

```
body { font: 12pt bold sans-serif }
```

There are other CSS terms that can be set. Test them in your browser and decide if the use of your styles will work for the majority of any HTML page using them. Remove the stylesheet from the HTML page and see how it displays without it. You may need to compromise how you use CSS for your presentation.

FileMaker Unlimited 6 comes with a demonstration of using CSS to display XML. Just as with the <body> element, stylesheets may be set to display an XML element such as <personName>. The position CSS term is used to set where to display the contents of the XML elements. Your browser may not support this CSS term. I have found that it is better to display as HTML and use CSS to format the text and colors.

The next chapter has examples of XML displayed as HTML. You can also find XSL and CSS examples in the FileMaker XSLT library at http://www.filemaker.com/xml/xslt_library.html.

Chapter 8

XSLT Examples for FileMaker Pro XML

This chapter will use all of the information presented in the previous chapters to show you how to use XSL stylesheets with FileMaker Pro 6 import, export, and XML web publishing. We will begin with some basic stylesheets and progress to more complex stylesheets.

8.1 Creating Databases from XML Sources

8.11 Create a Database with FMPXMLRESULT

This example shows how an XML document formatted in the FMPXMLRESULT grammar can be used to create a new FileMaker Pro 6 database.

1. Launch FileMaker Pro 6 and export XML with FMPXMLRESULT grammar from any of your databases or use the Export.fp5 database found in Chapter 2. Include a variety of field types, such as text, number, and date, and save the document as **Export0811.xml**.
2. If you specify Format output using current layout and have the field on the layout formatted to display two decimal places, your number fields will retain two decimal places in, for example, the data exported. If you prefer, perform the export again and use the field formats on your layout.
3. Close all databases but leave FileMaker Pro running simply to see the new database that you will create, rather than using the XML in an import to an existing database.

4. From the menu, choose **File**, **Open** and you will be presented with the Open File dialog. Change the Show pop-up to **XML Source** if it is not already selected.
5. The Specify XML and XSL Options dialog will appear. Choose the **File** radio button under Specify XML Source. If File is not already selected, you will get the Open dialog. If File is already selected, click the **Specify** button to get the Open dialog.
6. Navigate to the XML document you just created, select it, and click the **Open** button.
7. Now that you have selected the XML file to use as a source, click the **OK** button in the Specify XML and XSL Options dialog. You will get another dialog asking you to name the new database file. Call it **Export0811.fp5** and click the **Save** button.
8. The fields are created and the data is imported into the new database.
9. Take a look at the XML document Export0811.xml, and then compare its <METADATA> section and the Define Fields dialog in the newly created database Export0811.fp5. If you have a number field (TYPE="NUMBER" in the XML), that type is used to create the field. The other field types are determined by the TYPE attribute in the FIELD element.

Challenge: Export other field types (summary, calculated, and global) and look at the value of the TYPE attribute and the field type if you create a new database with your XML export.

8.12 Create a Database with FMPDSORESULT

An XML document that uses FMPDSORESULT grammar has to be transformed into FMPXMLRESULT grammar before it can be used to create a database. An XSL stylesheet is used to make the transformation. The elements in the XML will become the field names in the new database. The next section will demonstrate transforming FMPDSORESULT into FMPXMLRESULT. Since many XML documents have a similar structure (element names will become the field names), these examples will be helpful for some of the other examples in this chapter.

8.2 Transform FMPDSORESULT into FMPXMLRESULT

We'll use the FMPDSORESULT export along with an XSL stylesheet to transform into an FMPXMLRESULT document. These examples will work in small steps so that you understand how to build an XSL stylesheet.

8.21 Example 1: Find the Rows/Records and Display Some Text

Create a new text document and name it Transform1.xsl.

Add the prolog and the root element for all XSL stylesheets:

```
<?xml version="1.0" encoding="UTF-8" ?>
<xsl:stylesheet>
</xsl:stylesheet>
```

The stylesheet element has several attributes that we need to include. The version and XSL namespace for XSL have required values.

```
<?xml version="1.0" encoding="UTF-8" ?>
<xsl:stylesheet version="1.0" xmlns:xsl="http://www.w3.org/1999/XSL/
  Transform">
</xsl:stylesheet>
```

We'll add two more attributes. The first one is the namespace for the XML source document elements. The second attribute tells the XSL processor to not include this namespace with any elements we create in the resulting XML.

```
<?xml version="1.0" encoding="UTF-8" ?>
<xsl:stylesheet version="1.0" xmlns:xsl="http://www.w3.org/1999/XSL/
  Transform"
      xmlns:fm="http://www.filemaker.com/fmpdsoresult"
        exclude-result-prefixes="fm">
</xsl:stylesheet>
```

Add the top-level XSL output element and its attributes. For this example we want to show the result as text, so the method attribute has a value of "text". Later we'll show the result as XML. The output element shows us the version and encoding for the resulting document. The indent attribute probably should be "no" for most result documents. Any indentation in the stylesheet is added for readability in the code listings and should not be included when you create your stylesheets.

```
<?xml version="1.0" encoding="UTF-8" ?>
<xsl:stylesheet version="1.0" xmlns:xsl="http://www.w3.org/1999/XSL/
  Transform"
      xmlns:fm="http://www.filemaker.com/fmpdsoresult"
        exclude-result-prefixes="fm">
      <xsl:output version="1.0" encoding="UTF-8" indent="no"
        method="text" />
</xsl:stylesheet>
```

Now we need to do something with the XML elements in the source document, so we set up a template. The most common test is to find the root ("/") of the XML source document. From there, you can test for other elements as needed. We'll use the XSL element for-each to get every ROW element in the source document. We'll display the literal text "We found a row!" and a carriage return for every record in the source XML. If you would prefer to use a carriage return and a line-feed, add "
" after the "
". The following code shows the full stylesheet for transform1.xsl. Save this stylesheet in a convenient location and use it with an XML export.

Listing 8.1 transform1.xsl

```
<?xml version="1.0" encoding="UTF-8" ?>
<xsl:stylesheet version="1.0" xmlns:xsl="http://www.w3.org/1999/XSL/
  Transform"
      xmlns:fm="http://www.filemaker.com/fmpdsoresult"
        exclude-result-prefixes="fm">
      <xsl:output version="1.0" encoding="UTF-8" indent="no"
        method="text" />
      <xsl:template match="/">
            <xsl:text>TRANSFORM1.TXT&#13;Find our
              rows.&#13;&#13;</xsl:text>
            <xsl:for-each select="./fm:FMPDSORESULT/fm:ROW"><xsl:
              text>We found a row!&#13;</xsl:text></xsl:for-each>
      </xsl:template>
</xsl:stylesheet>
```

To create the XML export, choose File, Export Records and name the new file transform1.txt. Select FMPDSORESULT grammar and check Use XSL style sheet. Click the File radio button if it is not already selected. When you are prompted in the Open dialog to choose your stylesheet, navigate to where you saved the transform1.xsl file and click Open. The Specify XML and XSL Options dialog shows your stylesheet, so click the OK button.

You will be asked to select the fields for export. This is just a test of the stylesheet with the records, so only a few fields need to be used. Click the Export button and find the transform1.txt document you just created. When you open it in your text editor, you should see something like the listing below (two records in the found set).

```
TRANSFORM1.TXT
Find our rows.

We found a row!
We found a row!
```

8.22 Example 2: Display Something for the Fields

Here, we'll take the above stylesheet, name it transform2.xsl, and add another XSL element, <xsl:for-each>, to display text for the fields in the export. Just to make it easier to see what is happening, we'll use the name of the field elements as the text to display. Within the xsl:for-each loop for the rows/records, we'll add another xsl:for-each loop. The select attribute tells us to get any child element ("*") of the current path ("."). The XPath expression "name()" is a function that returns the name of each of these child elements.

Listing 8.2 transform2.xsl

```
<?xml version="1.0" encoding="UTF-8" ?>
<xsl:stylesheet version="1.0" xmlns:xsl="http://www.w3.org/1999/XSL/
  Transform" xmlns:fm="http://www.filemaker.com/fmpdsoresult"
  exclude-result-prefixes="fm">
      <xsl:output version="1.0" encoding="UTF-8" indent="no"
        method="text" />
      <xsl:template match="/">
            <xsl:text>TRANSFORM2.TXT&#13;Find our rows and show the
              fields.&#13;&#13;</xsl:text>
            <xsl:for-each select="./fm:FMPDSORESULT/fm:ROW">
                  <xsl:text>We found a row!&#13;</xsl:text>
                  <xsl:for-each select="./*">
                        <xsl:value-of select="name()" />
                        <xsl:text>&#13;</xsl:text>
                  </xsl:for-each>
            </xsl:for-each>
      </xsl:template>
</xsl:stylesheet>
```

Perform the same export as in Example 1, but select this new stylesheet and name the resulting document transform2.txt. Listing 8.3 shows the result for two rows and five fields from the Export.fp5 database used in Chapter 2. You can view your results in a text editor.

Listing 8.3 transform2.txt

```
TRANSFORM2.TXT
Find our rows and show the fields.

We found a row!
First_Name
Last_Name
City
State
Number
Date
We found a row!
First_Name
Last_Name
City
State
Number
Date
```

8.23 Example 3: Return an XML Result and Display Elements Instead of Text

Save a copy of transform2.txt as transform3.txt and make the following changes:

- method="xml"
- Don't include a title to the document, or make it a comment.
- Create a ROW element in the result XML that uses the MODID and RECORDID attributes from the source XML.
- Display the contents of the fields inside the <COL><DATA> </DATA></COL> elements. The transform3.xsl stylesheet is shown in Listing 8.4 and the resulting transform3.xml is shown in Listing 8.5. Use the same export as in Examples 1 and 2, but use the new stylesheet. You may select different fields if you wish.

Listing 8.4 transform3.xsl

```
<?xml version='1.0' encoding='UTF-8' ?><xsl:stylesheet version='1.0'
  xmlns:xsl='http://www.w3.org/1999/XSL/Transform'
  xmlns:fm="http://www.filemaker.com/fmpdsoresult"
  exclude-result-prefixes="fm">
      <xsl:output version='1.0' encoding='UTF-8' indent='no'
        method='xml' />
      <xsl:template match="/">
            <xsl:comment>TRANSFORM3.XML</xsl:comment>
```

```
        <xsl:for-each select="./fm:FMPDSORESULT/fm:ROW">
            <ROW><xsl:attribute name="MODID"><xsl:value-of
              select="@MODID" /></xsl:attribute>
              <xsl:attribute name="RECORDID"><xsl:value-of
              select="@RECORDID" /></xsl:attribute>
            <xsl:for-each select="./*">
                <COL><DATA><xsl:value-of select="." /></DATA></COL>
            </xsl:for-each>
            </ROW>
        </xsl:for-each>
    </xsl:template>
</xsl:stylesheet>
```

Listing 8.5 transform3.xml

```
<?xml version="1.0" encoding="UTF-8"?>
<!--TRANSFORM3.XML--><ROW MODID="3" RECORDID="5"><COL><DATA>Beverly</DATA>
</COL><COL><DATA>Voth</DATA></COL><COL><DATA>KY</DATA></COL><COL><DATA>1.00
</DATA></COL></ROW><ROW MODID="4" RECORDID="6"><COL><DATA>Doug</DATA></COL>
<COL><DATA>Rowe</DATA></COL><COL><DATA>FL</DATA></COL><COL><DATA>2.00
</DATA></COL></ROW>
```

8.24 Example 4: Transformation from FMPDSORESULT to FMPXMLRESULT Without the Fields

All that is left for us to add to the stylesheet is the other elements in the FMPXMLRESULT grammar. First we will add everything but the METADATA and FIELD elements. Example 5 will demonstrate how to get the field names from the source XML. Listing 8.6 shows the transform4.xsl stylesheet and Listing 8.7 shows the result, transform4.xml.

Duplicate or save the stylesheet from Example 3 and name it transform4.xsl. The easiest way to add the necessary elements is to export with the FMPXMLRESULT grammar and copy parts of the resulting XML. The name of the DATABASE, the name of the LAYOUT, and the number of RECORDS can be empty, so you can use an XML export from any FileMaker Pro database. Add an empty METADATA element and the start tag for the RESULTSET element. The FOUND value may also be empty. Don't forget to close the RESULTSET and FMPXMLRESULT elements.

```
    <FMPXMLRESULT xmlns="http://www.filemaker.com/fmpxmlresult">
      <ERRORCODE>0</ERRORCODE><PRODUCT BUILD="11/13/2002"
      NAME="FileMaker Pro"VERSION="6.0v4"/><DATABASE DATEFORMAT=
```

```
    "M/d/yyyy" LAYOUT="" NAME="" RECORDS="" TIMEFORMAT=
    "h:mm:ss a"/>
  <METADATA />
  <RESULTSET FOUND="">
  ...
  </RESULTSET>
  </FMPXMLRESULT>
```

Listing 8.6 transform4.xsl

```
<?xml version='1.0' encoding='UTF-8' ?><xsl:stylesheet version='1.0'
 xmlns:xsl='http://www.w3.org/1999/XSL/Transform'
 xmlns:fm="http://www.filemaker.com/fmpdsoresult"
 exclude-result-prefixes="fm">
    <xsl:output version='1.0' encoding='UTF-8' indent='no'
      method='xml' />
    <xsl:template match="/">
    <FMPXMLRESULT xmlns="http://www.filemaker.com/
      fmpxmlresult"><ERRORCODE>0</ERRORCODE><PRODUCT
      BUILD="11/13/2002" NAME="FileMaker Pro"
      VERSION="6.0v4"/><DATABASE DATEFORMAT="M/d/yyyy" LAYOUT=""
      NAME="" RECORDS="" TIMEFORMAT="h:mm:ss a"/>
    <METADATA />
    <RESULTSET FOUND="">
          <xsl:for-each select="./fm:FMPDSORESULT/fm:ROW">
                <ROW><xsl:attribute name="MODID"><xsl:value-of
                  select="@MODID" /></xsl:attribute><xsl:
                  attribute name="RECORDID"><xsl:value-of
                  select="@RECORDID" /></xsl:attribute>
                <xsl:for-each select="./*">
                      <COL><DATA><xsl:value-of select="."
                        /></DATA></COL>
                </xsl:for-each>
                </ROW>
          </xsl:for-each>
    </RESULTSET>
    </FMPXMLRESULT>
    </xsl:template>
</xsl:stylesheet>
```

Listing 8.7 transform4.xml

```
<?xml version="1.0" encoding="UTF-8"?>
<FMPXMLRESULT xmlns="http://www.filemaker.com/fmpxmlresult">
      <ERRORCODE>0</ERRORCODE>
      <PRODUCT BUILD="11/13/2002" NAME="FileMaker Pro" VERSION=
        "6.0v4" />
      <DATABASE DATEFORMAT="M/d/yyyy" LAYOUT="" NAME="" RECORDS=""
        TIMEFORMAT="h:mm:ss a" />
```

```
    <METADATA />
    <RESULTSET FOUND="">
        <ROW MODID="3" RECORDID="5">
            <COL><DATA>Beverly</DATA></COL>
            <COL><DATA>Voth</DATA></COL>
            <COL><DATA>KY</DATA></COL>
            <COL><DATA>1.00</DATA></COL>
        </ROW>
        <ROW MODID="3" RECORDID="6">
            <COL><DATA>Doug</DATA></COL>
            <COL><DATA>Rowe</DATA></COL>
            <COL><DATA>FL</DATA></COL>
            <COL><DATA>2.00</DATA></COL>
        </ROW>
    </RESULTSET>
</FMPXMLRESULT>
```

Try to import the transform4.xml you just created in Listing 8.7. You should be able to see the Import Field Mapping dialog, but there will be no fields listed on the left side! Cancel the process and proceed to Example 5 to see how we can extract the names of the fields and put them in the FIELD elements of the METADATA element.

8.25 Example 5: Get the Field Names for the Transformation

For this example, we will create the FIELD elements with <xsl:element>, extract the field names from the first record/row, and add them as attributes to the elements. Listing 8.8 shows the snippet to replace the <METADATA /> in Example 4. You can compare the following listing with Listing 8.2, "transform2.xsl," where we just got the field names.

Listing 8.8 Create the FIELD elements

```
    <METADATA>
        <xsl:for-each select="./fm:FMPDSORESULT/fm:ROW[1]/*">
            <xsl:element name="FIELD"><xsl:attribute
              name="NAME"><xsl:value-of select="name()"
              /></xsl:attribute></xsl:element>
        </xsl:for-each>
    </METADATA>
```

Listing 8.9 transform5a.xsl

```
<?xml version='1.0' encoding='UTF-8' ?><xsl:stylesheet version='1.0'
  xmlns:xsl='http://www.w3.org/1999/XSL/Transform'
  xmlns:fm="http://www.filemaker.com/fmpdsoresult"
  exclude-result-prefixes="fm">
      <xsl:output version='1.0' encoding='UTF-8' indent='no'
        method='xml' />
      <xsl:template match="/">
      <FMPXMLRESULT xmlns="http://www.filemaker.com/fmpxmlresult">
        <ERRORCODE>0</ERRORCODE><PRODUCT BUILD="11/13/2002"
        NAME="FileMaker Pro" VERSION="6.0v4"/><DATABASE
        DATEFORMAT="M/d/yyyy" LAYOUT="" NAME="" RECORDS=""
        TIMEFORMAT="h:mm:ss a"/>
      <METADATA>
            <xsl:for-each select="./fm:FMPDSORESULT/fm:ROW[1]/*">
                  <xsl:element name="FIELD"><xsl:attribute
                    name="NAME"><xsl:value-of select="name()"
                    /></xsl:attribute></xsl:element>
            </xsl:for-each>
      </METADATA>
      <RESULTSET FOUND="">
            <xsl:for-each select="./fm:FMPDSORESULT/fm:ROW">
                  <ROW><xsl:attribute name="MODID"><xsl:value-of
                    select="@MODID" /></xsl:attribute>
                   <xsl:attribute name="RECORDID"><xsl:value-of
                    select="@RECORDID" /></xsl:attribute>
                  <xsl:for-each select="./*">
                        <COL><DATA><xsl:value-of select="."
                          /></DATA></COL>
                  </xsl:for-each>
                  </ROW>
            </xsl:for-each>
      </RESULTSET>
      </FMPXMLRESULT>
      </xsl:template>
</xsl:stylesheet>
```

Listing 8.10 transform5a.xml

```
<?xml version="1.0" encoding="UTF-8"?>
<FMPXMLRESULT xmlns="http://www.filemaker.com/fmpxmlresult">
  <ERRORCODE>0</ERRORCODE><PRODUCT BUILD="11/13/2002" NAME="FileMaker Pro"
  VERSION="6.0v4"/><DATABASE DATEFORMAT="M/d/yyyy" LAYOUT="" NAME=""
  RECORDS="" TIMEFORMAT="h:mm:ss a"/><METADATA><FIELD
  NAME="First_Name"/><FIELD NAME="Last_Name"/><FIELD NAME="State"/><FIELD
  NAME="Number"/></METADATA><RESULTSET FOUND=""><ROW MODID="3"
  RECORDID="5"><COL><DATA>Beverly</DATA></COL><COL><DATA>Voth</DATA>
  </COL><COL><DATA>KY</DATA></COL><COL><DATA>1.00</DATA></COL></ROW>
```

```
<ROW MODID="4" RECORDID="6"><COL><DATA>Doug</DATA></COL><COL><DATA>
Rowe</DATA></COL><COL><DATA>FL</DATA></COL><COL><DATA>2.00</DATA>
</COL></ROW></RESULTSET></FMPXMLRESULT>
```

You will get an error if you try to import transform5a.xml, shown above. The EMPTYOK, MAXREPEAT, and TYPE attributes are required for import. We will create an attribute set for use with the FIELD element, although we could have entered the required attributes directly in the template. transform5b.xsl in Listing 8.11 shows this addition to the stylesheet and Listing 8.12 shows the resulting XML.

Notice how all of the fields will have a TYPE of TEXT. If you already have the fields created, the import should be fine. If you are using this method to create a database from XML, the field type will also be TEXT.

```
<xsl:attribute-set name="fieldStuff">
     <xsl:attribute name="EMPTYOK">YES</xsl:attribute>
     <xsl:attribute name="MAXREPEAT">1</xsl:attribute>
     <xsl:attribute name="TYPE">TEXT</xsl:attribute>
</xsl:attribute-set>
```

Listing 8.11 transform5b.xsl

```
<?xml version='1.0' encoding='UTF-8' ?><xsl:stylesheet version='1.0'
  xmlns:xsl='http://www.w3.org/1999/XSL/Transform'
  xmlns:fm="http://www.filemaker.com/fmpdsoresult"
  exclude-result-prefixes="fm">
     <xsl:output version='1.0' encoding='UTF-8' indent='no'
       method='xml' />
     <xsl:attribute-set name="fieldStuff">
          <xsl:attribute name="EMPTYOK">YES</xsl:attribute>
          <xsl:attribute name="MAXREPEAT">1</xsl:attribute>
          <xsl:attribute name="TYPE">TEXT</xsl:attribute>
     </xsl:attribute-set>
     <xsl:template match="/">
     <FMPXMLRESULT xmlns="http://www.filemaker.com/fmpxmlresult">
       <ERRORCODE>0</ERRORCODE><PRODUCT BUILD="11/13/2002"
       NAME="FileMaker Pro" VERSION="6.0v4"/><DATABASE
       DATEFORMAT="M/d/yyyy" LAYOUT="" NAME="" RECORDS=""
       TIMEFORMAT="h:mm:ss a"/>
     <METADATA>
          <xsl:for-each select="./fm:FMPDSORESULT/fm:ROW[1]/*">
               <xsl:element name="FIELD" use-attribute-sets=
                 "fieldStuff"><xsl:attribute name="NAME"><xsl:
                 value-of select="name()" /></xsl:attribute>
                 </xsl:element>
          </xsl:for-each>
     </METADATA>
```

```
        <RESULTSET FOUND="">
            <xsl:for-each select="./fm:FMPDSORESULT/fm:ROW">
                <ROW><xsl:attribute name="MODID"><xsl:value-of
                  select="@MODID" /></xsl:attribute><xsl:
                  attribute name="RECORDID"><xsl:value-of
                  select="@RECORDID" /></xsl:attribute>
                <xsl:for-each select="./*">
                    <COL><DATA><xsl:value-of select="." /></DATA></COL>
                </xsl:for-each>
                </ROW>
            </xsl:for-each>
        </RESULTSET>
        </FMPXMLRESULT>
        </xsl:template>
</xsl:stylesheet>
```

Listing 8.12 transform5b.xml

```
<?xml version="1.0" encoding="UTF-8"?>
  <FMPXMLRESULT xmlns="http://www.filemaker.com/fmpxmlresult">
  <ERRORCODE>0</ERRORCODE><PRODUCT BUILD="11/13/2002" NAME="FileMaker Pro"
  VERSION="6.0v4"/><DATABASE DATEFORMAT="M/d/yyyy" LAYOUT="" NAME=""
  RECORDS="" TIMEFORMAT="h:mm:ss a"/><METADATA><FIELD EMPTYOK="YES"
  MAXREPEAT="1" TYPE="TEXT" NAME="First_Name"/><FIELD EMPTYOK="YES"
  MAXREPEAT="1" TYPE="TEXT" NAME="Last_Name"/><FIELD EMPTYOK="YES"
  MAXREPEAT="1" TYPE="TEXT" NAME="State"/><FIELD EMPTYOK="YES"
  MAXREPEAT="1" TYPE="TEXT" NAME="Number"/></METADATA><RESULTSET
  FOUND=""><ROW MODID="3" RECORDID="5"><COL><DATA>Beverly</DATA></COL>
  <COL><DATA>Voth</DATA></COL><COL><DATA>KY</DATA></COL><COL><DATA>
  1.00</DATA></COL></ROW><ROW MODID="4" RECORDID="6"><COL><DATA>Doug
  </DATA></COL><COL><DATA>Rowe</DATA></COL><COL><DATA>FL</DATA>
  </COL><COL><DATA>2.00</DATA></COL></ROW></RESULTSET></FMPXMLRESULT>
```

8.3 XML to HTML

All HTML documents produced can be viewed in a browser. The pages don't need to be served by a web browser. You may find that some CSS and JavaScript may not render correctly, depending on the browser version. Test all the examples in this section to see your results.

8.31 FMPXMLRESULT to HTML

You can find two examples of transforming exported XML into HTML in the FileMaker Pro 6 folder FileMaker Examples\XML Examples\Export. You should study both of these stylesheets, as well as examples in the XSLT library, http://www.filemaker.com/xml/xslt_library.html, for more ideas on how to transform FileMaker Pro XML into HTML documents.

The simple_table.xsl stylesheet will create a basic HTML table showing the name of the database, the number of records, a row showing the field names, and one row for each record in your export. The complex_table.xsl stylesheet shows examples using the conditional <xsl:choose> and the functions position() and mod to determine the alternating background color of the rows.

8.32 FMPDSORESULT to HTML

This example is similar to the example in section 8.2. However, the output will be to method=HTML. The export and transformation will produce an HTML document. The data will be placed into an HTML table similar to the simple_table example. Instead of ROWs, we'll use the HTML element <TR>; and instead of COLs, we'll use the HTML element <TD>. This example will use the FMPDSORESULT instead of the FMPXMLRESULT export.

Example 1: Create a Simple HTML Table from FMPDSORESULT

1. First make a copy of the transform3.xsl file and rename it **dso2html1.xsl**.
2. Change the output method to "html" and indent to "yes".
3. We need to make this an HTML document, so add these tags just after <xsl:template match="/">:

   ```
   <html><head><title>DSO2HTML1</title></head><body>
   ```

4. The HTML document needs to be closed, so add these tags just before </xsl:template>:

   ```
   </body></html>
   ```

5. Just before the first <xsl:for-each>, add the HTML element <table border="1">. For convenience, we'll show the table borders. Just after the final end tag, </xsl:for-each>, add the table close tag, </table>.
6. Change the ROW element into the tr element. Don't forget the end tag! We won't use the MODID and RECORDID attributes at this time, so delete them from the stylesheet.

7. Change the <COL><DATA> elements into the <td> element. Change </DATA></COL> into the </td> element.
8. Save the changes to the stylesheet, as shown in Listing 8.13:

Listing 8.13 dso2html1.xsl

```
<?xml version='1.0' encoding='UTF-8' ?>
<xsl:stylesheet version='1.0'
  xmlns:xsl='http://www.w3.org/1999/XSL/Transform'
  xmlns:fm="http://www.filemaker.com/fmpdsoresult"
  exclude-result-prefixes="fm">
      <xsl:output version='1.0' encoding='UTF-8' indent='yes'
        method='html' />
      <xsl:template match="/">
            <html>
            <head><title>DSO2HTML</title></head>
            <body>
            <table border="1">
            <xsl:for-each select="./fm:FMPDSORESULT/fm:ROW">
                  <tr>
                  <xsl:for-each select="./*">
                        <td><xsl:value-of select="." /></td>
                  </xsl:for-each>
                  </tr>
            </xsl:for-each>
            </table>
            </body>
            </html>
      </xsl:template>
</xsl:stylesheet>
```

9. Export some fields from any of your databases or use Export.fp5, found in Chapter 2.
10. Choose **File**, **Export Records** and name your export **dso2html1.htm**.
11. Select the FMPDSORESULT grammar.
12. Check the Use XSL style sheet option and click the **File** button.
13. Use the stylesheet dso2html1.xsl and click the **Open** button.
14. Click the **OK** button and specify the fields to use in your new HTML table.
15. Click the **Export** button and look at your new HTML document in a text editor and in a browser. The transformed HTML document should look similar to Listing 8.14. Look at the <META> element added just after the <head> element. The XSL processor added this.

Listing 8.14 dso2html1.htm

```
<html>
<head>
<META http-equiv="Content-Type" content="text/html; charset=UTF-8">
<title>DSO2HTML</title>
</head>
<body>
<table border="1">
<tr>
<td>Beverly</td><td>Voth</td><td>KY</td><td>1.00</td><td></td>
</tr>
<tr>
<td>Doug</td><td>Rowe</td><td>FL</td><td>2.00</td><td>1/15/2003</td>
</tr>
</table>
</body>
</html>
```

Example 2: Create an HTML Table with Column Names from Field Names

The table in Example 1 above has just the columns of data and does not show what is in the columns. This example will create a header row with the field names from the first row, as in transform5b.xsl. We'll also use the concept of another template to process the header row and use it inside the main template.

1. Save a copy of dso2html1.xsl as **dso2html2.xsl** and make the following changes:

   After the <table border="1"> element, add the XSLT element below. We'll create another template to make the header row, but we must call it inside the current template.

   ```
   <xsl:call-template name="header" />
   ```

2. Create the template named "header" and place it after the first template in the stylesheet.

   ```
   <xsl:template name="header">
             <xsl:for-each select="./fm:FMPDSORESULT/
               fm:ROW[1]/*">
             <th><xsl:value-of select="name()" /></th>
        </xsl:for-each>
   </xsl:template>
   ```

The complete stylesheet is shown in Listing 8.15, and the result HTML is shown in Listing 8.16.

Listing 8.15 dso2html2.xsl

```
<?xml version='1.0' encoding='UTF-8' ?>
<xsl:stylesheet version='1.0'
 xmlns:xsl='http://www.w3.org/1999/XSL/Transform'
 xmlns:fm="http://www.filemaker.com/fmpdsoresult"
 exclude-result-prefixes="fm">
     <xsl:output version='1.0' encoding='UTF-8' indent='yes'
       method='html' />
     <xsl:template match="/">
          <html>
          <head><title>DSO2HTML</title></head>
          <body>
          <table border="1">
          <xsl:call-template name="header" />
          <xsl:for-each select="./fm:FMPDSORESULT/fm:ROW">
               <tr>
               <xsl:for-each select="./*">
                    <td><xsl:value-of select="." /></td>
               </xsl:for-each>
               </tr>
          </xsl:for-each>
          </table>
          </body>
          </html>
     </xsl:template>
     <xsl:template name="header">
               <xsl:for-each select="./fm:FMPDSORESULT/ fm:ROW[1]/*">
               <th><xsl:value-of select="name()" /></th>
          </xsl:for-each>
     </xsl:template>
</xsl:stylesheet>
```

Listing 8.16 dso2html2.htm

```
<html>
<head>
<META http-equiv="Content-Type" content="text/html; charset=UTF-8">
<title>DSO2HTML</title>
</head>
<body>
<table border="1">
<th>First_Name</th><th>Last_Name</th><th>State</th><th>Number</th>
  <th>Date</th>
<tr>
<td>Beverly</td><td>Voth</td><td>KY</td><td>1.00</td><td></td>
</tr>
<tr>
```

```
<td>Doug</td><td>Rowe</td><td>FL</td><td>2.00</td><td>1/15/2003</td>
</tr>
</table>
</body>
</html>
```

8.33 Subsummaries with FMPDSORESULT

Challenge: Revise the example XSLT subsummary.xsl to use the FMPDSORESULT. This stylesheet is found in the FileMaker Pro 6 folder FileMaker Examples\XML Examples\Export with the other examples. The stylesheet uses the <xsl:key> to group a particular column for summary. Hint: Instead of "fmp:FMPXMLRESULT/fmp:RESULTSET/fmp:ROW", use "fmp:FMPDSORESULT/fmp:ROW", and instead of "fmp:COL[1]/fmp:DATA", use the name of the element (field name) to summarize. Change other references to the XML elements as needed.

The subsummary.xsl stylesheet also is a good example for using the <xsl:variable> element. We'll use that element to set parameters for our version of a "fixed-width" text export.

8.4 Fixed-width Text Export

You can find an example of a text export for column widths to be of the same width. You can change the variable to be any width, but you don't have a way to change each column independently. This stylesheet is called fixed_width.xsl and is found with the other example stylesheets in FileMaker Pro 6. Our example will use <xsl:variable> to pass values and <xsl:param> to pass the width of each column.

8.41 Getting the Column Widths

Sometimes you will be given a map for the width of each column, such as in Listing 8.17. This map may also include default values to use or a format for text, like the amount column. Sometimes you may need to make a best guess by counting the characters in a sample output, as seen in Listing 8.18. This type of document may be in a monospaced font so you can see the columns. You can understand why it is much easier to determine the correct column width when you have a map!

Listing 8.17 Map of columns

```
begin (4) 'ORD '
firstname (20)
lastname (20)
state (2)
amount (9, 2) 000000.00
```

Listing 8.18 Sample text output

```
ORD Beverly             Voth                KY000001.00
ORD Doug                Rowe                FL000002.00
```

8.42 Setting Up Default Values

You may wish to use values multiple times within an XSLT stylesheet. These can be set by using the XSL top-level elements <xsl:variable> and <xsl:param> or by defining an !ENTITY before the <xsl:stylesheet> element. A good reason for using these methods is to allow quick changes to a default value, such as the end-of-line character or a delimiter. The difference between the <xsl:variable> and the <xsl:param> elements is that PARAM is used if a value doesn't already exist. We'll use both of these XSLT elements in our example, so you will see ways that they can be used.

The value of these elements can be global (used throughout the stylesheet) if set as top-level elements, or local if set within a template. In either case, the value of the variable or parameter is returned if the name is used in an XPath expression, by appending the "$" character before the name of the variable or parameter. For example, "$eol" returns the value set by:

```
<!-- end-of-line = CRLF -->
<xsl:variable name="eol"><xsl:text>&#13;&#10;</xsl:text></xsl:variable>
```

The value of an ENTITY is called by using the defined name of the entity between the "&" and ";" characters. Listing 8.19 shows how to define an ENTITY for use in an XSL stylesheet.

Listing 8.19 Define an ENTITY

```
<?xml version="1.0" encoding="UTF-8" ?>
<!DOCTYPE stylesheet[
     <!ENTITY eol "<xsl:text>&#13;&#10;</xsl:text>">
]>
<xsl:stylesheet>
...
</xsl:stylesheet>
```

We will use the <xsl:variable> for the fixed-width example. We need to define the end-of-line character and some "padding" characters for numbers and text. Start the stylesheet as in Listing 8.20. Change the end-of-line character to your preference. You may also define any other default values you may use throughout the stylesheet.

Listing 8.20 Begin variable_fixed.xsl

```
<?xml version="1.0" encoding="UTF-8"?>
<xsl:stylesheet version="1.0" xmlns:xsl="http://www.w3.org/1999/
  XSL/Transform" xmlns:fmp="http://www.filemaker.com/fmpxmlresult">
      <xsl:output method="text"  version="1.0" encoding="UTF-8"
        indent="no" />
      <!-- SET UP VARIABLES -->
      <!-- end-of-line = carriage return, change as needed -->
      <xsl:variable name="eol"><xsl:text>&#13;</xsl:text>
        </xsl:variable>
      <!-- space as text fill character -->
      <xsl:variable name="padSpace"><xsl:text>&#32;</xsl:text>
        </xsl:variable>
      <!-- zero as  number fill character -->
      <xsl:variable name="padNum"><xsl:text>0</xsl:text></xsl:variable>
      <!-- set your own default values here -->
      <xsl:variable name="begin"><xsl:text>ORD</xsl:text><xsl:value-of
        select="$padSpace" /></xsl:variable>
      <!-- main template here -->
      <xsl:template match="fmp:FMPXMLRESULT">
            <xsl:for-each select="fmp:RESULTSET/fmp:ROW">
            <xsl:value-of select="$begin" />
                  <!-- Begin each row with line start text -->
            <xsl:apply-templates />
                  <!-- see if there are templates for the columns
                     -->
            <xsl:value-of select="$eol" />
                  <!-- end each row with the end-of-line character
                     -->
        </xsl:for-each>
      </xsl:template>
</xsl:stylesheet>
```

8.43 Passing Parameters

The sample template shown here is used on each column to pass the desired width of the column and the padding character to use. <xsl:with-param> is used with <xsl:call-template> to pass this information. Our first column from the database is the firstname field and will be 20 characters wide padded with the space character. Each column will have a separate template match, so that we can pass different widths and padding characters. You may need to create a default template to handle any columns not specifically called.

Listing 8.21 Set up each column and default template

```
<xsl:template match="fmp:COL[1]">
     <xsl:call-template name="makeCol">
          <xsl:with-param name="colWidth" select="20" />
          <xsl:with-param name="colPad" select="$padSpace" />
     </xsl:call-template>
</xsl:template>
<xsl:template match="fmp:COL">
     <!-- do nothing for other columns, if any -->
</xsl:template>
```

8.44 Testing Data Length

For our example, a text string that is not long enough for a column will be padded on the right with additional spaces. If the text string is too long, it will be truncated to the column length. A number may need to be padded with leading zeros, as in our example, or with spaces. You must determine the padding character to use and whether it occurs before or after your text string. Use the <xsl:choose> element to test for the length of a string and what template to call for further processing.

Listing 8.22 makeCol template

```
<xsl:template name="makeCol">
     <xsl:param name="colWidth" select="0" />
     <xsl:param name="colPad" select="$padSpace" />
     <xsl:choose>
          <xsl:when test="string-length(fmp:DATA) &lt; $colWidth">
                    <!-- we will make another test here,
                      see Listing 8.21 -->
          </xsl:when>
          <xsl:otherwise>
               <xsl:value-of select="substring(fmp:DATA,1,
                 $colWidth)" />
          </xsl:otherwise>
     </xsl:choose>
</xsl:template>
```

Let's analyze Listing 8.22. This is a template named makeCol. Each column template in your stylesheet, as in Listing 8.21, calls the template. We will set the default parameters to use if we forgot to pass them to the template. You will get an XSL processor error if you use the parameters in the template and don't pass them to the template or set them within the template. The "colPad" parameter can use the global variable "padSpace", which was set at the beginning of the stylesheet.

Next we create an <xsl:choose> test to see if the width of the string value of the column is less than ("<") the passed parameter "colWidth". When the string is not long enough, we will test for the padding character, as in Listing 8.23. Otherwise we truncate the string by using the XPath function substring(). If the string value of the column is exactly the correct width, this function will just return the string value.

Listing 8.23 will be inserted in the makeCol template, above, where we need to make this test. We've passed a character to use for padding. When the character is the space ("$padSpace"), we want to have the output take the string value of the DATA element and call another template, textPad, to add the padding. We pass the parameter that tells us the number of times we need to add the padding character. If the padding character is the zero ("$padNum"), we want to call the textPad template, passing the "padCount" parameter, and then output the string value of the DATA element.

Listing 8.23 Test the padding character

```
<xsl:choose>
     <xsl:when test="$colPad = $padSpace">
          <xsl:value-of select="fmp:DATA" />
          <xsl:call-template name="textPad">
               <xsl:with-param name="padCount" select="$colWidth
                 - string-length(fmp:DATA)" />
               <xsl:with-param name="colPad" select="$colPad" />
          </xsl:call-template>
     </xsl:when>
     <xsl:otherwise>
          <xsl:call-template name="textPad">
               <xsl:with-param name="padCount" select="$colWidth
                 - string-length(fmp:DATA)" />
               <xsl:with-param name="colPad" select="$colPad" />
          </xsl:call-template>
          <xsl:value-of select="fmp:DATA" />
     </xsl:otherwise>
</xsl:choose>
```

Listing 8.24 makeCol template complete

```
<xsl:template name="makeCol">
     <xsl:param name="colWidth" select="0" />
     <xsl:param name="colPad" select="$padSpace" />
     <xsl:choose>
          <xsl:when test="string-length(fmp:DATA) &lt; $colWidth">
               <xsl:choose>
                    <xsl:when test="$colPad = $padSpace">
                         <xsl:value-of select="fmp:DATA" />
                         <xsl:call-template name="textPad">
                              <xsl:with-param name="padCount"
                                select="$colWidth - string
                               -length(fmp:DATA)" />
                              <xsl:with-param name="colPad"
                                select="$colPad" />
                         </xsl:call-template>
                    </xsl:when>
                    <xsl:otherwise>
                         <xsl:call-template name="textPad">
                              <xsl:with-param name="padCount"
                                select="$colWidth - string
                               -length(fmp:DATA)" />
                              <xsl:with-param name="colPad"
                                select="$colPad" />
                         </xsl:call-template>
                         <xsl:value-of select="fmp:DATA" />
                    </xsl:otherwise>
               </xsl:choose>
          </xsl:when>
          <xsl:otherwise>
               <xsl:value-of select="substring(fmp:DATA,1,$colWidth)" />
          </xsl:otherwise>
     </xsl:choose>
</xsl:template>
```

8.45 Looping to Add Padding Characters

The makeCol template calls the next template, textPad. You may begin to see how the XSL template is used very much like a Perform Script[subscript] in FileMaker Pro. Each template builds upon the one that calls it. We use a default parameter of "0" if none is passed and decrement a passed parameter throughout the loop. The <xsl:if> test will fail when there are no more padding characters to output. When all padding is complete, the stylesheet returns to the calling template, makeCol.

Listing 8.25 textPad template

```
<xsl:template name="textPad">
     <xsl:param name="padCount" select="0" />
     <xsl:param name="colPad" select="$padSpace" />
     <!-- template calls itself until all the required padding is
       included -->
     <xsl:if test="$padCount > 0">
          <xsl:value-of select="$colPad" />
          <xsl:call-template name="textPad">
               <!-- decrement the parameter -->
               <xsl:with-param name="padCount" select="$padCount - 1" />
               <xsl:with-param name="colPad" select="$colPad" />
          </xsl:call-template>
     </xsl:if>
</xsl:template>
```

8.46 The Complete Variable Fixed-Width Stylesheet

We'll put all the templates together, create a template for each column in our FMPXMLRESULT export, and save the stylesheet as variable_fixed.xsl. The width of each column is passed along with the padding character to another template.

Listing 8.26 variable_fixed.xsl

```
<?xml version="1.0" encoding="UTF-8"?>
<xsl:stylesheet version="1.0" xmlns:xsl="http://www.w3.org/1999/XSL/
  Transform" xmlns:fmp="http://www.filemaker.com/fmpxmlresult">
     <xsl:output method="text"  version="1.0" encoding="UTF-8"
       indent="no" />
     <!-- SET UP VARIABLES -->
     <!-- end-of-line = carriage return, change as needed -->
     <xsl:variable name="eol"><xsl:text>&#13;</xsl:text></xsl:variable>
     <!-- space as text fill character -->
     <xsl:variable name="padSpace"><xsl:text>&#32;</xsl:text>
       </xsl:variable>
     <!-- zero as  number fill character -->
     <xsl:variable name="padNum"><xsl:text>0</xsl:text></xsl:variable>
     <!-- set your own default values here -->
     <xsl:variable name="begin"><xsl:text>ORD</xsl:text><xsl:value-of
       select="$padSpace" /></xsl:variable>
     <!-- main template here -->
     <xsl:template match="fmp:FMPXMLRESULT">
          <xsl:for-each select="fmp:RESULTSET/fmp:ROW">
          <xsl:value-of select="$begin" />
               <!-- Begin each row with line start text -->
```

```
        <xsl:apply-templates />
            <!-- see if there are templates for the columns -->
        <xsl:value-of select="$eol" />
            <!-- end each row with the end-of-line character -->
    </xsl:for-each>
  </xsl:template>
  <!-- SET UP EACH FIELD/COLUMN WIDTH -->
  <xsl:template match="fmp:COL[1]">
        <!-- firstname -->
        <xsl:call-template name="makeCol">
            <xsl:with-param name="colWidth" select="20" />
            <xsl:with-param name="colPad" select="$padSpace" />
        </xsl:call-template>
  </xsl:template>
  <xsl:template match="fmp:COL[2]">
        <!-- lastname -->
        <xsl:call-template name="makeCol">
            <xsl:with-param name="colWidth" select="20" />
            <xsl:with-param name="colPad" select="$padSpace" />
        </xsl:call-template>
  </xsl:template>
  <xsl:template match="fmp:COL[3]">
        <!-- state -->
        <xsl:call-template name="makeCol">
            <xsl:with-param name="colWidth" select="2" />
            <xsl:with-param name="colPad" select="$padSpace" />
        </xsl:call-template>
  </xsl:template>
  <xsl:template match="fmp:COL[4]">
        <!-- amount -->
        <xsl:call-template name="makeCol">
            <xsl:with-param name="colWidth" select="9" />
            <xsl:with-param name="colPad" select="$padNum" />
        </xsl:call-template>
  </xsl:template>
  <xsl:template match="fmp:COL">
        <!-- do nothing for other columns, if any -->
  </xsl:template>
  <!-- TEMPLATE TO TEST FOR COLUMN WIDTH -->
  <xsl:template name="makeCol">
        <xsl:param name="colWidth" select="0" />
        <xsl:param name="colPad" select="$padSpace" />
        <xsl:choose>
            <xsl:when test="string-length(fmp:DATA) &lt; $colWidth">
                <xsl:choose>
                    <xsl:when test="$colPad = $padSpace">
                        <xsl:value-of select="fmp:DATA" />
                        <xsl:call-template name="textPad">
```

```
                              <xsl:with-param name="padCount"
                                select="$colWidth - string
                                -length(fmp:DATA)" />
                              <xsl:with-param name="colPad"
                                select="$colPad" />
                         </xsl:call-template>
                    </xsl:when>
                    <xsl:otherwise>
                         <xsl:call-template name="textPad">
                              <xsl:with-param name="padCount"
                                select="$colWidth - string
                                -length(fmp:DATA)" />
                              <xsl:with-param name="colPad"
                                select="$colPad" />
                         </xsl:call-template>
                         <xsl:value-of select="fmp:DATA" />
                    </xsl:otherwise>
               </xsl:choose>
          </xsl:when>
          <xsl:otherwise>
               <xsl:value-of select="substring(fmp:DATA,1,
                 $colWidth)" />
          </xsl:otherwise>
     </xsl:choose>
</xsl:template>
<!-- PADDING TEMPLATE -->
<xsl:template name="textPad">
     <xsl:param name="padCount" select="0" />
     <xsl:param name="colPad" select="$padSpace" />
     <!-- template calls itself until all the required padding
       is included -->
     <xsl:if test="$padCount > 0">
          <xsl:value-of select="$colPad" />
          <xsl:call-template name="textPad">
               <!-- decrement the parameter -->
               <xsl:with-param name="padCount" select="$padCount -
                 1" />
               <xsl:with-param name="colPad" select="$colPad" />
          </xsl:call-template>
     </xsl:if>
</xsl:template>
</xsl:stylesheet>
```

8.5 Export XML from Related Databases

It's fairly easy to pick related fields one relationship away and use them in your XML export. You may use FMPDSORESULT or FMPXMLRESULT to export related fields. See section 2.22, "XML from FileMaker Pro Related Fields," for the structure of each of these types of XML documents.

Walking the XML tree to get the <DATA> in each of the fields is not as easy. The XPath function position() can return a number relating to the child order of an element. The first <DATA> element in the <COL> element of a related field is "position() = 1" when you export with FMPXMLRESULT. The only difference of the <DATA> element in the FMPDSORESULT is that the name of the element is the name of the related field (including the relationship name). The first <DATA> element is still at "position() = 1". We will use this XPath function in our XSLT stylesheet to allow us to get each of the field contents in each of the portal rows.

Creating an XML document with data more than one relationship away is much more difficult. If you have a CUSTOMERS database and related ORDERS database, you may also have a related ITEMS database with all of the order items. A FileMaker Pro export from CUSTOMERS can yield the ORDERS fields in an XML export, but not the ITEMS fields. A FileMaker Pro export from the ORDERS database can get the CUSTOMERS information, but it will be repeated for every record/ROW in the found set.

Note: Indentation has been added for clarity in these examples. The actual export is not formatted this way.

8.51 Export as FMPDSORESULT

Step 1: Simple Export

Use the databases Customers.FP5 and Orders.FP5 for this exercise.

The script ExportCustomers in Customers.FP5 has a simple export of the Customer data, as seen in the listing below.

Listing 8.27 customers.xml

```
<?xml version="1.0" encoding="UTF-8"?>
<customers>
	<customer ID="1">
```

```
        <name>Herbson's Pices</name>
        <city>Monterey</city>
    </customer>
    <customer ID="2">
        <name>A Pealing Desserts</name>
        <city>New York</city>
    </customer>
</customers>
```

The stylesheet customers.xsl is shown in Listing 8.28. It's a simple stylesheet that converts the FMPDSORESULT into a slightly different XML format. The field ID needed to be placed as an attribute for the element <customer>. The other two fields are just placed within literal elements. The names of the fields (names of the elements) could have been used with <xsl:element> to create the element.

Listing 8.28 customers.xsl

```
<?xml version='1.0' encoding='UTF-8' ?>
<xsl:stylesheet version='1.0'
  xmlns:xsl='http://www.w3.org/1999/XSL/Transform'
  xmlns:fm="http://www.filemaker.com/fmpdsoresult"
  exclude-result-prefixes="fm">
    <xsl:output version='1.0' encoding='UTF-8' indent='yes'
      method='xml' />
    <xsl:template match="/">
    <customers>
        <xsl:for-each select="fm:FMPDSORESULT/fm:ROW">
            <customer>
                <xsl:attribute name="ID"><xsl:value-of
                  select="./fm:ID" /></xsl:attribute>
                <name><xsl:value-of select="./fm:Name" /></name>
                <city><xsl:value-of select="./fm:City" /></city>
            </customer>
        </xsl:for-each>
    </customers>
    </xsl:template>
</xsl:stylesheet>
```

Step 2: Export with Related Fields

The simple export in Step 1 does not contain any related fields or data. We revised the stylesheet to include the orders as a list with the order ID as an attribute. Listing 8.29 shows the revised stylesheet and Listing 8.30 shows the new XML document. The script to create the document is ExportCustOrders in Customers.FP5.

Listing 8.29 custOrders.xsl

```
<?xml version='1.0' encoding='UTF-8' ?>
<xsl:stylesheet version='1.0'
  xmlns:xsl='http://www.w3.org/1999/XSL/Transform'
  xmlns:fm="http://www.filemaker.com/fmpdsoresult"
  exclude-result-prefixes="fm">
      <xsl:output version='1.0' encoding='UTF-8' indent='yes'
        method='xml' />
      <xsl:template match="/">
      <customers>
            <xsl:for-each select="fm:FMPDSORESULT/fm:ROW">
                  <customer>
                        <xsl:attribute name="ID"><xsl:value-of
                          select="./fm:ID" /></xsl:attribute>
                        <name><xsl:value-of select="./fm:Name" /></name>
                        <city><xsl:value-of select="./fm:City" /></city>
                        <orders>
                              <xsl:for-each select="./fm:ID_Orders_
                                CustomerID.OrderID/fm:DATA">
                              <order>
                                    <xsl:attribute name="ID"><xsl:value-of
                                      select="." /></xsl:attribute>
                              </order>
                              </xsl:for-each>
                        </orders>
                  </customer>
            </xsl:for-each>
      </customers>
      </xsl:template>
</xsl:stylesheet>
```

Listing 8.30 custOrders.xml

```
<?xml version="1.0" encoding="UTF-8"?>
<customers>
      <customer ID="1">
            <name>Herbson's Pices</name>
            <city>Monterey</city>
            <orders>
                  <order ID="ORD2"/>
                  <order ID="ORD3"/>
            </orders>
      </customer>
      <customer ID="2">
            <name>A Pealing Desserts</name>
            <city>New York</city>
            <orders>
                  <order ID="ORD4"/>
```

```
        </orders>
    </customer>
</customers>
```

Step 3: Adding Other Related Fields

With the help of the XPath function position() we can set a variable to number the orders and also to use when getting the sibling <DATA> values. The ExportOrdersCust script in Customers.FP5 creates the XML in Listing 8.31.

Listing 8.31 OrdersCust.xml

```
<?xml version="1.0" encoding="UTF-8"?>
<customers>
    <customer ID="1">
        <name>Herbson's Pices</name>
        <city>Monterey</city>
        <orders>
            <order ID="ORD2">
                <num>1</num>
                <date>12-01-2002</date>
                <amount>23.54</amount>
            </order>
            <order ID="ORD3">
                <num>2</num>
                <date>01-06-2003</date>
                <amount>15.45</amount>
            </order>
        </orders>
    </customer>
    <customer ID="2">
        <name>A Pealing Desserts</name>
        <city>New York</city>
        <orders>
            <order ID="ORD4">
                <num>1</num>
                <date>11-15-2002</date>
                <amount>115.00</amount>
            </order>
        </orders>
    </customer>
</customers>
```

The stylesheet OrdersCust.xsl has a few changes to get the other related fields, as seen here:

```
<order>
     <xsl:attribute name="ID"><xsl:value-of select="." /></xsl:attribute>
     <num><xsl:value-of select="position()" /></num>
     <date><xsl:value-of select="../../fm:ID_Orders_CustomerID.OrderDate/
       fm:DATA[position() = $recNum]" /></date>
     <amount><xsl:value-of select="../../fm:ID_Orders_CustomerID.TotalAmt/
       fm:DATA[position() = $recNum]" /></amount>
</order>
```

The "../" expression in the code above is the XPath shortcut for "parent::". When you are on the first field in the first portal row, the path to the next field in that row is back up the tree to the grandparent and back down to the related field name and <DATA> element. If we did not specify the predicate for that element, you would get the first field in every portal row! The full XSLT stylesheet is shown in Listing 8.32.

Listing 8.32 OrdersCust.xsl

```
<?xml version='1.0' encoding='UTF-8' ?>
<xsl:stylesheet version='1.0'
  xmlns:xsl='http://www.w3.org/1999/XSL/Transform'
  xmlns:fm="http://www.filemaker.com/fmpdsoresult"
  exclude-result-prefixes="fm">
     <xsl:output version='1.0' encoding='UTF-8' indent='yes'
       method='xml' />
     <xsl:template match="/">
     <customers>
          <xsl:for-each select="fm:FMPDSORESULT/fm:ROW">
               <customer>
                    <xsl:attribute name="ID"><xsl:value-of select=".
                      /fm:ID" /></xsl:attribute>
                    <name><xsl:value-of select="./fm:Name" /></name>
                    <city><xsl:value-of select="./fm:City" /></city>
                    <orders>
                         <xsl:for-each select="./fm:ID_Orders_
                           CustomerID.OrderID/fm:DATA">
                         <xsl:variable name="recNum"><xsl:value-of
                           select="position()" /></xsl:variable>
                         <order>
                              <xsl:attribute name="ID"><xsl:value-of
                                select="." /></xsl:attribute>
                              <num><xsl:value-of select="position()"
                                /></num>
                              <date><xsl:value-of select="../../
                               fm:ID_Orders_CustomerID.OrderDate/
                               fm:DATA[position() = $recNum]"
                                /></date>
                                <amount><xsl:value-of select="../../
```

```
                                fm:ID_Orders_CustomerID.TotalAmt/
                                fm:DATA[position() = $recNum]"
                                /></amount>
                        </order>
                        </xsl:for-each>
                    </orders>
                </customer>
            </xsl:for-each>
        </customers>
        </xsl:template>
</xsl:stylesheet>
```

8.52 Export as FMPXMLRESULT

Similar XSLT can be used to transform related fields when you export as FMPXMLRESULT. The stylesheet OrdersCustXML.xsl is shown here. The results are the same as in Listing 8.31, OrdersCust.xml, but are called OrdersCustXML.xml. Compare the stylesheet in Listing 8.32 with this stylesheet.

Listing 8.33 OrdersCustXML.xsl

```
<?xml version='1.0' encoding='UTF-8' ?>
<xsl:stylesheet version='1.0'
  xmlns:xsl='http://www.w3.org/1999/XSL/Transform'
  xmlns:fm="http://www.filemaker.com/fmpxmlresult"
  exclude-result-prefixes="fm">
        <xsl:output version='1.0' encoding='UTF-8' indent='yes'
          method='xml' />
        <xsl:template match="/">
        <customers>
            <xsl:for-each select="fm:FMPXMLRESULT/fm:RESULTSET/fm:ROW">
                <customer>
                    <xsl:attribute name="ID"><xsl:value-of select=
                      "./fm:COL[1]/fm:DATA" /></xsl:attribute>
                    <name><xsl:value-of select="./fm:COL[2]/fm:DATA"
                      /></name>
                    <city><xsl:value-of select="./fm:COL[3]/fm:DATA"
                      /></city>
                    <orders>
                        <xsl:for-each select="./fm:COL[4]/fm:DATA">
                        <xsl:variable name="recNum"><xsl:value-of
                          select="position()" /></xsl:variable>
                        <order>
                            <xsl:attribute name="ID"><xsl:value-of
                              select="." /></xsl:attribute>
                            <num><xsl:value-of select="position()"
```

```
                                        /></num>
                                    <date><xsl:value-of select="../../
                                        fm:COL[5]/fm:DATA[position() =
                                        $recNum]" /></date>
                                    <amount><xsl:value-of select="../../
                                        fm:COL[6]/fm:DATA[position() =
                                        $recNum]" /></amount>
                                </order>
                                </xsl:for-each>
                            </orders>
                        </customer>
                    </xsl:for-each>
        </customers>
        </xsl:template>
</xsl:stylesheet>
```

8.53 Export to HTML

A stylesheet to create an HTML document can use the same principles shown in the previous two sections. Listing 8.34 shows the creation of a simple table. All orders are in a single row along with the customer information.

Listing 8.34 OrdersCustHTML.htm

```
<?xml version="1.0" encoding="UTF-8"?>
<html>
<head>
<title>Customers</title>
</head>
<body>
<table border="1">
<tr>
<td>1</td>
<td>Monterey</td>
<td>Herbson's Pices</td>
<td>ORD2</td>
<td>1</td>
<td>12-01-2002</td>
<td>23.54</td>
<td>ORD3</td>
<td>2</td>
<td>01-06-2003</td>
<td>15.45</td>
</tr>
<tr>
<td>2</td>
```

```
<td>New York</td>
<td>A Pealing Desserts</td>
<td>ORD4</td>
<td>1</td>
<td>11-15-2002</td>
<td>115.00</td>
</tr>
</table>
</body>
</html>
```

Listing 8.35 OrdersCustHTML.xsl

```
<?xml version='1.0' encoding='UTF-8' ?>
<xsl:stylesheet version='1.0'
  xmlns:xsl='http://www.w3.org/1999/XSL/Transform'
  xmlns:fm="http://www.filemaker.com/fmpxmlresult"
  exclude-result-prefixes="fm">
      <xsl:output version='1.0' encoding='UTF-8' indent='yes'
        method='xml' />
      <xsl:template match="/">
      <html>
      <head><title>Customers</title></head>
      <body>
      <table border="1">
            <xsl:for-each select="fm:FMPXMLRESULT/fm:RESULTSET/fm:ROW">
                  <tr>
                        <td><xsl:value-of select="./fm:COL[1]/fm:DATA"
                          /></td>
                        <td><xsl:value-of select="./fm:COL[2]/fm:DATA"
                          /></td>
                        <td><xsl:value-of select="./fm:COL[3]/fm:DATA"
                          /></td>
                              <xsl:for-each select="./fm:COL[4]/fm:DATA">
                              <xsl:variable name="recNum"><xsl:value-of
                                select="position()" /></xsl:variable>
                              <td><xsl:value-of select="." /></td>
                                    <td><xsl:value-of select="position()"
                                      /></td>
                                    <td><xsl:value-of select="../../
                                      fm:COL[5]/fm:DATA[position() =
                                      $recNum]" /></td>
                                    <td><xsl:value-of select="../../
                                      fm:COL[6]/fm:DATA[position() =
                                      $recNum]" /></td>
                              </xsl:for-each>
                  </tr>
            </xsl:for-each>
      </table>
```

```
    </body>
    </html>
    </xsl:template>
</xsl:stylesheet>
```

Challenge: Using the above XSL and the example "Hidden Portal Trick" found in the XSLT library, http://www.filemaker.com/xml/xslt_library.html, create an HTML page to show the customer information, followed by the related information in tables. Use <xsl:if> to show or not show the table, depending upon a record having related data.

8.6 Import XML into Related Databases

You may need to import an XML document into FileMaker Pro and the structure dictates the need for multiple databases, multiple stylesheets, and scripting to call the import routines to accomplish this. Go back and review Chapters 3 and 4 for more information about DTDs, schemas, and grammars. By understanding the structure of your document, you will know what elements will be used for import into any one database. Sometimes the data in an element will be imported into more than one database. Any field used as a relationship key may be shown once in the XML document but occurs in several databases. As a general rule, any element that repeats within another element probably is a good candidate for import into a related database. This section uses the Customers, Orders, and Items databases to import a single XML document.

8.61 The XML Source

The following listing is the document Orders.xml.

Listing 8.36 Orders.xml

```
<?xml version="1.0" encoding="UTF-8"?>
<customers>
    <customer ID="1">
        <city>Monterey</city>
        <name>Herbson's Pices</name>
        <orders>
            <order ID="ORD2">
                <num>1</num>
                <date>12-01-2002</date>
                <amount>23.54</amount>
```

```
                <items>
                    <item>
                        <productID>ABC123</productID>
                        <quantity>1</quantity>
                        <description>Oregano</description>
                        <price>23.54</price>
                        <extended>23.54</extended>
                    </item>
                </items>
            </order>
            <order ID="ORD3">
                <num>2</num>
                <date>01-06-2003</date>
                <amount>15.45</amount>
                <items>
                    <item>
                        <productID>23_45d</productID>
                        <quantity>2</quantity>
                        <description>Rosemary</description>
                        <price>5.00</price>
                        <extended>10.00</extended>
                    </item>
                    <item>
                        <productID>t456</productID>
                        <quantity>5</quantity>
                        <description>Thyme</description>
                        <price>1.09</price>
                        <extended>5.45</extended>
                    </item>
                </items>
            </order>
        </orders>
    </customer>
    <customer ID="2">
        <city>New York</city>
        <name>A Pealing Desserts</name>
            <orders>
            <order ID="ORD4">
                <num>1</num>
                <date>11-15-2002</date>
                <amount>115.00</amount>
                <items>
                    <item>
                        <productID>ABC123</productID>
                        <quantity>5</quantity>
                        <description>Lemon Zests</description>
                        <price>23.00</price>
```

```
                    <extended>115.00</extended>
                </item>
            </items>
        </order>
    </orders>
  </customer>
</customers>
```

8.62 The Databases

The example FileMaker Pro databases we used for exporting in section 8.5 are used here for importing the XML source shown in Listing 8.36. Each of the databases is described here, including field names, relationships, and import scripts. The field names do not match the element names in the XML source. To help create the XSLT stylesheets, you can make a simple FMPXMLRESULT export from each of these databases.

- Customers.FP5 fields: ID (number), Name (text), City (text)
- Orders.FP5 fields: OrderID (number), TotalAmt (number), OrderDate (date), CustomerID (number)
- Items.FP5 fields: CustomerID (number), OrderID (text), ProductID (text), Qty (number), Description (text), Price (number), cExtended (calculation, number = Qty * Price), ItemID (number)

Scripts (File Name, Script Name). These are the import scripts in each database. They are performed by a single script in the Items.FP5 database. The printed scripts don't show that all imports were performed manually with "matching names" and the criteria saved in the scripts. You also don't see that the ImportCustomers script uses the ID field as a match field and the import action uses the Update matching records in the current found set and Add remaining records options. When importing, we can be reasonably sure that the Orders and Items are new records to be created. We might already have the customer record and only need to update or add with the XML import.

Listing 8.37 Scripts

```
1. Customers.FP5, ImportCustomers
  Show All Records
  Import Records [ XML (from file): "Orders.xml"; XSL (from file):
  "ImportCustomers.xsl"; Import Order: ID (Number), Name (Text),
    City (Text) ] [ Restore import order, No dialog ]
2. Orders.FP5, ImportOrders
```

```
  Import Records [ XML (from file): "Orders.xml"; XSL (from file):
  "ImportOrders.xsl"; Import Order: CustomerID (Number), OrderID
    (Number), OrderDate (Date), TotalAmt (Number) ] [ Restore import
    order, No dialog ]
3. Items.FP5,  ImportItems
  Import Records [ XML (from file): "Orders.xml"; XSL (from file):
  "ImportOrders.xsl"; Import Order: CustomerID (Number), OrderID (Text),
  ItemID (Number), Qty (Number), ProductID (Text), Description (Text),
    Price (Number) ]
   [ Restore import order, No dialog ]
4. Items.FP5,  Imports
  Perform Script [ "ImportItems" ]
   [ Sub-scripts ]
  Perform Script [ Filename: "Orders.FP5", "ImportOrders" ]
   [ Sub-scripts ]
  Perform Script [ Filename: "Customers.FP5", "ImportCustomers" ]
   [ Sub-scripts ]
  Exit Script
```

Relationships (File Name, Relationship Name, Relationship, Related File). These relationships are not used with FileMaker Pro 6 XML import. You cannot select a related field in the import dialog.

1. Customers.FP5, "Orders", ID = ::CustomerID, Orders.FP5
2. Orders.FP5, "Customers", CustomerID = ::ID, Customers.FP5
3. Orders.FP5, "Items", OrderID = ::OrderID, Items.FP5
4. Items.FP5, "Customers", CustomerID = ::ID, Customers.FP5
5. Items.FP5, "Orders", OrderID = ::OrderID, Orders.FP5

8.63 The XSLT Stylesheets

The following stylesheets were created from the basic XML imports from each database. The field names and field order were used by placing the XSL elements in the same order. Look at the stylesheet for importing the items and see where the XPath uses the "../" (go to parent) notatation to walk back up the XML source tree to get CustomerID and OrderID information.

Listing 8.38 ImportItems.xsl

```
<?xml version='1.0' encoding='UTF-8' ?>
<xsl:stylesheet version='1.0' xmlns:xsl='http://www.w3.org/1999/XSL/
  Transform'>
     <xsl:output version='1.0' encoding='UTF-8' indent='no'
       method='xml' />
```

```
     <xsl:template match='/'>
<FMPXMLRESULT xmlns="http://www.filemaker.com/fmpxmlresult">
  <ERRORCODE>0</ERRORCODE><PRODUCT BUILD="11/13/2002" NAME="FileMaker Pro"
  VERSION="6.0v4"/><DATABASE DATEFORMAT="M/d/yyyy" LAYOUT=""
  NAME="Items.FP5" RECORDS="" TIMEFORMAT="h:mm:ss a"/><METADATA><FIELD
  EMPTYOK="YES" MAXREPEAT="1" NAME="CustomerID" TYPE="NUMBER"/><FIELD
  EMPTYOK="YES" MAXREPEAT="1" NAME="OrderID" TYPE="TEXT"/><FIELD
  EMPTYOK="YES" MAXREPEAT="1" NAME="ItemID" TYPE="NUMBER"/><FIELD
  EMPTYOK="YES" MAXREPEAT="1" NAME="Qty" TYPE="NUMBER"/><FIELD
  EMPTYOK="YES" MAXREPEAT="1" NAME="ProductID" TYPE="TEXT"/><FIELD
  EMPTYOK="YES" MAXREPEAT="1" NAME="Description" TYPE="TEXT"/><FIELD
  EMPTYOK="YES" MAXREPEAT="1" NAME="Price"
  TYPE="NUMBER"/></METADATA><RESULTSET FOUND="">
          <xsl:for-each select="./customers/customer/orders/order/
            items/item">
               <ROW MODID="" RECORDID="">
                    <COL><DATA><xsl:value-of select="../../
                      ../../@ID" /></DATA></COL>
                    <COL><DATA><xsl:value-of select="../../
                      @ID" /></DATA></COL>
                    <COL><DATA></DATA></COL>
                    <COL><DATA><xsl:value-of select="./
                      quantity" /></DATA></COL>
                    <COL><DATA><xsl:value-of select="./
                      productID" /></DATA></COL>
                    <COL><DATA><xsl:value-of select="./
                      description" /></DATA></COL>
                    <COL><DATA><xsl:value-of select="./
                      price" /></DATA></COL>
               </ROW>
          </xsl:for-each>
</RESULTSET></FMPXMLRESULT>
     </xsl:template>
</xsl:stylesheet>
```

Listing 8.39 ImportOrders.xsl

```
<?xml version='1.0' encoding='UTF-8' ?>
<xsl:stylesheet version='1.0' xmlns:xsl='http://www.w3.org/1999/
  XSL/Transform'>
     <xsl:output version='1.0' encoding='UTF-8' indent='no'
       method='xml' />
     <xsl:template match='/'>
<FMPXMLRESULT xmlns="http://www.filemaker.com/fmpxmlresult">
  <ERRORCODE>0</ERRORCODE><PRODUCT BUILD="11/13/2002" NAME="FileMaker Pro"
  VERSION="6.0v4"/><DATABASE DATEFORMAT="M/d/yyyy" LAYOUT="" NAME=
  "Orders.FP5" RECORDS="" TIMEFORMAT="h:mm:ss a"/><METADATA><FIELD
  EMPTYOK="YES" MAXREPEAT="1" NAME="CustomerID" TYPE="NUMBER"/><FIELD
  EMPTYOK="YES" MAXREPEAT="1" NAME="OrderID" TYPE="NUMBER"/><FIELD
```

```
  EMPTYOK="YES" MAXREPEAT="1" NAME="OrderDate" TYPE="DATE"/><FIELD
  EMPTYOK="YES" MAXREPEAT="1" NAME="TotalAmt" TYPE="NUMBER"/></METADATA>
  <RESULTSET FOUND="">
          <xsl:for-each select="./customers/customer/orders/order">
                <ROW MODID="" RECORDID="">
                      <COL><DATA><xsl:value-of select="../../
                        @ID" /></DATA></COL>
                      <COL><DATA><xsl:value-of select="@ID"
                        /></DATA></COL>
                      <COL><DATA><xsl:value-of select=
                        "./date" /></DATA></COL>
                      <COL><DATA><xsl:value-of select=
                        "./amount" /></DATA></COL>
                </ROW>
          </xsl:for-each>
</RESULTSET></FMPXMLRESULT>
    </xsl:template>
</xsl:stylesheet>
```

Listing 8.40 ImportCustomers.xsl

```
<?xml version='1.0' encoding='UTF-8' ?>
<xsl:stylesheet version='1.0' xmlns:xsl='http://www.w3.org/1999/XSL/
  Transform'>
    <xsl:output version='1.0' encoding='UTF-8' indent='no'
      method='xml' />
    <xsl:template match='/'>
<FMPXMLRESULT xmlns="http://www.filemaker.com/fmpxmlresult">
  <ERRORCODE>0</ERRORCODE><PRODUCT BUILD="11/13/2002" NAME="FileMaker Pro"
  VERSION="6.0v4"/><DATABASE DATEFORMAT="M/d/yyyy" LAYOUT="" NAME=
  "Customers.FP5" RECORDS="" TIMEFORMAT="h:mm:ss a"/><METADATA><FIELD
  EMPTYOK="YES" MAXREPEAT="1" NAME="ID" TYPE="NUMBER"/><FIELD EMPTYOK="YES"
  MAXREPEAT="1" NAME="Name" TYPE="TEXT"/><FIELD EMPTYOK="YES" MAXREPEAT="1"
  NAME="City" TYPE="TEXT"/></METADATA><RESULTSET FOUND="">
          <xsl:for-each select="./customers/customer">
                <ROW MODID="" RECORDID="">
                      <COL><DATA><xsl:value-of select="@ID"
                        /></DATA></COL>
                      <COL><DATA><xsl:value-of select=
                        "./name" /></DATA></COL>
                      <COL><DATA><xsl:value-of select=
                        "./city" /></DATA></COL>
                </ROW>
          </xsl:for-each>
</RESULTSET></FMPXMLRESULT>
    </xsl:template>
</xsl:stylesheet>
```

8.7 XSLT and Web Publishing

Many of the XSLT examples in this chapter may be used for output to the web. Read again in Chapter 5 about how to call a stylesheet in your HTTP request with a hyperlink or an HTML <form>. You may get unpredictable results depending upon browser anomolies. Generally the examples that exported and transformed to HTML work best with FileMaker Pro XML web publishing, but other examples (text and XML) may be viewed in a web browser.

You may add Cascading Style Sheet language to any XSLT that has HTML output. This is best placed within the <head> element of the HTML and called as a <link> to an external CSS stylesheet. CSS that is embedded in the XSLT stylesheet may produce parsing errors because of the nature of the text.

You may also test some of these examples by exporting the XML and placing the processing instruction at the top of XML document. An example is shown in Listing 8.31. The stylesheet dso2html3.xsl is a renamed copy of the stylesheet dso2html2.xsl shown in Listing 8.15, section 8.32, "FMPDSORESULT to HTML."

```
<?xml-stylesheet type="text/xsl" href="StyleSheetName.xsl" ?>
```

Listing 8.31 export.xml

```
<?xml version="1.0" encoding="UTF-8" ?><?xml-stylesheet type="text/xsl"
  href="dso2html3.xsl" ?><FMPDSORESULT xmlns="http://www.filemaker.com/
  fmpdsoresult"><ERRORCODE>0</ERRORCODE><DATABASE>Export.FP5</DATABASE>
  <LAYOUT>Form</LAYOUT><ROW MODID="4" RECORDID="5"><First_Name>Beverly
  </First_Name><Last_Name>Voth</Last_Name><State>KY</State><Number>
  1.00</Number><Date></Date></ROW><ROW MODID="4" RECORDID="6"><First_Name>
  Doug</First_Name><Last_Name>Rowe</Last_Name><State>FL</State><Number>
  2.00</Number><Date>1/15/2003</Date></ROW></FMPDSORESULT>
```

This renders correctly in some browsers but fails in the Macintosh version of Internet Explorer.

8.8 More XSLT Examples

Keep checking the XSLT Library, http://www.filemaker.com/xml/xslt_library.html, for more stylesheets to use with FileMaker Pro XML export, import, and web publishing.

Appendix A

Glossary of Acronyms and Terms

ACGI	Asynchronous Common Gateway Interface
API	Application programming interface
ASCII	American Standard Code for Information Interchange
attribute	Parameter to further define an element. Each attribute should be unique within a single element.
CDATA	Character data
CDML	Claris Dynamic Markup Language
CGI	Common Gateway Interface
ColdFusion	A web application development tool and web application server (http://www.macromedia.com/software/coldfusion)
CSS	Cascading Style Sheet
Daemon	An attendant that waits to serve, such as a mailer daemon on a server computer
DNS	Domain Name System (or Service)
DOCTYPE	Document Type Declaration
DOM	Document Object Model
DSO	Data Source Object

DSSL	Document Style Semantics and Specification Language
DTD	Document Type Definition
EBNF	Extended Backus-Naur Form
ECMA	European Computer Manufacturers Association
ECMAscript	See JavaScript
EDI	Electronic Data Interchange; a format for sending and receiving invoices, purchase orders, and other business transactions. New standards for using XML/EDI can be found with your favorite search engine.
element	Basic component of a tags-based text format document
entity	A character or series of characters that symbolize something
ERP	Enterprise Resource Planning
FAQ	Frequently Asked Questions
GREP	global/regular expression/print
HDML	Handheld Device Markup Language
HTTP	Hypertext Transfer Protocol
hub	A central location used to distribute data packets on a network
IETF	Internet Engineering Task Force
IP	Internet Protocol
ISO	International Organization for Standardization
JavaScript	Formerly LiveScript; a scripting language used to enhance HTML
JDBC	JDBC
JVM	Java Virtual Machine
Lasso	A development and application web server by Blueworld (http://www.blueworld.com/)
LDAP	Lightweight Directory Access Protocol
localhost	Default server alias for local access; also 127.0.0.1 IP address
metadata	Information about the data

namespace	Unique identifier for binding elements and attributes
NAT	Network Address Translation
network	An interconnection of computers and other devices; could be wireless
ODBC	Open Database Connectivity
parse	Translate the meaning of something, separate it out
PCDATA	Parsed character data
PDF	Portable Document Format
port	Connection ID for a server
PostScript	Adobe printing language
RAIC	Redundant Array of Inexpensive Computers
RAID	Redundant Array of Independent Disks
render	Draw, display
RFC	Request For Comment
root	Topmost location in a document
root element	Topmost element in a document
router	Hardware and/or software to switch connections on a network
RPC	Remote Procedure Call
RTF	Rich Text Format
SAP	Company with an integrated suite of applications for business transactions
schema	Plan or map of a document; outline
servlet	Small server application
SGML	Standard Generalized Markup Language
SMIL	Synchronized Multimedia Integration Language
SSI	Server-Side Include
SSL	Secure Sockets Layer
stateless	Does not maintain constant connection
stylesheet	List of elements to transform a document from one type to another
SVG	Scalable Vector Graphics
Tango/Witango	Application Web Server plug-in and development editor

TCP	Transmission Control Protocol
TCP/IP	Transmission Control Protocol/Internet Protocol
TEI	Text Encoding Initiative
template	Document with common elements that can be used as a basis for another document
UDP	User Datagram Protocol
Unicode	Method of encoding all characters, including pictogram languages
URI	Uniform Resource Indicator
URL	Uniform Resource Locator
URN	Uniform Resource Name
valid	Meets predetermined criteria. XML is valid if it conforms to DTD; FileMaker data is valid if it conforms to validation requirements in Define Fields.
W3C	World Wide Web Consortium
WAP	Wireless Application Protocol
WDDX	Web Distributed Data Exchange (ColdFusion)
WebObjects	Java-based Web development and Web server application (http://www.apple.com)
well-formed	Meets with the specifications. An XML document that conforms to the standards set forth by the W3C.
white space	Spaces, tabs, carriage returns, and linefeed characters
WIDL	Web Interface Definition Language
WML	Wireless Markup Language
WSC	Web Server Connector
XLink	XML Linking Language
XML	Extensible Markup Language
XPath	XML Path Language
XPointer	XML Pointer Language
XSL	Extensible Stylesheet Language or XML Stylesheet Language
XSLT	XSL Transformation
XUL	XML User Interface Language

Appendix B

Resources

Note: The author makes no assurance that these links are valid, as the Internet tends to change. Additionally, the author has no alliance with any of the contributors or products mentioned here.

Your first resource is the World Wide Web Consortium, http://www.w3.org. There you'll find the latest information about XML and XSL. For more specific information about XML and FileMaker Pro, your Internet travels should lead you to http://www.filemaker.com/xml/ and FileMaker XML Central. There you'll find documents about XML and FileMaker Pro, and links to the FileMaker XSLT Library, FileMaker XML Talk, and recommended books.

General Information about XML

Jeni's XML pages—http://www.jenitennison.com/

OASIS—http://www.oasis-open.org/

Patrick J. Kidd's Home page—http://csd1.dawsoncollege.qc.ca/~pkidd/xml_ref.htm

The Web Standards Project—http://www.webstandards.org/

XMacL—http://xmacl.com/

The XML FAQ—http://www.ucc.ie/xml/

Tools for Using XML and FileMaker Pro

Brushfire, Chaparral Software—http://www.chapsoft.com/products.html

CDML tools, FileMaker Inc.—http://www.filemaker.com/downloads/hqx/cdml_web_tools.zip

expat (XML Parser Toolkit)—http://www.jclark.com/xml/expat.html

EZxslt, Chaparral Software—http://www.ezxslt.com

FileBooks Link, HAPPY Software—http://www.filebookslink.com/

FireCracker, Regeneration (Owen Tribe)—http://www.regeneration.uk.net/firecracker.html

Interaction (Terje Norderhaug)—http://interaction.in-progress.com Interaction generates standard HTML pages on the fly.

Quark XML—http://www.quark.com/products/avenue/

RTF Converter, Logictran RTF Converter—http://www.logictran.com/

Style Master CSS editor for Windows and Macintosh, Western Civilisation Software—http://www.westciv.com/style_master/ Cascading Style Sheet editor for the Macintosh and Windows 95, 98, Me, 2000, and NT.

Visualizer, Waves in Motion—http://wmotion.com/visualizer.html

WebMerge, Fourth World—http://www.fourthworld.com/products/webmerge/ WebMerge generates static web pages from database files.

XPublish, Interaction (Terje Norderhaug)—http://interaction.in-progress.com/xpublish/

XMLSpy—http://www.xmlspy.com/

XSA (XML Software Autoupdate)—http://www.garshol.priv.no/download/xsa/

XML Tools—http://www.latenightsw.com/freeware/XMLTools2/index.html

XML Tools Scripting Addition—http://www.latenightsw.com/

XML Writer for Windows—http://xmlwriter.net/

Tutorials

FMWebschool (CDML and XML/XSL)—http://www.fmwebschool.com/

skew.org XML Tutorial—http://skew.org/xml/tutorial/

W3Schools Online Web Tutorials—http://www.w3schools.com
Recommended by Peter van Maanen.

XML Academy Courseware—http://www.xmlacademy.com/

XML tutorials—http://www.finetuning.com/tutorials.html

XSL concepts and practical use—http://www.arbortext.com/xsl/tutorial/tutorial.html

Zvon.org—http://www.zvon.org/

By Topic

- Accessibility

  Web Content Accessibility Guidelines 1.0, W3C—http://www.w3.org/TR/WAI-WEBCONTENT/

- Accounting

  FileBooks Link, HAPPY Software—http://www.filebookslink.com/

  QuickBooks, Intuit—http://quickbooks.intuit.com/

- ACGI

  Alias-of-FMP-as-an-acgi Trick, Chad Gard—Chad's example is on the book's web site (www.moonbow.com/xml).

  High-performance ACGIs in C, Ken Urquhart—http://developer.apple.com/dev/techsupport/develop/issue29/urquhart.html

- Apache XML

  Apache—http://xml.apache.org/

- AppleScript

  eBay Tracker, Jon Rosen—Jon's example is on the book's web site (www.moonbow.com/xml).

  XML Tools—http://www.latenightsw.com/freeware/XMLTools2/index.html

- ASP

  Microsoft—http://msdn.microsoft.com/
- Biztalk

  Microsoft BizTalk—http://www.microsoft.com/biztalk/
- Browsers

  Internet Explorer—http://www.microsoft.com/

  Microsoft XSL Developer's Guide—http://msdn.microsoft.com/

  Netscape—http://wp.netscape.com/browsers/future/standards.html

  Netscape DevEdge—http://developer.netscape.com/index.html

  Netscape developerWorks (XML)—http://www-106.ibm.com/developerworks/xml/

  Unofficial MSXML XSLT FAQ—http://www.netcrucible.com/xslt/msxml-faq.htm
- Calculated XML

  Cleveland Consulting Chart, John Sindelar—http://www.cleveland-consulting.com

  CC Chart Engine—An XML interpreter available on the book's web site (www.moonbow.com/xml)
- CDML

  CDML tools, FileMaker Inc.—http://www.filemaker.com/downloads/hqx/cdml_web_tools.zip

  CDML Reference.fp5, CDML Tool.fp5
- CERN and WWW

  World Wide Web and CERN—http://cern.web.cern.ch/CERN/WorldWideWeb/WWWandCERN.html
- CGI

  The Common Gateway Interface—http://hoohoo.ncsa.uiuc.edu/cgi/overview.html
- ColdFusion

  http://www.macromedia.com/
- CSS

  Cascading Style Sheets home page, W3C—http://www.w3.org/Style/CSS/

  Cascading Style Sheets, level 1, W3C—http://www.w3.org/TR/REC-CSS1

Style Master CSS editor for Windows and Macintosh—http://www.westciv.com/style_master/

Cascading Style Sheet editor for the Macintosh and Windows 95, 98, Me, 2000 and NT

- DDR (Database Design Report)

  ddr_grammar.pdf, FileMaker Inc—http://www.filemaker.com/downloads/pdf/ddr_grammar.pdf

- DOM

  Document Object Model (DOM) Activity Statement, W3C—http://www.w3.org/DOM/Activity

- Dreamweaver

  Macromedia—http://www.macromedia.com/

  Understanding importing and exporting XML and templates—http://www.macromedia.com/support/dreamweaver/ts/documents/templates_xml.htm

- ECMAScript (see also JavaScript)

  JavaScript standards—http://www.ecma-international.org/publications/standards/ECMA-262.HTM

- EDI

  XML/EDI—http://www.xmlglobal.com/consult/xmledi/index.html

- Electronic payment

  bill Xender, Ben Marchbanks—http://www.alqemy.com/products/billXender.htm

- ENCRYPTION

  Crypto Toolbox Plug-in, ProtoLight—http://www.geocities.com/SiliconValley/Network/9327/

  DES (Data Encryption Standard)—http://www.rsasecurity.com/

  Troi-Coding, Troi Automatisering—http://www.troi.com/

- ERP

  Enterprise Resource Planning (ERP)—http://www.cio.com/research/erp/edit/erpbasics.html

- HTML

  HTML HELP—http://www.htmlhelp.com/

  Hypertext Markup Language (HTML) Home Page, W3C—http://www.w3.org/Markup/

  HTML 4.01 Specification, W3C: http://www.w3.org/TR/html4

- I-mode (also see Wireless)

  NTT DoCoMo, Inc.—http://www.nttdocomo.com/home.html

  The unofficial independent imode FAQ—http://www.euro-technology.com/imode/faq-dev.html

  I-Mode and FMMobile—http://www.filemaker.com/products/mbl_home.html

- IETF—Internet Engineering Task Force

  http://www.ietf.org/

- ISO country codes

  ISO 3166-1: The Code List—http://www.din.de/gremien/nas/nabd/iso3166ma/codlstp1/index.html

- ISO (International Organization for Standardization)

  http://www.iso.ch/iso/en/ISOOnline.frontpage

- Java

  Java Servlet Technology—http://java.sun.com/products/servlet/

  jXTransformer, Greg Stasko, DataDirect Technologies—http://www.datadirect-technologies.com/products/jxtransformer/jxtransformer_index.asp

- JavaScript

  JavaScript.com—http://www.javascript.com/

  JavaScript Programmer's Reference DOM Objects—http://www.irt.org/xref/dom_objects.htm

  The JavaScript Source—http://javascript.internet.com/

- Lasso

  Web Data Engine, BlueWorld—http://www.blueworld.com/

  Lasso XML, BlueWorld—http://www.blueworld.com/blueworld/products/LassoWDE3.6/xml/default.html

- Macintosh

  XML for Mac users—http://xmacl.com/

- MAILTO protocol

  RFC 2368—http://www.ietf.org/rfc/rfc2368.txt

- MATHML

  W3C Math Home, W3C—http://www.w3.org/Math/

- Namespaces

  Namespaces in XML, W3C—http://www.w3.org/TR/REC-xml-names
- .NET

  Microsoft .NET—http://www.microsoft.com/
- PDF

  http://www.adobe.com/

  Ben Marchbanks—http://www.alQemy.com

  Dean Westover, Choices Software
- PERL

  XML2HTML, Roger W. Jacques—Roger's example is on the web site (www.moonbow.com/xml)
- PHP

  FXphp, A Free, Open Source PHP class for accessing FileMaker Pro data by Chris Hansen with Chris Adams—http://www.iviking.org/
- Plug-ins

  Crypto Toolbox Plug-in, ProtoLight—http://www.geocities.com/SiliconValley/Network/9327/

  doHTTP—http://www.genoasoftware.com/dohttp-gen.asp

  ExportFM, New Millennium Communications—http://www.nmci.com/

  FileBooks Link, HAPPY Software—http://www.filebookslink.com/

  GetHTTP, e4marketing, suggestion by Darwin Stephenson—http://www.e4marketing.com

  Search for a plug-in, FileMaker, Inc—http://www.filemaker.com/plugins/index.html/

  Troi-Coding, Troi Automatisering—http://www.troi.com/

  Troi-File, Troi Automatisering—http://www.troi.com/

  Troi-Text, Troi Automatisering—http://www.troi.com/

  XML Software Description (XSD)—http://www.troi.com
- RTF

  EZxslt, Chaparral Software—http://www.ezxslt.com

  Logictran RTF Converter, converts word processing documents to HTML and XML—http://www.logictran.com/

  upCast, Christian Roth—http://www.infinity-loop.de (Java Swing required)

- SAP

  http://www.SAP.com/
- Schemas

  XML Schema, W3C—http://www.w3.org/XML/Schema
- Search Engines

  Google.com—http://directory.google.com/Top/Computers/Data_Formats/Markup_Languages/XML/
- SMIL

  Synchronized Multimedia, W3C—http://www.w3.org/AudioVideo/

  SMIL and QuickTime, Apple Computer—http://www.apple.com/applescript/quicktime/
- Spinalot

  Apple Computer—http://www.apple.com/education/LTReview/fall99/spinalot/13index.html
- Styled text

  diStyler, Faustino Forcen—http://www.abstrakt.com/distyler.html
- TCP/IP

  Introduction to TCP/IP—http://www.yale.edu/pclt/COMM/TCPIP.HTM
- Techinfo—FileMaker

  http://www.filemaker.com/support/techinfo.html
- TEI—Text Encoding Initiative

  http://www.uic.edu/orgs/tei
- Themes

  ThemeCreator, Cinco Group—http://www.themecreator.com

  ThemeMonster, Steve Abrahamson—http://www.asctech.com/Products/ThemeMonster/
- Unicode

  Unicode home page—http://www.unicode.org/

  Unicode Transformation Formats (UTF-8 & Co.)—http://czyborra.com/utf/
- URI

  RFC 2396—http://www.ietf.org/rfc/rfc2396.txt

- User Interface

  XUL—XML User Interface Language—http://www.xulplanet.com/

  W3C User Interface domain—http://www.w3.org/UI/

- VOICEXML

  http://www.voicexml.org/

- WDDX

  OpenWDDX.Org—http://www.openwddx.org/

- Web Authoring

  Webmonkey—http://hotwired.lycos.com/webmonkey

- WebDAV

  WebDAV FAQ—http://www.webdav.org/other/faq.html

- Web Services

  FileMaker, Inc.—http://www.filemaker.com/xml/service_objects.html

- Wireless

  ALT Mobile—http://www.altconsulting.com/index.html

  Go.Web—http://www.goamerica.com/goweb/

  The unofficial independent imode FAQ—http://www.eurotechnology.com/imode/faq-dev.html

  Wireless Developer Network—http://www.wirelessdevnet.com/

  WirelessDeveloper.com—http://www.wirelessdeveloper.com/

- WITANGO

  http://www.witango.com

  XML-Extranet, Scott Cadillac—http://xml-extra.net/

- World Wide Web Consortium

  http://www.w3.org/

- XBRL

  Extensible Business Reporting Language (XBRL)—http://www.xbrl.org

- XHTML

  XHTML 1.0 The Extensible Hypertext Markup Language (Second Edition)—http://www.w3.org/TR/xhtml1

  XHTML BASIC, W3C—http://www.w3.org/TR/xhtml-basic

- XML

  Extensible Markup Language (XML) 1.0 (Second Edition), W3C—http://www.w3.org/TR/REC-xml
- XML Editor

  oXygen XML Editor—http://www.oxygenxml.com/index.html contributed by Dan Stein

  XML Editor 1.4—http://www.elfdata.com/
- XML Forum

  fmForum, Kurt Knippel—http://www.fmforums.com/
- XMTP

  XML Mail Transport Protocol (XMTP)—http://www.oasis-open.org/cover/xmtp.html
- XPath

  XML Path Language (XPath) Version 1.0, W3C—http://www.w3.org/TR/xpath
- XPointer

  XML Pointer Language (XPointer), W3C—http://www.w3.org/TR/xptr/
- XSL/XSLT

  XSLT.com—http://www.xslt.com/

  XSL 1.0, Extensible Stylesheet Language (XSL) Version 1.0, W3C—http://www.w3.org/TR/xsl/

  XSLT 1.0, XSL Transformations (XSLT) Version 1.0, W3C—http://www.w3.org/TR/xslt

Miscellaneous

The following submissions are not included in this book. The author appreciates all submissions and welcomes resubmission for the web site.

ASP—Campbell Green submitted examples of using ASP and XML from web-published FileMaker Pro.

CDML—Rob Sklenar contributed a CDML example of a Calendar solution.

CDML—Jane Chinn submitted a CDML example, Chem345.

CDML and JavaScript—ePortal by Dave Wooten is a method for displaying and updating portal records.

CSS—Fritz Kloepfel worked with displaying FileMaker Pro with CSS.

DOM—Shawn Larson submitted examples of XML-DOM for the Mac.

Firewalls—Dave Pong' s contribution on firewalls was not able to be included in this book.

Index

E

G

H

About the Companion Files

The companion files can be downloaded from www.wordware.com/fmxml and www.moonbow.com/xml. These files include examples discussed in the book, as well as demo plug-ins from Troi Automatisering, information on networking FileMaker Pro solutions, and examples provided by third parties.

The examples are organized into folders according to chapters. Simply copy the folders to your hard drive to work with them.

For more information about the contents of the companion files, see the CD index.rtf file included with the downloads.